The Greek State

VICTOR EHRENBERG

The Greek State

SECOND EDITION

LONDON

METHUEN & CO LTD

11 NEW FETTER LANE · EC4

First published in 1960 by Basil Blackwell Ltd, Oxford
This revised edition first published in 1969 by Methuen & Co Ltd,
11 New Fetter Lane, London E.C.4
Second edition © 1969 by Victor Ehrenberg

Printed and bound in Great Britain
by Richard Clay (The Chaucer Press), Ltd,
Bungay, Suffolk

SBN 416 12820 3

TO MY WIFE

Distributed in the U.S.A.
by Barnes & Noble Inc.

Contents

Preface to the First Edition

This book was first published in German. In producing an English version I was able to make a fair number of additions and corrections. I also hope that the book has generally gained in clarity. I have been frequently told by friends and reviewers that an English version would fill a serious gap, felt by scholars and students alike, both in Britain and in the United States. I shall be delighted if it will serve this purpose.

The English text is the result of the collaboration between my old friend Harold Mattingly and myself. I am very grateful to Mattingly for having done the initial spade work, and for discussing a number of passages with me. I also owe sincere thanks to Mr A. L. Irvine, who read the text in typescript and in proofs and did a good deal to improve its style. The final version remains my responsibility.

The problems of the Greek city-state have recently been discussed even in the Third Programme of the B.B.C. The debate among some distinguished scholars showed that agreement was out of reach. To some extent, this was so because the speakers differed widely even in their presuppositions. While nobody can hope to provide a clear-cut solution which might satisfy everybody, it may be useful to deal with the questions concerned in a wider context. That is, at least in part, what I have tried to do in this book.

In dedicating the book to my wife, I wish to thank her for forty years of married life, during which she has been my stand-by and my inspiration.

V. E.

London, May 1959

Preface to the Second Edition

This edition is based on the Second German edition (Zürich, 1965), though on account of more recent work in the field or more rethinking of my own, the book has been considerably extended and altered. I have also corrected some minor mistakes.

The book is again dedicated to my wife; it will be published some time after our Golden Wedding, and I can only repeat how much I have owed to her during these fifty years for guiding our and our sons' lives.

I am grateful to Messrs Methuen for their offer to publish the new edition, and especially to Mr Anthony Forster for the interest he took in the matter. I owe special thanks to my friend Professor Martin Ostwald and the Oxford University Press for letting me see the proofs of his important book *Nomos*.

V. E.

London, January 1969

Introduction

When we speak of the Hellenic State we are thinking of the political forms that grew out of the age of Greek immigration into the Aegean. I shall try to depict the development and character of these political units, and to establish the forms that in the course of history were decisive. Without anticipating too much, it may be worth while at this point – briefly and within the requirements of our theme – to distinguish what was essentially Greek from an earlier age and a surrounding world that were not. That the Greeks learnt and borrowed much from the East is an admitted fact; but there is no direct road leading from the territorial state of the East under its kings to the Greek community of citizens, even should it be established that the Mycenaean Greeks were under a priestly kingship, such as can hardly be imagined without Eastern influence. Another matter of special importance for the later Greek development, a matter, say, of social geography, is the extent to which the country was urbanized. The cities of the East, and indeed of the Minoans and Mycenaeans, found their centre in the royal palace; such a centre is not to be found among the later Greeks, even where there were kings. Nevertheless, it is possible that the typical city civilization of the East may have undergone changes in the Aegean before the Greeks came, and that it may have facilitated the transition to Greek forms of life. The influence of land and sea in the Aegean world had also shaped the predecessors of the Greeks. Out of this twofold inheritance – the preponderance of urban settlement and the geographical conditions – the new immigrants, hitherto bound to one another by the personal and social relationships of the tribe, created those new political forms of which the Polis, the Greek city-state, was the crown.

The question now arises: how far are we justified in speaking of 'the' Polis in general? We have to draw our picture of it from a number of states, and, to do so, we must recognize the unity that underlies the plurality. 'Polis' is to some extent an abstraction; it will be our task to describe what is typical, or what Max Weber calls the 'ideal type' (*Idealtypus*), without forgetting the differences that exist beside the common elements. Research in the last decades has vastly enriched our knowledge of the many Greek states and their constitutions in their almost countless varieties. It cannot be my task here to present the ever-growing material (especially of inscriptions), though I shall point out some references of particular importance; the main theme must not be forgotten or submerged under the mass of variations. I spoke of 'abstraction' as necessary; it is essentially a task set for all historical writing that is not purely chronological; and even chronological history, if it is to deserve its name of history, cannot be content to describe only what happened. The moment the historian begins to speak not of events but of conditions, he is forced to make abstractions and generalizations. In what follows we shall speak of 'the Polis' as we speak of 'absolute monarchy', of 'modern democracy' or of 'the society of the early or late Middle Ages'. In the same way, in the second part of this work, we shall deal with the 'Hellenistic State'. The emphasis must inevitably fall on what is common rather than on what is distinctive. Call it a compromise, if you will; but it is a compromise that is not only justified but absolutely necessary, if we are to win from the mass of detail a picture of the whole.

There is, however, another aspect not to be neglected when we try to regard the Polis as the historically decisive form of state. To the Greeks themselves the word 'Polis' was almost as general and vague as the word 'state' is to us. Greek political thought and public law, in fact, knew of very few, if any, unambiguous concepts. A word could have several different meanings (as, e.g., *perioeci*, *koinon*, *agora*), and several words could have identical or very similar meanings (e.g., *boule*, *synkletos*, *gerousia*). Difficulties will therefore occur, in particular when we wish to translate the Greek words. We shall try not to over-look these difficulties. They must, on the other hand, not prevent us from realizing the essential matters. It remains to be seen to what extent we shall succeed. After all, if the word Polis is often used in a vague and generalizing sense, it did represent to the Greeks a unique and largely uniform type of state, and it remained an essential factor within the Hellenistic state as well. In the following chapters we shall discuss what this type actually was like.

What we have said about the ambiguity of the concepts of public law in the Polis is to some extent true of the Hellenistic state as well. But the science and in particular the practice of law had meanwhile made considerable progress, partly as a purely Greek development and partly under the impact of various Oriental laws. The present book is not a work of legal science and the author is not a jurist. All that should be kept in mind by a generous reader.

PART I

The Hellenic State

CHAPTER ONE

The Origins of the Greek States

In this first chapter I shall try to sketch the conditions, geographical, ethnic, religious, social, and political, that led to the rise of the Greek states. There is much that is still unexplained, and the views represented here often remain mere assumptions, probable or perhaps only possible.

I. LAND AND SEA

I base the remarks that follow on the recognized fact that geography and history stand to one another in a relation of mutual influence, equally important whether we are thinking in terms of geography or of history. Of these two related elements one is essentially constant, the other essentially changing; the facts of space and nature remain constant through all the changes of time and history, yet vary in their significance and their effects. The history of the area first occupied by the Greeks, from the Helladic period down through Hellenic, Hellenistic, and Roman times into the Turkish period and the development of modern Greece, supplies unmistakable evidence both of changelessness and of change.

The region in which the Greek state had its original home embraces not only the peninsula that we call Greece, but also the islands and coasts of the Aegean Sea – the Aegean, as we call it for short. Sharply separated from the outside world by the open sea south of Crete and in the west, by the Balkan mountains in the north, and by the western edge of the plateau of Asia Minor in the east, this region may be regarded as a true geographical unit, with its base in its geological prehistory, when the land-bridge still existed between Europe and Asia. In the course of history, the Ionic migration (late in the second millennium or even later) and the ensuing movements from west to east over the Aegean Sea made this geographical unit a Greek unit, and thus formed, beyond all inner political frontiers, an area entirely Greek, the motherland of the multitude of Greek states. Its centre is the sea, but this sea is so thickly sown with islands, and the shores of Greece and the western coasts of Asia Minor are so broken up by the sea, that land and sea appear to be indissolubly connected; thus, the whole region is closely bound together by nature. Though it belongs to two continents, the Aegean is still a unit, for it is 'thalassocentric', centred on the sea and situated around the sea and its parts. A people that had no name for the sea when they first entered the Aegean area, learnt there to think of the sea as central, and never quite lost the habit.

The same geographical factors worked together to create a multitude of units and a great variety of forms. The fact that land and sea were so broken up led also to the erection of innumerable barriers. The land was torn in pieces by the bays, gulfs, and arms of the sea, and not less by the mountains which belong to a number of systems, created by mighty geological convulsions. Thus the Greek area displays an interlocked pattern of land and sea, mountains and mountainous districts, plains and valleys, islands and peninsulas, and the result is a wealth of small, sharply separated regions: nature sets an example of fragmentation that was followed and even surpassed by the political world. It was hard to find a place that offered any possibility for larger developments of power; even where (as, for example, in Asia Minor) extensive river plains might have served as a basis for it, the political and historical requirements were lacking.

We have indicated in the last paragraph the small extent of the natural and, even more, of the political districts. The whole area of the Aegean is very narrow in its scope; but the full meaning of this narrowness was only felt and realized when it was broken up internally into small and ever smaller divisions. For the sailor the sea never vanishes into infinity and, even where islands are scarce, some high peak like that of Athos or the Cretan Ida is always there as a landmark; so too on land there is never a plain that is not soon bounded by a mountain or an inlet of the sea. This among other things forced the political units to renounce expansion and led to a swift and complete seizure of the space available and to the early development of numerous political bodies. Painfully recoiling from its narrow boundaries and concentrated on itself, the state preserved a unity which displayed the features of a human community rather than of a political organization. The narrow space, admitting of little variation, produced a marked unification of the civic type and a very distinct political consciousness, limited though it was by its small scale. Neither power nor expansion could be the true aim of the growing state, but from the narrowness of space sprang high tensions that stimulated the creativeness of the community.

The limited space of the single political unit was again the main cause of Greek colonization and was responsible for the wide extent of the area of Greek settlements and the great number of their cities. The reason for the foundation of most colonies was the insufficiency of the homeland for housing and feeding a growing population. Political strife, either among rival groups of the ruling aristocracy or between nobles and non-nobles, could also be a cause of emigration. Even where trade and warlike energy led states to colonize, it was, in the last instance, the lack of a territory that could be exploited economically that drove men to the sea and created markets abroad. The age of colonization meant the spread of the Greeks of the Aegean over the whole of the Mediterranean and the Black Sea as well. A map, containing not only the Aegean, but the sea to the south of Crete, south Italy, east Sicily, the interior of the Balkans, and the coasts of Asia Minor, or, better still, a map stretching from Massilia to Sinope and from Cyrene to Olbia, will help us to realize that the Aegean is in the centre of an area, knit into one by the bonds of the sea and both limited and defended by the surrounding mountains, steppes, and deserts.

The sea, then, served as a safety valve for tensions within the narrow space, and so the exact position in relation to the sea was of decisive importance for political development. In the Aegean, in particular, the shores with their wealth of harbours called for trade and commercial intercourse and created economic prosperity and intellectual vitality, with a city-state as their living centre. Lands as close to one another as Argolis and Laconia, or Attica and Boeotia, illustrate the difference between regions that turn their faces or their backs to the sea. As the city developed, there emerged two characteristic forms of settlement – the settlement round a citadel, which was based on Mycenaean traditions, and the 'Phoenician' pattern, especially popular with the colonies, on a jutting peninsula or an island lying off the coast. A city's situation within the Aegean was no less important. The Aegean was a much frequented market between two continents; it was therefore of the highest importance for the individual state to be near the routes of traffic and points of intersection. A map will show that favourable position usually coincided with a favourable configuration of the coast. In general, it is the coasts that face the Aegean which are moulded into peninsulas and bays. It was here, then – in a historical movement from east to west – that those Greeks lived who held the political and cultural leadership; the western countries of the homeland were far behind and had hardly woken out of their sleep outside history when a new Greece,

B

intensely alive, had arisen still farther in the west. The slowing down of the pace of historical development in the Aegean world from Asia Minor to the islands, then to the east coast of Greece, and finally to her central and western districts played an important part in the manifold variety of the Greek world of states.

If we disregard some fertile plains, mostly small, Greece was always a poor country, poor in water – springs were especially important in determining settlement –, poor in arable land, poor in mineral wealth. The land trained the Greek peasant not so much to hard work and intensified methods as to frugality. The limitation and poor quality of the soil meant an early decline of grain crops in many districts and their replacement by vines and olive trees. The import of corn became necessary, while of wine and oil there usually was more than enough for the producer; the basic conditions of agriculture, remaining everywhere more or less the same, drove the peasant to the city market and, in time, increasingly to trade and seafaring.

The economic and political effects of the conditions innate in the soil were reinforced by the influence of the climate, the mild heat, the low rainfall, and the short winter. The climate took life out into the open. House and family were far less important for daily life and social meetings than the market and the wrestling-school. A man's profession too came to matter less. Public life was almost the sole environment of the citizen. Man proved himself to be indeed a ζῷον πολιτικόν, a creature bound to the Polis, the community both urban and political.

Natural conditions in the Aegean thus led to the creation of numerous self-contained communities, characterized as much by their rich variety and mutual rivalries as by narrow space and inner coherence. In the colonies, too, the type of state, developed in the Aegean, was in all essentials retained. Colonization depended entirely on the sea – in contrast to Rome which colonized by land – and was almost exclusively confined to settlements on the shore. Difficulties of navigation, lack of harbours, or of suitable land along the coast, occasionally discouraged the colonists. In other cases there were historical difficulties that made Greek colonization impossible, as, for example, in the south-east and on the north-west coast of Africa, where Phoenicians, the Assyrian power, or Carthage stood in the way. Conditions varied widely in the different areas of colonization. What the colonists sought chiefly were good harbours, fertile soil, and protection against pirates and hostile natives. Here, too, the life of the state was strongly directed inwards rather than outwards. The natural requirements were in all important points the same, and that despite the larger territories of the Greek cities in Italy and Sicily. Out of the character of the Mediterranean world, both in east and west, grew the Greek state that at once shaped and revealed the Greek character. The close packing of states inside the Greek world, and of men inside the states, was the essential cause of the universal urge towards the *agon*, the passion to compete with your neighbour.

2. TRIBE AND TOWN

Some of the Greeks, the Athenians for example, believed that they were autochthonous. In point of fact, it hardly admits of doubt that all the Greeks were forced south from their earlier positions north of the Balkans through movements of various peoples. More recently different views have been expressed, chiefly based on linguistic arguments. One is that the Greeks entered Greece and the Aegean from Asia Minor by way of the sea; another that the Greek language took shape in Greece after the invasion. In the latter case, the invaders would be pre-Greek Indo-Europeans; they might have entered Greece in several waves or in one only, since the dialects which might prove several waves of immigration would not yet have existed at that early stage. This kind of hypothetical construction is supported by uncertain evidence (archaeological or otherwise), and it is not yet the time for the historian to take a definite stand. There were, at any rate, Greeks in Greece from about the turn of the third to the second millennium. There they probably found an earlier Indo-European stratum, and above all 'Mediterranean' tribes which almost certainly had come from Asia Minor. The Greeks everywhere either absorbed or expelled the earlier population. Nothing is known of the political organization of these pre-Greek peoples except in Crete, where a mighty kingship existed. The Greeks themselves came into the land as 'tribes'. To what extent during the immigration and settlement large tribes divided or small tribes united lies outside our knowledge; the result certainly was that the tribe already in existence, or fragments that subsequently broke off, shaped themselves independently into a large number of political units. In this, the differences between the later main tribes (Dorians, Ionians, Aeolians) or any special characteristic of any one of them played a very small part.

The first immigrants, the Ionians and Achaeans, did not come in one wave, still less as one compact body. Freely mixing, it seems, with the original pre-Greek population, they became as rulers the exponents of the Mycenaean civilization which was spread most intensely over the eastern lands of Greece and was very much under the cultural influence of Crete. In the political life of the Mycenaean Greeks, as in their culture generally, we can establish a connection of Greek elements from the north with non-Greek elements from the east. Thanks to the decipherment of the documents written in the Linear script B, the political, social, and economic conditions of the Mycenaean age are becoming a little clearer, as the reading of the inscriptions proceeds; it is probable that these conditions were subject to non-Greek influence, perhaps not only Cretan but also Asiatic. The centre of the Mycenaean state was the royal citadel, and as the earliest Greek name for it was πόλις (πτόλις), it is very probable that the Polis as city and as state is derived from it. To the strong and walled citadel, of which the royal palace was the centre, was often attached a settlement which, though not fortified, usually gained much of the character of a town. Citadel and settlement (ἄστυ) formed a centre of courtly, political, and economic life, whereas mere citadels of refuge (Fluchtburgen) hardly existed; they only survived in north-western Greece. There was almost certainly beside the king a class of noble lords whose dwellings and graves lay near the royal citadel or in citadels of their own. Of the people we know little, but the gigantic buildings prove that a very numerous section of them – the subject pre-Greek population, of course, in the first place – were bound to forced labour. Kingship, the power of which is at once proved by its cultural achievements, had grown beyond tribal chieftainship into a strong monarchy, and often, as it seems, into supremacy over numerous vassal kings. The position of Agamemnon in the *Iliad* certainly shows traces of a kingship by the grace of God, but, in his relation to the other kings, he is only the commander-in-chief of the army. It is unlikely that there ever was a large Achaean empire on Greek soil. In spite of the unity of the Achaean civilization and language and the wide diffusion of the Achaean name, it is in no way certain that the Greeks of that age felt themselves to be a single people, still less a 'nation'.

From the fifteenth century B.C. onwards the Mycenaean Greeks pushed out in various directions, in a movement which led to struggles with Crete and Asia Minor, to the occupation of Crete, and the gradual settlement on the Aegean islands, on the south-west and south coasts of Asia Minor, and in Cyprus. The earlier period of this movement has been established by the tablets in Linear script B found in Cnossus and its dependencies. It received a new and stronger stimulus from the second large wave of immigration: that of the Dorians and the north-western Greeks (probably during the twelfth to eleventh century B.C.). This was the first attempt at colonization made by the Greeks and, by it, the Mycenaean Greeks to some extent freed themselves from their soil and their traditions. This process determined the form given to the cities that gradually rose on colonial ground. In Asia Minor in particular, where the Greeks settled among an alien population, on the fringe of a large non-Greek hinterland, usually attaching themselves to earlier places of habitation on peninsulas and isthmuses, everything tended towards urban settlement. Here, the Mycenaean Polis became a city in its narrow and most precise sense, with walls and, as seems evident at least from the example of Smyrna, with a planned layout based on axial streets from north to south. This takes us back as far as the eighth century B.C., and it would be proof of a forerunner, earlier than those in the west, of the later rectangular scheme of town planning connected with the name of Hippodamus. A city is not yet a state, but exercising its sway over barbarians, it must have become a state. It is likely, though by no means certain, that the type of political community, which we call the Polis, entered history in Ionia.

In the homeland, the collapse of Mycenaean Greece due to fresh immigration, together with the renewed tendency to split up larger units, brought with it a general revival of primitive conditions, with political forms to correspond; such conditions had already prevailed when the earlier immigrants arrived (as can still be shown in Arcadia), but had, in the main, been ousted by the Mycenaeans. Whether we can only now begin to speak of the genuine growth of a people is questionable; what is quite certain is that the motley world of Greek states only developed in the centuries following the Dorian invasion. The type of the Polis was in existence in the early eighth century; by then the Greeks physically and spiritually had become a Mediterranean people. After the internal and external decay of the Mycenaean age and its kingship, the tribal order came again into its own. Even where the tribes were not loosely settled in villages (κατὰ κώμας), as they often were, where they now dwelt in cities, usually walled, mostly in connection with a Mycenaean settlement, above all in eastern Greece, the tribal order gained a decisive importance; finally the colonial cities too adopted it, though more or less as a fiction. In Sparta (and similarly in Elis) the new settlement was deliberately founded away from the Mycenaean town; but even the unfortified settlement here, consisting of a number of neighbouring villages, can at least be described as half-urban. Under the general scheme of the structure of a tribal state new and clearly distinct types of states were concealed (see p. 22). But every settlement, whether in village or town, stood in virtue of its regional character in contrast to the 'personal' order of the tribe. This contrast became the more pronounced, as the ties that bound the tribe together were loosened by the establishment of a settled community.

The tribal order was based on the family as its smallest social unit. After settlement was complete, it formed the household (οἶκος), composed of free men and bondsmen. The household included possessions on a considerable scale (herds, valued metals, and land – in that order of importance) together with dependants of various kinds. The whole stood under the master of the house, whose power was very great, though never equal to the *patria potestas* of Rome. Beside him stood his wife – for Greek marriage rested on the principle of monogamy. The father had wide powers over his children, even more so, of course, over the slaves, known as ἀνδράποδα, who had no more rights than cattle, but at the same time were members of the household (οἰκέται). Only in Sparta did the state claim for itself the essential rights of the householder over his children and slaves. Everywhere it was the rule that property, mainly land, belonged to the family. As settlement took place the land was divided into 'lots' (κλῆροι), after special pieces had been separated off for the gods and the king (τεμένη); only hunting-land and pasturage remained common property. Private property, then, in the form of the lot was the economic basis of the household, which at first enjoyed a very high degree of self-sufficiency – it had hardly begun to give way in the Homeric age – but long remained bound to tribe and community; the master could not as a rule give away or sell its land at pleasure. The strict limitation of succession by inheritance was only decisively broken when division of the property among one's children, and also adoption, became possible – for instance, as provided for in the laws of Gortyn.

The independence of the family in law and economics was limited and restricted by certain social institutions, belonging to the primitive order of the tribe and persisting, above all in Sparta and Crete, into later centuries. Such were the communal life of the men, their common meals, and the age groups of the youths. But there were also, in ever-growing importance, other social units, built upon the family but set above it. It is possible that the clan (γένος, πάτρα) belonged to very early times, and that the individual family, the *oikos*, only gradually grew into a separate unit. The chronological order remains doubtful, but it is certain that later the clan was of far greater importance. It was generally tied to a narrow district – in Attica some demes bore clan names – and it was usually under the leadership of a single family, which supplied priests for the cults of the clan and occasionally a kind of official leader (ἄρχων). The clan was the chief means by which the nobles expressed and asserted themselves politically. At a later date, religious groups without bonds of kinship (such as the Salaminioi in Athens) might figure as 'clans' and enjoy their privileges. There had also always existed certain loose groups of kinsmen, but the oldest union of a number of families was the phratry; it was also the most important historically. In essence, though not in the underlying conception, there was no difference between phratry and clan, between a community of brothers and the group based on a common father; in all Greek dialects the Indo-European word for brother (*frater*) is only used for the member of a brotherhood (phratry), and not for a natural brother (*adelphos*); the fact is confirmed by the patronymic clan names of many phratries. There was also, for example in Caria, a group similar to the phratry, called *syngeneia*. The phratries went beyond simple connection by blood; the *patrai* are often found as their subordinate parts. It was probably at this point that there intruded upon the kinship organization of the tribe an association based on different foundations. This was the *Hetairia*, an association of men derived from the companionship of soldiers in the same tent and bound together by homoerotic relations; its place in the laws of Gortyn more or less corresponds to that of the phratry in other places. It was perhaps under the influence of the Hetaeria that the phratry became a 'band of brothers by blood', which again developed into a hereditary membership. Common possession of pasturage might also determine the character of a group that corresponded to the phratry, such as the συννομά in Rhodes, where the name indicated the fact of 'common pasture'. This implies another important element in early developments, namely neighbourhood. In a village the obvious duty of neighbours to assist each other would possibly prevail over blood relationship.

The phratries were as a rule included in the phylae (cf. *Il.* 2, 362) and, being thus given a place in the whole of the tribe, gained a political importance that went beyond the 'brotherhood'. Where a link between phratry and tribe did not exist, the tribe was the phyle; for that is really the name for the tribe (φυλή, φῦλον), and it seems that independent settlements occasionally coincided with a phyle. However, at an early time, the purely ethnical element ceased to be of real importance, though it never quite disappeared. The phyle was a personal association of kinsfolk, though one which only appeared when the tribe had consolidated itself in an urban settlement. The west of central Greece seems to have known no phylae. Sometimes in later periods, the phylae played a surprisingly great constitutional part; according to an inscription from Mylasa in Asia Minor (*Syll.* 167, fourth century B.C.) the decision of the Ecclesia had to be sanctioned by the phylae, though it remains doubtful whether this was – in Asia Minor of all places – a genuine survival of tribal organization.

Even where certain phylae were confined to a single district they should not be regarded as local bodies – except for certain later foundations, especially colonial cities. This becomes quite obvious when the same phylae appear in most states of one of the great tribal groups, the Dorian phylae of the Hylleis, Dymanes, and Pamphyloi, for example. These had once probably been independent tribes, the Hylleis perhaps Illyrian; the third, as its name implies, was already composed of a number of small tribal particles. In every state founded by the Dorians all three phylae seem to have had their place, a proof of the strong cohesion of the Dorians before the immigration. In some Dorian states other phylae appeared beside the three, presumably mainly representing the non-Doric part of the population; it might also happen that one or other of the Dorian tribes disappeared, and a conflict between the phylae might reflect a conflict between earlier and later groups of the population, as, for example, in Sicyon in the sixth century under the older Cleisthenes. Much the same is generally true of the four Attic or Ionian phylae, whose curious, half-significant names (Geleontes, Argadeis, Aigikoreis, Hopletes) perhaps originally denoted social groups of the Mycenaean age, though this cannot yet be proved. In Athens they were the only phylae; though the view is held by some that Athens only introduced them in artificial imitation of the Ionian model; in Miletus, and similarly in her colonies, there were two additional phylae, the Boreis and Oinopes (perhaps Aeolian). In Ephesus, on the other hand, we find only the Argadeis – not as one of the (five) tribes, but as a subdivision (a 'thousand'). In Erythrae there seem to have been only three phylae, and other pieces of evidence complete a picture that is anything but uniform. Still, if we think of the way in which the Ionian immigration took place, close agreement between the Ionian cities is by no means to be expected; there is no need to think of a late and artificial creation of the Ionian tribes. Such an explanation, however, does apply to the institution of a fifth tribe in Hellenistic Athens and to many of the other later phylae of which we know, whether they had an ethnical character as in Thurii or, as most frequently, were named after gods, heroes, or kings.

On colonial soil the political groupings of the homeland as a rule lived on, though subject to many changes largely due to the composition of the population, which often was rather mixed. Here, however, we are exclusively concerned with states with an urban centre, having little or no connection with an old tribal organization. Yet, through their youthful energy they might react on the homeland. In the colonies too, at an early date, probably earlier than at home, we find before the classification in kinship groups one into numerical groups of mainly military character. In many places a system arose, in which phyle and phratry were combined with 'thousands', 'hundreds', or 'fifties' (χιλιαστύς, ἑκατοστύς, πεντηκοστύς). A Hellenistic inscription from Delos, deriving probably from Dorian Asia Minor, shows the allocation of new citizens, not only to phyle and phratry but also to a group of 'thirty' (τριακάς) or a 'platoon' (ἡμιόγδοον). In Cos we find phyle, 'thirty', 'fifty', and 'a ninth' (ἐνάτα, perhaps a 'thousand', a ninth of the number of citizens). But in general the principle of kinship did not entirely disappear even under changed conditions.

Apart from these groupings by kinship and military units, which were soon taken over into the structure of the state, the tribe as early as the age of immigration had also its special political order, its 'constitution'. It rested essentially on three factors that may be regarded as common Indo-European. At the head of the tribe stood the chieftain or warlord (ἀρχός, ἀρχηγός); he was the military leader and was also priest and judge. It is noteworthy that the Greeks lost the Indo-European root word for king (reg-) and, to describe the ruler used various words, often of non-Greek origin (βασιλεύς, ἄναξ, κοίρανος). It is probable that the original Greek leader, whose title still survived in Sparta (ἀρχαγέτας), was something very different from the Mycenaean king. In the 'Homeric' kingdom can more of the former be found than of the latter; only Agamemnon's position seems to reflect the 'lord' (Ϝάναξ) of Mycenaean times. Immediately after the Dorian migration, the Greek kings were hardly different from tribal chieftains. Prince and people might often be bound to one another by an exchange of oaths of loyalty. The tribe itself was composed of its warriors, free men capable of bearing arms, who met in the assembly (ἀγορά) of army or people, and by acclamation chose the warlord, and whose agreement must at least have been needed for all peaceful transactions of importance.

Between these two the Council of the Elders (γέροντες) intervened at an early date – so early that they must always be taken into account in Greek history. The Council, which at this early stage can reasonably be compared with the Roman *patres*, was at first probably summoned by the king from the heads of the great families to advise him on important matters. It grew independent and embodied some limitation of the power of the king, and at the same time represented the class of nobles that rose above the ordinary free men. These three political factors in the constitution had not yet reached their final shape and importance, but for all time to come they determined the structure of the Greek state.

3. THE GODS

To the Greeks nature in all its manifestations was divine, and so all human life depended on its connection with the gods. There was no real community among the Greeks that was not also a religious community. All the groups in the social order of which we have spoken – family and clan, phratry and phyle, tribe and state, were also religious unions; each had one or more cults in which every member of the group took part, and whose direction and management fell to the householder (and his wife, for there were cults confined to women), to the eldest of the clan, the head of the phratry, the tribal king, or the state official. If we exclude an earlier age that can hardly be distinguished, in particular a priestly kingship that is likely to have existed in the second millennium, and also a few special places of cult such as Delphi or Eleusis, we find that the priests were always subordinates, engaged in technical functions only.

One most essential element in Greek religious life was its connection with the soil. The cults of the kinship groups, however, which often originated in the age of immigration, were in their very nature not tied to special places; they gained such a bond, if at all, as a secondary matter, possibly soon after the settlement. Only when an ancestor was worshipped as a hero (that is to say, at his grave) was any connection with the soil implied; this is true of the clan, which further gained a local centre in the residence of its head. Significant, too, is the question in the official Athenian test of new officials, the *dokimasia*: 'Have you a cult of Apollon Patroos and Zeus Herkeios, and where are these shrines?' (Arist. *Ath. Pol.* 55, 3). The double cult of the gods of the forefathers and of the hearth, which was valid for all Attic phratries and clans, lacked any fixed centre, but still could not exist without its holy place. Only the hearth (ἑστία) formed a real centre, originally for family and clan, and later for deme and state as well.

Locality became important in yet another way when the community was identified with a definite area: that is to say when the tribe had settled and become independent, and the state had come into existence. In whatever way the settlement had taken place in any particular case, the human group was of necessity bound within its territorial frontiers. Thus, the new local society like the old society of the tribe was a unit of cult. It is very remarkable that, whereas in the kinship groups within tribe and state the cult of the common ancestor was central, the special cults of tribe and state were not based on kinship. The worship of an eponymous hero of the tribe was probably always a late and artificial development; new creations of phylae and clans likewise had their adopted ancestor. The true cult of tribe and state belonged to the leading local god. To what extent gods, once identical, grew apart in this process, cannot now be determined; but it might happen that the local god was of foreign origin and character, for example the Artemis of Ephesus or the Apollo of Didymae. Excavations have shown that many shrines were placed on the top of older settlements, and that especially on sites within the Mycenaean tradition, as in Athens, Mycenae, and Tiryns, the temple of the god of the state was built where once stood the palace of the Mycenaean king. From this it has been correctly inferred that there was a continuity of cult – the palace god of the Mycenaeans becoming the city and state god of the Greeks. Down to the latest times an Athenian official still bore the royal title (ἄρχων βασιλεύς); he was avaliable for purposes of cult and competent to perform 'all ancestral sacrifices', being the immediate successor of the ruling priest-king of the Mycenaean age, of the type found also in Minoan Crete. The local tradition further involved not only the survival of altar and cult, but the turning of the house of the king into the house of the god; it is no accident that the architectural form of the *megaron*, which in Greece is first met in the chief rooms of the Mycenaean palaces, became compulsory for the Greek temple. The god himself took the place of the king; he became the monarch of a state that had ceased to be monarchical. In Athens there was a strange and striking ceremony, by which the peasant god Dionysus, much altered under foreign influences, was given his place among the gods of the state by his union with the wife of the 'king', the ἄρχων βασιλεύς; but this was probably a quite exceptional ritual. It was, on the other hand, a very general practice to ascribe the permanent leadership of a state to a god as 'leader' (ἀρχηγέτης or ἀρχηγέτις), sometimes, but by no means always, on account of a foundation legend.

The fact that an unusually large number of female deities appear as state deities has been explained as an outcome of the Mycenaean tradition; for in the cults of Crete and Mycenae the goddesses were preponderant. That is certainly not untrue; but such a succession could only occur because the fruitful earth was conceived of as a mother, and for the state god a close connection with the soil was essential. Gaia herself, however, never appears as state goddess – probably because she had early come to be thought of in a universal sense. That may have also been the reason, at a later date, why the supreme Greek god, Zeus, was nowhere the special god of a state and, even as πολιεύς, was only a general protector of cities. Originally, Zeus could not be considered as a state god because most likely he was a god of heaven and storms, dwelling on mountain-tops, and nowhere really bound to the soil. He could only become so by being linked to some local god or by being 'divided up', as in Sparta, into a lord of heaven and a lord of the land (Ζεὺς Οὐράνιος and Ζεὺς Λακεδαίμων). Probably this fact has been rightly interpreted, as indicating the change from the age of immigration to that of the new state, but it was the union of the two cults in one state that was historically the most important fact.

This leads us on to a more general religious development, which was of decisive importance for the state cult too. In the centuries after the migrations, there arose not only the world of the Greek states but also that world of gods at home on an Olympus, whether real or imaginary, which from its appearance in poetry is called 'Homeric'. This divine family represents a pantheon completely divorced not only from soil and nature but also from all local human groups; it is most intimately connected with the social sphere of the epic, and thus is part of the concept of the world held by the Ionian nobility. As epic poetry spread and exercised its influence also on the way of life of the nobility in the homeland, the Homeric world of gods, which once had entered on the rich inheritance of the divine world of the Minoans and Mycenaeans, now encountered many deities deeply rooted in life and belief, gods of nature and special places, gods of earth and soil, of hearth and clan. Their worship, indeed, during the archaic age often grew in strength and effect. Herein was mirrored at the same time the social process by which the non-noble sections of society rose in status and importance and the new form of state took firm root, bound to the soil and isolating itself from the Greek world at large. The extension and adoption of cults was a necessary concomitant of the formation and extension of political units; religious festivals formed a firm bond not only between citizens but also between mother-city and colony, or between states linked by a common origin of their peoples. Thus, in a variety of ways local cults became parts of wider contexts.

That spheres of religion, so distinct in their natures as the Olympian, the chthonic, and that of kinship groups, should have united without ousting one another is a fact of fundamental importance. It was from that process that the gods of the Polis arose; their new and peculiar form is also expressed in the emphasis on the divine image, renewed for the first time since the Mycenaean age had come to an end. It was only so that the god of a single Polis could bear the name and nature of an Olympian who had gained Panhellenic status; only so, on the other hand, that many a god, tied to some state or community, but to no Polis, could become a god common to all Greece. We think of gods such as Apollo in Delphi, Zeus in Olympia, or Demeter in Eleusis. It was Delphi that took an important part in spreading the worship of the Olympians and assimilating them to local deities. The heroes had their special importance. With the one exception of Heracles, who was a Panhellenic figure, they were by their graves and by the character of their cult more closely bound to the soil than most of the gods; they represented a strong element of intense religious life, and their cult formed the centre of many small associations, like most of the Attic groups of *orgeones*, but like Theseus could also grow into a kind of representative of the state. The majority of the heroes had once been great men of the epic stories and thus were intimately associated with the form of life which belonged to the times of the clans and their contests. They did their part in breaking Greece up into its many political units; in the mythical contests between heroes the actual fights between states found both model and expression. Thus, myth and cult, gods and heroes, helped to shape the new world of politics, in which the plurality of states yet never impaired the unity of the Greek character.

4. NOBLES AND NON-NOBLES

The contrasts in the religious world which, as we have seen, by a general process of transitions and unions formed the basis of the state cults, rested on a contrast both regional and social. We should have to assume this parallelism between the religious and the political and social spheres, even if we could not prove it. The 'popular' religion, bound up

with local cults, was predominantly the belief of peasants and shepherds
of the homeland; the Olympian religion, on the other hand, is best
understood as a product of a noble society, chiefly in Ionia, that had
largely freed itself from all tribal bonds. In detail, we cannot see how
this nobility arose; but we can say with some certainty that it arose out
of the conditions of the Mycenaean age. We are not yet sure how far
the documents in Linear script B open the possibility that the developments that I have now to describe had already started in the Mycenaean
age. The Greeks of the eleventh to ninth centuries B.C. in their primitive
conditions of culture and economy are clearly distinct from the Greeks
of Mycenae; the epoch marks an entirely new beginning. On the economic side, the nobility rose by land possession on the grand scale. In
politics, its rise was signalized by the decline of the army assembly,
which grew entirely dependent on the nobles and – as still later in
Sparta – had only the passive right of saying 'yes' or 'no'; but also by
the decline of the monarchy which, as Alcinous in the *Odyssey* shows,
lost its exclusive position. The distinction of title between the overlord
or warlord and the vassal kings or noble chieftains (cf. I 2) disappeared
and, instead of one king, we find a number of them (οἱ βασιλῆες).
Only in a few states did kingship last into later times, in Cyrene for
example, or in the special form of the double kingship in Sparta – the
latter perhaps due to an original union of three tribal kings, one of
whom later disappeared. We can certainly point in all quarters to a
gradual limitation of the royal power; that it was gradual, that
monarchy, unlike tyranny, never came, as in Rome, to be the object of
hate and outlawry, is characteristic for the development of the Polis. It
is also very doubtful whether the transition from monarchy to aristocracy had anything to do with the beginnings of the colonization; this
view has recently been expressed, but it is refuted simply by chronology. The new ruling class of the 'kings' was a society distinguished by
birth and wealth (ἀγαθοί, ἄριστοι or ἀριστῆες, εὐπατρίδαι),
owning most of the land (γεωμόροι) or breeding horses (ἱπποβόται).
In the thoughts and actions of these nobles, the state was for long
almost forgotten behind the class. It was, above all, in the
Council that the nobility found its unity and its active expression in the
state; but in reality they had no close relation to the state that they
dominated, and hardly any to the kinship groups within the state. It is
only thus that we can understand the religious world of these men; at
the same time, as always, the political and military spheres were closely
allied. Single combat which – almost exclusively – ruled the tactics of

the age and which survived in the name of the 'knights', the *hippeis*, reflected the loose relations between the 'kings', who might prefer not to fight in the retinue of the king but go out for booty on their own account. So far as these 'heroic' individuals recognized any community at all, they found it in the framework of the social life of the nobility; in this the companionship, the *hetairia*, had a large place beside the clan. The standards of this common life were set by noble custom, which was called *themis* because it grew out of the commands of the 'charisma' of the king, of his '*themistes*'.

In many districts, as for example in Thessaly, the rule of the nobility stood in contrast to the rising cities; Thessaly remained the country of cavalry ($\iota\pi\pi\epsilon\hat{\iota}s$), and that meant predominance of the nobles. Generally, however, it was the nobles who concentrated in the cities. Settlement in towns grew continually in political as in economic importance; the increasing urban concentration was one of the main reasons for the decline of the monarchy and, after it, for the slow break-up of the rule of the nobles. The power to rule was still bound to military valour and landed possessions; but the city ($\pi\acute{o}\lambda\iota s$) – within the area of the state ($\delta\hat{\eta}\mu os$) – was now a living centre, where government was carried on and justice administered, where the 'Agora' developed from an occasional assembly into a permanent market, where the economic isolation of the household and the class isolation of the individual noblemen were slowly but steadily undermined. The word 'polis' had not yet got the meaning of 'state'; so we cannot describe this rule of the nobles in a class society as a Polis, only as a first step towards one; the ever-growing importance of the urban element implies this too. The part of the population that was not noble, the ordinary free men, were partly settled as farmers or tenants on the land, but they too became increasingly town-dwellers. In the town settled also the artisans and pedlars who had hitherto been without a fixed home, and in the town everything went to undermine the pure class structure. A rule of the nobles over the non-nobles might develop into a rule of town over country; in Asia Minor, in the midst of a non-Greek population, that came as a matter of course. It was in the town that the class state changed into the community of citizens.

The whole of this development, which included the passing of the tribal organization into the Polis, was most decisively realized in the eastern parts of the homeland – the main area also (and this is significant) of the geometric style; at the same time, as was only natural, the influence of the advanced urban forms on colonial soil was very marked.

There the tendency to think things out rationally had set in strongly at an early date and enabled men to emancipate themselves more decisively from the social and political traditions of the tribe. A similar development was expressed by the changes in the methods and conditions of military, economic, and political life, changes which may not always have happened at the same time or in the same order, but as a whole they formed parts of a single process, closely linked to one another, and all belonging to the second half of the eighth and the seventh centuries. In place of single combat came the tactics of the closed phalanx of hoplites. That was only possible when the knights with their bearing of proud independence disappeared, when the military order based upon equality found its counterpart in a political order as a community of free men. Actually, in those states in which the nobility had not freed itself so completely as in Ionia from the bonds of clan and state, the contrast with the non-noble population heightened the family pride of the nobles and led to a very strong emphasis on the quality of belonging to the Eupatridae, the descent from noble fathers. The clan came more and more to form the fundamental community of the nobility; it determined their conceptions of law (inheritance, blood-vengeance, etc.) and taught its members a strong sense of solidarity. It meant a great step forward, therefore, when the nobles found themselves compelled so far to broaden the clan organization of the state as to admit non-nobles to its ranks. In Athens, probably in consequence of a law of Solon, the members of private cult associations (θιασῶται) or other non-noble persons (ὀργεῶνες) were enabled to take part in the cults of the clans, taking their place with equal rights beside the sons of the noble families; these were called clan members (γεννῆται) or, at an earlier stage, milk-brothers (ὁμογάλακτες). Later it might happen that they were members of a religious association which claimed or pretended to be a clan, such as the Salaminioi. The most important duty of the phratries was, by the religious sanction they provided, to watch over the admittance to citizenship.

The rule of the nobility, so often arbitrary, contributed a good deal, especially in the matter of jurisdiction, to awaken and strengthen the urge of the non-noble classes to have a share in the state. Hesiod is our earliest witness, and a very impressive one at that, who reveals a society in the process of transition from a stateless existence to that of the representative of Polis unity. Outside and beyond their social cohesion the nobles discovered the fact, more and more decidedly emerging, of a wider political community. It must not be overlooked that the nobles themselves, by limiting or abolishing blood-vengeance, clan feuds, and the right of taking the law into their own hands, had entered the path that led to their incorporation in the state even before the non-noble elements broke through. We do not know to what extent the nobles were acting upon their own free decision, to what extent they were under compulsion by the rise of other groups of the people. Anyway, when they renounced blood-vengeance and self-help, the road was opened which led to the legal supremacy of the state. Without that, there would have been no criminal jurisdiction by the state nor even a simple administrative organization. Naturally, it was the free peasants who first announced their political aspirations. They shared with the nobility the principle that citizenship rested upon the possession of landed property – a principle that still retained its importance in the Polis, when the social and economic development had gone much further and the folk without any land of their own had their share in the state. The community itself now owned land which was no longer an object of dispute among the noble families. To the mutually related changes in politics and the army corresponded the economic development which led to two results: the nobles appropriated to themselves small private properties, thus robbing the peasants of their economic and political basis ('Bauernlegen'), and trade and handicraft rose to be factors of increasing importance. The issue of these two tendencies was that a steadily growing class of men without landed property worked its way into the state – a shift of emphasis in politics and social life that began in the age of colonization and found vigorous and direct expression in the sixth century.

With this, the forms of noble life passed beyond their original sphere. Released from their class restriction, they became of decisive importance for the rising mass of citizens and with that for the life of the state in general. On the other hand, as the civic community grew, a new sense of justice made itself felt. The unquestioned validity of the noble code was replaced by the will to a justice that extended to all (δίκη). The Greeks had taken the road by which the state, as a community at once political and religious, became the one and only power to form rules of life, to create a tradition of jurisdiction, and to establish a system of legislation with written codes of law. All that made 'Nomos' the expression and the master of the state. In general, however, the nobles were able to adapt themselves to the political development – though less, and hardly ever of their own will, to the social and economic one – and so to retain the leadership in the changed state.

c

5. FORMS OF STATE

Those varied historical phenomena and developments of which we
have up to now been writing were the reason why the many Greek
states that came into being had such very different forms. They are
described here as 'forms of state' in contrast to the different 'forms of
constitution' that may exist within one form of state (see pp. 43 ff.).
Inside their world of states the Greeks themselves knew of two main
forms: *ethnos* and *polis*, which are usually rendered, not quite accurately,
as tribal state and city or community state, but which might be better
described as state without and state with an urban centre. Both grew
out of the tribal constitution of early times, but the process of consolida-
tion must have taken a considerable time. It is likely that the Ethnos,
which was so much closer to the tribal society, was established earlier
than the Polis which can be shown as early as the eighth century to have
existed as an autonomous political and economic unit, especially in
Ionia, on the islands of the Aegean, and in the eastern districts of the
Greek mainland, wherever Mycenaean castles and cities had existed.
The Polis could also be a mother-city, sending out colonies, that is to
say, new Poleis, all over the Mediterranean shores. Beside it stood the
Ethnos. Under these two contrasting forms of state is hidden a great
variety of states, differing from one another in more than mere detail.
Despite this, scholars have done well to follow the generalization; in
those two forms we can find expressed the essentials of all Greek states.
Sparta, so peculiar in many respects, represents a difficulty; but following the practice of antiquity, which surely recognized what was essential, Sparta too is dealt with inside the framework of the Polis.

If in the following chapter we are to treat the Polis as the essential
Greek state, we must try to justify this further generalization. It will be
well to begin by discussing the other state form, the tribal or cantonal
state. It is understood that the Polis never was the only type of state
among the Greeks, and though it will be the centre of our description
of the Hellenic state, the Ethnos always existed beside it. This more
primitive form of political community was peculiar to the western and
some of the central districts of Greece – that is to say, it generally occurred where traces of Mycenaean settlement are either rare or altogether lacking. It was a form of state immediately connected with the
age of migration; the word ἔθνος actually denoted that it belonged to
some tribe, what we might call 'nationality' (cf. e.g. Her. VIII 45;
Thuc. III 92, 5). The origin of independent tribal states followed both

the Achaean migration, for example in Arcadia, and the north-western Greek immigration, for example in Aetolia, Acarnania, and Elis. Tribes, sometimes divided into sub-tribes, settled in a manner usually determined by the natural conditions of the district in question, and the country took its name from the tribe (as, for example, Locris and Achaea). In Epirus originally fourteen tribal subdivisions existed, and in the Delphic Amphictiony twelve (see below, p. 109), all once independent. Men lived in homesteads or open villages ($\kappa\hat{\omega}\mu\alpha\iota$, $\delta\hat{\eta}\mu o\iota$), often widely apart from one another; thus the cohesion of the tribe was loosened, and the political elements of the constitution of the tribe completely or almost completely disappeared. With the exception of the Macedonians and the non-Greek kingdom of the Molossians in Epirus, no traces of the tribal kingship can be pointed out in these states. The memory of its disappearance lasted longer on the sites of the mighty Mycenaean monarchy; as a general rule, tradition is easily lost under the primitive conditions of loose regional unions. Occasionally, neighbouring settlements united to form a joint village community or a kind of cantonal union which in 'citadels of refuge' might possess common places of safety in times of war. Such unions or communities might often gain a certain independence, even to the extent of waging war separately from the tribe, of having their own laws and concluding treaties with one another (cf. Tod, 24; 34); that is to say, actually winning their own full rank as states. Local potentates, too, might occasionally make themselves independent. Normally, however, the unity of the tribe remained alive and generally acknowledged, particularly when supported by a common centre of worship of the tribal god. Still, as we have seen, a firm political connection was often lacking. In Boeotia, on the other hand, unity was either enforced by the leading Polis (Thebes), or disrupted by the other autonomous Poleis; it was a struggle between Ethnos and Polis within the framework of an Ethnos (see pp. 122 f.). From other evidence we learn that a tribe could wage war on its own, and conclude treaties (e.g. Thuc. I 107, 2; II 22, 3; III 114, 3); we do not know, however, how far the tribe was really concerned as a whole. Anyway, it will certainly be understood from what has been said that, in contrast to these states, it was the Polis that was the state which had historical significance. That remains true although such tribes as the Aetolians and Acarnanians, to say nothing of the Macedonians, played an important part in Greek history from the fifth century onwards, above all in the internal wars of Greece. The full strength, however, of the tribal states belongs to the time of the large federal movements in the fourth and third centuries (on this, see pp. 120 ff.).

Between the two forms of state, there were some intermediate forms which may in part be regarded as special forms of the Ethnos. The canton often tried to escape from the political weakness of its primitive organization, especially by establishing an urban centre and thus, in fact, finding a way of transition to the Polis. That happened, it is true, usually within sub-tribes of small extension; otherwise no Polis could have risen. It could also happen that a single settlement rose to become the capital of its district and brought at least part of the rest of the tribe into dependence on it (e.g. Opus in Locris). The Greeks described such an occurrence as a *synoikismos*, that is to say a single deliberate act of 'settling together'; this might happen in states other than the cantonal ones. In whatever manner such a 'synoecism' took place, it certainly meant a union in administration (cf. Thuc. II 15) as well as in religion; religious union consisted in the common recognition of one or more city gods (θεοὶ πολιοῦχοι). Often it was a city already in existence that destroyed the political existence of the other independent places of the area (e.g. Lesbos in 428 B.C.). This meant the merging of a number of Poleis into one; it was essentially a matter of politics and law, a *sympoliteia*, and only involved a certain slow loss of population to the capital. Synoecism seems to be foreshadowed in a law of the fifth century (*Syll*. 45), in which Halicarnassus and a small place, Salmakis, still appear as practically independent of one another. Sometimes a process of the past that had taken place gradually was interpreted as a single synoecism (e.g. Athens). There was no basic difference when in later times the synoecism was often linked to the creation of a new city (e.g. Rhodes); though in such cases a large part of the population had to be resettled on the site that had hitherto been unoccupied. There might be an even more marked shift of population, when the inhabitants of some open places were drawn together into the nearest Polis (e.g. Thebes after 431 B.C.); but this was a military measure, without real political significance. On the other hand, the creation of a city as a new and single political centre for a district so far settled in villages and homesteads only (e.g. Mantinea, Megalopolis) was something rather different. It was not a mere shift of population; it was not a union confined to law and politics; it meant that a city was actually created out of nothing. In Mantinea, under pressure from Sparta, there later occurred the opposite of a synoecism, a temporary *dioikismos*; for a time the city of Mantinea ceased to exist (Xen. *Hell*. 5, 2, 7). Synoecism was the most important means by which a tribal state could pass into a Polis. But it is wrong to regard it, even though we may include all its varieties, as the only or even as the principal cause of the origin of the Polis.

All these changes, which belong partly to early times, and partly were as late as the fourth and third centuries B.C., reflect the decisive importance of the Polis; always and in every way it influenced the more primitive political formations. This is true even of countries like Achaea, in which the number of ancient cities prevented any one of them from becoming the capital. Having more than one chance of starting political life, the people here, at an early date, turned the cantonal organization towards a league (κοινόν); out of Polis and canton arose a third form, which in its constitution was entirely determined by the Polis (cf. pp. 120 ff.). The Polis was by far the most common and politically effective type of state; this remains true even though the Greek cities in Italy came under strong constitutional influence from Italy and Rome, and the colonies on the shores of the Black Sea generally experienced the growth of a mixture of Greek and barbarian civilizations. The Polis it was that everywhere expressed and carried Greek culture. This has two meanings; on the one hand, it was the Polis alone that accomplished the great historical deeds, the Polis alone that led the Greek spirit to its supreme cultural achievements after Homer; in the second place, the Polis represented the Greek form of life in surroundings that were not Greek – first of all in Asia Minor, then by colonization over the whole of the Mediterranean, and, finally, by the foundations of Alexander and the Hellenistic kings, even at much later times, far in the heart of Asia. It comes to this: we have the right to regard the Polis as 'the' Greek state. Polis here is, of course, an abstraction from a great number of real states and the vicissitudes of a long history. The Greeks saw in the Polis the normal form of their state, the philosophers even saw it as the normal form of any and every state, and the political development of several centuries made it – beyond any doubt – the predominant form of state. In the next chapter we shall try to disentangle from the variety of countless Poleis – many of them most imperfectly known – the common and essential elements.

CHAPTER TWO

The Polis

I. BASIC FACTS

(a) *Territory*. When Aristotle wants to discover the essential qualities of a Polis he mentions as the first: community of place. That implies, above all, the unity of space and the identity of the territory of the state with the land of the citizens. Where this region lay was in a sense irrelevant. Themistocles could threaten in sober earnest that the Athenians would transfer their Polis to Italy, and that is not the only time that we hear of such plans for a completely new settlement. Because of those geographical conditions of which we spoke above (I 1), the territory of the Polis is to be thought of as a narrow and closed region lying round an urban centre, bounded by mountains and sea and the territories of neighbouring Poleis. 'So long as the Polis grows without losing its unity, let it grow – but no further' (Plato, *Rep.* 423b). The passion for expansion, which is common to every form of state, but which is very weak in the Polis because of its character as a human community and its tendency to isolate itself, did occasionally break through these bounds; but this did not happen to any great extent, and in general it occurred only late. Still, it has been shown that there were towns, called Poleis, whose territory belonged to another state. They were dependent on that state which, on the other hand, guaranteed their existence. Thus, the territory of a Polis was sometimes extended, mostly by colonization, though in a somewhat concealed manner. A comparatively common form of expansion was to add land of 'Perioeci' or for an island state like Thasos or Rhodes to take possession of a piece of land on the mainland opposite (Peraea). All such things were more likely to happen because, both in time and in principle, the state as a community came before the state as territory. The latter was important, but less as a possession than as the extent of political power.

Sometimes a Polis succeeded in enlarging its territorial area. Syracuse held under her power a considerable territory with several dependent cities; Argos, as late as the fifth century B.C., destroyed some smaller states such as Mycenae and Tiryns, and thus was able to make the whole of Argolis her territory. The most important examples of this kind are, in their different ways, Athens and Sparta. Athens united all Attica under her rule. This was said to have happened by the synoecism ascribed to Theseus, but it was really the result of a lengthy process, ending with the inclusion of Eleusis as late as the eighth century B.C. This synoecism meant that Athens reduced the Attic communities from Poleis to demes (cf. the Tetrapolis round Marathon), and thus extended the unified territory of the Polis over the whole country. The principle of territorial unity was not destroyed but asserted; all Attica became citizen land. Only the crossing to Salamis – at all times an object of dispute between Athens and Megara – may be thought of as a certain violation of the principle of territorial unity, but this did not happen before the sixth century B.C. and after long fighting.

In Sparta, on the other hand, the relation of state and land was different. Here, the territory of the state and the land of the citizens were not identical; the land was divided into the real property of the Spartiates, cultivated by the Helots, and the 'surrounding' land of the Perioeci. To the circle of land of the Perioeci – which, however, was broken at several points – belonged the great island of Cythera, lying some way off the mainland. The land of the Spartiates, apart from its original modest extent in the Eurotas valley, lay in the plains of Messenia, separated from the Eurotas valley by the mighty walls of Mount Taygetus and, in places, by land of Perioeci. Here too the principle of unity was broken; the state was not the territory of Sparta, though, in a purely political sense, this pseudo-city was the centre of the state and the seat of government. Characteristics of the Polis and of the Ethnos unite here, together with some additional creative features, to form something unique – in some ways a territorial state.

In fact, the territory of the Polis varied greatly in extent. Apart from Athens with rather more than 1,000 square miles of territory, including Salamis and Oropus, and Sparta with about 3,300 square miles, including Laconia and Messenia, there was hardly a Polis of the homeland or the islands with more than 400 square miles. Some, and some of importance, had less than 40. Corinth had 340, Samos 180, Sicyon 140, Aegina 33, Delos (less than 2) with Rheneia $8\frac{1}{2}$ square miles. Many districts which are usually spoken of as political units contained a considerable number of single Poleis; e.g. Boeotia with about 1,000 square miles had ten (later as many as twenty), Phocis with 630 had twenty-two, Lesbos with 680 had six, Crete with 3,300 had, it is said, as many as a hundred. Of the colonies, certain Poleis in Asia Minor and, above all, some in South Italy and Sicily, possessed a really considerable territory: thus Syracuse, including Leontini, had about 1,830 square miles, Acragas 1,670, Gela 660, Selinus and Himera between 430 and 470. For comparison we may quote a few modern examples (in round figures): Scotland has 30,400, Massachusetts 8,300, Luxembourg 1,010, Greater London 700, the Orkney Islands 375, the canton of Geneva 110, St Helena 50, Manhattan 30, San Marino 24, Monaco 9, Gibraltar 2 square miles.

'Community of place' was also expressed by the fact that town and countryside equally belonged to the Polis. The Polis was not just plain city-state; but there was only one single town. This town, as a rule a walled city, contained the state hearth (ἑστία), the temples of the state cults, the offices of the highest magistrates, the Agora; frequently, though not always, it included a citadel. But this city lived off its land and, although that land in its narrowness and poverty was often insufficient, the Polis never ceased to rest on an agrarian basis. Many of the peasants lived in the country, but often, especially where the hinterland was very small or where a non-Greek population remained as serfs, the 'yeomen' lived in town but had their fields outside. For Athens we may assume that it was only after the Decelean War that the population of the countryside was no longer more numerous than that of the town (see below, p. 32).

The territory, small as it might be, required for carrying on its administration some principle of subdivision. At first, the fact that the members of a clan usually lived close together might make any special local distribution unnecessary; but soon this changed, and place began to count for more than kinship. Mostly, however, we can no longer comprehend the development in any detail. Where the principle of kinship was still upheld, it was rarely more than a fiction. It is significant for the unity of town and country that the Polis was never divided into those two parts, but that all local divisions included both. From earlier times, there is evidence in the Attic naucraries for a division of the territory of the state that must have existed before Solon; in them the personal principle was combined with the local one in some way unknown to us. These forty-eight divisions, originally, it seems, an organization designed to let the citizens take part in the building of warships, became administrative districts of a general character, and their presidents (πρυτάνεις) might on occasion play an important role in politics; the naucraries were distributed twelve to each of the four phylae – which shows that some regional meaning was not quite absent even from these. Aristotle (*Ath. Pol.* 8, 3; cf. frg. 5) knows also of twelve *trittyes*, the three parts into which each phyle was divided; they were units between the phylae and the naucraries. The existence of the trittyes is not in doubt, but their character, especially their relation to the original twelve Poleis of Attica, is a matter of dispute. Certainly in them as in the whole development which, even before Solon, had begun to push the kinship groups of society into the background, we see the increasing importance of the local element and the imperfect way in which it was linked up with a state still based on tribal structure. A further step followed, when the political and social division of the people came to be mainly determined by the regional principle, which might work hand in hand with the local influence of noble factions or of cult centres – as to some extent in Attica where the groups of the Pediaei, Paralii, and Diacrii, the men of the plain, the coast, and the hills, played distinctive parts, although the political unity of each group ('party') must not be taken for granted. Cleisthenes then brought the local principle to complete victory over the kinship principle. What was essential in his 'reform of the phylae' was the division of Attica into ten phylae, each composed of three trittyes, taken from the three sections into which Attica was divided: city, coast, and interior. This ingenious division did not turn the phylae into closed administrative units but it did make them – and with them the tenths of the council derived from each tribe, the Prytaneis – into mixed bodies in which the Eupatridae no longer held the upper hand. We should add that the many demes, urban or country boroughs, became political bodies and formed the basis of a new order of the state. The regional connections of kinsfolk and clans were decisively destroyed, although the fact that membership of the deme was inherited introduced a new element of purely personal connection that took no account of actual future residence. Moreover, the local principle was to some extent over-shadowed by what Aristotle defines as Cleisthenes' chief aims, the 'mingling of the people'. Much in the distribution within the local units looks illogical; anomalies in the system might, however, be deliberate in order to disrupt earlier bonds, and to secure support for a democratic order. It was neither by descent nor simply by the place of residence, still less by profession, that the citizen population was divided. It was to be treated as a homogeneous unit. That was the ideal, though reality was slightly different. The power and influence of the nobles were by no means broken nor the importance of the city of Athens reduced. On the contrary, the citizens of the urban trittyes were the most active and politically influential section of every phyle. Even so, Cleisthenes' final aim – never achieved, but decisively approached – was the political unity of the Athenian people within the whole of Attica.

It was probably under Athenian influence that the old local units, the κτοῖναι, in Rhodes, which perhaps were kinship units at the same time, were changed into demes. As in Athens, but usually in a less complicated and consistent form, the phyle everywhere came to contradict the very meaning of its name and became a purely local district. Even in Sparta, it seems, the local principle found an early expression in the division of the settlement of Sparta into five villages or 'obae' (ὠβαί). A curious further development, probably quite artificial, must have occurred in Alexandria, where there were 5 phylae, 60 demes, and 720 phratries. The fact that phylae, phratries, and demes might have their separate local self-administration and their own possession of land, must not be taken as evidence that they had once been independent settlements. The principle of divided territory rather than divided population generally asserted itself and confirmed the close relation of the Polis to the soil.

(b) *Population*. The population of the territory of the Polis consisted of free and non-free. Among the free, there were citizens and non-citizens, among the non-free there were serfs and slaves. The origin of these distinct classes of the population goes back partly to the fact that all Greek states (even Athens, which had forgotten the fact) were conqueror states, and that accordingly there was a contrast between old and new inhabitants; on the other hand, the later economic and social developments also played their part.

To form any opinion of the divisions of the people, we need some knowledge of the numbers, absolute and relative. All our estimates, being based on very inadequate and chancy material, will give us at the best approximate figures; we can only try to determine something quite general and typical. In most cases, our sources mention numbers not of citizens but of soldiers only, sometimes of colonists. The amount of possible error when we use those incidental and occasional figures is almost unlimited. In the following tables, I do not try to compete with any attempts at reaching exact figures. All I wish to show are typical figures and the approximate course of the general development. As examples, I will give estimates for Athens as a Polis highly developed and economically flourishing, for Boeotia as a purely agrarian district, corresponding in area to Attica, but in the fifth century B.C. containing

ATHENS

	c. 480 B.C.	c. 432 B.C.	425 B.C.	c. 400 B.C.	c. 360 B.C.	323 B.C.	313 B.C.
Citizens	25–30 [35]	35–45 [43]	[29]	20–5 [22]	28–30	[28]	21 [21]
Citizens with families	80–120 [140]	110–80 [172]	[116]	60–100 [90]	85–120	[112]	60–85 [84]
Metics	4–5 [?]	10–15 [9·5]	[7]	6–8 [?]	10–15	[12]	10 [10]
Metics with families	9–12 [?]	25–40 [28·5]	[21]	15–25 [?]	25–50	[42]	25–35 [35]
Slaves	30–40 [?]	80–110 [115]	[81]	40–60 [?]	60–100	[104]	30–60 [?]
Total population	120–50 [?]	215–300 [317]	[218]	115–75 [?]	170–255	[258]	140–90 [?]

BOEOTIA

	5th cent. B.C.	4th cent. B.C.
Citizens	28–30	35–40
Citizens with families	85–95	110–25
Metics with families	5–10	5–10
Slaves	20	30
Total population	110–25	145–65

SPARTA

	480–460 B.C.	371 B.C.	3rd cent. B.C.
Spartiates	4–5	2·5–3	2–2·5 (?)
Spartiates with inferior rights	0·5 (?)	1·5–2	1·5–2 (?)
Spartiates with families	12–15	7–9	6–8
Perioeci		40–60 (?)	
Helots		140–200 (?)	
Total population		190–270 (?)	

ten, and later even more, independent states, and finally for Sparta as a peculiar type of an extreme oligarchy. All the figures that I give are uncertain, those of the slaves hardly more than guesses. To make plain how uncertain these figures are (but also to show that they have some elation to reality) I add (in square brackets) to my figures for Athens those adopted by A. W. Gomme; his arrangement differs from mine, but I have fitted it to my tables, without, I trust, making any serious alterations. All numbers are in thousands.

The figures for each country reflect in their variations the course of historical events. At the same time, the comparison between different types of state is very significant for each form, especially for its economic and social life. One of the most remarkable facts is the comparative thinness of population in Boeotia as compared with Attica, above all, of course, in metics and slaves. That was so although in Boeotia a number of different states are included, among them the powerful city of Thebes. We should be also interested to know the distinct figures for town and country population, but they are far too uncertain even for Athens. Practically all we can say is that before the Peloponnesian War barely two-fifths of the population lived in the city and the Peiraeus; at an earlier date the number was considerably smaller, while in the later fourth century B.C. it rose to over a half. The number of the Athenian metics outside city and harbour must always have been very small. We sometimes hear of a Polis of the Ten Thousand (πόλις μυρίανδρος); that was an ideal form of state, but as a limit not to be exceeded by an important, if average Polis, the number of ten thousand can be regarded as realistic. In a similar way, the political theorists, dealing with the needs of their ideal cities, were thinking of numbers that were within the limits of reality; Plato, Laws 771A, speaks of 5,040, Aristotle, Nic. Eth. 1170b, 31, of neither ten nor a hundred thousand citizens. They confirm the principle that too large a population would endanger the unity of the Polis. It is quite possible that Pericles' law of 451 B.C., by which only those retained the citizenship whose parents were both citizens (ἐξ ἀμφοῖν ἀστοῖν) was designed, in part at least, to check the dangerously rapid increase of the citizen body. The experience of the Polis taught the Greeks the need for restriction, in numbers no less than in territory. 'Who could be general of such an unwieldy mass or who could be a herald, unless he had a voice like Stentor?' (Arist. Pol. 1326b, 5; cf. also Xen. Hell. 2, 4, 20). Moreover, direct democracy, as the Greeks knew it, was impossible without restricted numbers of citizens. In the course of time the oppo-

site, that is to say, the decline of the number of citizens, became a
more serious danger. We know of that particularly in Sparta, but it
was a phenomenon that at different periods occurred at other places as
well. Aristotle, *Pol.* 1272a, 22, could even believe that the small
numbers in some Cretan states were caused by the practice of
paederasty.

The division of the non-free population, as stated above, into serfs
and slaves has recently been attacked because there was no strict
demarcation line between the two groups. This is true, but it can be
maintained that there were different degrees of non-free status, for
example slaves without any rights and slaves with certain privileges;
above all, there were intermediate positions 'between free men and
slaves' (Poll. 3, 83). The situation, complicated in itself, has become more
so by frequent contradictions in our sources; Aristotle's systematic
scheme, for example, is more than once refuted by our primary evidence. Crete provides equally rich and contradictory evidence.
Athenaeus' sources (VI 263 e–f) distinguished, on the one hand, between
public and private slaves, on the other between domestic slaves and
prisoners of war. This means that two different categories, the nature of
slavery and its origin, are mixed up. In the Law of Gortyn the words
for domestic slaves ($οἰκεύς$) and slaves in general ($δοῦλος$) are used
indiscriminately; there too some legal rights of slaves are mentioned
which did not exist in other states. It is uncertain to what extent the
law code of Gortyn was valid even only among other Cretan states, and
as there is no definite divergent evidence it seems better not to generalize
from that one codification.

We therefore follow the division otherwise recorded for Crete into
slaves and clarotae. It is probably significant that in the passage from
Pollux quoted above, which may go back to Aristophanes of Byzantium, several different groups are all included under the common head-
ing of $μεταξὺ ἐλευέρων καὶ δούλων$, that is to say, the Spartan helots,
the Thessalian penestae, the Cretan clarotae (who were settled on the
klaros, their master's inherited property), and the *mnoïtai*, the public
slaves. It seems impossible to define, and to distinguish clearly between,
the many Greek words for the non-free; but the view ought to be upheld that, apart from slaves who were simply owned by their masters,
there were others, peasants who only paid regular duties and were
bound to the land. We are inclined to call the latter 'serfs', but must
admit that the expression is taken from the conditions of medieval
feudalism and therefore not completely appropriate; but a better name

has still to be found. Moreover, as antiquity knew something very similar to medieval enclosure (*Bauernlegen*), the word serfs (= *Hörige*) is not too misleading. We thus accept the traditional names for the various groups of non-free people.

Slavery first gained in the Polis, and through the economic development of the sixth century B.C., that great importance which is suggested by the numbers given above. Before that, as Homer shows, we find domestic slavery on a modest scale in which women were more numerous; it rested on exposure of children, kidnapping, and prisoners of war. Its form and spirit were essentially patriarchal, and its economic significance was almost negligible. Later on, owing to the changes in economic conditions and methods, the slaves as a cheap form of labour became a very important part of property. The main contingent was now supplied by foreign slaves who were bought from slave traders; but there were, of course, Greeks too, among them in earlier times free citizens who had fallen into slavery through debt. Slave revolts hardly ever occurred in Greece before Roman times. It seems that in the third century and even earlier there were revolts in Chios which was notorious for her masses of slaves, and in the Decelean War more than twenty thousand slaves ran away from Attica (Thuc. VII 27, 5); most of them will have been workers in the mines. The lack of revolts was due, not so much to the very motley composition of the whole body of slaves as to their treatment which in general was good, and also because slaves had a chance of gaining economic independence and enjoyed certain rights at law. We have many pieces of evidence about the position of Athenian slaves and their chances of rising economically; but they were by no means the best off; in Crete, for example, slaves were admitted to take the oath, while in Athens they could only testify, if at all, under torture. Beside private slaves, there were almost everywhere public slaves (δημόσιοι), who frequently were important assistants of the officials. It comes out clearly that the slaves were an indispensable element in the structure of the state and, as such, dependent on the state as well as on the individual master. Slavery, on the whole, increased with the progress of Polis development. Slaves were needed through the growth of trade and manufacture as well as by the increasing share of all citizens in political life. Must we therefore speak of a 'slave-holders' society'? Certainly not in the sense frequently used. If the Greeks could not do without slaves, these were never the only workers, or even the most important. The poor among the citizens had always to work for a living; they normally regarded the slaves as fellow-workers (cf. Xen.

Mem. 2, 3, 3) rather than as competitors; naturally, whoever could afford it held slaves. All comparisons with the slavery of the American South are out of place, except perhaps as far as the large estates in Sicily and Italy are concerned. Slaves, if not under that name, have in fact existed at all times and in all forms of society.

Remarkable again for the Greek conditions is the small number and slight importance of the freedmen (ἀπελεύθεροι). Manumission might come by the private decision of the master, but sometimes also as an official reward for some useful service, in war or by the denunciation of a criminal offence; it was usually done under the form either of a dedication or of a sham sale to a god (Olympia, Delphi, Poseidon at Taenarum), and was often burdened with restrictions or conditions. The position of the freedmen at law was, in contrast to Rome, at best equal to that of the foreigner. In this we perceive the unbridgeable gulf that separated citizen and slave; it also explains why there was in general no great urge on the part of the slaves to be freed.

Slavery was the most common, but not the only negation of freedom in the Polis. In many places, through the subjection of an earlier population by conquest, a class of serfs arose, peasants, as they have been described before, who had to pay with part of their harvest. To this class belonged the Thessalian penestae and the Cretan clarotae. The Attic hectemorii, who – according to the predominant modern view – were required to pay a sixth of their crops, though in a similar position, were free men who had sunk through debt and loans on their property into serfdom. To what extent the laws of Gortyn referred to slaves or serfs remains disputed; but certain is that the class mentioned there had almost complete independence in matters of family law, might even marry free women and have free children; they also had some legal rights in public life.

Among the same group of serfs we must reckon the Spartan Helots (εἴλωτες), though in the peculiar structure of the Lacedaemonian state they held a position of their own. In Laconia they were mostly the conquered pre-Dorian population, in Messenia the Dorian Messenians, conquered in the eighth and seventh centuries B.C. They were all settled on the land of the Spartiates, allotted to some individual Spartiate to cultivate his estate and to render personal service; they were bound to the soil, but allowed to use the surplus of the crop for themselves. The individual master could neither liberate nor sell them; they were exclusive property of the state, which had the most extensive rights over them: think of the Crypteia. They, and they alone, bore the whole burden of agriculture; only their existence made it possible for the Spartiates to be nothing but a military class. Economically, the Helots may have been no worse off than the serfs in other states, but they not only lacked any power to act at law, they were completely without its protection. It can easily be understood that in our sources they frequently are simply called slaves. The arbitrary treatment by the Spartiates kept them in constant fear, but that worked either way. Every year there was an official proclamation of a state of war between Spartiates and Helots, which made the murder of a Helot a permissible act of war; this situation led to frequent dangerous revolts, and Sparta's policy was largely determined by fear of them.

For a looser kind of dependence we may refer to certain border districts, mostly mountainous country, surrounding the more level territory of the interior and, therefore, appearing necessary for the defence of the state. Here we find Perioeci, 'dwellers round', usually independent peoples or communities, required to serve in war and render various other services. Perioeci are found, for example, in Thessaly, Crete, Argos, and Elis, probably also in some of the colonies. Their position varied from place to place; some of them can be described as 'dependent' Poleis or tribes (like those mentioned above, p. 26); others were simply neighbours or allies. In Thessaly they were subject allies; in Crete, where they were called ὑπόβοικοι or ὑποῖκοι, we hear nothing of service in war. It also seems certain that the expression Perioeci was often used in a rather vague and unprecise way (cf. e.g., Arist. *Pol.* 1303a, 8; *FGrH.* 310 F 6). In Sparta alone were the Perioeci inseparably bound up with the body of the state; though it is improbable that they were ruled by Spartan harmosts. In lasting struggles during the eighth to sixth centuries B.C., occasionally also by voluntary union or by colonization, a ring of dependent territory was drawn round the land of the Spartiates. The Perioeci who dwelt in these regions were for the most part Dorians themselves, were settled in independent communities called Poleis, were owners of their own land, which, however, was usually not very fertile, and had their own dependants and slaves. They were called 'Lacedaemonians' and owed service in war to the state, though they enjoyed no active political rights, since they were not citizens of Sparta, but of their own towns; in view of the numerical decline of the Spartiates they were more and more called on to serve as officers and officials abroad. Their further importance to the state lay in the fact that they shut off the Helots from the outside world. It appears from Thuc. V 54 that it was a right of the kings, not of the ephors, to call the Perioeci out on military service; this is perhaps a surviving trace of an old royal prerogative. A state hostile to Sparta, such as Argos in the fifth century B.C., could give the privilege of 'proxenia' to a Perioecus, and in doing so, call him 'Oenuntian' as a citizen of his home town Oenous, not a Lacedae-monian, let alone a Perioecus; but that has little relevance to the actual constitutional position inside the Spartan state, except for confirming the fact that the towns of the Perioeci were regarded as Poleis. The common view that the Perioeci carried the burden of trade and crafts must, to a large extent, be modified. Sparta's foreign trade was small, crafts were mainly domestic and depended on Helot labour. The Perioeci were 'yeomen', who naturally went in for some local crafts and petty business. In matters of taxation they seem to have been put on the same plane as the Spartiates.

Sparta was to an unusual degree self-sufficient. This made it possible to exclude on principle the activities of foreign elements, and on occa-sion to banish by arbitrary decision all foreigners present in the state. In all the other Greek states, though more particularly where trade and crafts played a larger part than in purely agrarian communities, strangers (ξένοι) were a section of the population that counted for much economically. The Polis so far took account of this as to modify the original lack of legal rights, in a varying degree; in particular, to allow the freeborn foreigner who had settled permanently, to form a closer connection with the state, and thus at the same time make better use of him for state purposes. This practice was consistently followed through in fifth- and fourth-century Athens, after Solon and Cleisthenes had already given citizen rights to many foreigners – slaves and freedmen, it is said, among them (Arist. *Pol.* 1275b, 36). Foreigners became *metoikoi*, metics, 'co-dwellers' (also σύνοικοι, or later πάροικοι) by an act of admission, to which they were often compelled after a period of residence which probably varied from state to state. Originally, all these settlers were Greeks; but from the fourth century B.C. there was a certain percentage of non-Greeks among them. By their acceptance as metics they gained the right of residence, the protection of the law for their persons, a share in cults and festivals as well as freedom to practise their professions; on the other hand, they were required to pay a low poll tax (μετοίκιον) and to take their share of public burdens – some-times, to serve in the army. At Athens a list of all metics was kept in the office of the Polemarch (*SEG.* XVIII 153, 30 f.). They remained non-citizens, they had to be represented in court by a citizen as 'prostates',

D

and the right to own land (ἔγκτησις γῆς or οἰκίας) could only be granted as a special privilege. Such grants of privilege might lead to other improvements in their status, especially to freedom from taxation (*ateleia* or *isoteleia*). In Rhodes there was a privilege called ἐπιδαμία, presumably a preliminary to the grant of citizenship in the next generation.

All these groups of the population of which we have spoken so far, great though their importance may have been in numbers as well as in economic and also in social life, had no active and legal share in the state. In some cases, they were only linked to it through their relationship to some individual citizen. Constitutionally, the Polis was the state of the citizens and none other; only the express conferment of citizenship could break through the barriers that existed for everyone who was not a citizen. Even in Sparta the 'people' (δᾶμος) of the Spartiates were the sum total of citizens; the Perioeci, as we have said, though Lacedaemonians, were not citizens. The fact that slaves, metics, and the rest played such an active and independent part in the state's economic life, made it largely possible for the citizen to devote his life to the state, to be indeed a ζῷον πολιτικόν. Still, we must not generalize too much; the idea of 'state pensioners' is hardly apposite even for the Athens of the fourth century B.C. The relative figures (quoted on p. 31) show that not only in the oligarchies, but even in the advanced democracies, the rule of the citizens was the rule of a minority – a minority that frequently tended to diminish, partly as a result of the exposure of children, partly through civil and foreign wars. It was essential for this ruling minority that the population, other than citizen, should not form a unity, either in origin or in social life. Thus, to take an example, the Helots and Perioeci never combined against the Spartan supremacy, and Aristotle (*Pol.* 1262b, 1) can say of the peasants as the subordinate class that their disunion is advantageous to the state. We see here how the Polis as the community of citizens rested on assumptions that might become dangerous to it, and that, at any rate, could make its policy, both at home and abroad, narrow and narrow-minded.

2. POLITEIA

(a) *Citizenship*. The Greek word for citizenship is πολιτεία. The same word also describes the citizen body and the constitution, the whole structure of the state (cf. Plut. *Mor.* 826 C–E). In this usage we find two things expressed: one, that the state, whatever its constitution, rested on the fact of citizenship and the way in which it was distributed; that is to say, the type of constitution depended on the number and quality of those who were citizens (cf. pp. 44 ff.); second, that something more than citizenship was involved. The abstract word *politeia* reflected the unity of the citizens, not only the sum of the individuals but the living body composed of rulers and ruled, and the political life that was the very life and nature of the citizens. The use of the same word for individual participation in the state and for its general structure shows that the participation was in the main not a purely legal act between individual and state; it reflected the vital adherence of the individual to the citizen body, as also to the other communities inside the state (pp. 11 ff.), and therewith was bound to them, bound to religion and soil.

This implies that a purely legal answer to the question 'who is a citizen?' does not do justice to it. Descent is, of course, the first requirement – the fact of being born into family, clan, and deme and growing up into phratry and civic community; but it is remarkable that the strictest definition of descent (for example, ἐξ ἀμφοῖν ἀστοῖν, or by regular marriage with a foreigner only if based on a special treaty of ἐπιγαμία with the state in question) was not original and did not occur before democracy came into being. Even not every democracy had such severe laws, and states in non-Greek surroundings would frequently admit legal marriages with native women (e.g. Cyrene; cf. *SEG.* IX 1, 2 f.). In conservative Sparta it was the possession of a *klaros* and the sharing in *Agoge* and *Syssitia*, that is to say, in the common life of the Spartiates, not legitimate birth, that made the fully qualified Spartiate. The system of state education, with its age groups going back to prehistoric times, attained decisive importance only in Sparta and Crete; but the possession of land was in general and for a very long time a prerequirement for citizenship. To prevent a diminution in the number of citizens, the acquisition or sale of property was forbidden in many states, or a maximum was fixed for the possession of land. Connection by kinship and connection by locality, for all their distinctness, could exist side by side, and this was reflected in the varied use, often quite arbitrary, of patronymic and demotic names (apart from Athens, for instance in Rhodes). This 'natural' citizenship was still limited to a minimum age (18–21, ἀφ' ἥβης), but in aristocracies frequently to a much higher number of years. Even grown-up sons needed the confirmation of their rights as citizens; at Athens they had twice to be accepted into the phratry, first after birth and again when they came of age; after that they registered with the deme to which the father belonged.

In earlier times the nobles might admit to their ranks a foreign nobleman who had given evidence of his goodwill, without any express conferment of citizenship; but from about the seventh century B.C., social events and changes made it necessary to fix more rigidly the qualifications for citizenship. Above all, some restriction was indicated as a reaction against the growing freedom with which citizenship had been conferred – in Athens, for example, after the tyranny and after Cleisthenes; for both had swelled the body of their adherents by the reception of many new citizens. In general, the conferment of citizenship on an individual followed from special services to the state, but grants to whole bodies of men were also made as a result of special political conditions. For a long time, the rule held that such a grant could only be made to men without 'Politeia' – whether to such as had for some reason lost their own civic rights, or to foreign despots with whom till then the question of citizenship had simply not arisen. Against too easy admission of new citizens there were many safeguards; the rapid increase of grants of citizenship as early as the fourth century B.C. represented a decline both of the Polis and of the value of citizenship. With the award of citizenship to non-citizens, the strict meaning of Politeia was destroyed; by authority of the ruling citizens, a legal act could extend the circle of the members of the community. This formal grant of citizenship naturally implied that the newcomer was also admitted to the subordinate groups of the community; but this subsequent act of admission could not create the firm bond of membership by birth. Finally, when it became possible to gain a new citizenship without losing the old, the original sense of joining one's kinsfolk and their cults, as well as the whole local relation, was virtually abolished. What had once been the whole basis of a man's life was sadly reduced, now that several citizenships could exist side by side; at the best it was a measure useful in the relations of states to one another; finally, it became an honour for which you paid rather dear. Thus the Polis gave up all resistance to the destruction of its fundamental social order. We do, however, find even in later times rare examples of a contrary tendency; for instance, Gortyn and Cnossus declined to receive back into their state former citizens who as mercenaries had gained the citizenship of Miletus.

Even older than the right of the state to make new citizens may have been its opposite – the right to expel a citizen from the community.

This withdrawal of citizenship was called Atimia (ἀτιμία). It is clear that it grew out of the original Atimia, the principle in the times of blood-vengeance among the clans that the killing of the man who had been declared an outlaw was not punishable. With the changes of law and the growth of the power of the state, Atimia took on a different meaning. It might be total or restricted to certain rights, pronounced for life or with a time limit; it always meant the cancelling of political and religious rights as well as the confiscation of property, but not the loss of legal personality and not, necessarily, the denial of residence at home. Both of these punishments might, however, be linked to it (disenfranchisement: ἄτιμος καὶ πολέμιος, or similarly; banishment: ἄτιμος καὶ φυγάς). Atimia was the public penalty, above all, for serious political and religious offences; the man who truly offended against the state was thrust out of it. It was a very different thing when the conditions for citizenship by birth and census were decisively changed as, for example, by Pericles in 451/0 B.C. Citizens on such occasions were simply turned into non-citizens, and we can well understand that over such a question many legal cases arose (γραφαὶ ξενίας). Perhaps as early as after the expulsion of the tyrants, possibly in 445/4 B.C., and certainly by the decree of Demophilus (346/5 B.C.), there was frequent reviewing of the list of citizens (διαψηφισμός).

Aristotle (Pol. 1277b, 34; 1278a, 36) links the conception of citizens to a share in the government (κοινωνεῖν ἀρχῆς), and ἀρχή here includes not only the Council but in a democracy the assembly and law courts as well. He narrows down citizenship to the full (or active) citizens and leaves the reduced (or passive) citizenship out of account. Citizen and not a kind of metic, as Aristotle says (Pol. 1278a, 38), was also the man who, though having no share in government, belonged by descent or special grant as a free man to the state and its subordinate groups, and therefore enjoyed the rights of residence and ownership as well as full legal rights. To the citizens of lesser rights belonged those classes which in oligarchies or timocracies were limited in their political status by social or economic restrictions. Thus, for example, in the Athens of Solon the thetes were admitted to the popular assembly, but not to any office (Arist. Ath. Pol. 7, 3); in Sparta, the hypomeiones, as they were called, were a group which, although Spartiates, had through the loss of their klaros suffered what looks like an almost complete loss of their political rights. It might happen that the citizens of full rights were lifted as a special body above the general mass of citizens (cf. the Politeuma of the Myrioi in the constitution of Hellenistic Cyrene;

SEG. IX 1). In Thebes, a law was in force that only he was a full citizen who had not traded in the Agora for at least the last ten years; that rule hit the small peasants in particular. In many places, the *banausos*, the man who earned his livelihood by manual work, was limited in his rights. In oligarchies men of uncertain descent were sometimes given a partial share in the rights of citizenship, for example at Sparta the *mothakes* and *nothoi*, sons of a helot or foreign mother, as far as they took part in the *agogē* (*trophimoi?*), perhaps also the *neo-damodeis*. In democracies, however, the same restriction hit men who sprang from the marriage of a citizen with a foreign woman, and it could even happen that all intermarriage with the reigning Demos was forbidden to its political opponents (Thuc. VIII 21). In Rhodes there was a special group of ματρόξενοι, who seem to have corresponded to the Athenian νόθοι ἐκ ξένης, the sons of a foreign woman.

In a legal sense – though by quite a different line of thought – the younger men too were not full citizens. Mostly, during the years between coming of age and thirty, the citizen still lacked the right and obligation to take an active part in the government (ἀρχή). Women and sons under age were, of course, subject to a restriction of their civil rights and duties merely by the position of the father as the head of the family; this could amount to a complete lack of legal capacity. They might sometimes be distinguished from the citizens (*politai*) as the 'townsfolk' (*astoi, asté*); but that is an ambiguous notion. Archilochus, for example, speaks (7, 1 f.) of the *astoi* as the members of the Polis, though he also mentions them as *politai* (52), and Tyrtaeus (2, 2; 9, 24) twice calls Sparta an *asty*. A woman was a citizen (*politis*), although, as in Athens, she might not even have the right to plead in court or to hold property (ἔγκτησις); citizenship was, as it were, latent in her and found expression, for instance, when the question arose of the legal descent of her children. In many states, for example in Sparta, the woman could own property and as an heiress (ἐπίκληρος) could gain an importance that went beyond private law. Even more rights were granted to women at Gortyn; they could not only own property, but act on their own in court. Finally, a limitation of civil rights might be produced by a partial Atimia.

Civil rights implied civil duties. We meet this most clearly in the oaths of the ephebi and the officials, generally preserved in late versions, but going back to earlier ones. The duties included, among other things, the defence of the state against external enemies and the defence of the laws against internal foes, obedience to the laws, loyalty to home cults and to ancestral beliefs. With any restriction of civil rights went a similar limitation of obligations – at least, where the two were indissolubly connected, as in the taking over of offices.

We have thus had to distinguish not only between citizen and non-citizen but also between citizens of full and of lesser rights, that is to say, between ruler and ruled; herein is expressed the general fact that every community rests on some form of rule. On the other hand, in the identity of the requirements for all citizens – free birth and belonging to the people of the state – we see the lively tendency in the civic community to put all its members on equal level. Thus it was that two opposed principles, that of rule and that of equality, were the two creative forces which, on the basis of civic freedom, determined the political form of the Polis. They were revealed above all in the gradations of citizenship, and that is why these gradations determined the different forms of constitution. The connection between Politeia as citizenship and Politeia as constitution, which Isocrates (VII 14) calls the soul of the Polis ($\psi v \chi \grave{\eta} \pi \acute{o} \lambda \epsilon \omega s$), finds here its deeper foundations.

(b) *Forms of Constitution.* The Polis was the state of its citizens, the *Politai*. There was always identity between state and citizens, but only the full citizens possessed unrestricted rule in the state, roughly what we call sovereignty. Democracy, then, as the rule of the whole people meant the perfection of the Polis. It was the number and quality of the full citizens that decided that structure of the state which, if we avoid the modern meaning of the word, we may call constitution. Greek thought usually started from the number of the rulers and therefore distinguished monarchy, oligarchy, and democracy, the rule of one man, of a few, or of the whole people. Yet beside and even before the notion of quantity stood that of quality. The question of political and social character, for example, found its expression in the popular party names ($\chi \rho \eta \sigma \tau o \acute{\iota}$ and the like), or in such earlier terms as Eunomia and Isonomia. Out of this rose numerous variations of the three main types of constitution. The change from names indicating a good or bad order or equality (*-nomia*) to the statement of rule (*-archia, -kratia*), whether of the few or the many, was more than a mere change of names: it implied the realization of the factor of power in politics and in constitutional life. We shall return to these questions. Since, however, the identity of the citizens with the state was the leading idea of all constitutions, and since they all had the same main institutions (citizens' assembly, Council, and officials), the forms of constitution are not to be regarded as independent forms of state, but as different expressions of one and the same Polis.

On the main types of constitution the political philosophers based their doctrines. Aristotle's division of constitutions by ethical standards is an example, with his three good constitutions: πολιτεῖαι, and three bad ones: παρεκβάσεις. So again is the search for the best state, appearing very early and in the typically Greek form of an 'agon', a contest, or the theory of a cyclic movement of constitutions that grew more and more into shape between Plato and Polybius. All these concepts show the importance that the notion of a constitution had in Greek political thought. However, even if they have a kernel of historical and empirical truth, they cannot serve as a framework in which to draw a picture of the real state. As against them we must emphasize how far from sharp the boundaries between the single constitutions were, and how the many intermediate stages only confirm the truth that, as far as we are concerned, the different constitutions are ultimately aids towards our understanding of the true nature of the Polis.

The view we have expressed that the rule of the citizens with full rights was the essential feature of the Polis, and that thus in every constitution, as Aristotle saw (*Pol.* 1294a, 11), the will of the majority – naturally of the citizens and not of the population – was decisive, implies that no monarchical constitution was compatible with it. The kingship of early times, whether as tribal leadership, as pure monarchy, or, finally, as rule of the king as the first among equal nobles, continued to exist in later centuries with the northern peoples of Macedon and Epirus only; moreover, in point of date, it came before the Polis, in which it survived, if at all, at best as a faded relic, for instance in some religious officer like the ἄρχων βασιλεύς who in Athens had the presidency in trials for murder and so retained an original function of the king, or in the Attic 'kings of the phyle' (φυλοβασιλεῖς), the heads of the four old phylae. In other places, too, we find 'kings' as officials. There are, it is true, a few isolated examples of the continuance of the monarchy, especially in Sparta with its strange double kingship, in which, as in other peculiar features of the Spartan constitution, the Polis age and the pre-Polis age blended; it was in part a hereditary and sacred dignity, in part an executive office, entirely dependent on the state. As for tyranny (τυραννίς), the second form of monarchy in Greece, its name – and perhaps more than the name – was probably imported from the Lydian monarchy into the Greek conditions of the seventh century B.C. (cf. Archilochus, frg. 22; 70). In the traditional explanation, tyranny meant the usurpation of the rule of the Polis by an individual, but in itself it was no proper form of constitution. The existing constitution almost always formally continued, whether the tyrant held an office already in existence but now clothed with special powers, or ruled simply in virtue of his own personal ascendancy and influence. The tyrant stood, as it were, beside, not outside, the Polis and its constitution. Even when the constitution was suspended, that is to say, when the normal life of the state was no longer functioning – as might happen as a rare exception – again it is true that tyranny did not mean a new form of constitution, but an arbitrary interruption of the rule of law in the state. The fact, however, that it could come at all to the rule of an individual – and so frequently – speaks volumes for the nature of the previous constitution and its deterioration, above all in its social structure; it shows how gravely at times the inner equilibrium of the Polis could be disturbed. No tyranny lasted longer than into the third generation; that shows, just as the survival of Polis institutions, that the community was in the end stronger than the individual. The conflict of the two was, after all, at the bottom of the whole phenomenon.

It is no accident that the early political rise of the individual belonged to an age in which individuality found its decisive expression in lyric poetry; but it would be a mistake to regard tyranny exclusively from this personal standpoint. The tyranny of the earlier times (seventh and sixth centuries B.C.) was above all a phenomenon of social, not of political, history, although those who adhered to it or profited by it might be men of less than full political rights as well as belonging to the socially and economically depressed classes of the free population. It was in the fields of social life and culture that the great achievements of the tyrants lay. The Sicilian tyranny of the fifth century B.C. was distinguished from the earlier tyranny in the east by its predominantly military character, which again was largely determined by its special task – to defend the Greeks in Sicily against Carthage.

A special and peculiar form, something between legal kingship and tyranny, is seen in the kingship of the Battiadae in Cyrene which lasted with interruptions down to the middle of the fifth century B.C. What was illegal in tyranny was not so much its arbitrary rule – a factor not always in evidence – as the fact that it was usurped. This it was that distinguished tyranny from the *aisymnetia*, according to Aristotle an 'elected tyranny'; unlimited powers were conferred on an individual, who might be called 'arbitrator' (αἰσυμνήτης) or 'mediator' (διαλλακτής) or plain 'lawgiver'. This again was no special constitution; it merely meant the creation of an exceptional position for an individual, based on a special mandate, an individual universally accepted as arbitrator in the strife (στάσις) between different groups of the people; he tried, in Solon's words, to overcome the social crisis 'by force and by law'. The lawgivers most famous in antiquity were the legendary Lycurgus in Sparta, Draco and Solon in Athens, and Zaleucus and Charondas in the West. The activity of Lycurgus is reflected in the document called the 'Great Rhetra' (Plut. *Lyc.* 6), the date and significance of which has been much debated, and even more definitely in the final social order of Sparta. On the borderline between tyranny and aesymnetia stood, it seems, Pittacus of Mytilene. It was the fact of usurpation and the supreme rule by one man, making void the freedom and sovereignty of the citizens, that caused the Polis to regard tyranny as one of the worst crimes, punishable with death or Atimia; consequently it glorified tyrannicide. This was equally true of nobility and Demos, and that though people were quite aware of the prosperity and peace that reigned under the tyrants. The theorists then made the tyranny a particular, though evil, form of constitution. This fact was caused in part by the recognition that a single ruler was sometimes necessary for a state; thus, to estimate the possibility of a one-man rule, and to justify it, became a legitimate task of political thought. Another fact that counted was that, purely as a historical event, tyranny and aesymnetia were of singular importance and, in fact, often provided the transition from oligarchy to democracy, either by adopting a hostile attitude to the nobles or by trying to bridge the gulf between nobles and non-nobles. Moreover, the kingship of primitive times had always stayed in Greek memory through the myths of the heroic age; at the same time, from the beginning of the fourth century B.C., a new age of monarchy began, and with it a new type of tyrant made its appearance, the military usurper and dictator, whose rule transgressed the bounds of the Polis; of this class the most notable example is Dionysius the First. In him, the ἄρχων Σικελίας, the ruler of a Polis and the ruler of Sicily and even of parts of Italy were one.

There were Greek states which never had a tyrant or an arbitrator. Their constitution – usually oligarchic – was so firmly established that they were able to solve within its framework the most urgent social and economic problems, without the need of using force. Chalcis may serve as an example where the ruling class of noble and wealthy landowners, by sending out colonies on a grand scale, reduced the numbers of those without land to such an extent that they were no longer dangerous either economically or politically. Another example is provided by Aegina which never founded colonies and yet managed without a one-man-rule; this will have been possible because from early times transit trade created good opportunities for most of the people to earn a living.

If it is true that it was the body of privileged citizens, that is citizens with full rights, which held the sovereignty in the state, whether we speak of oligarchy or of democracy will depend on whether these citizens were a minority in the sum total of citizens, or whether, in principle at least, they were identical with it. We must, however, emphasize that those in possession of sovereignty were not necessarily identical with those who held supreme power in the state (τὸ κύριον); for that supreme power usually lay with a special body, chosen from those privileged citizens. This means that the two forms of constitution were, in fact, only separated from one another by degrees. For all that, the resulting difference in political structure and in the political part played by the various institutions might be so great that it is justifiable to speak of an essential difference between oligarchy and democracy. For the Greeks themselves, the question whether the whole population or only a privileged section shared in the rule, was one of supreme importance and the cause of the most passionate civil wars. It goes without saying that economic and social interests played a large part in these matters, but in Greece they were rarely stronger than political forces and principles.

With regard to the course of constitutional history, it naturally developed very differently with different tribes and states. One may speak of a typical historical sequence which goes back ultimately to a scheme of Aristotle (especially *Pol.* 1286b, 10), though it had been prepared by theories of corruption of each type of constitution as documented by Herodotus (III 80 ff.). The scheme of order is: kingship – aristocracy – oligarchy – tyranny – democracy. The historian may be able to use this sequence with discretion, without being in danger of falling into some form of determinism, which can be traced in its impressive development from Aristotle and Polybius to Spengler and Toynbee. If, as suggested above, we may disregard the early kingship, the first event of constitutional importance in the development of the Polis was the differentiation between aristocracy and oligarchy – the former meaning the rule of a nobility of birth, the latter that of a nobility of wealth. No clear separation of the two types seems possible;

in both of them, one has to do with essentially the same group of the population, exalted first by birth, then by wealth, but still more or less the same in their way of life. The fact, however, of the distinction may be taken as a definite landmark in public law no less than in the social development. The nobility of the Homeric age, that society which had a life largely outside the state, had learned indeed how to find its place within the state; but they still held fast to their character as a class, which meant that nobody who was not a nobleman could share in the rule of the state. When the change in military methods and economic possibilities had shaken the principle of class, aristocracy as the state of a nobility by birth frequently passed into oligarchy, in which full citizenship was bound up with the evidence of a certain amount of wealth. The two principles were combined when, as tradition often records, elections were held on the basis of nobility and wealth ($\dot{a}\rho\iota\sigma\tau\acute{\iota}\nu\delta\eta\nu$ $\kappa a\grave{\iota}$ $\pi\lambda o\upsilon\tau\acute{\iota}\nu\delta\eta\nu$). As long as wealth meant wealth in land only, the breach with the principle of class was legal rather than actual; but things became very different in the sixth century B.C., when money economy began to prevail.

The simplest, probably also the earliest, form of oligarchic constitution was that in which the possession of a certain amount of landed property constituted the basis of full citizenship. That was the law even in a mercantile city like Miletus in the sixth century B.C.; but in general there were the most diverse variations. The principle of plutocracy, which had forced its way through in oligarchy, together with the growing tendency to rationalize politics, might lead, for example, to the gradation of citizenship by definite census groups ($\dot{a}\pi\grave{o}$ $\tau\iota\mu\eta\mu\acute{a}\tau\omega\nu$) and so to timocracy, or to the gradual process by which movable wealth (goods, slaves, money) was put on equal level with the possession of land. In addition, there were combinations with the principle of mere numbers; we find as particularly popular the 'thousand' ($o\acute{\iota}$ $\chi\acute{\iota}\lambda\iota o\iota$; cf. p. 13). Above all, military changes were decisive. Just as in earlier times only those had full citizen rights who could keep a horse ($\dot{\iota}\pi\pi\epsilon\hat{\iota}s$), so now, with the change of tactics, by which single combat of knights was replaced by the citizens' phalanx of hoplites, full citizenship was tied to the capacity to supply one's own armour and to fight in it for the state. This was the state of the 'providers of arms' ($\ddot{o}\pi\lambda a$ $\pi a\rho\epsilon\chi\acute{o}\mu\epsilon\nu o\iota$); the hoplite was at the same time the *polites*, the citizen. Probably on account of this fundamental fact, the 'people' could quite often be called the 'army' ($\sigma\tau\rho a\tau\acute{o}s$). The 'Polis of Hoplites' – in Opuntian Locris probably identical with the 'thousand' – existed also in early

Athens in the combination of the pre-Solonian Hippeis and Zeugitae; Sparta, on the other hand, can hardly be called a pure hoplite city, as the Perioeci, though they too served as hoplites, did not belong to the citizen body. Towards the close of the fifth century B.C., the state of the 'providers of arms' became a pet ideal of the moderate oligarchs (cf. the draft of 411 B.C. and the so-called constitution of Draco); its influence lived on in the pages of political philosophers. In comparing these things, we must not forget that decisive structural changes had taken place between the state of the age of aristocracy and oligarchy and the oligarchies of later times. It is noteworthy that the citizen body of 411 B.C. was to be one of five thousand, but that in the final drawing up of the list the number rose to nine thousand. The restriction to those who could provide their arms was no longer a guarantee against democracy; the extreme oligarchs regarded even the constitution of the five thousand as democratic (Thuc. VIII 92, 11; cf. 86, 6).

Against the rule of nobility and wealth, the urge towards equality among the citizens that was inherent in the concept of 'Politeia' steadily gained ground. In this process, the principle of common property of the clan, which in most states, except extreme oligarchies or radical democracies, prevailed for a long time, was abandoned in favour of that of private property, and oligarchy could defend itself with the claim that all property belongs to those who have earned it, not only to the ruling class (Ephorus, FGrH. 70, F 149). The social struggles of the seventh century B.C., the aesymnetae designed to produce peace and reconciliation, last but not least the tyrants who usually rose as leaders of the lower classes and took a decisive part in freeing the peasant class, in the social and political rise of the citizens without land, and in the general levelling of the citizens – all these were steps on the road to the democratization of the Polis. Of special importance further was the increase in the numbers of the lower classes in town and country; the upper classes tended to diminish in numbers through the excessive strain of service in the army. To this we may add that the internal conflicts that had originally been connected with the rise of social groups and their leaders took on a new character when the leaders stood out as individual persons and, in place of the old clan followers, separate social and political groups were established, which with some justification may be called 'parties'. When this happened, a large part of the aristocracy seems to have withdrawn from politics, but the noble hetaeriae – by then a kind of oligarchic clubs – played a new and considerable political role, especially behind the scene. The speed and quality of the democratic development varied widely, partly on account of oligarchic resistance and partly through its own inner impulses. Thus, the idea of democracy could embrace a great number of constitutional forms.

The idea of democracy requires that all citizens not only shall be the sovereign power but shall in fact rule – that is to say, have their equal share in the use of political power. One aristocratic trait, however, remained undiminished in the democratic Polis, its exclusiveness towards all who were not citizens: democracy may be conceived as a kind of extended aristocracy. For a long time many nobles continued to be leaders in the democratic state, while others as 'oligarchs' cherished the bitterest enmity towards democracy and would no longer regard the Polis in its present form as their fatherland. Such an attitude was, however, essentially futile, and democracy usually forced its way through. Even in the most extreme democracies the ideal goal of absolute equality was never attained, and distinctions in political rights always remained; for example, in fourth century B.C. Athens, the thetes were still excluded from the archonship. However, the popular assembly and the law courts, the supreme authorities to which all the rest must answer, were open to all citizens and, through continual change in the citizens who were called on to serve in Council and public office, it was ensured that uncommonly large numbers should be politically active. We still speak, it is true, of democracy when the differentiation of political rights was much stronger and the census excluded many citizens – the majority, it might be – from certain rights. Here then, as we have said, no clear distinction from a moderate oligarchy is possible. There were other differences as, for example, those between colonists and the citizens of the mother-city; in Olbia, the Milesians had either equal rights with the citizens, or they held the privilege of freedom from taxation; in the latter case they could not serve as officials at Olbia (Tod, no. 195). The magnificent development of Athenian democracy, which dominates our literary tradition and actually from the fifth century B.C. onwards exercised a strong influence on other states, must not make us forget that it was an exceptional case and that there were many grades of a more or less moderate democratic constitution. Still, when we say that Athens was an exception, we do not mean, as some have meant, that democracy was not the inner goal of the constitutional development of the Polis, the 'perfection' of the Polis. It is remarkable that, in spite of tyranny and civil war, we cannot speak in archaic Greece of any genuine revolution. Democracy developed organically out of the state of the nobles – though this, of course, did not exclude resistance and strife – and radical democracy developed not less organically out of the more moderate forms.

We have the right to distinguish between fundamentally different forms of constitution, but, as we have several times suggested, this right must be used with discretion; this is confirmed by the slogans that were employed when, in the course of the history of the Polis, the constitution was changing its form. The state of justice, of δίκη – for so we must understand the Polis by the idea that gave it shape – was really a picture of wishful thinking, to which one might hope to approximate through good order and peace. 'Good order' (εὐνομία) expressed a striving for a state conceived of as a 'kosmos', a harmonious whole (Solon, Sparta). It is important to realize that this kind of order was ultimately divine, set as a task to the citizens in their aim at achieving justice. Eunomia did not denote any special and peculiar constitution, but a firm order and coherence, in which the resistance to all *hybris* led to discipline, moderation, and balance. Not only in the activities of the aesymnetae but also in the Spartan system we find operating in the constitution a movement towards democracy, even though not actual democracy itself. It was of special importance that the legal tradition arrived at fixed norms. The codification of law, which in most Greek states took place in the seventh and sixth centuries B.C., made law the expression of the will of the state; what originally was 'laid down' or 'set up' (θεσμός) could become the inevitable and traditional norm (νόμος). 'Good order' gave way to 'good laws'; but no Eunomia was possible without freedom (ἐλευθερία) and equality (ἰσότης). They were necessary concomitants of every Politeia; only their scope varied with the rights of full citizenship, and such excessive demands as those for equal share in wealth and power (ἰσομοιρία) were repelled. Against tyranny and against the oligarchic rule of the rich families was raised the plain demand for Isonomia which – whether as 'equality of distribution' or 'equality of political rights' – became the expressive symbol of a democratic constitution. Inside democracy the principle of equality could imply a variety of different contents (ἰσοψηφία, ἰσηγορία, ἰσοτιμία, ἰσοτέλεια). Eunomia, on the other hand, became the ideal symbol of oligarchic constitutions; in Hellenistic Crete a college of officials could bear the title Eunomia – here probably an echo of the traditional collective κόσμος. The ever more pronounced contrast between Eunomia and Isonomia mirrored the contrast between the two forms of constitution, and thus between Sparta and Athens. That

contrast was at the same time an expression of political theory of which
our sources otherwise do not tell us anything; it was, as in later theory,
even then concerned with the ideal of the 'best' state.

The close connection of Politeia and Nomoi at which we have
hinted changed in political theory into a contrast between them –
Politeia meaning the constitution of the state, Nomoi the laws of other
than political character, private and religious. This distinction was alien
not only to the original use of language; it was also directly contrary
to that unity, characteristic of the Polis, of political, legal, and religious
norms. Both words, Politeia and Nomoi, meant the same thing, the
Polis, but from two different points of view, as the community of
those who were citizens, or as the exponent of those norms by which
the citizens had to live.

3. POLITICAL STRUCTURE

The existence of distinct successive forms of constitution ultimately
depended on a shifting of the centre of political gravity from one to
another of the three elements which were inherited from the age of
migration and which determined the structure of the Polis. After the
monarchy had been almost completely ousted, it was the highest
college of officials that inherited the monarch's place; but in the
aristocratic states the weight shifted more and more to the Council,
and the officials usually and exclusively became the executive, not
characteristic for any particular form of constitution. We may say, with
only a slight exaggeration, that in aristocracies and oligarchies the
political power rested with the Council, in democracies with the
popular assembly. It was not till Roman times and largely under Roman
influence that it became usual, in letters to a Polis, to address the officials
(οἱ ἄρχοντες) before Council and Demos; there are one or two earlier
examples from the Hellenistic age. There were other developments
under the Roman empire, such as at Athens the prominence of the
Areopagus and the introduction of an elected leading official, the
'Hoplite General' (στρατηγὸς ἐπὶ τὰ ὅπλα). It must be said that the
constitutional bodies as described in the following pages, were often not
sufficiently effective and could be pushed aside by the initiative of individual political leaders who might, or might not, have an official position. We shall now and then refer to these matters.

(a) *The Assembly of Citizens*. The army in assembly (*Wehrgemeinde*),
the assembly of all free men able to fight, was still fully alive in Homer

in the assembly of the army or the people. But the epic also shows un-
mistakably its close dependence on king and nobles. The identity of the
whole people and the community, even under a tribal leader, belonged
to the past; but it lived on as an idea and, finally, as a fiction only, long
after the actual power in the state had passed to the nobles, and the possession of full citizenship based on birth or wealth determined the
composition of the citizen assembly. It may nevertheless be said that the
assembly of citizens, of the community or the people, expressed the
fundamental idea of the state as the community of the citizens, that is to
say, that the state rested on the immediate share of all its citizens in
political life.

In many states this assembly (ἀγορά, in Doric usually ἀλία, ἀλιαία,
or simply δᾶμος) was restricted in numbers; full citizenship, then, only
meant that a man might be called to make up the assembly. This
introduction of numbers as a framework for state corporations shows a
clear tendency to rationalize conditions in the state; but it may go back
to very early times. In the aristocracies of birth son followed father as a
member of the citizen assembly only after the father's death; membership might be restricted, as in Locri Epizephyrii, to the 'hundred
Houses'; in one case, that of the rule of the Bacchiadae in Corinth, to a
single clan. In oligarchies, too, there was often an assembly of the
'thousand' or, later, the 'ten thousand', which, in view of the smallness
of Greek states, might mean a very moderate oligarchy, or even the
rule of a majority; but we know also of assemblies of 600 (Heraclea
Pontica) or 180 (Epidaurus). In such cases we may hesitate whether or
not to call such an assembly a Council; but it will be better only to
assume a Council where it is recorded beside a larger assembly; that is
the usage of the ancient tradition, though the Council of the 600 in
Massilia is an exception. In the Ithaca of the *Odyssey* there was no
Council, and the Geomori of Samos met collectively in the bouleuterion, the Council chamber. The possibility of a single ruling body
existed only for the citizen assembly, not for the Council, which was an
ἀρχή, and as such always something distinguishable from the citizen
body. It is clear that in very small popular assemblies the institution
had somewhat deteriorated, but even there it represented the sovereignty of the state. Perhaps Aristotle (*Pol.* 1298a, 40) is thinking of such
a constitution when he mentions the case of the citizen assembly in
an oligarchy transferring its competence to a body elected from its
midst.

Of the full power of the citizen assembly in aristocracies and
E

oligarchies, we know very little; it must be measured by whether there was or was not a Council in existence beside it. Such a Council usually, but not always, did exist; when it did not, the assembly retained full freedom to debate and decide. Much more frequently, however – and always in fully developed oligarchies – the chief power lay in the hands of the Council; the citizen assembly at the most decided as the final authority in the more important cases. The assembly had, as a rule, no right to debate and only met at the calling of the Council or an official; in some states, however, a fixed number of regular meetings might be prescribed. At any rate, the political centre of gravity in an oligarchy hardly ever lay with the sum total of the citizens with full rights, even if their numbers were severely limited.

The same is true of the assembly, which was essentially the assembly of all free men or warrior citizens, the Apella of Sparta. The oligarchy of Sparta consisted in the domination of Spartiates over Perioeci and Helots, not in that of a nobility over non-nobles; thus the inner organization of the 'peers' (ὅμοιοι) could be democratic. Even the establishment of the sovereignty of the Damos in the 'Great Rhetra' (late eighth or early seventh century B.C.) need not be an anachronism and does not contradict the dominating position of the Gerusia. Economic and social distinctions within the unified Damos came to count from an early date and the oligarchic character of the state in general had its influence. The ruling 'people' became a small upper class, which expelled from its body more and more men of lesser right; the Apella fell into dependence, first, as the rider to the 'Great Rhetra' (seventh century B.C.) shows, on the kings and the Gerusia, later on the ephors. Like other oligarchic assemblies the Spartan Apella lacked the right of initiative, but it could – at least from the fifth century – hold a debate. Voting took place by acclamation, and the louder shout decided; only in exceptional cases was this method of voting, which Aristotle (*Pol.* 1271a, 10) describes as 'childish', replaced by open decision through division in 'lobbies' (cf. Thuc. I 87). The competence of the Apella was mainly limited to the vote for or against a declaration of war, the making of treaties of peace or alliance and the election of gerontes and ephors; but it obviously held a fair amount of power, and the part played by the Gerusia was reduced as compared with, say, the sixth century.

The dominating position of the citizen assembly could only be given full effect when it was combined with that of the whole people and, thereby, embodied the actual power in the state – in a democracy. It is true indeed that the lines of transition between moderate oligarchy and moderate democracy were very faint; but it is equally true that it was a new departure when the identity of Polis and 'Politai' was realized in its institutions – when the ruling assembly was now open to all free men over twenty years of age and so to the lower classes, with their preponderance in numbers. The assembly of citizens really became the assembly of the people and, in principle, all citizens could now decide all business of the state (Arist. *Pol.* 1328b, 32). Thus, 'direct' democracy had come into existence, as was only possible in a state that was strictly limited in space and numbers. As the expression of the Polis-community the popular assembly was a natural and, in a sense, a necessary institution; it existed even in places where never even so much as a majority of the people could be present. It was not till the beginnings of a representative system that the principle of direct democracy was abandoned, and then with much hesitation. It is hard to decide to what extent a reasoned belief in the positive value of the collective judgement of the masses played a part.

The name of the popular assembly was Ecclesia (ἐκκλησία), both in Athens and, following her example after the fifth century B.C., almost everywhere. It was the assembly of the ἔκκλητοι, those 'called out' – originally, it appears, of those who were called out of their houses by the cry of the herald and assembled in the Agora or in some other agreed place. Apart from the regular meetings, which took place monthly or even more frequently (Athens eventually had forty during the year), there were also extraordinary meetings on special occasions (σύγκλητοι) – certainly more than the average citizen, especially the peasant, could attend without serious economic loss. In principle, the Ecclesia might consist of all citizens; but the regular attendance of the poorer population, as well as of some of those who lived at a distance from the city, only became possible when payments were introduced, which might to some extent make good a day's lost earnings. This, however, only happened when democracy had been in existence for some time, in Athens after 400 B.C.; together with the excessive number of sessions, it led to the final preponderance of the urban masses. Yet, even after the introduction of payment, so large a part of the citizens was often missing that quorums had to be introduced to make decrees valid. These were inevitable results of carrying out the democratic idea, but they do show that, even in the extreme democracy, there was no escape from certain restrictions on the Ecclesia. The summoning and direction of the assembly – the latter a very important political function – were everywhere in the hands of men not appointed by the Ecclesia out of its own members. Usually it was the chairman of the Council, or of the section of the Council that was in session, who held this function; occasionally a high official. The daily change of chairman, such as we find in Athens and elsewhere, prevented any permanent influence either way between the Ecclesia and its leader. When in Athens, in the fourth century B.C., the Ecclesia was presided over, not by the committee of the Council, the prytaneis, but by the 'prohedroi', chosen by lot from the nine-tenths of the Council not in session, that meant not only a limitation of the power of the Council and a splitting up of authority characteristic of extreme democracy, but also the most decisive form of an ultimate autocracy of the popular assembly; still, it remained exceptional. The requirement, on the other hand, that every ordinary meeting, with its agenda partly prescribed by law, must be announced some days in advance, and the impossibility of holding an extraordinary meeting without express summons, provided some safeguard against any caprice or overhastiness of the masses.

The strongest check on the Ecclesia consisted in its constitutional connection with the Council, expressed most clearly in the common formula introducing a decree of the people ($\check{\epsilon}\delta o\xi\epsilon\ \tau\hat{\eta}\iota\ \beta o\upsilon\lambda\hat{\eta}\iota\ \kappa a\grave{\iota}\ \tau\hat{\omega}\iota\ \delta\acute{\eta}\mu\omega\iota$), which normally replaced the older formula mentioning the demos alone, and implied that every decree of the people must be preceded by a preliminary decision of the Council (probouleuma). In this way, the debate in the popular assembly was generally directed and the initiative of the Ecclesia seriously limited. Between Ecclesia and officials, as in all dealings of the individual citizen or official with the Ecclesia, the Council intervened as a restraining intermediary. Still, it was always possible to tell the Council what kind of probouleuma they should produce, to decline it or to change it by amendments, till it could be almost reversed; thus the Ecclesia regained a good part of its freedom.

Its debate was characterized by a general freedom of speech ($i\sigma\eta\gamma o\rho\acute{\iota}a$, $\pi a\rho\rho\eta\sigma\acute{\iota}a$), a constitutional fact which may have been introduced – though gradually by custom rather than by decree – about the middle of the fifth century. The debate led up to the vote in which numbers were counted either by show of hands ($\chi\epsilon\iota\rho o\tau o\nu\acute{\iota}a$) or, in secret ballot, by 'voting-pebbles' ($\psi\hat{\eta}\phi o\iota$). A simple majority decided. In general, every decree of the Ecclesia was called a psephisma. This name need not imply that secret ballot was an earlier method than the more informal show of hands; but it probably does mean that the introduction of the

ballot was a very important step in the development towards democracy. A Psephisma was bound to carry the force of law; the sharp
distinction that Aristotle (cf. *Pol.* 1292a, 33) made between Psephisma
and Nomos did not exist, although some modern scholars in varying
ways have followed Aristotle. In Athens the only *nomoi* were the ancient
laws of Draco and Solon, or their renewal in the codification of 403/2
B.C.; they were originally called *thesmoi* (see p. 51), but became
'Nomoi' because they belonged to the traditional order – and that was
the true meaning of Nomos. All other laws were *psephismata*, including
the decisions moved by extraordinary commissions (ξυγγραφεῖς; cf.
e.g. Tod, 74). On the other hand, in fourth-century Athens, beginning
it seems in 403/2 B.C., there were boards of special officials, called
'lawgivers' (νομοθέται, at other places also νομογράφοι); their decisions
were called Nomoi, though there is nothing actually in their content
to explain that use. We do not see that there was more than a purely
formal distinction; the laws of the nomothetae, too, had to be ratified
by the Ecclesia, and so the sovereignty of the people remained intact.
The Nomos, it is true, always ranked above the Psephisma and could
displace it (cf. Andoc. I 87). The legislation by nomothetae may be
regarded in general as an attempt to check the arbitrary making of laws
by the Ecclesia, a restriction imposed by the people upon themselves.
Even over the popular assembly, then, stood a higher instance, 'the
law', of which all single laws were parts and reflexes.

It must be remembered, on the other hand, that the Ecclesia was a
mass assembly which was bound to obey the laws of mass psychology.
That meant, above all, that it was influenced and guided by political
leaders, the 'people's leaders' (demagogues) or 'orators' (rhetors).
These 'demagogues' do not generally deserve a title which nowadays
is clearly derogatory. It was they who largely determined state policy,
and their power usually depended on their success. As long as they held
high office at the same time, as for instance Pericles, they were – at
least theoretically – compelled to render account to the Ecclesia or
some commission appointed by it. For a long time, they belonged to
aristocratic families and were therefore, even if genuine democrats,
descendants of a long aristocratic tradition. At Athens, it was with
Cleon that leaders began to emerge from the middle classes, from trade
and manufacture; that brought about a new radicalism, though usually
in methods rather than on principle, and members of noble families
still continued to fill most of the leading positions.

If we ask what was the competence of the Ecclesia, we find that its fundamental power of decision on all matters was in practice considerably limited. In the Ecclesia was embodied the supreme power of the state, in debate and decision; the Ecclesia was lord over war and peace, treaties and alliances with other states, legislation and jurisdiction, grants of citizenship and privileges, death, banishment, or confiscation of property of the citizens, election and audit of officials, grants of taxes and loans (Arist. *Pol.* 1298a, 3, a little amplified). In principle the Ecclesia was entitled to reverse its own decrees (ἀναψηφίζειν); in practice, this seems to have happened very rarely, although it was not illegal. The mighty prerogative of the popular assembly was limited in fact, but not in principle, by such arrangements as the probouleuma of the Council or the boards of lawgivers; but it was the vote of the Ecclesia that always gave the final decision. Things were not quite the same with the control and dismissal of officials; for this there were almost everywhere special control officers, who had to report either to the Ecclesia, to the Council, or to a court of law. An unusual form of self-limitation by the democratic Ecclesia existed, for example, in early Mantinea (Arist. *Pol.* 1318b, 23); the people here elected out of their own ranks electors who then elected the officials. Even more essential was the limitation of jurisdiction. The Ecclesia often retained the right to try certain political offences, thus affirming its claim alone to represent the state. With the progress of democracy, however, almost the whole of jurisdiction passed to the popular courts. It was the same people that sat in the Ecclesia and the courts of law (though in the latter only those over 30 years of age), but the renunciation of the Ecclesia gave expression to the fact that every government, even the people acting as such, was subject to the legal authority – though that again was the people. For all that, the fact remains that in direct democracy the people themselves were the rulers. It goes without saying that 'government' was under the sway of an easily misguided multitude. The 'tyranny' of the Demos could lead to similar misdeeds as that of an individual ruler, and it is significant that later *demos* and *demokratia* were deified.

One right of the people, that did not exactly fall under the conception of jurisdiction, was Ostracism, a verdict 'by potsherds' introduced probably by Cleisthenes, that in similar forms (like the Petalismos in Syracuse) was also used in other states. Every year, the assembly with a minimum quorum of six thousand was given the opportunity to banish an individual for ten years, with no prejudice to his honour or possessions. It could only happen when a popular politician felt strong

enough to appeal to the people in order to remove a rival from the
political scene. The original meaning of the institution was most likely
the protection of democracy against tyranny or against the power
of the noble clans; but when it was first employed (487 B.C.), it
had become a moderate and human instrument of politics within
the democratic state. For some time it proved very effective, though
it soon was misused and exhausted its usefulness. The ostracism of
Thucydides, son of Melesias, in 443 B.C., was the last of decisive
political importance; it established Pericles as supreme in the state.
When Hyperbolus was banished instead of either of the two leading
statesmen, Nicias and Alcibiades (417 B.C.), ostracism had become a
farce and was never employed again. It was not an essential part of
democracy.

There is a clear line that leads from the old army assembly by way of
the citizen assembly of oligarchy to the Ecclesia of democracy; it is
linked to the fact that the whole body of men bearing arms was the
people of the state, and also to the fact that only the citizen, present in
person, could exercise his political rights. But beyond this, no influence
of the original assembly of warriors can be traced in the development
of the Polis towards democracy.

(b) *The Council*. The Council as an official authority grew out of the
institution of the 'Elders' (γέροντες) – or, according to another
explanation, of the γερῶχοι as either 'the recipients of gifts of honour'
or 'the holders of the honourable position of a γέρων'. In early times the
Elders stood as an informal advisory body beside the king, including
men distinguished by age and nobility. Quite soon, however, especially
in times of war, it was power and nobility rather than actual age that
marked out these 'counselling old men' (γέροντες βουλευταί; *Il.* VI
113); the 'Council of Elders' (*Il.* II 53) thus became Council simply,
that is the *boulē*. In this Council sat the Elders of the noble clans and
families; in many states the description of Council of Elders, Gerusia,
persisted. Apart from its power of advice, which it possessed by its
very nature, it had also the power of criminal jurisdiction, as can be
seen from the court scene on the Shield of Achilles. As the Council was
the true exponent of nobility, it was almost a matter of course that in
the state of the nobles it took over the supreme power in general. It
was no longer a college of advisers, but one of ruling lords, all of equal
rights. Only where the full assembly of the nobles was strong – that
usually meant where it was small – was there no place for a Council.
The change from aristocracy to oligarchy, from nobility by birth

to nobility by wealth, found particular expression in the Council; for then it was again a minority out of the ruling class that was selected.

The composition of the Council showed very great variety in quality and numbers. The formation of a Council in a noble society followed almost automatically, either by birth or co-option. In an oligarchy it soon proved necessary to elect the members; this was usually done by the citizen assembly. As conditions for election, there might be a fixed age limit, a census, higher than that of the ordinary full citizen, perhaps a special scrutiny of descent, or the previous holding of some high office. The Councillor in Massilia, for instance, must be able to show citizen descent for three generations and must have children; the Areopagus in Athens was composed of those who had been archons, the Cretan Council (βολά) of former *kosmoi*. Often there was limitation of numbers, but at very different levels; there might be twenty, as probably in archaic Drerus, or several hundred. Where the Council appeared too large – and this could occur in aristocracies at a comparatively low figure – a small ruling committee was often chosen from it, a sort of oligarchy inside an oligarchy; such were the *probouloi* who seem, as a preparative committee, to have done for the Council what the democratic Council did for the Ecclesia. It must be defined as a special form when there was only one assembly in the state, called the 'Council', and no real assembly of citizens; but of the Council only a section was at any time in office and was itself called 'Council'. There were thus two Councils, a larger and a smaller, but it would be more correct to speak even here of a citizen assembly and a Council; for the 'great Council' might have several thousands of members. Examples may be found in the Boeotian constitution between 447 and 386 B.C. (*Hell. Oxyrh.* 11) and the so-called constitution of Theramenes in Athens (Thuc. VIII 97, *Ath. pol.* 30, 32 f.), which both show the unmistakable influence of Athenian democracy, however strongly they were in conflict with it. It is because of this anti-democratic tendency that the large assembly was called Council, not Ecclesia; thus we have here a variety that may be regarded as secondary, not as characteristic of oligarchy. Generally, both in aristocracies and oligarchies, membership of the Council only expired at death. The Council, then, as an instrument of government, had great steadiness and a conservative outlook. At the same time, as there was no fear of being called to account, the temptation to autocratic arbitrariness was very great. Against this, precautions were taken in some places: the Council, for instance, might be elected only for a limited term, mostly for a year, though this already means a transition towards democracy.

The Council of aristocracy and oligarchy usually had a very wide competence, the greater as less weight was carried by the citizen assembly. In Athens, for example, before Solon, we hear nothing of the latter, whereas Aristotle says of the Areopagus (*Ath. Pol.* 3): 'The Council of the Areopagites had the constitutional task to see to the maintenance of the laws; it dealt with most important state business; at its discretion it checked and punished all offenders against public order.' Here, then, beside its general political power, the Council had a sort of right of supervision over the citizens, characteristic of a state which was meant to be a *kosmos*. But when Aristotle goes on to say: 'The election of the archons followed birth and wealth, and from their number, the members of the Areopagus were appointed,' we may doubt whether this method of appointment of the Areopagites really goes back to the age before Solon; it would indicate a dependency of the old Council on the popular assembly, which in the time of noble rule is improbable. Even after Solon we must think of an ascendancy of the Council over the Ecclesia. In pre-democratic times the preamble to a decree could take account of the Demos only (as at Athens) or of the Polis (as at Drerus) – not, as was usual later, of Council (or kosmoi) and people. That implies that the Council or the leading officials acted for the popular assembly, which had at most a purely formal share in all decisions. The use of the earlier formula probably also indicates that the Council of the time had not yet a truly probouleutic competence.

Sparta again was the state in which the oldest form of Council was preserved at its purest. The Spartan Gerusia remained the council of the king, even when by the 'Great Rhetra' its numbers were fixed at thirty (with the two kings) and it was elected by the Damos. It would, however, be a mistake to regard this as a sign of democracy, just as the election of magistrates by the *comitia* did not make Rome a democracy. The small body of the Gerusia, chosen for life from Spartiates over sixty years old, no longer available for service in the field, but distinguished for their worth and authority, was the real State Council, which joined the king and ephors in debating the most important business before it was laid before the Apella; in earlier times, it could, acting with the kings, even annul a decision of the Apella. Further, the Gerusia was the court for all more serious offences. The Ephorate pushed it more into the background, but as the Gerusia controlled the current business of government and in the case of important decisions could perhaps lay a Probouleuma before the Apella, it remained of importance, even in later days when its dignity suffered by the notorious venality and partiality of its members.

The advance of democracy found as a rule its main enemy in the competence and power of the Council. It was the deep roots of the Council, largely religious, that frequently saved it; for, where its change into a democratic Council encountered invincible internal difficulties, a compromise was arrived at, by creating two Councils. If the old Council was called βουλή, the new one had to have a special title; in Chios, for example, in the first half of the sixth century B.C., there was a 'people's Council', a βουλὴ δημοσίη (Tod, no. 1). Or else the new Council might be designated by the fixed number of its members. Whether Solon really created a Council of the Four Hundred beside the one on the Areopagus is much debated. In the democracy of Argos things were different; there was a Council and apart from it, the body of the 'Eighty', undoubtedly oligarchic in character; both Councils beside the leading officials were engaged in the oath confirming such an important act of state as the treaty of alliance with Athens (Thuc. V 47). It was especially the religious importance of the oligarchic Council that survived, as it did with the *basileus*; there are several examples. Our most exact knowledge, of course, concerns the two Councils of Athens, the Council on the Areopagus and the Council of the Five Hundred. Complete as was the transfer of political power to the democratic Council – it took place in several stages, the latest in 462 B.C. – the Areopagus retained an aura of holiness, as Aeschylus showed in the *Eumenides* in 458 B.C., and by its mere existence, as also by its main surviving functions as court for murder trials, it remained a factor not to be neglected in politics. When Athens in Roman times was again an oligarchy, the Areopagus, which had never ceased to exist, again became the leading authority, though the other Council was not abolished.

The relationship between Council and citizen assembly in a democracy did not differ widely from what it was in an oligarchy; the general principle remained the same. If the citizen assembly had always been – at least in theory – the sovereign of the state, the Council now remained the actually ruling authority. A kind of intermediate constitution seems to be reflected in an Attic inscription (*IG.* I², 114), in which essential rights of Council and Heliaea are restricted in favour of a 'Demos in full assembly' (δῆμος πληθύων), consisting of at least six thousand citizens; unfortunately, the date of the inscription and its exact relevance are quite uncertain. The inscription of Chios, to which we have already referred, shows how the democratic Council of this early democracy acted for the Demos (τά τ' ἄλλα πρησσέτω τὰ δήμο). In places where no second Council was created, but the oligarchic Council was recast in a democratic mould, tradition had its strong influence. Moreover, considerations of statesmanship made it necessary, especially in a democracy, to establish some ruling authority which could act as well as deliberate, and against a ruling body of a few individual officials spoke the fear of tyranny and the mistrust typical of democracy. On the other hand, the democratic principle demanded that the Council should only be the instrument through which the Demos ruled. All citizens were to have their share in the government, the ἀρχή, both Council and offices, and this could only be secured by making them generally accessible and by constantly changing the holders. The Council, which usually consisted of four to six hundred members, was elected or chosen by lot in and from the subdivisions of the state. In this way, a domination of the countryside by the town was avoided, and sortition prevented as far as possible any tampering with the election. As a man must always announce his candidature in person, the economic difficulties, which might have been an obstacle, had to be removed; the councillor therefore received payment. The turn-over within the whole body of citizens was ensured by having each man elected for a fixed period only (mostly a year, and never more) and by restricting re-elections; in Athens, for example, no one could be councillor more than twice in his life. Thus, even in the extreme democracy, the Council was never a mere committee of the Ecclesia but, being elected out of the whole state and its subdivisions, a truly representative body; always, also as the representative of the Demos, the Council possessed a certain independency of the Ecclesia.

Even the Council was still too large to be able to manage the regular business of the government. For this reason, sometimes, a committee, changing once a month or less often, was formed; in Athens the year was divided into ten prytanies, corresponding to the ten phylae. The principle of alternation was retained; all councillors sat once in the actual government. The same principle is seen driven to extremes, when in Athens the chairman of the prytany who in the fifth century B.C. was also chairman of the Ecclesia ('President of the Republic'), only held this office for twenty-four hours. It is obvious that through continual changes the actual work was made much more difficult. A certain stability was provided by the important office of

Secretary to the Council (γραμματεὺς τῆς βουλῆς), which in many states was an annual office, though in Athens in the fifth century B.C. it changed with the prytanies; in his department at least the tradition of a documentary style was created and preserved. The Council carried on all negotiations with foreign states and received ambassadors; it directed foreign policy. In internal affairs, too, almost everything was under its care; the officials had to report to it; it had supreme authority over all financial matters. Finally, its judicial functions had not entirely gone, although they were severely limited, to the gain of the popular courts; the Council had a certain right of punishment, especially over officials.

The co-operation of Council and Ecclesia was mainly realized in that preliminary consideration of matters by the Council, the probuleuma, of which we have spoken several times. It seems that round about 600 B.C. this form of co-operation became so prominent that it finally determined the part played by the democratic Council. It implied a truly universal competence of the Council in all spheres of legislation. It might happen that the Council abstained from its special function and that the Ecclesia passed an independent decree (ἔδοξε τῶι δήμωι, a formula which no longer meant the same as in the sixth century B.C.); they might either reject the recommendation of the Council or entrust it with the task of producing a probouleuma on some specific question (cf. Tod, no. 154). As the highest organ of government the Council also had a share in the executive; it was charged by the Ecclesia to carry out its decrees and had, in case of need, to enlarge them. Thus, the well-known law about the mysteries at Andania (Syll. 736) ends thus: 'If in this law any detail about the carrying out of the mysteries and the sacrifices is not written down, the synhedroi [i.e. the Council] shall decide – without, however, changing anything in the provisions of this law that might possibly lead to dissolution of the mysteries. Otherwise their decree shall be invalid; but this law shall be valid for ever.' The far-reaching independence of the Council remained restricted by the unquestionable authority of the popular assembly.

The Council, which had once been a body of the heads of the noble clans and later the ruling body in the oligarchic state, eventually became the one institution in the Polis that could be interpreted as some kind of representative government, especially as in Athens, probably from the time of Cleisthenes, councillors were chosen by lot in the demes of each phyle in approximate relation to the number of citizens in each deme. The number of councillors from each deme could sometimes be revised, and very small demes remain without representatives.

Even so, the system must not be regarded as truly representative in the modern sense; it was only the external form of representation that can here be detected; the central idea, the representation of the will of some body within the state (deme or phyle) by an individual – naturally elected and not chosen by lot – and the gathering of such individuals into a body to represent the general will – this was something the Polis never knew, and perhaps, being what it was, never could know.

(c) *The Officials.* The old kingship had changed in the aristocratic state from its more or less 'charismatic' position into an office, filled by the community, though at first for life. The very general title that it now bore (ἄρχων, πρύτανις, δαμιουργός, κόσμος, etc.) expressed its universal competence and its dominating character as well as the renunciation of hereditary kingship. The office of *tagos* in Thessaly, a feudal tribal state, combined in a very unusual way duration for life and a purely temporary expedient in times of emergency. In general, however, in the position of a lifelong leader so much of the royal position was still preserved that the nobles and their political organ, the Council, were bound to strive for its limitation. That is why, from the beginning, their policy tended to divide the original kingly power. The three main functions of the king – religious, military, and judicial – formed the foundation on which a body of officials, gradually including more and more distinct offices, was built up; this body did not altogether cease to represent the unified administration of the state, as is confirmed by the usual comprehensive titles (ἀρχαί, τιμαί, οἱ ἐν τέλει), which could be stretched to include the Council. The tendency to division sometimes set in so early and so vigorously that the state never went through the stage of one single universal office, but was ruled by a number of leaders of equal rights. In Cos, on the other hand, there was even in later times an eponymous magistrate, called μόναρχος. The principle of 'specialization' was more and more expressed in the titles of the officials; it also meant a change in the concept of office, which ceased to express political leadership and became the conscientious performance of a set task. Moreover, besides specialization, two more restrictions with similar effects came into play: limitation in time, which stood in marked contrast to the lifelong membership of the Council and brought the offices into decisive dependence on that body, and a collegiate character of each office, by which each individual official was placed under the control of colleagues who shared his competence with equal rights. In contrast to Rome, however, which also was familiar with time limitation and colleagues in office, there was no *cursus honorum*, no hierarchy of office, and in contrast to the Roman empire there was no bureaucracy. The official was just a citizen who, apart from his share in the popular assembly, the Council, or the courts of law, temporarily discharged a task set him by the state.

For Athens, Aristotle gives us a somewhat stylized picture of the whole development on which the nature of *archē* in Greece consists, so different both from Roman magistracy and from modern office; but we must not forget that in Aristotle's account, which is schematic and purely constitutional, the outstanding importance of the noble families, which in all aristocracies very largely controlled the election of officials, is left out of account. According to Aristotle, beside the king came first the polemarch, the leader in war. Kingship was next divided into political and religious functions; the highest cult officer retained the name of *basileus*, while the actual leader of the state received the title of archon. The basileus thus took second place. We should, however, say that the polemarch as a yearly official (i.e. as something more than a representative of the king for an *ad hoc* purpose) is likely to be later than the archon, whose very title expressed the departure from monarchy. The competence of the archon, still very extensive, was later considerably limited by the transfer of his jurisdiction to a board of six men inside the body of archons, the thesmothetae. The offices, we are told, were originally for lifetime, then first limited to ten years, and then to one. This looks like artificial construction, but at the same time the board of 'archons' developed from three to nine members, among whom from 683/2 B.C., after the introduction of an annual calendar, the archon in the proper sense, the 'first archon', was eponymous, that is to say, he held the right to give his name to the year, and for some time to come, retained the main power. That was why, even after Solon, political struggles ranged round the position of first archon; it could be regarded as a possible step towards tyranny. The archonship of ten members in 580 B.C. (*Ath. Pol.* 13), if it is really historical, shows a strange and ephemeral attempt to bring into one body representatives of the original groups of the people (nobles and non-nobles, people with and without landed property). Occasionally, especially in small oligarchies like those of Crete, the leading college of officials was able to maintain its position even against the Council. In some states the right to name the year was not tied to any political office, but to some religious one, often to that of basileus, or, as in Miletus, to the president of the guild of singers. The explanation of this may be found in the connection of the calendar with the sphere of religion, though in

Ionia this was often bound up with the principle of social standing; at any rate, the right to name the year must never be taken as evidence for a political importance of the office in question.

What we have just said is true also of Sparta, where the right of one of the ephors to name the year, which existed from about the middle of the eighth century B.C., was probably connected with an original religious competence in the office. In the course of the late seventh or early sixth century B.C., the ephors became the highest authority. It is important that kingship here survived; that meant that a contrast which in other places was expressed by succession in time here took the form of coexistence in rivalry. On the other hand, the special character of the Spartan state, in which the 'kosmos' was expressed in its strictest and most rigid form, gave the ephors an authority in politics, administration, jurisdiction, and police that went far beyond the usual; they ruled the whole life of citizens and non-citizens alike. The kings, apart from their religious functions and their share in the Gerusia, retained only their control of military operations – and that was sometimes restricted; it must, however, be admitted that some of the kings, because they were great men, could and did exercise strong political influence. The five ephors, elected each year from and by the whole body of Spartiates, could thus be described by Aristotle as both democratic and tyrannical. The Ephorate was in no way typical of the Polis office in general, but it indicated a possibility latent in it, against which the democratic Polis had to safeguard itself.

It is especially characteristic of Crete that the chief officials, the κόσμοι, might be termed ὁ κόσμος as a collective unity. Here, more clearly than in other places, the original character of the aristocratic leadership of a community found expression; its ideal task was to maintain an orderly and traditional system. On the other hand, it was in Crete, too, that specialization was early introduced; in Gortyn, in the sixth century B.C. there was not only a κόσμος ἰαροργός, probably corresponding to the Athenian ἄρχων βασιλεύς, but also a κόσμος κσένιος ('praetor peregrinus'!), who decided all cases in which metics and serfs were involved.

The new and big tasks set to the Polis, in particular by the political and economic development of the seventh and sixth centuries B.C., made an increase, if only on a moderate scale, of offices necessary, even in oligarchies. Besides the highest political and military officials, there appeared, above all, special officers for law, police, and finance. All officials were elected; sortition remained a rare exception. Usually, election was by and from the citizens of full rights; occasionally, as in Mantinea (see p. 58), there was indirect election, or else the Council elected, either from those qualified or from its own numbers. The method described by Aristotle (*Ath. Pol.* 8, 2) as original – that of the Areopagus testing officials for fitness and selecting them – is probably part of aristocratic political theory in the fourth century B.C. and not historical. Some offices were tied to a very high census; the taking of any office, inasmuch as it was not paid, involved a readiness to make material sacrifices. In the oligarchic Polis office was something voluntarily undertaken for the community (*leiturgia*); but, of course, the holding of an office might procure personal advantages. From the number and kind of offices many variants of oligarchic constitution might arise, but the common features predominated. There was a danger that a chief official might retain his office for a number of years (as Damasias did in Athens in 582–580 B.C.) and thus gain tyrannical power; to prevent this, it was frequently forbidden to hold office more than once, at least within a certain number of years; we find this as early as *c.* 600 B.C. in Drerus. The Polis very early gave up choosing its officials as men specially suited to office. This meant that they really forfeited their independence and became simply executives, liable to give account, under the supervision of the Council.

The one test to which every official, indeed the members of the Council, as well, had to submit was the *dokimasia*. We only know of it in Athens, where it was probably a legacy from early times, taken over by democracy, but something similar must have existed elsewhere too. The test was held either by the Council or more usually by one of the popular courts, and was first concerned with a citizen's legal birth and his bond with the Polis by ancestry and cult. But the second question was whether the man treated his parents well, paid his taxes, and had taken part in military campaigns. This provided a more exact account of what being a citizen really meant; there must be no question of parents being left destitute, and care for their graves was also enjoined. Such requirements as these may have originated among the old nobility; but they became part of the general ethical standards of the Polis, which were based on the unwritten commandments that you should honour the gods, your parents, and your guests. Later evidence shows that there was also a *dokimasia* for new citizens and even for rhetors, that is for politicians.

Democracy did not change the character of Polis office; but it did very greatly increase the number of officials, and consistently continued to limit their powers. As the introduction of pay for officials, too, became necessary in democracy – though that did not extend to the highest and most important offices – the principle of voluntary performance was clearly restricted; the Leiturgia became a sort of taxation of the rich, even of men who were not citizens, and thus one of the main causes of the bad financial policy of the Polis. The multiplication of officials, again, did not mean any drastic change, as neither a bureaucratic hierarchy nor a *cursus honorum* was introduced; all offices, important or not, stood on an equal legal level and were all alike directly dependent on Council and Demos. Here again we encounter the fundamental truth that every official was no more than a citizen, accidentally, as it were, and for a limited period engaged in some special service for the state.

The limitation of the power of officials resulted chiefly from the increasing specialization of their competence, and in addition from the actual removal of certain rights – for example, the right to deal directly with the people, the right of jurisdiction and of inflicting punishments. Equally effective with these limitations of competence were those of a formal character, for example the almost universally adopted principle of having collegiate boards of officials. In fourth-century Athens the Secretary to the Council was the one individual official of importance, but it is significant that there were soon a whole number of clerks (γραμματεῖς) or, as they should more properly be called, secretaries. Further, there was the limitation in time, almost always to one year; together with the liability to give account (εὔθυνα) and the prohibition to hold the same office more than once, the restriction to an annual office worked definitely in a democratic direction. A position that must be surrendered after a year and under a strict rendering of accounts was no good foundation for personal power. Even the little-regarded under-secretaries (ὑπογραμματεῖς) were forbidden to be employed more than once by the same authority (Lys. 30, 29) – a proof that citizens who made their living in the service of the state were not professional officials. Through all this, the principle of regular change which we have already established for the democratic Council, was maintained for all offices, and thus the idea of democracy as the people ruling through all its members was preserved.

In the same direction worked the method of appointment by lot; it excluded influence of any kind and any regard for persons; in combination with the prohibition of re-election, it produced the greatest possible turn-over within the citizen body in the holders

F

of office; thus, it emphatically served the principle of democratic equality and contributed further to reducing the importance of the offices. As the composition of the authorities, including the Council and the courts of law, as well as the sequence of the phylae in office, and many other things were determined by lot, the Greeks naturally saw in it a necessary element of democracy and carried it to technical perfection by a variety of complicated methods, including some very ingenious devices for casting lots. Against the dangers into which the hazard of the lot might plunge the state, a number of precautions were taken. In earlier times lots were sometimes drawn among a narrower circle of elected qualified persons (κλήρωσις ἐκ προκρίτων); for certain offices of a technical character, especially the military and the most important financial offices, pure election remained the usual method of appointment, even in radical democracy. For those officials who were appointed by lot there were strong safeguards both in the limited competence of most of them and in their liability to render account. In Athens this led to a continuous control by the introduction of the *epicheirotonia*; in each prytany the officials had to be confirmed after the Ecclesia had been asked whether they had administered their office well. Furthermore, against every decision of an official an appeal to the people was possible; in Athens, Solon himself introduced the popular courts for this purpose, while in Chios at the same time there was appeal possible to the popular Council, the βουλὴ δημοσίη. However, it would be a mistake to conclude from these various safeguards that the Greeks regarded the lot as a kind of necessary evil. Socrates' criticism of the lot stood almost by itself. Sortition was regarded as an entirely normal way of appointing officials in a democracy, and it worked. The part that each individual played as a matter of course in the Polis, and in democracy in particular, produced a minimum of qualification, which was helped out by the technical knowledge of the state slaves employed as assistants in most offices. But appointment of officials by lot did not stop at being a possible method; it became something like a necessity in a state where the equality of the citizens was the first principle, and the official was just one of these citizens, chosen by chance and for a short term to carry out the will of the Demos.

The early degradation of the political authorities involved a separation between politics and administration, and this rendered some other form of political leadership necessary. In many democratic states the old form of the highest office lost all political importance. Such importance was now concentrated on elective offices, especially on those for which re-election was unrestricted; this was the case with the Athenian strategi and, perhaps, in Chios with the polemarch. This did not mean that the purely military character, for instance, of the *strategia* disappeared; there were still strategi who were commanders of armies and fleets and nothing else. Outside Athens, there were strategi to whom special and general authority was granted (στρατηγοί αὐτοκράτορες); at Athens they occurred as Commanders-in-Chief of the Sicilian expedition; otherwise they could not claim that rank, and they certainly were not tyrants in disguise. Frequently, on the other hand, the strategi were simply citizens of importance; in some cases, the strategia was linked to the position of the political leader that democracy required, the advocate and protector of the whole people in all fields of politics and administration. Holding at the same time an office, and thus liable to be called to account, he still fitted into the order of the Polis. At Athens, the position of a strategus chosen 'by all' (στρατηγὸς ἐξ ἁπάντων) was a fairly frequent method, by which one phyle was represented by two strategi and one by none; it was a legal, if irregular way of creating a special position for a leading politician. In the fifteen years' strategia of Pericles, that kind of leadership based on a particular office found its classical form and its historical justification. He never rendered accounts as he was re-elected year by year, whether by his own phyle or by all phylae. He frequently imposed his will on the people by rather autocratic methods. He failed in the end when, in the distress of war, invasion, and plague, the people refused to follow his guidance any further. Even this form of leadership was finally discarded by the radical democracy, through the exaggeration of its principle of allowing no power to any official, and through the divorce of the individual from the ties that bound him to the Polis. Strategi could still be of great influence in fourth-century Athens, though not as officials, rather as commanders of mercenary troops. Men like Timotheus, son of Conon, or Chares tried to revive Athenian imperialism. Still, more and more the state was given over to demagogues who held no office and therefore were without legal responsibility; but they could be outstanding orators such as Demosthenes or good administrators and financial experts such as Eubuleus and Lycurgus, and they gained authority even in office. It was then that the title 'guardian of the people' (προστάτης τοῦ δήμου) came to be the obvious description of the leading politician; in retrospect it was also applied to the leading statesmen of earlier times.

(d) *The Popular Courts*. Administration of justice in the Polis lay entirely or mainly with those holding the actual political power. Jurisdiction by the whole body of citizens therefore came in only with democracy; in quite a number of democratic states the Ecclesia enjoyed extensive juridical competence. Besides, there were single judges, largely as an inheritance from the period of aristocracy and oligarchy, and likewise jurisdiction by the old Council (Areopagus, Gerusia). To counterbalance them, democracy created a court of appeal, for which, of course, only the people itself could be competent; in Athens this happened as early as Solon. It was then that the popular courts were born. The name usual in Athens, Heliaea (= assembly), suggests that at first it was just the Ecclesia that met as a court of law. In the course of further development, the court of appeal came to be the first and only court of law in all cases of importance, and thus relieved the Ecclesia of some of its duties. It was, it is true, virtually the same men who were active as members of the sovereign Ecclesia and as members of the courts of law. Yet, gradually, the guiding principle seems to have asserted itself that government and jurisdiction ought to be separated and that even the popular assembly as the organ of government should be under judicial authority. Perhaps it was of some significance that the minimum age was twenty for the Ecclesia, but thirty for the courts. With them a new factor of political importance was created, the only one that was not common to all forms of Polis constitution, but belonged to democracy alone.

The popular court, as we know it best in Athens, was in a sense a jury; for each judge (δικαστής, ἡλιαστής) took a special oath and the court met under the presidency of an official who was not entitled to vote (thesmothetes). But the description 'trial by jury' is misleading; there was no contrast between laymen and professional lawyers; for such did not exist. What was important was that the people, identical with the state, were represented in the popular courts. Just as the Ecclesia in principle contained the whole body of citizens, just as year by year practically all citizens took their turn in sitting in the Council, so too were the individual courts of law composed out of the whole body of the citizens. In Athens members were taken from men over thirty years of age by a complicated form of sortition, which frequently changed. Some states showed divergences from the Athenian norm, both as regards the method of appointment and the minimum age; but for democracy in general the principle held good that the member of a court of law was not an official; he was no ἄρχων according to the ordinary view at any rate, except in the sense that as a member of the Ecclesia he was part of the ruling Demos.

In the fifth century B.C. at Athens six thousand of the men offering themselves were chosen by lot and then, by further casting of lots, assigned to the various courts, which had their special names. Later, when the number of citizens had declined, all who entered their names were accepted, and a man might, it seems, sit in more than one court and so draw several payments. Pay for the judges was introduced by Pericles and raised by Cleon to three obols a day. The courts in Athens were of considerable number and size. Apart from the five courts for murder and homicide, which were managed by the Areopagus and the Ephetae, there were, in the fourth century B.C. at least, ten precincts for court sessions. As judges in private cases a body of 201 was normal, in special cases of 401; for public cases the numbers were as big as 501, or 1,001, or even 1,501. The moderate oligarchy of Hellenistic Cyrene had for capital cases a court of no less than 2,101, including the Council of 500 and the 101 Gerontes. Except for festivals and days of ill omen, and from the fourth century B.C. also the days when the Ecclesia met, the Athenian courts sat very frequently, quite often daily. After speeches by both parties the court gave its decision, voting with pebbles by simple majority.

The courts, then, made great demands on the Athenian Demos. This is clear enough from the fact that apart from trifling cases the courts had all jurisdiction in their hands; their verdict was without appeal and came into immediate effect. It was disastrous that the political will of the Demos came to find stronger expression in the courts than in the assembly; one main reason was that the courts decided whether any particular proposal or psephisma was or was not illegal. The courts gained actual legislative power by the way the con-cepts of illegality (γραφὴ παρανόμων) or inappropriateness of a bill (νόμον μὴ ἐπιτήδειον εἶναι) were used; the many uncertainties and gaps in the existing laws (ἀσαφεῖς νόμοι) had the same effect. Thus prosecutions, designed for the protection of democracy, became weapons in party strife, far too freely employed and often abused. The highest authority at law finally became the highest in politics: 'As master of the vote, the people became master of the state' (κύριος γὰρ ὢν ὁ δῆμος τοῦ ψήφου, κύριος γίγνεται τῆς πολιτείας) (*Ath. Pol.* 9). Aristotle, rather as an anachronism, carries back into the age of Solon what in the late fifth and the fourth century B.C. was a fact. An institu-tion that had arisen through the separation of legal from political power – though the same persons might share in both – now witnessed their new union and thus became the most decided representative of the democratic Polis, the protector and representative of the Nomos – little as it was suited to the task. The great courts now became, especially in public cases, the happy hunting ground for demagogic orators and informers. Such a development seems to have taken place in Argos even earlier than in Athens. Democracy reached its perfection by making the people judges of everything; but in doing so, it brought grave discredit upon itself.

4. FUNCTIONS OF THE STATE

We distinguish three branches of state activity: legislation, jurisdiction, and administration. So far as political functions in the stricter sense are concerned, in legislation and executive, what really matters has been said in our third section; it was not feasible to separate the living organs of government from their functions. Of the forms of foreign policy, again, we shall have more to say in the section of inter-state relations (p. 103). But we have still to make some reference to those functions that, though a necessary part of the life of the state, were confined to some special area of duties of a fundamentally non-political kind.

(a) *Religion and Cult.* Religion as the essential form of intercourse between man and god was bound to the community. Thus the Polis, with its subdivisions and tribal groups, its societies and associations, was concerned with cult, and the state itself probably of greater importance than all the smaller bodies. This may be seen in several ways. The Polis with its organs and institutions rested on a religious basis; again, it concerned itself to a considerable extent with public worship and exercised some kind of control over it. We have already spoken (cf. I 3) of the role played by religion in the origin and growth of the Polis; we have still to show how later on the Polis in general discharged its religious duties.

For most of the public sacrifices fixed calendars were used in which annual regular sacrifices and those more rarely performed were clearly separated. These sacrifices had economic importance, because they provided for the ordinary citizen the chance – not very frequent otherwise – to have a good dinner with ample meat, and on public expense at that.

No political action of any importance, no assembly of the people, no meeting of a board of officials or a court could take place without an introductory sacrifice and prayer. If the sacrifice proved unfavourable, the meeting or whatever it was had to be postponed. The religious act was always performed by officials of the Polis, not by priests, who never appeared at duties outside their sacred shrines and their very strictly confined area of activity. In Greece, therefore, except in such states as Delphi, the religious sphere never dominated the political one, closely though the two were united. Religion was not independent of the state, but neither was the state independent of religion. On this fact rested the peculiar importance of the oath for the state. The curse pronounced by a man on himself in case of perjury, implied as it was in every oath, whether expressed or not, was a means by which the state could use the fear of divine punishment to reinforce effectively the ties that held its citizens together. Men bound themselves to the state by making the gods their sureties; the words of the orator Lycurgus (*Against Leocr.* 79), that it is the oath that holds democracy together (τὸ συνέχον τὴν δημοκρατίαν ὅρκος ἐστί) is true of non-democratic states as well.

Certain deities, mostly as a trinity, were officially recognized by the Polis as the guardians of oaths. Oaths were taken by citizens (ephebi), judges, and officials, before the court, by contestants and umpires at agonistic competitions, also to confirm especially important decrees of the people or treaties with a foreign power. Not rarely we hear of an oath of allegiance to the existing constitution, taken by all citizens, to restore political security after some internal crisis; a not dissimilar purpose was served by the monthly exchange of oaths between the kings and ephors in Sparta. In all these cases – except that of the oath before the court – the oath was of a promissory nature; it meant a guarantee for the future. The oath was mainly concerned with secular matters; much the same was often true of the curses which could be pronounced on behalf of the state against the transgressors of certain norms, and which formed a sort of complement to the oath. For example, by a law of Solon, the archon had to pronounce a curse on those who evaded the official prohibition of export. The immediate connection of the Polis with religion found further expression in the fact that the state, as much as any individual, might be defiled by murder and needed purification and atonement. At certain sacred times, no executions were allowed to be carried out as, for instance, in the case of Socrates. Of course, as religious beliefs gradually lost their strength, these measures of assurance lost much of their value, though no real reduction in their use can be observed.

Just as the life of the Polis rested on religious foundations, so the state god reigned over the whole community; by him stood a host of other deities, who all enjoyed state worship. To each of these deities official sacrifices were made on certain holy days; to many of them great public festivals were devoted. Everywhere, the number of these state gods underwent gradual change and extension. There was in a special sense a deity that guarded the city (πολιάς, πολιοῦχος); there was Hestia so intimately connected with the life of the state as goddess of the state hearth – or it might be, some other deity of the hearth; there also were gods of market and assembly (ἀγοραῖοι); there were the local deities of various sites, mostly identified with Olympian names and figures; the heroes, bound to the soil; usually also the half-foreigner Dionysus, early and completely Hellenized; finally, there were the deities of private cult associations and foreign origin, that had been adopted into the Pantheon of the Polis. Athens and her goddess show to what an extent state and state god could be identified, and how, out of inherited myth and cult, a new official, largely 'secularized' worship could develop. The Parthenon and the statue of gold and ivory were less religious symbols than representative objects of cult; this meaning can be most impressively recognized in the frieze where gods, heroes, and citizens are united to celebrate the great festival of Athena. Here religion had become the expression of that cultural patriotism which Pericles above all tried to teach the Athenians. True religious worship of Athena of course continued to exist – but not in the Parthenon.

Our discussion of state cults has already introduced the second form of interaction between Polis and religion. Between the Polis and its god there was a definite legal relationship, which imposed serious obligations on the state. The Polis took care of the cult, mainly by financing it, as the temple revenues and voluntary liturgies were as a rule not sufficient. The state determined the number and character of the sacrifices, arranged for the making of necessary cult utensils, administered the temple property, guaranteed the protection and maintenance of the shrines, watched over the right of asylum, and much else. All these matters were a regular part of the agenda (τὰ ἱερά) and engaged the attention of officials and popular assembly; a number of special cult officers, often with the basileus at their head as the heir of the religious position of the king, carried out what was needed. The only duty left to the priests – themselves for the most part also appointed by the Polis – was the maintenance of the special rites of their own individual shrines; even over that the Polis exercised a certain right of control and, as we see from many sacred laws, would on occasion concern itself with details of ritual. It was a favourite practice to leave the actual instruction to some religious authority of weight, Delphi above all others. Even over the mysteries of Eleusis which could not be a state cult because its 'community' included foreigners and even slaves, Athens exercised a right of supervision through special officials, though this did not impair the rights of the old priestly families.

The care by the state for the cult was sometimes bound to include protection against possible attacks. There was, of course, no orthodox dogma to defend; all talk about 'tolerance' and 'intolerance' in Greek religion misses its real nature. Any defence, like everything else, grew from the intimate connection of the state with its cults. Yet, public prosecutions for 'impiety' (ἀσέβεια) were not only directed against notorious religious offenders but might even attack 'beliefs', if these threatened the unity of political and religious traditions. As guardians of such a tradition and as representatives of a citizen body, whose citizenship was inseparable from 'piety', we may understand the accusers of Anaxagoras and Socrates.

(b) *Law*. The Polis, which by creating a tradition of jurisdiction and by codifying the law had overcome blood-vengeance and the claim to take the law into one's own hands, undertook, as a state based on law, to bring the laws into force and administer justice. The right, originally general, of the father of the family over life and death of its members was preserved in the formula 'he shall die unavenged' (νηποινεὶ τεθνάτω), used for certain offences committed inside the house. When the state had taken over the main part of jurisdiction, and the legal privileges of the noble families had been decisively checked, there was need of judicial and police officers and of a developed system of legal procedure. As judges we find at first everywhere individual officials as well as certain boards. In the course of political development, jurisdiction was often taken over by Council, Ecclesia, and, above all else, by the popular courts (pp. 72 f.). Certainly in the democracies, but also in many oligarchies, the officials were only left with the presidency of the Law Courts (ἡγεμονία δικαστηρίου); in this capacity they had to test the admissibility of a charge, to conduct the preliminary examination, and to take the hearing of witnesses. Beside the ordinary courts, in particular those of jurymen, there was special lower jurisdiction by various officials, who in the more important cases took over the presidency of the ordinary court in question. There were also police and executive officers.

The religious character of the Polis and the deep connections between law and religion explain why, especially in early times, both in the demonstration of proofs and in passing sentence, sacred ceremonies, such as oath and curse, played a large part. On the other hand, we cannot deny a growing secularization of the law; originally, it is probable, divine revelation – whether by utterance, oracle, or ordeal – was if not the only yet the most important source of law. In the heyday of the Polis the religious and non-religious forms existed side by side. The legal administration and executive, for instance, were mainly supplied by the Polis officials; very few of them were of a religious bent, and the exegetae who would explain the religious side of a case, were not state officials. It was otherwise with verdict and punishment. Oaths were commonly taken from the parties to a case, the witnesses and the judges; actual ordeal hardly ever occurred. Slaves could act as witnesses, though usually under torture, and the same seems sometimes to have happened to non-citizen Greeks. Among the penalties, money-fines, devoted to sacred purposes, played a considerable part, though normally fines were secular and went to the state. In Athens, it seems, prison was not only for safe custody till the day of trial or till the carrying out of the death penalty but also, though rarely, as an additional penalty, especially for state debtors. Lastly, capital jurisdiction kept its special position, marked by the retention of old forms of an essentially religious nature. In Athens it continued for a long time in the hands of the Areopagus and the fifty-one Ephetae, the latter essentially for cases of unintentional homicide.

The attitude of the state was especially shown in the fact that it regarded a very large part of legal cases as of public concern, even when the offences in question were by no means directed against the state as such; in cases of homicide, there might be the danger of 'pollution', threatening the whole community. There could be both public and private actions (δημόσιαι δίκαι – in Athens 'written suits', γραφαί – and ἴδιαι δίκαι). Procedure in the two, though different in detail, was not in principle distinct; but only in public cases could the verdict touch a man's person and honour. For a time at least, after 401 B.C., it was the rule that civil cases should first come before an arbitrator; if no agreement between the parties could be reached, he acted as the first court of jurisdiction. The nature of a public charge was chiefly marked by the fact that normally there was no public prosecutor. Any citizen with full rights (ὁ βουλόμενος) was entitled to prosecute in the public interest; in private cases only the man immediately concerned could prosecute. In certain special cases, one or other official might have the duty to prosecute; rarely, when the state itself seemed to be endangered public prosecutors might be elected; but these were only exceptions confirming the rule that prosecution lay open to every fully qualified citizen. The state rewarded the successful prosecutor in public cases by special grants; on the other hand, it tried, though with only limited success, to check frivolous prosecution by the threat of punishment. It is important to note that in public cases the prosecutor could not withdraw his charge, as he could in private cases right up to the verdict. In his rights as his duties the individual was bound to the Polis. Here, perhaps, more clearly than anywhere else we see the largely non-legalistic character of the Polis; it was no abstract conception above the citizens, but their community.

In its separation of public and private charges, which does not correspond to the modern contrast between public and private law or that between criminal and civil law, Greek law took some very strange paths. To the class of public charges belonged, of course, all actual offences against the state, such as high treason and deception of the people (ἀπάτη τοῦ δήμου), all charges of illegality (παρανόμων), of neglect of duty in office, or military offences. It is understandable that *asebeia*, too, fell into this category. But to the same group were assigned many offences which were directed against individuals, though in some sense they concerned the state; such were charges of adultery, procuring, prostitution of boys, informing, even of theft – all these, however, only in certain aggravated cases, where it was regarded as a 'violent outrage' (ὕβρις); this might find expression in a variety of ways, but always marked the offender as a transgressor against the community. Murder and manslaughter, on the other hand, certainly more serious charges, which surely concerned the citizens as a whole, were left to the next of kin to prosecute; here, the old law of blood-revenge still made its impact. There was a logical inconsistency here. It can be compared with the position in family law; while as a whole it came under private prosecutions, certain cases, such as injury (κάκωσις) to parents, orphans, and heiresses, in Athens even idleness and extravagance, were treated as public charges. It seems that here the existence and possessions of the family were threatened, and the family was a group of vital importance for the state in a political and even more so in a religious sense. Incidentally the fact that in many private charges a public interest was involved is further expressed by the surrender of half the money penalty to the state.

The whole legal system of the Polis (especially in Athens, where alone we know much of it in detail) was highly complicated and developed. It is, however, certain that laws and legal rules considerably differed among Greek states. We need not repeat what we have said at several occasions in this book on the differences of public law and the rights of citizenship; but it ought to be pointed out how strongly, for example, the code of Gortyn differs from Athenian law in matters of family and property law. The Greek passion for litigation had some very unfavourable results; but we must regard it as really remarkable that the Polis devoted such a large part of its energies (in men, time, and money) to the practice of jurisdiction. The principle of personality ruled. Only the fully qualified citizen had full standing at law and in court; women and metics usually needed a representative in court (κύριος, προστάτης), while the slave was simply the property of his master. It was to the citizens only that the entire legal system was adapted. The laws formed its foundation; in all public cases the citation of the laws formed an essential part in the proofs offered by both sides. The leading principle was not only to protect the life and property of the citizens but also by fitting the individual citizen into the system of jurisdiction (even in oligarchies he could at least be a prosecutor), to preserve that community of the citizens that rested on justice (δίκη) and stood under the Nomos. There is significance, therefore, in the fact – and not only as a symptom – that in the Hellenistic age the Polis ever more frequently had to call in foreign judges to decide even private cases. This may often have been because their own courts were overburdened; but the decisive consideration must have been that a more impartial verdict might be expected from external judges than from those whose material interests might, if only indirectly, be involved. Few other facts show as clearly as this how far the Polis of a later age had sacrificed its independence, even in home affairs (see below, pp. 105 f.). In early times, on the other hand, the perfect 'state of justice' (Rechtsstaat) remained an ideal never fulfilled. Still, ideals exist not only in order never to be realized; they are born out of reality and they reshape reality.

(c) *The Armed Forces*. The Polis had derived from the people in arms; it was essentially the state of the citizens. Both facts made the defence of the state the true concern of its people. There was no question of compulsory military service; it was the other way round: the capability to serve constituted the fully qualified citizen. This capability was both physical and economic; the supply of arms and other equipment was the business of the individual. War service, therefore, remained the privilege, though also the obligation, of the propertied classes, that is to say, of those who provided their own arms, the ὅπλα παρεχόμενοι. In the age of single combat among the nobles, that meant the knight with his chariot or horse, in the Polis proper it meant the hoplites. They were the decisive army and, at the same time, the military expression of the Polis ('Hoplite Polis'; on its origin see above, p. 20; cf. also p. 49). The light-armed troops who, like the cavalry in most of the states, played by comparison a very slight part in war, were recruited from the lower orders, who as a rule had not full citizen rights. The phalanx of hoplites, like the body of citizens, was divided into a number of self-contained units, often called *phylae* (cf. e.g. Tod, no. 41, 5), and with the phalanx the Polis fought its battles. Its military discipline and tactical training were first brought to perfection by Sparta in the seventh century B.C., where military education was essentially identical with the pattern of life; largely from Sparta the new tactics were carried over to a number of other states, though inevitably with many necessary changes. In democracy, defence of the state rested on the whole people. As the poorer classes could not afford armour, they were used partly as light-armed troops, but mainly as crews for the fleet. In Athens fleet and democracy lent one another mutual support.

The citizens, at least as far as they were hoplites, were entered on an official list (κατάλογος). Their term of liability to service in general embraced forty years, the period between the ages of 20 (or 18) and 60. It is obvious that the youngest and still more the oldest classes only took the field in moments of the most urgent emergency; the officials and councillors were, during their term of office, exempted from military service. It was a corollary of military duty in democracy that pay was generally given to everyone who served as long as a war lasted. With the one exception of Sparta, the Polis gave insufficient attention to military training. That meant that the cavalry, which required a more thorough training both of the individual and of the tactical unit, was generally of very small military value. Not till the fourth century B.C. did Athens, after earlier, probably only half-official beginnings of military education and the employment of the young men as περίπολοι or νεότατοι, establish the 'Ephebia'; that is to say, in order to educate the young for the citizen army, the years from 18 to 20 were made a period of training, organized by the state and directed by officials and picked teachers. This institution of the Ephebia became a general Greek feature, though in somewhat divergent forms; in the Hellenistic age its military character almost entirely disappeared, and it remained as no more than a system of general education.

The chief command in war, once held in early times by the king, was in the Polis usually entrusted to elected generals. At first there might be a single officer only, but he was mostly replaced by a board; in Athens after 500 B.C. the ten strategi gradually ousted the polemarch. At Marathon the polemarch had still the final decision, but a strategos like Miltiades could be something more than the commander of the regiment of a phyle. In Sparta, where originally both kings took the field, though after the sixth century B.C. only one, their powers were severely limited by the ephors and by 'advisers' (σύμβουλοι) who were sent out with him. Thus in Sparta, but even more so in the democratic Polis, the general was frequently also a politician and often, therefore, released from the actual command of the troops. Still, these conditions led to a good deal of trouble. A separation of army and politics, desirable as it might be in theory, was not really possible, because army and Polis were identical. The members of the Athenian college of strategi were more or less prominent citizens and, as soldiers, often neither trained nor qualified. This is true, for example, of Sophocles; it is not certain whether the historian Thucydides, who theoretically knew so much about warfare, was a good admiral. Anyway, the high command of both army and fleet became involved in politics. The real officers, however, the leaders and lieutenants of the army units and the squadrons of the fleet seem to have retained their purely military character, and in the fourth century B.C. the strategi too were mainly professional soldiers. The Athenian trierarchy was of a peculiar character; financial capacity seems to have counted for more than warlike efficiency. That was even more so when in the fourth century a new fleet was to be built and maintained.

By nature as by training the Greeks varied vastly in their quality as soldiers. Against the view often expressed that they were almost entirely unsoldierly, we may point to the appearance as early as the seventh century B.C. of Greek mercenaries, for example in Egypt and Asia Minor; later they served as instrument of the tyrants, and increasingly after the Peloponnesian War, as soldiers in the service of the Poleis, beside or instead of the citizens; the latter, even if financially capable of serving, steadily declined both in numbers and in their zest for service. Only in relatively few cases were the mercenaries non-Greeks; but Greeks stood everywhere in the pay of barbarians. We cannot even speak of a decline in soldierly qualities, though the decline

of the citizen armies proceeded hand in hand with the general symptoms
of decay in the Polis, in particular with the growing materialism and
apolitism of its citizens.

(d) *Finance*. For a long time the Polis had no financial supremacy in the
true sense of the world. The income of the community belonged to the
multitude of individual citizens. As was only natural, it soon became
clear that certain needs of political and social life set limits to that
principle. However, it survived into the fifth century B.C. at least, in the
form of public distributions of state surpluses to the citizens; for smaller
units like phylae and phratries examples are found even later. To the
collective profit of the citizens a collective obligation often corresponded. Gradually and to an increasing extent public revenues and
public expenses became the reserve of the state. The slowness of this
development was largely responsible for the primitive character of
the financial policy of the Polis. The earliest Greek coins (sixth century),
on the other hand, were most likely not used to foster foreign or retail
trade, rather to help public payments; the change-over from bullion
into coinage could easily become a source of public income.

Budgeting of state finances was not known before the Hellenistic
age. This was practicable because of the very simple character of the
financial administration, just as this again was made possible by the
fact that at first the financial needs of the state were small; the manifest
shortage of precious metals was an additional reason. Some spheres, in
which the modern state is financially concerned, practically did not
exist for the Polis (e.g. education, social services, public transport);
others were at least partially left to be provided for by individuals. Such
were military equipment and the various forms of 'liturgies', to which
in oligarchic states we may add service as official, councillor, or judge.
The liturgy was a voluntary contribution undertaken by wealthy
citizens for the state. Some liturgies were required each year (ἐγκύκλιοι,
Dem. 20, 21), above all the choregia, the presentation of the dramatic
chorus; others, of which the trierarchy, the equipment and maintenance
of triremes (built by the state), was the most important, were often
demanded, though not regularly. The state thus abstained from
financing important public duties, which were left to depend on
private willingness to make sacrifices. This was the chief reason why,
even in fifth-century Athens where public expenses had risen to great
heights, there was no budget. Therefore, because the Polis lived, so to
speak, from hand to mouth, it was the more necessary to keep a strict
watch over both income and expenditure. It was customary to divide

state finances over a number of separate chests, each reserved for special purposes. In general, there was not one main treasury, not even a state reserve; it was a feature of the financial policy of Pericles in the years before the Peloponnesian War, as important in its effects as it was revolutionary, to assemble a very considerable sum on the Acropolis and keep it for times of need. This measure as well as others made the financial administration more complicated. Beside the Ecclesia which held financial supremacy, and the Council, which seems everywhere to have been the chief financial authority, ever more officials sprang up, employed in the collection, or the farming out, of taxes and customs-duties, in administering the various chests and farming out public works, also in receiving and checking the accounts. This form of organization, primitive and in a way unreasonable as it was, did, however, make it possible to view details more clearly and to restrict the dangers of unsound or dishonest action to comparatively small areas. Yet, it was out of the question to obtain an idea of the financial position as a whole and so to make proposals in advance.

The primitive form of public finance would perhaps not have been possible, if the Polis had not had the support of the temple treasures. The temples drew big revenues from the yield of the large landed possessions of the gods, from votive offerings, from their share in the war booty, from tributes and fines. They were the first – partly again as heirs of the Mycenaean kings – to practise the accumulation of treasures and, by accepting deposits and by lending out money especially to the state, to set themselves up as 'banks'. A strict distinction was always made between the possessions of the temples and of the state; but usually, even in early times, the state took control by official treasurers of the administration of the temple treasures; thus any possibility of an independent policy was ruled out, which might use the wealth of the state gods for purposes of its own. The money that a temple lent to its own state – or to a foreign state, as happened at some of the Panhellenic shrines such as Delos and Delphi – was regarded by the state as a loan, carrying interest and, if possible, repayable. Frequently, it is true, especially in times of war, the Polis, while nominally borrowing, actually used up the temple treasures, without any thought of paying interest or repayment. Gradually, besides the temples, other states and private individuals emerged granting loans of money.

The expenses of the city in earlier times were almost all concerned with the cult, with sacrifices and festivals, cult utensils, statues, and temples. These items always remained important; only through them did the Greek state become the great creator and protector of art. But besides the sacred embassies that went to festivals or oracles, there were embassies of a political character; besides the sacred buildings secular ones; besides the dedications to the gods, honorary gifts to citizens and foreigners. Political life, too, involved a growing financial burden, as the publication of laws and decrees on stone or bronze multiplied. Even more vital, the development of army and fleet necessarily led to state action; the building of ships, in particular – as distinct from their equipment – could not be effected through the voluntary action of individual citizens. In democracy, the action of the state tended altogether to replace private action; the relation of Polis and citizens was even reversed, when the citizens for their very existence became more and more dependent economically on the state, receiving pay as soldiers in war, as Councillors and judges, eventually even for attendance in Ecclesia and theatre. Beside these regular expenses there were the extraordinary ones – first of all for the conduct of war, later frequently also for the reduction of the price of corn and for distributions of corn to the people. It has been said that democracy and Parthenon were 'luxuries'; but this view, even if not implying a sharp criticism, forgets not only that building gave employment but above all that to the Greeks economy was never an end in itself; the *raison d'être* of the Polis lay in what has been called luxury.

Within the organization that we have sketched a balance was usually effected by meeting current expenses out of current income, extraordinary expenses by extraordinary revenues. The regular income was, of course, to begin with small enough. Neither the sale of the skins of sacrificial animals nor the legal fees and fines, so far as these were not actually devoted to the gods, yielded much. Even the landed possessions of the state were, as a rule, not large, though in many states the yield of the mines was considerable. At Athens in 483 B.C. Themistocles, following an earlier example of the island of Thasos, stopped the distribution of the silver from Laurion among the citizens and used it to build the Athenian fleet. Everywhere, in fact, more or less decidedly the Polis claimed for public ends what had once profited the individual. It was in the spirit of the Polis community that this should as little as possible involve any direct burden on the citizens. Occasionally, we hear of a tax on agricultural produce, especially the tithe on corn (δεκάτη σίτου), but not knowing the special conditions and reasons we cannot generalize. Such caution seems particularly justified by the fact that most tyrants introduced direct taxes like the tithe (or sometimes lower

G

rates) on produce, or even a poll tax. Thus this form of taxation was reserved for conditions under which the constitution of the Polis was irregularly suspended, and the general rule was that there were direct taxes for metics and foreigners, either on the person or on business. State monopolies – which were rare enough and as a rule only temporary – were monopolies of sale; sometimes they might concern the hiring out of public slaves. Indirect taxes were fairly common, for instance market dues and in Athens a tax (ἐπώνιον) on sales at auction, especially of land. But the main yield did not come from taxes of any kind, but from the customs duties; levied on imports and exports, in harbours and straits, they were purely maritime and particularly hit the traders, who were mostly not citizens. Connected, it seems, with this tendency of the Polis not to raise money directly from its citizens, was the general rule that monopolies, taxes, and customs, frequently domains and mines as well, were leased out to private individuals; the Polis thus received a fixed rent, which was guaranteed. To the sources of income that we have listed we may add various dues and taxes on traffic, the legal fees that had grown considerably in democracy, the war booty, the tributes from subject and allied states. Sparta (Thuc. I 80, 4) was not the only place where money for immediate use was seldom available: for exceptional cases and extraordinary expenses special revenues might be voted by simple decree of the people. The main tax of that kind was a general property tax (εἰσφορά), which was levied in time of war and had to be voted anew on each occasion; in the fourth century it was reorganized as a regular tax. It was the only direct tax of importance and hit metics and citizens alike; but it seems that it was less oppressive than, as a rule, is assumed from the moving complaints of those who were most concerned. On other occasions, the state might resort to expropriation and confiscation, and in general it can be said that the means adopted to meet sudden financial crises usually brought only momentary relief and were sometimes most questionable both from the economic and the ethical point of view. This is even more true of the loans and other financial measures of the Polis in its decline. If we look at Athens in the fourth century B.C. – for there we have our fullest evidence – we see that the sore difficulties of financial policy were at least largely due to the very understandable unwillingness of the well-to-do to contribute to the costs of the extreme democratic rule. The suggestion by Aeneas Tacticus (12 f.) to make the wealthy responsible for the recruiting and the maintenance of the mercenaries was clearly impracticable. Still, after Chaeroneia (338 B.C.), the sound financial policy (διοίκησις) of Lycurgus established for some years a fair balance.

It was in the nature of the financial policy of the Polis, that it was economically unproductive. The Polis knew no protective duties to encourage home production, whether on the land or in the workshops; it did not grade the customs-duties according to the goods, but as a rule had a uniform rate of 2 per cent; occasionally, as on the Bosphorus, the Athenian toll might be as much as 10 per cent. The Polis had no trade policy to benefit a civic merchant class. Behind its financial measures was a predominantly fiscal way of thinking, though its effects were mitigated by the fact that the state was identical with its citizens. As far as the relations between Polis and individual were determined by financial considerations, they rested on two strangely contradictory principles. On the one hand, the Polis largely depended on the voluntary services of its citizens; on the other, the mass of the people was ever more tending not to live for the Polis but on it. Only the fact that economic interests played a minor part for the individual citizen made possible that general and intense sharing in the state that characterized democracy. To meet the demands that we have mentioned, the state had often to take severe measures against the well-to-do, which has led some scholars to talk of an economic tyranny of the Polis. Although the complaints of some of the wealthy were partly responsible for this verdict, it goes too far completely to deny such an economic tyranny. Above all, on account of it, the liturgy gradually lost its character of a voluntary service, though when it became a direct tax, it became also necessary to allow challenge and revision. By what was called in Athens *antidosis*, the individual citizen gained the right to shift the tax off to another citizen, while offering to exchange property with him; this meant that the state left the establishment and control of the liability to pay mainly to private initiative. Here is clear evidence how hard the Polis still found it to tax its citizens directly.

We see how public spirit and readiness for sacrifices on the part of the citizens, and a ruthless financial policy on the part of the state worked together, but the whole system finally broke down through the decline of taxable values and the limitation of consumption, through the excessive demand for pay for citizens and foreign soldiers, the understandable reluctance, as well as actual impoverishment, of a considerable section of the well-to-do, and through the inability of a primitive and awkward organization to act. Moreover, the economic revolution of the third century B.C. with its complete shifting of trade routes, with the change, almost as complete, of the methods of production and trade, the devaluation of money, and the rise of prices, which in Greece was not balanced by a corresponding rise in wages, led to a terrible intensification of financial distress and of social conflicts. The Polis was in no position to deal effectively with this situation. Thus social revolutions sometimes broke out, as in Sparta with the revolutionary kings Agis and Cleomenes who tried to restore the 'Lycurgan' constitution; for all the new human values and new thought that inspired them, the appeal was still to the 'ethos' of the old Polis, in an attempt to overcome a tradition of the Polis itself that had become fossilized and had lost its true meaning.

5. THE NATURE OF THE POLIS

The Polis was the state of the *politai*, the citizens. This is expressed by the fact that the name of the state was taken from the sum total of its citizens in both town and country (οἱ 'Αθηναῖοι, cf. Thuc. III 92: Δωριῆς, ἡ μητρόπολις τῶν Λακεδαιμονίων. Also I 107, 1, in contrast to Her. VIII 31 who takes the χώρα as the metropolis). Mostly as in Athens, the description of the state by the name of its people derived from the name of the urban settlement; in other cases, it was the land in which the settlement was situated that gave its name to the state (as in Elis). These differences did not affect the nature of the Polis. The Greeks took their idea of the state as a whole not from the territory and not from any more or less abstract concept (*res publica*), but from the free men who sustained the state. "Ανδρες γὰρ πόλις (Thuc. VII 77, 7): it is the men that are the Polis. There were no subjects. Even under a tyrant the Polis knew of no subjects in the meaning of a real monarchy. The structure of the constitution was decided by the share the citizens took in the popular assembly, in the Council and the courts. The dangers of radicalism were at least restricted by the joint effects of these institutions. The definition – 'state of the citizens' – can thus be drawn from the very existence of the Polis, but we have already seen (pp. 38 f.) that this must not be understood merely as a union of individuals. The individual was a citizen only in virtue of his membership of family and phratry, of deme and phyle. The state, then, was built on individuals only through the medium of subdivisions, in which even those citizens who seldom came to town were still assured of a personal share in the state, at least by the frequent elections. Society, on the other hand, was based on the personal groups, in which the same men were united for worship and social intercourse.

There was, then, identity of state and society, at least as far as the citizens alone were concerned. This implied a problematic issue at the heart of the Polis. For the state is and must be one, whereas society is a plurality, an order of social grades. This clash of opposing forces was experienced all the more violently in the Polis, because the narrowness of space made the individual permanently and forcibly realize his bonds with state and society. To arrive at inner harmony, either the state had to accept the setting of social grades and entrust the leadership to the highest class (aristocracy and oligarchy), or society had to fit itself into the unity of the state and permeate it (democracy). This contrast was never fully realized by the Greeks, because in the unity of the Polis they could not see the distinction between state and society. On the same contrast rests, for example, Aristotle's polemic (*Pol.* 1261a, 10) against Plato's 'one state' (μία πόλις, *Rep.* 462b). In fact, the class differences of Polis society were never fully removed, even not by radical democracy. In Plato's dialogues we find Socrates, the son of a stone mason, in the midst of his aristocratic disciples. There was a tension which was overcome by two concepts, *eros* and irony. The former was based on Socrates' understanding of the human soul, and the love of his disciples for the admired master; the latter was largely self-irony and, above all, the greatness of Socrates' mind. The social facts remained under the surface; a social unity was not achieved.

Sparta stood in a position by herself; the oligarchic principle dominated the state of the Lacedaemonians, the democratic the body of privileged citizens, the Spartiates. This led also to the curious fact, which must not be explained by the analogy of some of the leagues (see pp. 120 ff.), that here the name of the state (οἱ Λακεδαιμόνιοι) was not identical with the designation of its citizens; the Perioeci too, not only the Spartiates, who were tied to the city, were Lacedaemonians. This shows how Sparta stood in contrast to the typical Polis; Athens, on the other hand, embodied the type, though not in its average, yet in its perfect form. In the contrast of the oligarchic and the democratic forms of state were displayed the two basic tendencies of the Polis – rule and equality.

These somewhat abstract considerations will come to life, I hope, if we realize what the nature of Polis society was: it was mainly composed of the urban population, that limited number of men who usually knew one another, who were generally linked – even as political opponents – by interests and thoughts running in the same direction, and whose life was lived in the open, in market and street, palaestra and public hall. Although the social power of the well-to-do was never and nowhere completely removed, the character of this society implied the demand for political equality of the citizens: free speech between man and man produced freedom of speech in politics (ἰσηγορία), as realized in fifth-century Athens; the rich man was not very differently housed from the poor; if a woman displayed too much luxury, if a tomb was too extravagant, the state stepped in to interfere. The citizens were assembled like one large family round the hearth of the Polis, a life in common which received its inner tension from the natural self-assertion of the individual and its urge towards competition (ἀγών), but was seriously threatened only by the degeneration of that competitive spirit, by internal strife (στάσις). The gravest cause for disunity was the struggle between rich and poor. Plato (Rep. 422e, 551d) could actually speak of two cities within one Polis, and the facts were even more complex than that. The conflict between rich and poor involved, above all, the estate owners versus indebted peasants and agricultural labourers, secondly the beati possidentes of trade and manufacture versus artisans and retailers, possibly also the free citizens versus foreigners and slaves. Against any claims of non-citizens the citizens might maintain a closed front, 'because the whole Polis comes to the aid of each of its citizens' (Plato, Rep. 578d). Still, we must not forget that Polis society came to include at least part of the metics, that is to say that the citizens' body and Polis society moved away from one another. It is therefore not quite accurate to speak generally of the identity of state and society.

Inequalities of power and possessions did, however, drive the social groups time and again into conflict, despite the striving of the city to serve political equality by continual exchange between the rulers and the ruled. 'It is always the weak who strive after equality and justice; the strong cannot be troubled about them' (Arist. Pol. 1318b, 4). The fact that these attacks gradually gained ground meant that the Polis was developing towards an ever more radical democracy; and in it, eventually, the many and the poor were 'the strong' – which explains occasional oligarchic reactions. These social struggles, which in many places eventually became regular fights between political parties – especially when the parties more and more attached themselves to foreign powers – directly threatened the Polis in its very existence as a community of citizens. The community feeling that could once be taken for granted was lost; that is how 'concord' (ὁμόνοια) came to be an ideal deliberately striven for, though often combined with a strong distrust, not only of secret opponents of the existing constitution but also of all foreigners, even official envoys.

The Greeks had all too good reason to know why they condemned στάσις, civil war, so passionately. Not only were internal party fights in the state very common, they also took on methods which could hardly be exceeded in fanaticism and cruelty (cf. the famous picture that Thucydides gives of Corcyra). Greek patriotism changed its character; it ceased to be an inborn love of home and a natural attachment to one's own community, and became a moral demand, only too often forgotten in party strife. Here once more, as so often in this discussion of the nature of the Polis, we must realize how easily any generalization runs the risk of mistaking the ideal for the real. The funeral speech of Pericles and the *Republic* of Plato are the outstanding, though not the only, examples of a process of idealization, which makes a sober historical estimate very difficult. In recognizing the danger we cannot always be sure of avoiding it; moreover, every ideal has a reality underlying it that must not be neglected.

Equality and justice appear as weapons of the oppressed, but also as directing principles of the Polis in its development. Here we discover the mutual relations of state and individual; on them, modern judgements have often been rather one-sided. We must not think of those relations as meaning either the complete self-surrender of man to the Polis or simply the breeding of the free individual. In the good days of the Polis there was no real individual life apart from the Polis, because it was a community embracing all spheres of life, and because the citizens were also the rulers, and their interests, properly understood, coincided with those of the Polis. Certainly the Polis had to defend itself against selfishness and private interests; in some places it was the law that in debates on a war those whose estates bordered on enemy country must not take part (Arist. *Pol.* 1330a, 20). No one ever doubted that it was not the individual citizen who exercised political rule as judge, Councillor, official, or member of the Ecclesia, but the whole body of citizens, represented by law court, Council, office, or popular assembly. The public spirit of the citizens, which really held the Polis together, rested on their identity with the state – that is to say, on the basic fact of 'Politeia'. This is also the reason why the representative principle remained alien to the Polis. It was essential that the individual should share in the life of the state directly and personally. The Polis was not only the soil from which the autonomous individual arose – lastly in conflict with it, though never without it – but it was the citizen of the Polis in his voluntary and unquestioned devotion to the state that represented Greek man in his perfection. As we have seen, this did not necessarily mean that every citizen of a Polis was a great patriot. The egotism of party or class or the will to power of the individual often enough led men to make a stand against the community. It remains true, however, that at least before the close of the fifth century B.C. the Polis was the strongest force – even at the period when the individualism of the tyrants no less than that of the lyric poets opened to the Greeks new paths into the future. To quote the selfishness and love of glory of the Greeks as evidence against their public spirit means forgetting that the Greek in general undoubtedly was a realist, but that his personal advantage and reputation were most intimately connected with the advantage and reputation of his Polis. It will be sufficient to remember the part played by the Olympian victors, perhaps even more Pindar's description of those who had not been victorious (O. 8, 69; P. 8, 85). The career of Alcibiades remains an exception like that of his rival Lysander; it revealed unmistakable evidence of decay in the Polis community and the growing independence of the great individual, although neither of them actually aimed at *tyrannis.* In principle, and even – imperfectly – in reality, the forces were balanced; man was a ζῷον πολιτικόν, a creature bound up with the life of the state; the Polis was the community of the citizens (κοινωνία τῶν πολιτῶν). Willing sacrifice here, state compulsion there – the boundaries became confused. Although some laws cut deep into the private life of the citizens, it was the society of citizens that gave itself these laws. It is evident that the state despotism of Sparta no less than, in the Athenian democracy, the individualism that finally cut itself loose from the state (ζῆν ὡς βούλεταί τις) were both extreme cases, and only represented possible ends of Polis development.

If for a long time the freedom of the citizen found its limit in the εὖ ζῆν, the well-ordered life, of the Polis, the state was restricted in its expansion by its inability to neglect the fact of the unity of its citizen body. This, after the geographical conditions and the bond to the urban centre, was the third reason for the narrow self-centredness of the Polis as it was also a direct result of it. It has rightly been said that the face of the Polis was almost completely turned inwards. Yet, the close neighbourhood of states meant that they were always in a condition of rivalry, a kind of contest, above all, in the struggle for Hegemony. Of course, sheer will to power and power politics played their part, especially in the predominance of strong states over weak neighbours, but usually not to the extent that our modern conceptions would lead us to suppose. As the competitive spirit in politics weakened, it was left to the will to freedom in the individual state to offer an ever-weakening resistance to power politics. The tension between power and freedom is perhaps the dominant theme in all history, but no state has succeeded so far as the Greek Polis in finding a balance between the two, which only suffered final shipwreck in the fight between the freedom of the Polis and the power politics of monarchy. In freedom, in the independence from any foreign power, all citizens had their share, even the poor (Arist. *Pol.* 1280a, 5); only in a free state could the freedom of the citizens rise to unlimited devotion to the state and, at the same time, lead to the political initiative of the individual. On the other hand, the idea of freedom contained an element that tended to go beyond the single Polis, to include the whole Greek world in its scope. At the time of the Ionian revolt, most of the Greek states of the motherland may still have imagined that the fight for liberty on the part of the Greeks of Asia Minor was no concern of theirs; but they soon were to learn that they were mistaken. The battle-cry calling upon the 'sons of the Greeks' at Salamis was a cry for freedom (Aesch. *Pers.* 402), and the special Panhellenic festival of deliverance, the 'games of liberty' ('Ελευθέρια), at which the victor in the armed race even in later ages was called 'the best among the Greeks' (ἄριστος 'Ελλήνων), was held in Plataea in memory of the battle that had freed the soil of all Greece; it is, however, true that this festival was probably not inaugurated before the fourth century B.C.

External and internal freedom were, to begin with, hardly distinguished in Greek thought; 'freedom' (ἐλευθερία) was the contrast to tyranny as well (Her. I 62) and thus often synonymous with 'autonomy' (Her. I 95, VIII 140a). But gradually men learned to understand autonomy in its true meaning, as the right and capacity of the Polis to enjoy its own laws and not, in such a matter as that of the constitution, to model itself on some other Polis. Autonomy could thus be conceived of in its specific sense; the fact that the Polis might be independent in finance and jurisdiction could expressly be stated in an official document (Thuc. V 18: αὐτονόμους καὶ αὐτοτελεῖς καὶ αὐτοδίκους). The demands of autonomy properly embraced the whole life of the state; the formula used by Thucydides therefore implies a devaluation of the original conception of autonomy, caused by the conditions of the Athenian empire; Athens had to a large extent made a monopoly of finance and law. She exercised her authority mainly through cleruchies and control officers. Just as Corinth had to some extent done in her Adriatic colonies and in Potidaea, Athens created several types of colony, standing somewhere between an autonomous colony (ἀποικία) and a cleruchy, which was – at least in its original form – a garrison of Athenian citizens. The tension between autonomy and hegemony, of which we shall have to say more later (see below, section III 3), which each time led to the dissolution of hegemonial alliances, also created new forms that may perhaps be regarded as variations of the Polis. However, the will to autonomy probably remained the strongest force in Greek politics, and it is true, in general, that while the freedom of one Polis largely depended on that of all, autonomy was also the expression of 'particularism' in the world of Greek states, of the will of each Polis to shut itself off and to isolate itself – the cause of the endless internal wars of Greece. In early times, some states, above all Athens and Sparta, had succeeded in destroying the other towns in their district or in depriving them of their autonomy; it happened elsewhere, too, that towns which once perhaps had been independent Poleis were kept subservient to one ruling Polis. Still, in most cases the attempt came to grief, as with Thebes, or was never made. The right of self-determination appeared as a concept of equal standing beside that of freedom and, even more than that, it became the slogan of internal war in Greece and the crucial problem of alliances and leagues. The concept of autonomy was stretched, especially in the Hellenistic age; often not even the presence of a foreign garrison was regarded as an infringement of autonomy; it was enough if the communal life of the Polis was undisturbed – or might seem to be.

Autonomy meant the right of political self-determination, at first sight a somewhat negative thing. It led to an egotism of the Polis which of course found its most obvious expression in an egotistic attitude of the citizens; it may be held responsible for many abuses and many extreme developments. Yet this concept of autonomy, so fundamental for the Polis, must be regarded also as the expression of strong forces of a positive nature. We shall see later how closely it was bound up with the Nomos; but it meant, above all, a community, self-absorbed, closely united in its narrow space, and permeated by a strong political and spiritual intensity that led to a kind of special culture of every Polis. There existed a very pronounced particularism of culture, although it was only on the ground of culture that Panhellenism was a strong element in the Greek mind. Actually, in art, literature, and philosophy certain genres were confined, at least for certain periods, to one only or a few states. It is doubtful whether here the special character of a tribe still found an expression that in politics was as good as lost; I believe that neither the Dorian nor the Ionian character (if there was such a thing at all) was responsible for the differences in the cultural field. The special culture of a Polis, on the other hand, was essentially marked by its unity. The reason for this is that all expressions and forms of spiritual as well as artistic life were closely bound up with the political and religious existence of the Polis, a fact revealed at its grandest in Athenian tragedy. Communal life in every one of its various forms was expressed in the works of art and thought. It is remarkable how very strong the participation of all citizens was in the culture of their Polis, and that is true not of Athens alone. What a passionate attachment existed between the victor at Olympia or Delphi and his Polis! And how without such attachment could there have been a Sparta, whose special culture consisted in the discipline and achievement of a race of soldiers that despite all symptoms of decay held its own for centuries?

It is a much discussed question to what extent the freedom of the Polis could include the freedom of the individual. At any rate, it meant freedom *within* the state and not freedom *from* the state. That was to come later. But even as a citizen's right, it clashed with the claim of equal rights, in democracy no less than in oligarchy. It was a Spartan who told the Persian king (Her. VII 104): 'The Spartans are free, but not in all things; for above them as their master is the law.' We shall have to speak of that Nomos which restricted individual freedom, until the two completely separated, and the freedom of the citizen became the freedom of the individual, as preached by Sophists and Stoics.

Perfect freedom and autonomy could only be thought of when the Polis was independent of any outside power, including any non-political one; that is to say, in particular, when it enjoyed economic self-sufficiency ($a\vec{v}\tau\acute{a}\rho\kappa\epsilon\iota a$). Obviously this was an ideal never fully to be realized. But self-sufficiency had its meaning, not only in theoretical debate but also in reality. By far the greater number of Greek states were based on the land; for it was the union of town and country that made the Polis. Everywhere, there was a definite tendency to satisfy supply and demand on the home market. At this point, the Polis could intervene to reduce the demand for, and the import of, goods from abroad. Solon had issued a general prohibition to export; only oil was exempted. Very few Poleis, however, were in a position even to feed their citizens, let alone supply them with all that was required for a civilized life. Import of grain and wine, of raw materials and commercial products, in varying degrees and ways, could not be avoided; it implied a corresponding production and export of home goods. The satisfaction of these necessities of life, the τροφή, thus became a vital basis of foreign policy, though by no means the only one or even the most important. Only very slowly, and by no means universally, did the Polis change over from a community of consumers to one of producers. The supremacy of politics over economics was hardly ever in doubt; but the more decidedly the Polis isolated itself politically, the fiercer grew the tension between political and economic forces. As a result, a large section of the citizen population, in spite of the growing intensity of economic life, for a long time abstained from participation in trade and business. In oligarchies such participation was mostly left to the citizens of inferior rights, in democracies increasingly to metics and slaves. When it became clear that Polis economy could not possibly be self-sufficient, the Polis as the community of the politai stood aloof from economic life. It has been rightly emphasized how strong and diverse an element free labour represented, even outside husbandry, and how the payments granted for participation in political life were not sufficient, generally and permanently to supply the poorer classes with a livelihood without the need of earning. The prohibition for the citizens to engage in a handicraft, mentioned by Xenophon (*Oecon.* 4, 3) and taken over by Plato (*Laws* 846d), only existed here and there (ἐν ἐνίαις τῶν πόλεων); but we must maintain the view that without metics and slaves the Polis economically could hardly have existed at all – apart, perhaps, from a few outlying, purely agrarian states. A little way back we were regarding public payment for a majority of the citizens as both effect and perfection of the democratic idea; but it was also a necessary consequence of the economic structure of the Polis, which had the duty to feed its citizens. That task grew more and more urgent and, at the same time, more difficult, as the number of farmers gradually decreased, a fact very obvious in Attica during the fourth and third centuries. The dream of the citizen to live on allowances without working, and the contempt for manual work, expressed the trend of the Polis towards self-sufficiency, though they did not always and everywhere have the same force; in modern discussions, under the influence of Greek political theories, they are often seriously overrated.

Nowhere do we find these phenomena developed in such an extreme degree as in Sparta. The form of its economy was in any case unique, since the Spartiates themselves did no work on the land, but as owners of the land drew their rent. The state here was not compelled to rely for its economic needs on metics and slaves, as it had Perioeci and Helots as integral parts of its population. It is a mistake, however, to regard the *Rentnerideal*, the dream of a life based on public pay and no work, as specifically aristocratic. Again, the view commonly held that in Athens the 'public rentiers' were the result of political imperialism can hardly be maintained. When we are told that Aristides is supposed to have advised the Athenians to 'grasp hegemony, to leave their fields (!), and to live in the city' (Arist. *Ath. Pol.* 24, 1), the facts clearly testify that nothing like that ever happened, even to a limited degree. Those rentiers, so far as they existed at all, belong to the fourth century B.C., when there was no longer an Athenian empire. True enough, however, the Polis concerned itself with economics only so far as they really affected the community as such, the inner economic life of its citizen body. For that, state support was often forthcoming. Compulsory measures, such as the official regulation of prices, or the fixing of a maximum for landed possessions, or attempts to restrict the free disposal of a man's own property, also most forms of economic agreement with other states – all served in the first place to supply the citizens with the necessities of life. Such measures were largely due to the passion of the Polis for self-sufficiency; here we may see the seeds of a 'welfare' policy, which was, if rather modestly, expressed in Pericles' social measures and in the care for those wounded in war and for surviving children of the fallen. Slavery, of course, was not merely an economic necessity, it was vital to the whole social and political life of the citizens; but we should not judge it in a Pharisaic spirit. Within the limits prescribed by their time and environment, the Greeks handled this inhuman institution with as much humanity as possible.

In the fourth century B.C., and even more in the Hellenistic age, we meet with two new phenomena; in a world of large monarchical states the Polis lost in political power, and its society, more and more under the influence of economic motives, tended to disintegrate. The constitution of the Polis lived on; it did so by undergoing changes and innovations, which in general will not be treated here in any detail. The autonomy of the Polis was something always being claimed and, in theory at least, always admitted. But the bourgeoisie that now ruled, though it might appeal with an honest enthusiasm to a glorious past, was no true heir of the citizens of the old Polis; any community life now was more and more concentrated in smaller bodies and associations.

We come to a similar result from a different point of view. No community – least of all one whose form of life is determined by autonomy – can be imagined without some moral content. That cannot be realized without some binding norms, whether they be religious or ethical, legal or conventional. Without such norms the community of citizens simply could not exist. It is essential for it that law, religion, morality, and custom were not really separated; in the last principle at least, they coincided. For the Polis, this principle was the Nomos. In it, as the expression of the many 'Nomoi', were united norms of law and morality, norms sacred and profane, norms written and unwritten. Thus, the rule of the Nomos meant something more than that the Polis was based on justice, though that in itself was important enough. Venerable in age, yet new every day, the Nomos could be experienced by every citizen as a tangible reality; it preserved the sacred traditions of his ancestors, originating from the aristocratic tradition as it did, and kept the past alive; as the will of the gods it ensured the future; it expressed, in fact, a sense of eternity that united the citizen with his ancestors and descendants. The Nomos was embedded in history, yet it was also a constructive principle. The law of the lawgiver, ancestral customs and religious usage, the rule of divine order – all, as representatives of state, society, and 'church', built up the unity of the Nomos, which reflected the unity of the Polis and dominated it. The citizen assembly as the political ruler and the god of the state as the divine king, were brought together in what expressed the will of both – in the Nomos, which really became 'Nomos the king'. The Polis as 'church' never became a theocracy; equally, the Polis as 'state' was not given over to the caprice of the ruling masses, until the belief in the Nomos and its dominance broke down and any decree of the people could take its place. 'The people should fight for their Nomos as for their walls.' These words of Heraclitus (frg. 44) reflect the force of the Nomos – binding and including, but also secluding – as aristocracy had created it and democracy taken it over. Autonomy, as the framework for the special political and spiritual being of each Polis, was possible because the Nomos existed and ruled. That harmony of state and society which was ever being aimed at was centred on the belief of the citizens in the Nomos, as well as on the single Nomoi that radiated from the one Nomos. 'Where no Nomoi rule, there is no Politeia' (Arist. *Pol.* 1292a, 32).

The Polis itself endeavoured to fight against the dissolution of the Nomos. In many states any alteration of the existing political conditions was forbidden under heavy penalty; there were special laws against attempts to set up a tyranny; officials and Councillors – in Sparta the kings, too – were bound by oath to be unfailingly true to the constitution. Yet, it was itself a first symptom of decay if one had to preserve artificially a Politeia, threatened already in its existence and undoubtedly in need of reform. Crete and Sparta had a more modest rule (Plato, *Laws* 634d): the young were not allowed to criticize the laws. It is understandable that the aristocratic enemies of democracy led the fight against the Nomos, and on the other hand, the resistance that won freedom and autonomy for the individual sprang from the freedom and autonomy of the Polis. 'In the end they trouble no longer about the laws, written or unwritten, because they do not want to have any master' (Plato, *Rep.* 563d). The Nomos changed from sacred tradition to a purely human convention, against which 'nature', the φύσις of the autonomous individual, rebelled.

Plato in one passage (*Rep.* 590e) compares the influence of the Nomos on the citizens with the education of children. He saw the deep truth that the Polis was a pedagogic community. Simonides had already said: 'The Polis educates man' (frg. 53D). Again it is not the compulsory state education of Sparta that was characteristic, though perhaps it may be regarded as the most extreme consequence of the view of 'Paideia' which was alive in the Polis. The Polis educated, not through any state organization or through schools and teachers – we only find that rarely, and more commonly only in the Hellenistic age – but through the Nomos as the foundation of its concept of man. Sometimes there were deliberate prohibitions and prescriptions, for example laws against luxury or increased punishments for offences committed when drunk (Arist. *Pol.* 1274b, 19; *Nic. Eth.* 1113b, 31); later, officials could be appointed to guard the laws (νομοφύλακες), or to supervise the behaviour of women (γυναικονόμοι) and the education of boys (παιδονόμοι); the intention of the lawgiver, ethical and educative, cannot be mistaken. In the main, however, education, which was not confined to the young, was achieved unintentionally and unprofessionally through the community life, both intimate and public, of the citizens. This Paideia, largely assisted by the agonistic contests in the gymnasia and by erotic relations between men and boys, was no matter of pure intellect; it was education in its full sense, embracing graceful behaviour as well as inner morality, special knowledge as well as human perfection, aiming at a free balance between spirit and body; as 'Kalokagathia' it had been the ideal of the age of aristocracy.

It was most important that Homer – and this happened for the whole of Greece only through the Polis – was at the same time the inspiration and the instrument of this education. The heroic ideal of the epic could not simply conform with the ideal of the citizen of a Polis; yet, the ethics of a nobility which gradually came to merge in the state could and did develop into the ethics of the Polis. The object of any education, practised by the community as such, could be no other than to make the pupil a true member of that community (cf. Plato, *Laws* 643e). The Polis educated the polites, its citizen.

At an early time, education by the Polis instinctively, as it were, produced that minimum of organization and control that was needed. In the 'sacred band' of Thebes, for example, or in Crete, each man had entrusted to him by the state the lad who was both his pupil and his beloved. The Areopagus in Athens, which was felt by the citizens to be the 'guardian of the laws', was in a high degree an educational institution. Later, there was the service of the ephebi, especially for military training; in many places various officials were given pedagogic tasks. But, by then, the good days of the Polis were over. The connection with public life appeared still close; but what may still be called a state organization was in Hellenistic times really no more than a local affair. Moreover, instead of education through the community there was now education *to* it, and the idea of education for citizenship was replaced by an ideal of general culture. It was the Sophists who partly started this change, partly resulted from it.

This brings us to the question: how are we to think of the Polis in its relations with the whole of the Greeks? It is a question of the relations between state and nation. The old view was that Greek 'particularism' prevented the formation of a unified nation; a more recent view is that in reality every Polis was, in fact, a nation, while Hellas was a unity above the nations, like modern Europe. Neither of these views corresponds to the facts. When, in the fourth century B.C., we find Panhellenism as a force in politics, albeit not a very important one, it was in part a sign of natural exhaustion and the desire for peace, in part little more than a slogan in the battle against a foreign foe – like the awakening national consciousness of the age of the Persian wars. The general tendency to create larger political units was a result of growing power-politics and the self-assertiveness of the Polis; it had nothing to do with a 'national' policy. But we can certainly point to one influence at work, which, with little influence on politics, was a unifying bond beyond all political divergencies: the Greeks were ever learning afresh,

especially in contrast to a 'barbarian' world around them, the value of
those common traditions, created and carried on by the noble societies
of the eighth to the sixth centuries B.C. – origin, language, poetry,
religion, custom, and above all, the Nomos which had become equivalent to the sum total of the common Nomoi of Hellas. The contrast
to the 'barbarians' had its roots in the archaic age, but grew enormously
in strength by and after the Persian wars. Hellas was not so much a
geographical as an ideal concept, as Herodotus, for example, often
enough shows (not only in VIII 144). The Panhellenic policy of Pericles
(see III 1) and the literary Panhellenism of the fourth century B.C.
imply some strength in common Greek feeling even during the fifth
century, if not earlier; it was strengthened in particular by the influence of
Delphi and her Amphictiony (see pp. 109 ff.). The Greeks felt themselves
as one people, though they could never be one nation. The essential
nature of the Greeks came to life in the Polis; that is why even the
modern contrast between the political and the cultural concept of a
nation (*Staatsnation* and *Kulturnation*) is not entirely relevant. The
tensions, on the other hand, that arose between the Polis and the whole
Greek people were not strong enough to give a deeper sense to the
course of Greek history. In their way of forming state and people as in
other things the Greeks were *sui generis*.

The self-destruction of the Polis – we have on various occasions
pointed to its symptoms – was the main reason why the idea of the
Polis retreated into the realm of the spirit. Greek political theory began
maybe with Hesiod, certainly with Solon, and from then till Aristotle
it was no matter of quiet reflection, but of passionate desire to establish
norms; its greatest impulse came from the catastrophe of the Polis and,
in the execution of Socrates, its Pyrrhic victory over the individual.
The most prominent idea was some kind of 'communism', as depicted
in Aristophanes' *Ecclesiazusae*, in Hippodamus' ideal state, in Plato's
Republic. The latter found the word for it, Utopia, the state of 'no
place' on earth. Even Aristotle, the realist, tried to design an ideal state
(*Pol.* bks VII–VIII). In a different sense, on the other hand, but with
similar justification, we may speak of the political theories of both
Plato and Aristotle as resting on a basis of experience. We may indeed
discover frequent references to real conditions; but it is more important
to recognize that the philosophers' pictures of the state always retained
the main characteristics of the Polis. When they tried to depict the
'best' state, they were not creating empty Utopias, but, as it were,
intensified descriptions of the Polis as it existed, descriptions that might

H

even be thought realizable, as an 'example of a good Polis' (παράδειγμα ἀγαθῆς πόλεως, Plato, *Rep.* 472d). The nature of the Polis, however magnified, was reflected in those books.

Still, we should mistake the essence of Greek political theory, if we did not realize the decisive part played in it by the concept of constitution. In Plato's state, it is true, the whole of political and social life is included; and yet, the question of the 'best' state is largely one of constitutional structure. We see this particularly in the great interest with which the political philosophers treat various existing constitutions and their relations to one another, as well as the concept of the mixed constitution. The quest of the ideal state involves the recognition that better and worse constitutions of necessity shared in those relations, that the boundary lines between them are often vague, that mixtures may arise and even may appear desirable, and that there may be an inevitable sequence of various actual constitutions following one another.

Plato's *Republic* and *Laws* as well as the political writings of Aristotle, and the states imagined by earlier and contemporary writers, of whom we have only indirect knowledge, were aimed at the Polis and at it alone. As Greek thought knew of no state worth the name but the Polis, political theory could not serve some picture of general humanity, such as could be and sometimes was imagined. 'For no Lacedaemonian troubles himself about how the Scythians order their state' (Arist. *Nic. Eth.* 1112a, 28). Despite this, the effects and the dissemination from these imaginary states did overstep the limits, both in time and in space, of the Polis, and reached out to the remotest human possibilities. Therein is revealed not only the genius of their creators but also the genius of the Greeks in general; the forms and norms of their state, for all its obvious limitations and its confinement to a particular age, contained so much of general humanity that they could affect thought and imagination everywhere and for ever.

Federations of States and the Federal State

I. INTER-STATE RELATIONS

The will of the Polis to be autonomous and self-sufficient was always contrasted with the necessity for the states to live together. How this necessity found its expression in a number of ways can here only be hinted at, but the point must not be omitted; it reveals an essential part of the foreign policy of the Polis, and without some bridge between state and state the attempts to form units going beyond the single state, of which we have soon to speak, would hardly have been possible. The primitive idea that the foreigner is the foe had been for a long time past controlled only by the ancient customs of hospitality. In this, even the non-Greeks were included. Gradually, however, firmer relations between Greeks and Greeks developed, which crossed the boundaries of the single community and depended, in the first instance, on the similar way of life among the noble society of the early age. Beyond the sphere of chivalry of that society, there were closely related religious forms, the appeal of the suppliant, and the grant of asylum; they were also valid for other strata of society. Slowly, too, the Greeks became more conscious of those 'national' feelings of which we have spoken (pp. 100f.). The metics, Athena's 'foster-children', in many states because of their wealth an important element outside the citizen body, gained great influence, especially in Athens; but we cannot tell whether or how far they built a bridge to their former homelands; in general, they were more inclined to adapt themselves as closely as possible to the new home of their choice. For a time, at any rate, the individual human being seemed better able than the state to form connections beyond the bounds of the Polis. What it came to was that personal relations between man and man were a preliminary stage from which strictly political relations might develop. On the material side, the custom of exchanging presents, well known to the Homeric age, led on to ever more varied forms of social and economic connections. Trade relations came early to count for much; they grew beyond the personal sphere into that of the community. The sea did its part in strengthening such relations and hastening on their confirmation in law. The trade disputes of later times (δίκαι ἐμπορικαί), which in Athens came under the jurisdiction of the nautodikai, concerned demands in civil law, arising from treaties between citizens of different states; one at least of the parties would be trading by sea.

The most important form of such relations between states was the *proxenia*, the official 'guest-friendship', by which the citizen of another state was honoured, but at the same time was won over to represent the interests of the state and its citizens honouring him. As early as the sixth century, the Demos of Corcyra erected a cenotaph for a *proxenos* drowned in the sea, who is called 'friend of the Damos' (Kaibel, 179). An influential proxenos might count for much in improving the trade relations between two states (cf. e.g. *Syll.* 185). Sometimes, awards of proxeny might be very numerous at one and the same time (cf. *Syll.* 492); they must be explained, at least partially, by the special liveliness at the moment of trade and commerce. In Hellenistic times, the proxeny was readily conferred on foreign judges (see below). In many cases, though not of necessity, the personal relations with the proxenos led to political results. Quite early, it is true, proxeny came to be conferred together with other mere tokens of thanks and honours such as the description of 'benefactor' (*euergetes*), or somewhat later together with real privileges such as the right of ownership, personal security, freedom from taxation (ἔγκτησις, ἀσφάλεια, ἀτέλεια), or it could be conferred as a mere compliment perhaps on doctors and poets. All this showed how proxeny began to lose in real value. The activity of the individual proxenos as a 'consul' became less important as states concluded treaties of friendship and trade. When, as was frequently the case from the fourth century on, proxeny was conferred together with the citizenship, and when it became possible to hold more than one citizenship at the same time, the end was reached, and the true meaning of the institution was lost. Beside it, and replacing it, came the honour of a golden wreath or a statue.

It is hardly necessary here to talk of the usual forms of diplomatic relations; they developed comparatively late out of the heralds of early times. It is perhaps worth mentioning that the invitation offered to citizens of great merit in Athens to dine in the Prytaneion (ἐπὶ δεῖπνον) was extended to the ambassadors of foreign states (ἐπὶ ξένια), and thus became an honour granted by one state to another. The forms of personal relationship might early be extended to whole states, but otherwise the relations between state and state went beyond the personal forms. A kind of borderline case is that of the *symbola*, agreements on legal aid to be granted to the citizens of one state in the other state. They meant, above all, assurance against violence and robbery of any kind (συλᾶν), a kind of ἀσυλία, something like a non-religious asylum. Temple asylum, of course, continued to have its own great importance, and in the Hellenistic age it even gained in value in a time of war and plunder (cf. e.g. Welles, nos. 25–8; *SEG.* XII 37 ff.). As it was chiefly foreigners who engaged in trade, the symbola became primarily commercial treaties; they hardly ever had an actual political meaning. More vital for relations between states were certain forms of treaty, which originated from the chivalry and religion of an earlier age and concerned war and peace; they did not in the first place serve the ends of power-politics. In the form of a solemn vow (σπονδαί), they confirmed an armistice that was to be a preliminary to peace negotiations (ἐκεχειρία) and the actual peace itself. The latter was often fixed for a definite period and gradually raised to a hundred years or eventually for ever (ἐς ἀεί); thus the mere termination of hostilities became an actual treaty of peace. In the gradual extension of the state of peace is reflected the process of moving away from the concept that war, and not peace, was the normal condition. Another way of concluding a peace treaty was that two states by exchange of oath were made allies (συμμαχία), either to gain some distinct aim in war or to last for a longer period and contain some definite political clauses.

The development of inter-state relations was, of necessity, affected when some states gained greater power and thus rose above the common level. Even colonization created between mother-city and colony a tie that usually left autonomy intact on both sides, but involved certain rights and privileges, mainly of a religious nature; moreover, the colony was often required to preserve a constitution modelled on that of the mother-city, and the chief colonizing states rose in their general standing among the Greeks. Corinth, in particular, in her colonies such as Corcyra and Potidaea, claimed a position of non-religious influence, extending to domestic politics (cf. Thuc. I 38, 2; 56, 2). In this context, we ought to speak of a custom, used from early times (cf. Her. V 95.; Plut. *Sol.* 10; Tod, no. 33), that was frequently practised and thus became traditional (κατὰ πάτρια); it happened frequently that a third city (sometimes called πόλις ἔκκλητος), or even a king, was invited to decide between two contending states. It might be a question of a leading, 'hegemonial' city

deciding a case within its alliance (see below, pp. 111 ff.), and some of
the cases quoted for the sixth and fifth centuries B.C. may even not be
historical; but sufficient examples remain to show, in the settlement of
a military dispute by arbitration, at least a dawning consciousness of a
law above that of the state. Arbitration is best understood as a secular
version of an originally religious act, the appeal to a deity. It was the
same as within a state: arbitration, at a very early time, had taken the
place of a divine decision. It is noteworthy that very often Delphi was
taken as arbitrator – not only because of its religious importance, but also
because of its character as a Panhellenic institution above the individual
states; in one case (Thuc. I 28, 2) the choice was left open between a
decision by the League and the Delphic oracle. In choosing an arbitrator, it was natural that the city chosen should be of high reputation;
by arbitrating a city might even gain higher esteem. Many of these
cases that came to arbitration were about boundaries (περὶ ὅρων).
When Sparta and Argos could not agree about Cynuria (Thuc. V 41, 2)
they concluded a peace treaty for fifty years and, at the same time,
reserved the right to contest the region debated under 'agonal' conditions, that is to say that they would fight only if and when neither
state suffered from sickness or was at war. Here we may really speak
of a localization of the danger of war by diplomacy. During the
Hellenistic age, the employment of judges from abroad increased
greatly; we have evidence of this, not only in the surviving arbitra-
tions but also in honorary decrees, all of them similarly worded. In
the whole procedure there was a basic contradiction of the autonomy
of the Polis, and this became acute when the method was also applied
to purely domestic disputes (see p. 80), and when there was no recognition of a higher law, but sheer incapacity to decide for oneself.

We see, in fact, that the conception of autonomy was shrinking: not
only did the inter-state relations gain more scope, but actual authorities
above the single Polis were recognized, and that opened the door to
possible forms beyond and above the state. As a kind of prelude to
this development we may think of *Isopoliteia*, by which the citizens of
one Polis were given full citizen rights in another (as, e.g., between
Athens and Plataea); though often this was the merely nominal result
of a treaty of friendship and alliance between two states (cf. the treaty
between Aetolia and Acarnania, *IG.*² IX 1, 3). The granting of citizenship to a whole Polis, whether one-sided or (as more usual) mutual,
meant a breach of the principle, if not of the formal fact, of autonomy;
later it showed a way in which several states might be combined in a

higher unit. Out of Isopoliteia grew Sympoliteia. But long before that happened, unions transcending the state had already been formed, whose nature was determined either by a religious centre (Amphictyonies) or by power politics (hegemonial alliances) or by public law (Leagues).

Before we go into details about these unions, we must speak of what was a kind of preparation for them. It meant a decisive advance in inter-state relations when bilateral agreements were replaced by agreements among a number of states. That could still be in the form of a simple bilateral treaty such as the alliance between Athens on the one hand, Argos, Mantinea, and Elis on the other (Tod, no. 72 = DSDA. II, no. 193); but what more frequently happened was that one state at war gained allies by a series of bilateral agreements with several states. Military alliances of this nature existed from early times; in myth we have, for instance, the Trojan War and the Seven against Thebes, in history, the Lelantine War between Chalcis and Eretria, which led to coalitions on both sides. It needed, however, a common extreme danger from abroad to create a new form of inter-state co-operation – an interhellenic congress at which the necessary measures were decided on by deputies of many states.

The first congress of this kind was that of 481 B.C., which in a true confederacy united a large part of Greece against the Persian invasion and, above all, ensured peace at home. This military alliance was concluded in the first place to ward off an immediate danger; no exact aim and therefore no time limit was fixed; the league was still, in theory, in force in 462 B.C. (Thuc. I 102, 1; 4) and in 427 when negotiations were going on with Plataea (Thuc. III 63, 2). Yet, this military alliance was, in a legal sense, no independent entity; it had no official name and no regular organization; the allies were bound, not by treaties, but only by oath. Sparta took the lead because she was προστάτης τῆς Ἑλλάδος, that is to say, held the position of recognized military, though not really political, leadership (Thuc. I 18, 2); we may compare it with the religious leadership of Delphi. Sparta, who carried her own self-sufficiency and autonomy further than any other state, was by her power and reputation raised to a position in which the defence of the rest of the Greeks became her necessary task and duty.

Congresses and treaties, naturally, came more and more to be used as weapons in inter-state politics. The exceptional plan for a Panhellenic congress, suggested by Pericles (Plut. Per. 17), stands by itself and came to nothing. Its aims were to secure the restoration of the burnt temples,

to keep the freedom of the seas, and to ensure peace – all destined to
serve the cause of Athenian greatness; but it contained the kernel of
the idea of 'common peace' (κοινὴ εἰρήνη), which set the tune for the
numerous congresses of the fourth century B.C. When Pericles, at the
height of Athenian power, was working for unity he hardly paid any
regard at all to the autonomy of the several states. The King's Peace of
387 B.C., on the other hand, made the autonomy of the individual
state and the common peace the poles round which the debates at the
congresses of 375, 371, 366, and 362 B.C. revolved. Our sources reflect
an intense diplomatic activity in the Greek world in the fourth century
B.C.; congresses, treaties, and leagues (see below, sections 3 and 4) were
all attempts to ensure the common peace. To achieve this, it was
essential that there should be not merely a conclusion of peace but that
states which had not taken part in the war could join in. We cannot
deny a certain influence here of the Panhellenic movement, as propa-
gated mainly by men of letters; but what counted for much more were
the elementary political and economic needs and forces in the individual states. There was also the Delphic Amphictyony to serve as a model
and guide. In 340 B.C., on the other hand, Demosthenes tried, with
only partial success, to bring about a Panhellenic coalition against
Philip and thus once again revive the form of a purely military alliance.
After Chaeronea it was the congress of Corinth, convened by Philip,
and the League there decided on, that were more successful in attaining
the pacification of Greece. By including the idea of the κοινὴ εἰρήνη
in the whole of his treaty (see below, section 3), Philip freed himself
and later rulers from any idea of peace as something that could be won
independently, without a Hegemon.

2. AMPHICTYONIES

The word ἀμφικτυονία or ἀμφικτιονία (= union of 'dwellers around')
was given to religious associations of a number of states, mostly near
neighbours. Its beginnings go back to early times; in some cases, the
Amphictyony may have grown out of an original tribal or cantonal
state (see pp. 23 f.). We know of the Boeotian Amphictyony of Onchestus; that of Calauria, lying round the Saronic Gulf, but including
also Orchomenus in Boeotia; the Panionion, probably founded soon
after the colonization of the west coast of Asia Minor; the Amphictyony of Delos as the religious 'union of the Ionians and the population
of the isles nearby' (Thuc. III 104); the Amphictyony *par excellence*,

that of Pylae and Delphi. Each of these unions had the shrine of a god as its centre – Poseidon at Onchestus, at Calauria and on Cape Mycale (Heliconius), Apollo at Delos and Delphi; the Delphic Apollo succeeded Demeter, who had been worshipped at Thermopylae. Membership of these unions usually belonged to twelve Poleis or, in the case of Delphi, to twelve tribal states (*ethne*). This shows that the Amphictyony of Pylae must have arisen before the full development of the Polis, which, however, in the area of Thessaly and central Greece was late. Before and after 200 B.C. several of these unions were renewed; it is not impossible that it was only then, under the influence of the Delphic Amphictyony, that some of them received the name of Amphictyony.

The primary aim of the Amphictyony was purely religious; it was an association for providing the festivals and sacrifices to the patron god. This, however, presupposed common religious ties and was bound to have its effect on the political and economic relations of the states to one another. We find it true here too, as always in Greece, that to make an absolute separation between the spheres of religion and politics does violence to the facts. It is at once significant that during the festivals there ruled the 'Truce of God'. It was perhaps here that the idea of peace found its first home; not without reason may Calauria once have been called 'Eirene' (Arist. frg. 597). The shrine was also an asylum, a centre radiating lasting peace; that was something that the similar 'Truce of God' of the Panhellenic festivals, which took place only every few years, could not do. The prominence of Poseidon indicates how important the religious union could be especially for maritime states; the Amphictyony of Calauria, whose members were mostly small seafaring states, probably did its part in checking piracy. The Panionion underwent a change into an organization of political influence (see below), and when Delos became the centre of the Athenian League and, later, a member of the Athenian empire, its Amphictyony stood frequently under a predominantly Athenian administration (cf. Tod, no. 85; 125). Apart from the maintenance of cult, it was the special task of the Amphictyony to guarantee certain rules of behaviour between different states. Their federal centre was not a Polis; Calauria belonged to Troezen, and in Delphi it was not the Polis of that name, but the 'sacred land' that was the centre of the union. It was the fact of a common cult that bound the states together, even though, within the limits of the rules of the Amphictyony and outside it generally, each state was completely independent both in politics and in waging war. The alliance of Athens with the

Delphic Amphictyony (*SEG.* XII 7, XXII 2) shows that body engaged as a whole in an active foreign policy (*c.* 458 B.C.).

The ties which bound the individual states to the higher unit were religious, but their close cohesion found expression even in the official name of the union (οἱ ᾿Αμφικτύονες, τὸ κοινὸν τῶν ᾿Αμφικτυόνων). It is significant that the centre of an Amphictyony might help to create unions of a different nature and thus exert an indirect but manifest influence on the formation of political leagues; this was the case with Delos in the First Athenian League and the Koinon of the Islanders, and at times with Onchestus in the Boeotian League. Again, we can hardly understand the Amphictyony of Pylae, except by assuming that it was also concerned with the freedom of the pass of Thermopylae, which, for political as well as economic reasons, might affect its members. From Delphi we know the oath which every state had to take and by a curse on itself to guarantee. By piecing together the various, partially supplementary traditions (*DSDA.* no. 104; Tod, no. 204) we can make out that they swore 'not to destroy any Polis of the Amphictyones, or starve it out, or cut off its running water, either in war or in peace; if anyone transgresses these rules, to take the field against him and call up[?] the Poleis, and if anyone plunders the property of the god or is privy to such robbery or has any designs against the sanctuary, to take vengeance for it with hand and foot and voice and all one's power'. The words and the spirit of this oath influenced warfare even outside the Amphictyony. The obligation by oath was the basis of any military action by the Amphictyony itself either against disobedient members or foreign enemies of the sanctuary. An amphictyonic war was, of course, an extreme measure of compulsion, which could hardly be considered by any of the other Amphictyonies. There were also money fines and religious punishments, especially exclusion from the temple.

The fact that the Amphictyony had power, in whatever form, implied a certain degree of organization. We only know of it in Delphi. Here, each of the twelve members had two votes in the assembly of the Pylaea, which took place twice a year; the number 'two' possibly originated in the fact that distant states such as Sparta and Athens were admitted and then the original tribal votes were doubled; but the question remains obscure. The members sent representatives on the occasion of the Pylaea, the hieromnemones, pylagori, and agoratri, who were appointed in various ways as officials of their own states. They formed the Council (συνέδριον), the leading authority, acting also as a court; they could come to decisions even when not complete, but they met only twice a year. An inscription (*Syll.* 145; *SEG.* XVI 104; XXIII 75) tells us about the oaths and the activities of the twelve hieromnemones, who were primarily concerned with the protection and care of the sacred precinct. The most important authority of the Amphictyony was composed of officials from its member states; here the idea of representation is, it seems, cautiously attempted. Besides the Council there was probably an Ecclesia, composed of all citizens of the allied states who chanced to be present in Delphi; we know nothing certain about its competence. Grants of honours and privileges were made either by the Council or by the Ecclesia. Other officials were employed by the Amphictyony, but had limited powers. The relation of the Amphictyony to the Polis of Delphi was not clearly defined in principle; frequent co-operation, however, must have taken place. The religious union, as we have already emphasized, exercised influence in various directions on inter-hellenic politics; occasionally it concluded treaties itself, but a political role, in a stricter sense, was only gained by the Delphic Amphictyony, when its authority was, for instance, used by Philip in his power politics, and later by the Aetolians. In the Hellenistic age even purely political leagues were sometimes called Amphictyonies.

If we study the structure of the Delphic Amphictyony – and in many ways that of the other Amphictyonies will have been similar – the most important fact is that the Amphictyony had no real power to proceed against individual citizens of its member states and could not avoid the local authorities; but with the consent of the member state, the Amphictyonic court could at once act. In cases of violation of the laws of the Amphictyony, if the offenders were extradited by their home states, the latter would be declared free of guilt. The autonomy of the individual state, therefore, was hardly touched by the power of the Amphictyony; but in the event of a religious offence, the state like the sinner was defiled (ἐναγής), and had to atone at least by delivering up the culprit. The rule of religion was the force above the state to which the members of the Amphictyony submitted themselves.

3. ALLIANCES UNDER A HEGEMON

The unions between states, even as far as we have been dealing with them, occasionally gave some of their component states the chance to acquire a leading position. Frequently, it was not a long step further

to a leadership defined in terms of law (ἡγεμονία). When Herodotus
(VI 98) speaks of the struggles of the chief states of Greece for the 'rule'
ᾰρχ‑ε (ἀρχή), he does not mean such a supremacy as Sparta traditionally held
(προστασία, see above, p. 107), nor the actual domination over Hellas,
which would have been Utopian, but a partial leadership, giving the
state in question a preponderance of power. The only possible form
that such a 'Hegemony' could take was that of an alliance.

The Symmachia began as a comradeship in arms or a military alliance
concluded for a longer period, that is to say, as a normal inter-state
relation. From the middle of the sixth century B.C. a new form arose,
though the old still survived. This new form was an alliance of a leading
state with a number of others, not limited in time or by any specific
aim, implying a leading position of the one state in war, and soon also
in politics, loosely organized at first, but clearly an attempt at a unit
transcending the single state. We shall describe this form as an 'alliance
under a Hegemon' and shall assign to it the Lacedaemonian or Peloponnesian League, the First and Second Athenian Leagues, and the League
of Corinth. However varied they may have been in structure, development, and aim, it is as with the Polis itself: the differences do not cancel
out what is common in the basic type. We retain the name in general
use, but we are clear in our own minds that these 'Leagues' were no
federal units. In the two older Leagues we are not even sure how far
there was any constitution definitely fixed; but the events make it
possible to recognize the principles.

Three elements appear essential to the alliance under a Hegemon.
The first is the duality of its structure, with its two parts side by side –
the hegemonial state and the allies. This is expressed in the name of the
League (οἱ Λακεδαιμόνιοι καὶ οἱ σύμμαχοι, etc.). We are hardly
justified in concluding from the title of the hellenotamiae, the treasurers
of the First Athenian League, that the League was called 'the Hellenes';
that was the unofficial title of the war alliance of 481 B.C.; occasionally the name is given by Thucydides to the Athenian allies, but never
to the League itself. The title of those officials is simply an abbreviation
that could not be avoided (see below). The fundamental duality of the
alliance was the essential thing; it rested on oaths or treaties concluded
by the leading state with each of the allies. These individual treaties
were drawn up for an unlimited time, but, like any other alliance,
could be terminated by notice – unless, as was often the case, secession
was made a religious offence by oath and religious ritual. The treaties
then became 'permanent alliances'. What the sacred oath in the treaty

mainly determined was the duty of the Hegemon to protect the allies, that of the allies to follow him in war. The League thus became an offensive and defensive alliance. In the Corinthian League, the protection by the League was extended to include internal revolution. An alliance between members of the League was possible; in the Peloponnesian League a member could wage its own war, or two allies could even fight one another so long as the League itself was not at war at the time. Only in the Second Athenian League, which was marked by deliberate self-denial on the part of Athens, was every member at once *symmachos* of all the other members. In the Corinthian League, too, it seems, and certainly in its revived form of 302 B.C., all members were in alliance with one another. The inevitable dualism led in the Second Athenian League to its having two heads; as a principle, this was also retained in the Corinthian League. The structure of this League diverged from the norm because the Hegemon here was no Polis, but the king of Macedon; he held his position as a power outside the League. In strict law there may have been a Panhellenic League (οἱ Ἕλληνες); but it only gained political effect through its connection with the Hegemon, whose position included his descendants. The title of the League was Φίλιππος καὶ οἱ Ἕλληνες, and in 302: οἱ βασιλεῖς καὶ οἱ Ἕλληνες.

In the second place it was characteristic that there was no common citizenship of the League. The individual was always citizen only of his own state; the League was not strictly an entity of public law, it had even no definite religious centre. The connection of the First Athenian League with the Apollo of Delos did not last for long and had no marked influence on the quality of the supreme power of the League. That power, held by the Hegemon and representatives of the allies, was only concerned with foreign policy, especially, as the idea of 'Symmachy' suggests, with leadership in war. The Hegemon, of necessity, stood in contrast to the federal elements of the League and the freedom and autonomy of the allies, though all this belonged to the fundamentals of the alliance. That leads to our third fact: there was a tendency for the supreme power of the League to pass entirely into the hands of the Hegemon, and for the autonomy of the allies to be reduced and eventually annulled. That means a tendency to change the alliance under a Hegemon into an ἀρχή, a united empire based on domination. This tendency found vent in various forms and degrees; but it was everywhere present. To quit the League now meant not merely the breaking of an oath, but a political revolt.

The territory of the alliance was in no way fixed, it had no unity, it could vary in extent as new allies came in or old allies fell away. That remains true even though the area of the First Athenian League was more accurately defined by its division into tributary districts, while the Corinthian League embraced all Greece except Sparta. The members of the League were states (πόλεις, rarely ἔθνη or κοινά), in the Corinthian League also combinations of states. Commonly, but not invariably, the alliance of a state with the Hegemon coincided with its entry into the League. There was great variety in the character and importance of the organs of the League. A League assembly never existed, for there was no League citizenship; but there might be some kind of League Council. In the Peloponnesian League, the envoys who were sent to represent their home Ecclesia at Sparta formed a body that only met on special occasions, that was convened and presided over by the ephors; its decision preceded that of the Apella of Sparta. Formally, then, Sparta alone made the decision, though she could not easily disregard the vote of the assembled delegates, in which she had not taken part. It speaks volumes for the loose ties that bound the allies that Sparta in the Peace of Nicias of 421 B.C. proceeded alone and afterwards tried in vain to induce her allies to accept it. Just as there was no fixed organization, so were there no League officials. In contrast to this, the form of the Athenian confederacy of Delos was firmer and more elaborate. True, the League Council, which was not regularly in session and probably never met in full numbers, had no great importance in Delos and still less later in Athens; originally, it seems, it had one regular annual meeting, and at first it certainly had a share in some 'Athenian' decrees, for instance, in those that concerned the use of the tribute. Athens like every member of the League had only one vote, but was clearly in a position to ensure a majority of votes, especially from the smaller states. The main reason for a stricter organization was that instead of contingents in men and ships there was a money contribution, the φόρος, fixed by Athens in agreement with the single members. These tributes flowed into the League chest, which had Athenian treasurers; their name, hellenotamiae, indicated their rank outside mere state officials. The amount of the tributes and its variations seem to have been influenced less by political than by economic considerations; but the mere fact of a *phoros* was felt as an infringement of autonomy. In the Second Athenian League, whose basic rules were also fixed documentarily (Tod, no. 123), the Council (Synhedrion), which met regularly in Athens and in which each state apart from Athens was represented by one vote, had at least a share in the exchange of oaths at the admission of a new member. The Synhedrion was summoned by an Athenian ἐπιστάτης τῶν πρυτάνεων, but elected its own president. Its decrees (δόγματα τῶν συμμάχων) came either directly or through the Council of the Five Hundred before the Athenian Ecclesia; or the Synhedrion could consider a Probouleuma of the Council. Whether the Synhedrion in the latter case (ἔδοξε τοῖς συμμάχοις) had final legislative power or whether, as was certainly the normal procedure, the decision was with the Athenian Ecclesia, cannot be decided. Anyway the *dogmata* of the allies were dated by the Athenian archon and by the month and day of the Athenian calendar, though not by the prytany, and there was no mention of the Secretary or the President. We get the impression that Athens was sure of her Hegemony, but at the same time made an earnest attempt to organize an effective League. In the Corinthian League, in a strictly legal sense, it was not the Hegemon who had the executive in his hands, but the Synhedrion, which passed the decisive decrees and could also act as a court and take steps against infringements of the statutes of the League. In this Synhedrion the states or groups of states had not all the same voting power; that varied with the strength of the military contingents they supplied. The Hegemon or his deputy convened the Synhedrion, but had no vote in it himself. The Synhedrion had a clearly representative character and stood for the sum total of all Greeks.

The relations between the leadership of the Hegemon and the autonomous allies were seriously affected by military necessities, which easily led on to political compulsion. When the hegemonial Polis interfered in the internal affairs of the allies and demanded that they should adapt their constitutions to its own, the autonomy of the allies had virtually ceased to exist. But that happened only at the end of a long development, though this, one way or another, repeated itself for every League. Anyway, the two principles of hegemony and autonomy never reached a final harmony. In the Lacedaemonian League the position of Corinth was for a long time very significant for the independence of some of the allies. Notably in 432 B.C., she exercised a decisive influence on Spartan policy. When, however, Sparta decided to send out officers to take charge of the allied contingents (ξεναγοί), it meant the beginning of a growing Spartan dominance. From the last years of the Peloponnesian War this meant, for new allies, garrisons, harmosts as the local commanders, tribute, compulsion to adopt an oligarchic constitution, and eventually a subject position as a member of an actual empire. Even so far as the older members were concerned, Sparta, without consulting them, could conclude treaties that involved the League as a whole. In the Athenian empire, the tendency to move from the unquestioned autonomy of the allies to the complete Hegemony of the leading state reached its perfection. Although, compared to the Peloponnesian League, the elements of federation were at the outset here much stronger, Athens from the first was in a much more powerful position over against her allies than Sparta to hers. Revolt and defection soon sharpened Athens' dominant position. The most important step in the reduction of the allies to subjects (ὑπήκοοι) was the removal of the League treasury to Athens (454 B.C.); Athens had now the free disposal of the tributes; a sixtieth was at once devoted to the goddess Athena. After the Peace of Callias (448 B.C.), the raising of tribute by Athens could, it seemed, no longer be fully justified by the need to watch over the peace of the Aegean. Worse still, the new assessments of the allies were made by Athenian officials only and, in case of complaints, the Athenian court would decide; cleruchies – colonies of Athenian citizens – occupied allied territory and so in many places ensured Athenian supremacy; there were Athenian garrisons with their commanders (phrourarchs), often, no doubt, for protection against local tyrants or against Persia; lastly, Athens tended to interfere in the internal factions of the allies and to enforce democratic constitutions. On the other hand, we must not forget that the Demos in the allied states generally preferred the rule of Athens to that of their domestic opponents. Where oligarchies were allowed to continue, the internal contrast only intensified the external coercion, which found further expression in the fact that Athens held jurisdiction in important cases and that even in private cases between citizens of allied states, the court of appeal was at Athens. With the unification of law thus effected went a unification of coinage, measures, and weights. When in 413 B.C. the tribute was replaced by a 5 per cent customs-duty in all harbours of the empire, that meant some relief, especially for the overburdened landowners, and also in the method of collection; but it was yet another step towards the full unification of the empire. In the end, only Lesbos, Chios, and Samos enjoyed autonomy; there was no common citizenship, and Athenian citizenship remained confined to the Demos of Athens till just before the collapse.

In the two Leagues of the fourth century B.C. the strengthening of the Synhedrion meant at first a protection of autonomy. The contributions of the allies in the Second Athenian League (συντάξεις) had not the character of a tribute; the payment of tribute (φόρον φέρειν) was expressly forbidden. The Synhedrion fixed the date and the amount of the contributions, which perhaps were at first voluntary; they were again administered by Athens, but could only be used for League purposes. Major legal cases were decided by the Synhedrion and the Athenian popular court, both acting together (Tod, no. 123, 55); the procedure of this common jurisdiction is not known, though the trials naturally took place at Athens (Tod, no. 142, 73). Of confiscated property a tenth went to Athena; but the money might be collected by the state of the offender, and any debts had to be paid to the League (Tod, no. 154, 10 f.). Gradually, however, the military and financial dominance of Athens reduced the Synhedrion to a mere consultative body, and with cleruchies and garrisons the methods of the Athenian empire returned. Still, the methods of the First Athenian League were here only used now and then; in the Corinthian League, the Council (συνέδριον τῶν 'Ελλήνων) itself, which was dependent on the Macedonian king, became a menace to autonomy; for, on the basis of the League constitution, it could force the League to interfere in the internal conflicts of a Polis. This was of especial importance, as no state was allowed to alter its constitution or tolerate revolutionary intrigues; there was, on the other hand, ample reason for a possible intervention by the League, since the social and economic conditions could easily threaten the domestic peace of many states. The direction of the policy of the League in the sense desired by Macedon was ensured by the maintenance of Macedonian garrisons in a number of strategic cities, despite the autonomy of the allied states. The allies were also subject to an unconditional following in the field, when the Synhedrion had received a request to that effect from the Hegemon.

In general, as we have said, the alliance under a Hegemon grew from a number of separate alliances. Thus, the Peloponnesian League began with a treaty between Sparta and Tegea, the wording of which, misunderstood by Aristotle (frg. 592), proves that Tegea had to drive out all Messenians and was not allowed to make any of them citizens of Tegea. Herein we see a regulation characteristic of all alliances under a Hegemon; the interest of the Hegemon and the obedience of the other state are implied. It was in the half-century following the treaty with Tegea (c. 550 B.C.) that the Peloponnesian League gradually developed; we cannot, in my opinion, pin down its establishment to any one year. In a similar way, Athens built up her Second League and Philip the

I

Corinthian one on agreements with the single states. In general, the alliances under a Hegemon showed very different structures and developments; the reason is that we are not dealing here with a uniform type of constitution, but with unions of a mixed military and political character, which may have been shaped and modified as the changing situation demanded. Accordingly, the aims of each of the Leagues was different. With Sparta, League policy was her method of political expansion, taking the place of regional extension for a state essentially complete within its own borders. It was her means of establishing the strongest forces on land, without decimating her always threatened store of Spartiates, and so becoming Hegemon first of the Peloponnese, and after 404 B.C. of all Greece. The sworn confederacy of the Persian War was, it is true, based on the Lacedaemonian League, but that did not follow from its nature; the later union was a pure war alliance without any political organization; we have already spoken about it in another context (p. 107). On the other hand, it was the Panhellenic resistance to Persia, though also the contrast between Athens and Sparta, that was responsible for the creation of the First Athenian League. That is to say, it was by no means within the frame of the same anti-Persian alliance that the Hegemony simply slipped from the land power, Sparta, to the sea power, Athens. What now arose was a new League, in a new form from the first moment and with allies largely new. Both Leagues were for war, but only the policy of Athens, basing itself on the principle that the allies must recognize the same enemies and friends (Arist. *Ath. Pol.* 23, 5), with its strong emphasis on the idea of an offensive against Persia, aimed beyond the narrow boundaries of the Polis. Yet, the Panhellenic feeling of the time of war left the Polis fundamentally unchanged, and the 'empire' in which the 'alliance' finally became a mere fiction broke down as much because of the tyrannical will to power of Athens as of the stubborn will to autonomy of her allies.

Quite different was the picture in 378 B.C. The aim of the new Athenian League was peace, not war. This meant a reversal of the essential meaning of the Symmachy. Certainly, peace was to be guarded against Sparta, but only in order to secure autonomy; since the King's Peace that had to be the presupposition of every League policy. Even non-Greek states could join this League; for in its organization, for the first time, the idea of a real League of states was taken seriously by creating a strong federal authority apart from the power of the Hegemon. However, even this attempt was shipwrecked on the inability of the Polis to moderate its love of autonomy and fit itself into a larger whole. It was only external force that finally reached this goal by overcoming the Polis. The League of 337 B.C. – quite apart from its importance as a political weapon in the hand of Philip – was set on one purpose, to ensure the common peace, the κοινὴ εἰρήνη. As before, the means employed was the Symmachy, the armed alliance of autonomous states, who in principle were free from being garrisoned and from paying tribute. Peace and Symmachy conditioned one another. The 'common peace' meant that civil wars as well as wars between Greeks were forbidden, and that help from all sides was forthcoming against any breaker of the peace. To the idea of ensuring common peace was added that of a war against Persia. Philip, with his idea of a war of revenge, linked up with the events of 480 B.C., perhaps also with the general truce of 481 B.C. If the treaty between Philip and the League already contained the provision that 'the Greeks should have the same enemies and friends as the king', that would prove how important the idea of an offensive war was; but it is not certain whether it did, though it appears in the renewal of the League in 302 B.C. and is an analogy to the First Athenian League. At any rate, at least as strong was the connection with the tradition of the κοινὴ εἰρήνη, so characteristic of the fourth century B.C. What was new in 337 B.C. – apart from the political situation – was the fact that a Panhellenic combination of a League of Peace and a Symmachy stood under the leadership of a monarch as Hegemon – and one who ruled over a country which the Greeks regarded as barbarous. To speak of a union of Greece under Philip would mean to mistake the nature both of the Polis and the Symmachy; but, as a body that could administer justice to the citizens of its member states or could appoint a member as arbitrator between two states, the Corinthian League was something more than a mere Symmachy. The building of the bridge that led to the federal state had begun. Antigonus and Demetrius Poliorcetes in 302 B.C. and again Antigonous Doson in 224 B.C., came back to the idea of an alliance among the Greeks for peace and war. The League of 302 B.C. (*IG.*² IV 1, 68) provided for close co-operation between the individual states and the Synhedrion, but ensured the representatives sitting in the Synhedrion against having afterwards to give account in their own Poleis. The creation of a leading board of five prohedroi enabled the Synhedrion to transact the business of the League in earnest, though it is true that for a time a number of member states was under the control of Macedonian garrisons or imposed

tyrants. In the League of 224 B.C. power had further shifted in favour
of the allies. The king of the Macedonians was now a member of the
Synhedrion, whose decrees had to be expressly ratified by the individual states, a fact that resulted in frequent lack of unity. The power of
Philip V and the rivalry of the two great Leagues, the Achaean and
the Aetolian, deprived the all-Greek alliance of its importance. It
remained a dream. Generally, the Hellenistic Leagues from 337 onwards, directed or opposed by Macedon till the Roman intervention,
rounded off a process of which the historical coherence and unity are
unmistakable, quite apart from all that was conditioned by the time
and the special circumstances of each case.

4. TRIBAL AND REGIONAL LEAGUES

Sparta and Athens had succeeded at an early date in making political
units out of Laconia and Attica; even as late as the fifth century B.C.
independent states like Mycenae and Tiryns were merged in the state
of Argos, or Rhodes as a state came into being from the union of three
states on the island. There was frequently the tendency now, within
the limits of a country, or only of part of it, to subordinate the autonomy of the Poleis to a higher political instance, if not entirely to
destroy it. In this way, a tighter political union could be formed, even
where there was no leading Polis, but only the loose bonds of a tribal
or cantonal state which, however, would never have quite lost a
common political spirit. A genuine unified state was never achieved;
but there were various grades of federation, which in part at least
achieved political strength. Seen as a whole, it was a single process.
Primitive and loose political forms (as in Thessaly, Acarnania, Aetolia,
Phocis, Locris, Arcadia) were transformed into a closer union, to a
'Koinon' which, like the tribal state, was often bound to a common
shrine and not seldom continued to bear the name of ethnos. Yet, the
members of such a union were autonomous entities (πόλεις or ἔθνη).
This federation of states was distinguished from the Amphictyony by
the presence of central authorities of a political and military character,
from the Symmachy by its actual unity. As even here the supreme
authority of the union was still feeble, the development often went
further and led to a form truly beyond the isolated individual state, to
the creation of a new state on a federal basis, with its own sovereignty
and its own citizenship. This new creation of a 'federal state' may be
thought of as a συμπολιτεία, but the title was by no means fixed.

The boundary between a federation of states and a federal state was not always very clear.

Tribal cohesion and local connections had been responsible for the creation of the old federations of the Greeks in Asia Minor: the Dorian Hexapolis, of which we know practically nothing, the Aeolian League, probably of twelve cities, the existence of which has only been deduced from Her. I 149 ff., and the League of Ionian cities (12 or 13, later 9), whose centre, the sanctuary of Poseidon Heliconius on Mycale, bore the name Panionion. If the religious league of autonomous cities had the character of an Amphictyony (see above, p. 109), from an early date they also showed some ethnical unity and a certain political activity. The reason for this was the contrast between the colonial Greeks and the foreign powers of the hinterland, and also the rival Greeks of different tribes; they may have been supported by an Ionian monarchy in the post-Mycenaean age (Strab. 14, 633). Attempts at political co-operation lasted down to the time of the great revolt of 499–494 B.C. Of the nature and power of the central authority, we know very little; in particularly it is not known whether there was a federal body permanently in session. Still, the possibility of effective action by the League and the common discussion of the most important questions of foreign policy are manifest, above all in the alleged proposal of Thales (Her. I 170) to found a common Council hall (*Bouleuterion*). After its dissolution under Persian rule the Panionion was revived late in the fourth century B.C. (Welles, nos. 3, 52).

In Thessaly primitive forms long survived. The tribal state here was composed of four cantons, the tetrads or tetrarchies, which originally were territories rather than tribes; they primarily had military significance and represent an earlier division of the whole state into regions. Since the Thessalians took part in the First Sacred War and the Lelantian War, they as early as that had a position of considerable power. We must assume that latest in the seventh century a firm tribal organization existed, ruled over by the noble clan of the Aleuads. Shortly before 500 B.C., Thessalian influence dominated Boeotia up to the frontiers of Attica; they also ruled over Phocis and played an important part in the Delphic Amphictyony. The whole state was based on agriculture both of nobles and free peasants; it had its own armed assembly and war leader (*tagos*; see p. 65). It was to some extent unified, but this unity was based on feudal foundations and early impaired by the rise of numerous cities. Still, a loose connection of tribes always persisted, and from a recently discovered inscription we know that as early as the middle of the fifth century there were polemarchs (four?) as eponymous magistrates. That means that they were annual officials, probably elected by the federal assembly. It follows that earlier than usually assumed, feudalism and the regal position of the *tagos* had given way to a more democratic sympolity. After a period of weakness, a League of the Thessalians (κοινὸν τῶν Θεσσαλῶν) was created; in the fourth century it had, under Boeotian influence, a federal organization of considerable strength, also financially. There was an assembly and a supreme official (*archon*) as well as polemarchs and a federal army. How far feudal estates still counted outside the cities, we do not know; the latter seem to have surrendered the harbour and market duties to the federal government (Dem. 1, 22). After the Lamian War, Thessaly lost its independence to Macedon. In Roman times, that is after 196 B.C., there were only Poleis left, and they had a fair amount of freedom; above them rose a unified League, with its own, albeit limited, federal citizenship, its Synhedrion, and its exclusive right to issue coins. Similar was the development in Epirus, where the independent states of the smaller tribes (ἔθνη) and their kingship long survived. Among them was the κοινὸν τῶν Μολοσσῶν, a League of the Molossians with its own citizenship; from it began, in a way we cannot really discern, the unification of Epirus into a federal state, composed of several leagues (κοινά), and under a monarchy of limited rights, later changed into republican rule. In Arcadia, too, the original tribe had split into cantons and cities, even before historical times. Still, in the fifth century B.C., there were perhaps federal coins, and the worship of Zeus Lycaeus had always a binding force, though only over part of the country. The main hindrance to unity lay in Sparta; it was only after Leuctra that a regular League, officially called τὸ κοινὸν τῶν Ἀρκάδων, came into being which by synoecism created its capital Megalopolis. There were federal authorities, a board of fifty damiurgi, elected in proportion to the size of the single states, and the federal assembly of the Ten Thousand, the μύριοι; but the centrifugal forces in the individual states could not in the long run be suppressed. In similar fashion, though varying with the conditions, the development proceeded in Acarnania where both Poleis and Ethne were members of the Koinon, in Phocis, Locris, and other smaller countries.

In Boeotia the conditions were different. Religious connections within the tribe are proved by the Amphictyony of Onchestus (pp. 108 f.) and by the festival of the Pamboeotia at the shrine of Athena Itonia. In a political sense, however, the tribe was obscured behind the independence of many country towns, and it was only the will of Thebes to take the political lead that brought about a certain unity as early as the seventh century B.C.; though this was hardly more than a symmachy. Under Theban supremacy stood a federal army under the command of Boeotarchs. Notable among the various vicissitudes of Boeotian history is the federal constitution (*Hell. Oxyrh.* 11), which was introduced earliest in 447, but probably somewhat later, and in a strange and artificial way combined the preponderance of Thebes with the claim to equal standing, raised by at least the most important of the other cities. Thebes was only one among the nine (later ten) League members, but of the eleven parts ($\mu\acute{\epsilon}\rho\eta$) of the land of Boeotia, on which the constitution was built, Thebes after the destruction of Plataea owned four; other cities formed two or one of these parts, several of the smallest only a third each. These parts were at the same time elective bodies. It has recently been made likely that in 447 it was Orchomenus which held political supremacy, and that Thebes then owned two of the parts of Boeotia. In the main, however, Thebes did dominate the country down to 386 B.C. The supreme authority of the League was very strong; the autonomy of the individual cities was decidedly limited by the compulsion to adopt a certain moderately oligarchic constitution. Yet, it seems that there was no federal citizenship, though the League was called 'the Boeotians'. The special characteristic of this League was that the government of the individual cities and, it seems, of the League as well, was in the hands of a Council, divided into four sections, which took turns to transact business. The eleven parts of the land shared in the federal Council, in a way roughly corresponding to their populations, as also in the executive board of the eleven Boeotarchs. The total Council was an assembly based on the representative principle, and it enjoyed the sovereignty that usually belonged to the primary assembly (cf. Thuc. V 38, 2). Its sessions were held on the Cadmeia. After the dissolution of the League in 386 B.C., with the liberation of Thebes (379 B.C.), a new epoch began, when the Theban Hegemony found its most consistent form. It has been suggested that at this time a unified Boeotian state may have been created. That there was a federal citizenship is, at least, doubtful, though we can be sure of the existence of federal officials with their seat in Thebes; of the seven Boeotarchs three were Thebans, and we have evidence of an eponymous archon (e.g. *Syll.* 179. 201). The Theban Hegemony, which sometimes extended beyond the borders of the land, rested on the Koinon of the Boeotians, based on tradition and tribal connection;

it remained in existence even after the Hegemony of Thebes broke
down in 338 B.C. It was now a League of Poleis of equal rights, with a
double citizenship for each individual. A similar form, with a Hegemon
as its head, appeared even earlier in the Chalcidice. Olynthus (in 432
B.C.) created a unified state and a League of Χαλκιδεῖς round it; it
contained a number of members, equal in rights and severely limited
in their autonomy. This strictly organized state did not rest on an old
tribal community; it was remarkable as probably the earliest attempt
to advance beyond the Polis by way of a genuine federal state. The
two Leagues of the Boeotians and the Chalcidians are the oldest
examples of which we can point of a strong tendency towards federation in the fifth century B.C.; they too carried out for the first time the
idea of representation in a practical form. It may be that this movement
was influenced by oligarchic political theories; it seems certain that
the thought of proportional representation, which we could not admit
for the Polis, found its natural soil in federal unions and perhaps first
grew out of that soil.

What these Leagues most clearly expressed, and most decidedly
where one Polis as Hegemon gave the lead, was the will to political
power, which grew in the struggles between the Poleis, but above all
in the resistance to the position of Athens or Sparta as Hegemon. In
an enhanced degree, the age of the Hellenistic great powers demanded
a territorial extension, such as the single Polis could never know. It was
tribal leagues from which, as they extended in a powerful and consistent
progress beyond the boundaries of tribe and country, the only great
powers of Hellenistic Greece developed, the Aetolian and the Achaean
Leagues. Their unity was guaranteed no longer by the cohesion of
tribe or country, but by political power. Between them and the
Leagues that we have been discussing there was a big difference in
territorial extent, in political importance, and even in structure, in so
far as they were built on the equality of the member states. Some
likeness in constitutional structure existed nevertheless.

The Aetolian League grew out of a tribal state, which despite its
loose settlement in villages and its division into three sub-tribes was a
firmly coherent unit (Thuc. III 94 ff.). The sacred district of Thermos –
not a Polis – was later the centre of politics; but the League was held
together by something more than religious bonds; that is shown by
the policy of expansion that early set in. An inscription, found in the
Athenian agora (Tod, no. 137), seems to prove that the League was in
existence as early as 367 B.C., and that its government was in a position

to call a member state to account for violating a treaty (σπονδαί) made with Athens. The interpretation of the inscription, it is true, is not quite certain, but on the whole it seems likely that the League at that 367 time had become a federal state, and that this did not happen as a result only of the conflict with Macedon. Its members were cities and villages, the latter, it seems, as country districts set on a level with the cities; of the sub-tribes we hear no more, but ἔθνη are mentioned as late as the time of Alexander (Arr. I 10, 2). A constitution that was consistently organized, together with the warlike strength of the people, gave the League an energy which in the third century B.C. made it the master of central Greece. Far beyond the territory of Aetolia, from the Ionian to the Aegean Sea, Poleis and Koina were either merged into the League by *sympoliteia*, or attached to it by *isopoliteia*, the 'mutual grant of potential citizenship'. The latter, sometimes combined with *epimachia*, was in use particularly in the case of separate areas. The League was strong enough to allow a large degree of independence both to cities and tribal bodies. In the League, then, a political whole arose in which tribe, cities, and allies were bound together into a higher unit, into one single state.

The Achaean League was from ancient times a League of cities (12, later 10) whose immediate reason for cohesion probably lay in their common tribal stock; they had, however, a religious centre in the temple of Zeus Homarius near Aegium. These Amphictyonic beginnings had little influence on the later development. It is probable that a political unity with common citizenship existed here as early as the fifth century (cf. Xen. *Hell*. IV 6, 1). Details are lacking, but the federal state preceded the late entry of the Achaeans into the general affairs of Greece, when the League, by including Calydon, thrust out beyond the Corinthian Gulf (c. 390 B.C.). After a period of weakness it was the struggles of the age of the Diadochi that forced the Achaeans to a new union, at first of only four cities. Aratus, then, by bringing in Sicyon, Corinth, Megara, Epidaurus, and other states, made the League the mistress of almost the whole of the Peloponnese and the strongest state of the Greek homeland; at times it covered an area of about eight thousand square miles. No less than sixty Poleis were members of the League; no Koinon as such was admitted, and territory dependent on the individual cities (κῶμαι, etc.) was usually converted into independent members of the League. Here we see a marked tendency to keep the power of the member states weak and to hold them in balance, while strengthening the power of the League. The

division of the League territory into administrative districts (συντέλειαι)
served the same purpose. Member states had often to receive garrisons
of federal troops; sometimes they even asked for them. Nowhere else
was the permanence of the bond to the League so strongly emphasized;
withdrawal counted as revolt, just as in the First Athenian League on
the basis of an alliance in war.

Of a federal constitution in a strict sense we can only speak when
the stage of a 'federal state' had been reached. The earlier stages of the
general development were only preliminaries; there may have been
single federal authorities, but no uniform type of constitution had yet
developed. That indeed, despite considerable differences, is significant
for the federal state in its final forms. We can best characterize the
structure of this federal constitution by regarding it as an adaptation
of the Polis constitution. As the constitutions of the single states still
persisted, there was a duplication of all essential political factors. Here,
too, the relation of the individual to the state rested on his citizenship;
but now it was a federal citizenship (συμπολιτεία), and the citizenship
of the single Polis existed beside it. The organs of the League, as of
the Polis, were the citizen assembly, here too as a rule a primary one,
the Council (mostly συνέδριον, σύνεδροι, or βουλή), a body very
diversely appointed in the different Leagues, but generally of some
independence. In this body, the idea of representation, already suggested though never accomplished in the Polis Council, partially
materialized; for here the Councillors did actually represent their
states, the individual members of the League. Finally, there were the
officials, frequently called by the same names as Polis officials (strategos,
archon, damiurgos, etc.), sometimes expressly marked as federal
officials (Boeotarchs); at any rate, the nature of their offices corresponded to that of the Polis officer (annual tenure, liability to give
account, prohibition or limitation of re-election, etc.). The extent of
the League territory and the composition of the whole state meant that
the citizen assembly seldom met and that even the Council did not sit
permanently. That made the position of the officials all the stronger;
thus there was an almost complete reversal of the Polis constitution,
with the dividing line between the Council and the board of highest
officials not always clearly fixed. Beside the leading board, which was
usually not large in number (Boeotarchs, apocletae in Aetolia, damiurgi
in Arcadia and Achaea) and could be regarded as a smaller Council,
stood a single man, the strategos, as the leader in war and often enough
in politics too. He was the decisive leader of the executive, who,

especially in the two large Leagues of Hellenistic times, held extensive competence and combined in his person military and civil power. His position reflected an essentially monarchical age.

In other ways, too, the transfer of the Polis constitution to the League did not mean that its character went with it. Citizenship of the League gave the citizens of each member state full citizen rights, not only the private rights of freedom to own property and to marry (ἔγκτησις and ἐπιγαμία), but also the essentially political rights of active and passive franchise within the whole League territory, that is to say, for all member states; the actual exercise of citizen rights in the several states may, however, have depended on residence. Anyway, it is a fact that here arose the citizen of a truly territorial state. I believe we must, for the time being, recognize this fact, even though later, in the Lycian League, citizenship of the League may have been confined to ownership of property and freedom of marriage. It would alter the picture considerably, if even in the older Leagues the individual had active political rights in his own Polis only. For the citizens of the member states, as a rule, the primary right might be citizenship in their own Polis, and they could gain federal citizenship only by the entry of their Polis into the League, that is to say, by origin and descent, just as in the Polis itself; but the autonomous conferment of citizenship by the League could mean that a foreigner might first become a citizen of the League and could then choose his Polis. Thus, at least some restriction was put on the right, so precious for the autonomy of the Polis, of free decision in the conferment of citizenship. The citizen, on the other hand, had the right to own land and to take up his residence in any Polis of the League, and to get himself a wife from any League city; that meant that the population of the League in their personal relations, and with that the many member states, grew into a true political unit, into a true state.

The character of the League is largely determined by the relations between the central League authority and the member states. It was no matter of indifference whether their constitutions were oligarchic or democratic; the League must obviously try to produce some uniformity in the constitutions of its members. This was no longer so difficult; for by then the old contrast between oligarchy and democracy was much less strongly felt. In fact, the two forms of constitution, under the name of δημοκρατία, were often classed simply as republican and contrasted with monarchy. Constitutional uniformity was achieved, for example, in Boeotia and Achaea, while in the Aetolian League, with its very motley constituents, the question never arose. The federal constitution itself, which was based on the equality of the member states, had at once a certain democratic character; but this was balanced by a more oligarchic structure of the constitution. Several requirements might be needed for full citizenship, such as age and income; but no federal constitution could be defined as belonging to any fixed form of constitution. Much more important was the division of competence and functions between central power and single states. Matters for the League exclusively were foreign affairs, including conferments of citizenship and of proxeny, and the decision on war and peace. So too was the army; but the contingents from the single states in the federal army usually stayed undivided and unmixed under their own commanders. The election of federal officials was made by the federal assembly, except where it was a question of representatives of the member states or subdivisions of the League. Legislation and jurisdiction lay in the hands of the League so far as they actually concerned it, otherwise they were left to the members; if there were disputes among the members the League had the power to arbitrate. It also had the supreme right of coinage; but in addition there was often coinage by the member states, though always of one and the same standard. Political and administrative activities, then, were shared between the two groups of authority; but federal authority was always dominant and, in case of doubt, decisive. This was even true in relation to the individual citizen, who was bound by the federal laws before those of his own Polis. In military service each citizen was bound to the League, not the individual state. Accordingly, in financial matters, the League seldom relied on fixed quotas from the member states, rather on taxes levied directly on the citizens, whether regular or called for at special occasions. Thus, in many aspects, the Polis became a mere organ of the federal authority.

In the individual Leagues, there were many deviations from the typical forms that we have sketched. Above all, if there was one single Polis as Hegemon, as in Boeotia, this altered conditions considerably. The peculiar constitution of the Boeotian League after 447 B.C. has already been briefly described (see above, pp. 122 f.); but even when in the fourth century B.C. more normal forms recurred, the real power in the League was with the League assembly that met at fixed times in Thebes. It was virtually equivalent to the Theban popular assembly and was called δᾶμος; we have no evidence of any Council beside it. Here, we see, the idea of the Polis still prevailed. It is much harder to realize the relations of citizen assembly and Council in the Achaean League. Its much discussed constitution seems to have undergone a reform (probably in 217 B.C.). The names that we find in our authorities beside βουλή and ἐκκλησία, namely σύνοδος and σύγκλητος, cannot immediately be equated with those usual words, and they seem themselves to have changed in the course of time. The most probable explanation is that Synhodos and Synkletos were not the official names of the two constitutional bodies but denoted regular and irregular meetings of either Council or assembly. The vague use of the names in our tradition makes all explanation very difficult; but when we hear of four *Synhodoi* in the year 220 B.C., it is probably sessions of the Ecclesia that are meant. Later, on the other hand, there were only extraordinary assemblies of the people – no regular ones – and they were called *Synkletoi*; they never met except for a few vital decisions, as for war and peace. Similarly, the two names were used for the Council, in whose hands the real government lay; this Council sat with the leading officials in regular sessions (σύνοδοι), advertised in advance, but also in extraordinary ones (σύγκλητοι). The Council was not a 'probouleutic' body, with powers of pre-deliberation; it was the ruling assembly, which, among other things, elected the officials. As the Council is probably to be regarded as a representative assembly, the Achaean constitution displayed a strengthening of the representative principles, which in other Leagues, as for example the Aetolian, had been used and later given up again.

A peculiar form can be found in the Cretan League, the κοινὸν Κρηταιέων, which in the late third and the second centuries united many Cretan cities under the leadership of Cnossus and Gortyn in a common jurisdiction (κοινοδίκιον). It seems to have had no federal army, no federal citizenship, no federal officials, though there were a Synhedrion and an assembly. This position, somewhere between a Symmachy under a Hegemon and a proper federation of states, is to be attributed mainly to the special position of Crete in the Hellenistic age. Attention, however, has also been called to a συγκρητισμός of early times, though it is not very well attested (Plut. *de frat. amore* 490b. Etym. magn.).

Here, too, we may mention the Island League, the κοινὸν τῶν Νησιωτῶν, which was distinguished from other Leagues in having no connected territory, in standing under the changing control of the Hellenistic rulers, and in having as its highest official (νησίαρχος) a non-islander, nominated by the protecting power – a further expression of the lack of independence in this League; it seems that he might be even subordinate to the Ptolemaic commander, the nauarch. The League thus appears partly as a continuation of the type of Symmachy under a Hegemon (cf. the Corinthian League); as a Koinon without strong federal power it was a kind of federation of states; and because it had a citizenship valid in all the islands (ἐν πάσαις ταῖς νήσοις, *Syll.* 939) – though this might not be quite a genuine federal citizenship – it was a special variety of the federal state. Because of its religious centre in Delos it has even been explained as an Amphictyony. This vague nature of the Island League really derived from the fact that it was no independent political entity, but a tool in the politics of the great powers, borrowing some of the forms of federation.

Of the many Hellenistic κοινά we may still mention the Lycian League, which at times seems to have been a member of the Athenian empire. Later, it can be shown at various times to have been a unit, resting on an ethnical basis. According to Strabo (XIV 664 f.), the League had a Synhedrion in which the member states were proportionally represented; later inscriptions speak of an elective assembly (ἀρχαιρεσιακὴ ἐκκλησία), apparently not a primary assembly. As federal officials we find a high priest and a Lyciarch, probably one and the same office. As another example of representative government in the form of a federal state we may mention the four republics into which Macedon was divided in 167 B.C. Polybius alludes to this when he says (31, 2, 12) that the Macedonians were not accustomed to a 'democratic and representative constitution' (δημοκρατικὴ καὶ συνεδριακὴ πολιτεία).

There was, we may say, a development culminating in the territorial League. The primitive forms of tribal or cantonal state out of which mainly that development arose, were absorbed, while the Polis was inserted in and subordinated to the new form of state. Thus was completed a process from within, which the great powers of the Hellenistic world had brought about by their very existence and their overruling might, the process of overcoming the old Greek state. Outwardly it might look as though the organization of the Polis had been transferred to a federation; Polybius had seen in the Achaean League 'a single Polis' (2, 37, 11), and the treaty of 212 B.C. between Rome and Aetolia speaks surprisingly of the Aetolian Politeuma. But⁺ what did it really mean? A system of proportional representation was partially introduced; assembly and Council were enfeebled to the advantage of the power of the officials; there was now dual citizenship, and taxes were paid directly to the League; there was a territorial state with its natural policy of expansion. In brief, it was an attempt to change the Polis from within in order to meet the requirements of a new age; although in the Hellenistic age the Polis did play its special and important part (see below, pp. 190 ff.), fundamentally the federal development meant the end of the idea of the Polis.

PART II
The Hellenistic State

CHAPTER ONE

The Origins of the Hellenistic World of States

The Hellenistic age – according to the most general view, which is also the most sensible – includes the three centuries between Alexander and Augustus; but its really creative period, especially in the political field, was restricted to little more than the first half of this period. The Hellenistic state was a creation of the late fourth century B.C. and the early third, that is to say, of Alexander and of the two generations of his successors, the 'Diadochi' and the 'Epigoni'. All that ensued was essentially the outcome of this creative epoch; new states then entered the picture and new features were developed, while some of the medium-sized states were organized on similar lines, but reached their prime later, when internal decay and external forces undermined and finally destroyed the big powers, and eventually the Hellenistic state as such. To a very large extent, however, its form still lived on in the empires of Rome and Byzantium.

From what had been said before follows that the Hellenistic state, as understood in the second part of this book, is the territorial monarchy. Not all states in the Mediterranean world during the Hellenistic age were 'Hellenistic' states in that sense, not even inside the Greek world and in the East. It cannot be our task to discuss here, for example, the Hellenistic Polis and the Hellenistic League. Even when they had political power, they still continued the forms of the 'Hellenic' state and so belong to the first part of this work; we shall mention them in this part only as far as they were of importance for the character of states that were truly Hellenistic. These, however, cannot all be treated in one and the same manner. Quite apart from the question of evidence which for most of them is very scanty, any attempt to demonstrate what is common and typical must concern itself primarily with the great powers, the more so as they usually supplied the models for the smaller states. The important differences between the various states must, of course, be taken into account.

The Greeks always knew of monarchy as a form of state. We have mentioned in Part I the kingdom of early times and its after-effects; we have also dealt with the *tyrannis*. Moreover, there always was the kingdom of non-Greek peoples, which generally was regarded by the Greeks as despotism, that is to say, as alien and hostile to the very idea of the Greek state and its freedom. Even so, some of the Greek states had legal and friendly relations with eastern and northern kingdoms. Moreover, from the time of the Sophists, Greek thought took real notice of the problem of monarchy, and a theoretical discussion started in which monarchy was one among several possible constitutions. Individualism was spreading, and many ancient bonds of the Polis began to lose their firm hold; eventually they more or less disappeared. That was the soil from which grew a new plant, the idea of a reasoned one-man leadership, the rule of a man trained and advised by philosophers. In Isocrates' monarchical treatises, although they kept close to reality and in fact were not without triviality, monarchical theory found a basic form. In Plato's philosopher-kings, the development reached a second and higher summit.

The theory of a 'good' monarch of the Polis found its completion in reality. Not only the petty kings of Cyprus, for whom Isocrates wrote, but great rulers such as Iason of Pherae and, above all, Dionysius I of Syracuse were 'tyrants' who outgrew the earlier form of Polis tyranny and founded territorial monarchies. About Dionysius, we know a great deal and we realize that he, at the beginning of the fourth century, to a large extent anticipated the Hellenistic monarchy. His was a dynastic policy; he was called ruler of Sicily (ἄρχων Σικελίας), and he governed his territories through military officials; in the Polis of Syracuse, the constitutional bodies survived, but had little say, and the ruler was chiefly advised by 'friends' (φίλοι) who were half courtiers and half officials. All these features we shall meet again in the Hellenistic kingdoms; the analogies will be best explained as deriving from a similar situation rather than from connections across several generations and a wide geographical distance. In Agathocles, about a century later, Dionysius, it is true, found a really 'Hellenistic' successor.

Plato's attempts at gaining decisive influence on the Sicilian rulers were bound to fail. There is hardly any direct connection between the ideal states of the philosophers and the founders of the new monarchies of the third century. The analogies which some scholars have tried to discover are caused by the fact that monarchy was 'in the air'. Both political theory and political reality were bringing monarchical rule closer to the Greek mind; at the same time, democracy was more sharply criticized. When the Macedonian kings entered Greek politics, they found fanatical resistance, though also pro-Macedonian partisans; the old Isocrates welcomed Philip as the champion of Panhellenism. We do not know for certain whether Philip or Alexander was actually influenced by Isocratean ideas – more likely they were not. We do know that Aristotle had no understanding for the new form of state, and it is hard to imagine that Plato's deep and unrealistic ideas could guide the conquering kings and generals. No safe bridge led from the Polis of the 5040 or that of the *Laws* to the Hellenistic kingdom, though it is true that the Greeks gradually recognized Hellenistic monarchy as a legitimate form of government.

The present description of the Hellenistic state is part of a whole, entitled 'The Greek State'. It might seem that I am associating myself with a view, taken by others, that in the Hellenistic state we see an exclusively Greek phenomenon. This is not at all how I see it, and I must add a few words to what I have said. The theory just mentioned takes no account of what stands first in the Hellenistic state, both in order of time and importance: the rule over non-Greek people and the non-Greek inheritance, whether from Macedon or from the East, that so decidedly helped to shape the new political creations. The most important states were ruled by Macedonians; later, there were new foundations by Hellenized Orientals and a few Greeks. These facts alone should be sufficient to prove that we cannot regard the Hellenistic monarchy as something purely Greek. The Macedonians may go back to a 'Greek' origin, but in historical times they were always, even by their own rulers, regarded as barbarians, and only a small section – king and part of the nobility – were 'Hellenized', For the Greeks of the third century, it is true, the Hellenistic world was only an extension of the earlier Greek world; that in itself is perhaps sufficient justification for including the present discussions under the one general title. There is more to add. It was Greeks who most strongly determined the general spirit and the cultural form of the Hellenistic age. It was the Greek spirit which, nourished and merged in the stream of Greek evolution, took over the local influences – yes, even the creative achievements of non-Greeks such as that of Zeno who founded the school of Stoicism. This is true in some measure of politics too, but the importance of the non-Greek element as creative and formative was greater here than anywhere else, except in the sphere of religion. Therefore, when I let the Hellenistic state appear as something subordinate to the general title 'The Greek State', I do so not without some serious reserves. The Hellenistic state never was an Hellenic state.

The empire of Alexander the Great, from its very beginnings when, at his landing in Asia, he 'threw the spear' and thus based the future on his right of conquest, set the conditions for the new type of state and served as its model – and that although to the last it was itself still growing and, as the heir of many and varied empires and states, it never attained its final shape, quite apart from what Alexander's last plans may have included. In the first place, it was simply the historical connection of the Hellenistic states with Alexander's empire that made it possible for them to exist at all. The death of the great king, who was the only sure centre of his empire, released those centrifugal forces that had so far been with difficulty controlled. The long and bitter struggles among the great Macedonians, who at first as satraps took over the provinces of the empire, meant a clash between the unity of the empire as a whole and the establishment of the satrapies as independent states. After the rapid decay of the central government Antigonus again took up the idea of imperial unity – no longer in the service of the old royal house, but as a purely personal aim. He too came to grief; with Ipsus (301 B.C.) the first period of conflicts came to an end. The decision between universal empire and single states had been taken – it had, in fact, been taken already in the 'Year of the Kings' (306–305 B.C.) when the satraps finally became kings. Thenceforward it was a matter of forming and consolidating the single states under the Ptolemies (Lagidae), Seleucids, and Antigonids, while other creations like Lysimachus' empire had a merely ephemeral character and rose only to fall again. By 280 B.C. the new political world had assumed its definite shape: a system of states under three leading great powers.

We may properly speak of a system of states, though the word 'system' must not be pressed too far. What seems to be essential is the existence of a society of states, within which, despite all its internal conflicts, a certain political balance cannot be mistaken. The empire of Alexander was in the main divided between the three great powers. There were zones in which the three states bordered on one another and could make contacts, and these zones gave room for fights between them (for parts of the Aegean and Asia Minor and for Syria), but gave room also for the creation or maintenance of smaller states, especially in Asia Minor and on the eastern border of the Seleucid empire. Thus it came about that a number of states of middle size were fitted into the system, or gained their independence out of the decline of the great realms. We think in the first place of the kingdom of Pergamum, founded by the Paphlagonian Philetaerus, as early as about 280 B.C., even though not at first truly independent. Independent, or only temporarily under Seleucid over-lordship, were some of the princedoms of Asia Minor under their Hellenized Oriental dynasties, such as Cappadocia, Bithynia, Pontus, Commagene; the territory of the Galatians became a state of the same type. The weakening of the Seleucid empire later made possible the creation of the Bactrian, Indian, and Parthian states in the East, and still later the political independence of Judaea. As a kind of forerunner of such states, with a similar structure, we may regard the kingdom of the Crimean Bosphorus, which arose from similar conditions, but always lay outside the Hellenistic world of states. This then was the society of states, including dynasties that were not Greek but stood under Greek cultural influence, that embodied the Hellenistic type of state. It goes without saying that many institutions, when they were adapted to the different conditions of the smaller states, somewhat changed their appearances. Out of the political unity of Alexander's empire, though divided into numerous states, grew the unity of the Hellenistic world with its new form of state.

In this process, the boundaries of Alexander's empire had in some places been crossed; but how much more was this the case when the Hellenistic type of state began to have effects far beyond its original sphere and exert its influence even in the western Mediterranean! Alexander may have intended to conquer the West, but he died too soon. Epirus, the neighbour of Macedon, and its great king Pyrrhus may be regarded politically as a bridge to the West, though, like Macedon itself, they had grown into the Hellenistic scheme on the basis of an ancient popular kingship. The kings of the little Athamania, lying between Macedon and Epirus, in a decree which in form and content tried to imitate the decrees of Hellenistic rulers (Welles, 35), prided themselves on their descent from a mythical ancestor, who was a son of Hellen – just as the kings of Macedon and Epirus derived their origin from heroes of Greek myth. Then again in Sicily, Agathocles created an empire which displayed features generally in conformity with the contemporary Hellenistic monarchies of the East; the policy of Agathocles against Carthage was an attempt to repeat Alexander's designs on the West. Under Hiero II the Sicilian empire enjoyed a second heyday – its last –, and here the borrowing from Eastern and Hellenistic models was unmistakable. On the other hand, Carthage and Rome, the two strongest powers in the west, in spite of strong Hellenistic influence in the field of culture, maintained their old political forms, which they developed in their own independent ways. These two states and empires were not shaped on the Hellenistic model, though the foreign policy of Carthage may perhaps be regarded as Hellenistic in the sense that it protected the existing society of states, and that the unity of the Hellenistic age included the western Mediterranean until Rome finally upset the equilibrium.

The heirs of Alexander's empire were heirs of his position; their states were in essential features heirs of his state. Naturally, however, there were inevitable variations of selection and change, due to the smaller space, the deliberate setting of boundaries, the historical situation, and further developments. Philip had brought Macedon out of her previous position on the edge of the Greek world and almost outside history, when he made her a great power in Greece; in extending and organizing his rule over Thrace and Illyria, where cities with a mixed population had existed before, he showed himself a precursor of his son and the Hellenistic kings, just as the Greek tyrants and the dynasts of Asia Minor in the fourth century B.C. can be regarded as their forerunners. Still, it remained for Alexander to create the new form of state. He did not discover completely unknown countries, but he did open up to the Greeks an expanded world and made the Macedonian people master in it. His attempts to fuse the Macedonians with the Eastern ruling people, the Iranians, did, it is true, come to nothing; but it illustrated a typically Hellenistic problem, expressed by the generally prevailing fact of a state with mixed population. We have said that the Greeks themselves regarded the Hellenistic world as a mere extension of the Greek world; but that was not true of Alexander and his Macedonians. In his personal position he combined the popular kingship of Macedon and the hegemony of Greece with the absolutism of the Achaemenids, the kings of Persia. We find a similar combination in the shaping of the royal court and central offices, the organization of the army and the administration of the empire, although the original elements might combine in various ways and there was frequent change, in which the varying aims and methods of Alexander played their part. The effects on the successor states varied too, though to some extent they were unified by the unity of Alexander's person. It may be obvious, but is nevertheless worth noting, that for the Seleucids the model and forerunner was essentially the world ruler of the last years, while for the Ptolemies it was the master of that 'first empire' of 332 B.C. that embraced the eastern Mediterranean, the founder of Alexandria.

Moreover, we must not overlook the fact that, between the empire of Alexander and the final establishment of the states of his heirs, stood, in point of time, the ephemeral but powerful and important empires of Lysimachus and, above all, of Antigonus Monophthalmus. They formed at once a bridge and a zone of division; their peculiar forms will occasionally be mentioned in our description.

Alexander and the Macedonians carried Greek civilization into the East. It is, I believe, a historical fact that a command was issued by the king to the Greek states to worship him as a god; with this the monarchy took a new form, which went far beyond the Macedonian or Persian model, and which was destined to have immense importance in world history. How far Alexander deliberately tried to Hellenize the East remains uncertain; I am inclined to regard the idea of a Greek 'mission' as a likely initial motive on Alexander's part, but in the main as an interpretation *post eventum*. However, the outcome certainly was that he opened up the world to a Greek people which in spirit as well as in numbers had burst the narrow bounds of its homeland, and could now supply to the new states the class needed to provide leaders in social and cultural life. The spread of Greek individuals and Greek culture was assisted not only by the mere existence of the empire but above all by the many cities founded by Alexander. He thus provided the powerful and decisive impulses to that twofold development by which the world, the οἰκουμένη, became Hellenized, and the Greeks became citizens of the world. This furnishes the broad historical stage on which the creation and history of the Hellenistic states was enacted. Close relations to old Hellas, beyond its much reduced importance in the Aegean, became for the new monarchies an aim sought again and again to be established. From Antigonus onwards freedom and autonomy of the Greek states became a weapon in the struggles of the kings with one another, especially against the efforts of the Antigonids to revive the Corinthian League.

Whatever the particular connection with Alexander, it was decisive for the historical uniformity of the Hellenistic states that a process of continuous development and growth, hitherto held together only by the genius of a single ruler, now became a stable and impersonal form – in fact, an institution. The many differences that existed between the various Hellenistic states and often even between the reigns of different rulers in the same state must not, of course, be overlooked. But even the supreme distinction between the national kingship in Macedon and the new dynasties of Macedonian-Greek rulers in non-Greek territory could not destroy the unity of the new type of state. This new type became the model for states, Greek and non-Greek, in East and West, and modified the character of the Macedonian kingship itself. We tried, in the first part of this book, to work out the type of the Polis from a number of Greek states: we must now try something similar inside the framework of the Hellenistic world of states. The political history of the centuries from Alexander to Augustus, the Hellenistic age in pre-Roman times, forms a unity in itself. In the same sense there was a unity of Hellenistic civilization, and as civilization and state are in so many ways indissolubly allied, there must have been a unity in the form of the state, which can and should be demonstrated.

CHAPTER TWO

Basic Facts

I. TERRITORY

The state founded by Alexander was a universal empire and so from its very nature intolerant and exclusive, allowing no other states beside itself to count; yet, in fact, it embraced barely half of the territory that lay within the geographical vision of the Greeks. Alexander's empire followed the claims to universal rule of the great empires of the East, but had a stronger justification for its claim, since it united territories in the Mediterranean and in Hither Asia, while its incorporation of the West may actually have been the ultimate intention of its ruler. This final aim was never achieved, but it was only through the collapse of the 'world' as united by Alexander that the coexistence of a number of states with equal rights in the whole area of the Mediterranean and the Near East was made possible. It is important to note that the new rulers – generals and satraps of the school of Alexander – governed exclusively and from the first very large areas, and that thus a wide extent of state territory was accepted, both as a basis and as an aim, even by the most determined champions of the idea of separate sovereign states. The states that now arose were, indeed, of very varied sizes, but in so far of the same type as each of them was large in comparison with all Greek states, and not small even if related to the space actually available in the inhabited world of the Oecumene. Only so was it possible that a small number of states could maintain a balance of power that might be unstable, but was never seriously disturbed until Rome intervened; it was this equilibrium that determined the politics of the age and thus its general character; this remains true in spite of what has been called the 'hegemonial efforts' of the great powers, which applied, if at all, to Greece and the Aegean only.

Alexander's empire reached a size of about two million square miles. Of the successor states the Seleucid empire at its greatest extent included about one and a half million square miles, the western provinces (Mesopotamia, Syria, Asia Minor) by their dense population and their position the political heart of the empire, some two hundred and fifty thousand square miles; even after the Peace of Apamea and the loss of Asia Minor, about one hundred and twenty-five thousand still remained. The empire of the Ptolemies, on the other hand, at its greatest extent (excluding the deserts) contained about sixty thousand square miles, the Macedonian empire not more than forty thousand. The ephemeral empire of Lysimachus probably embraced some hundred and sixty thousand square miles, Pergamum after 189 B.C. about seventy thousand. In contrast to the figures of the Greek states and Leagues – even the Achaean League after 188 B.C. had only about eight thousand square miles – it appears at once that in these simple figures and sizes an entirely new type of state had come into being. This is true, not only of the empires in their greatest extent but also of their central areas. Pergamum alone in the third century B.C., even after the great gains of Eumenes I, was hardly more than a large Polis, with less than three thousand square miles of territory; much the same is true of Hiero II's Syracuse. Macedon, however, and Egypt had each, apart from their dominions, about twelve thousand square miles. Even the middle-sized states of the Hellenistic age, such as Bithynia (over eighteen thousand), Galatia (sixteen thousand), Judaea (twelve thousand) reached a size which permits us to regard them as the same type of state as the great powers. The eastern successor states of the Seleucid empire, the Graeco-Bactrian empire of the third to second century, and the Parthian that struck out so vigorously from the beginning of the second century B.C., contained mighty territories, almost reaching the half-million. Finally, we may note that Carthage, before the first war with Rome, ruled over an area of about sixty thousand square miles of coherent territory in Africa, and about the same in its provinces, and that Rome, as a result of the First Punic War, grew from about fifty thousand to about seventy thousand square miles.

The quality and character of the land varied enormously within each single empire. River-land and desert, high mountains and low plains, interior and coast, they occur in all the states in varied and wide-spaced coexistence; there were correspondingly powerful variations in the climatic and cultural conditions. There is no need to illustrate these points in detail. It was, of course, in the continental empire of the Seleucids, extending from the Mediterranean over Mesopotamia and the Iranian plateaus to the mountains of inner Asia, that the union of lands and economic units of completely diverse character were most manifest. On the other hand, the uniform character of the land of

Egypt, the valley and the delta of the Nile, and its separation from the outside world, allowed at least in the central part of the Ptolemaic empire the possibility of a strict and centralized organization; though the empire as a whole felt both the advantages and the drawbacks of a state based essentially on the sea. What has been called the 'originality' or uniqueness of Egypt rests above all on the position and the nature of the country; they were responsible no less for its self-sufficiency and seclusion than for the conservatism of its culture and its over-emphasis on organization and officialdom. No other Hellenistic state was quite in the same degree shaped by its territory as was that of the Ptolemies.

The clear distinction between central and outlying districts may be seen in the Seleucid empire in the division first into the districts west of the Iranian mountains and the Irano-Bactrian East, the 'upper satrapies' (αἱ ἄνω καλούμεναι σατραπεῖαι), and again into the Mediterranean to the west and the continental Asiatic regions east of the Euphrates line (the last two more or less balancing one another). These distinctions express the haphazard, even artificial, way in which the state's territory could be composed. We may think of the relation of Macedon to Greece or of the possessions of the Ptolemies, at one time extending from Cyrene over Crete and the League of the Nesiotae – an ally only in name – as far as the south and west coasts of Asia Minor and even the Thracian Chersonesus. We realize that in cases like these we cannot speak of trunk and limbs of the same body. Nor were these states centred on the sea, like the First Athenian League, in which geographical unity was achieved only through the sea. Now, the sea was a hotly contested battleground, as were the lands of Syria and Palestine between the Seleucid and Ptolemaic empires. Even the empire of Lysimachus, which lay on both sides of the Hellespont, was for all its apparent cohesion so far from being a unit that it soon broke up again into its European and Asiatic parts. It was only the middle and small states that did not suffer from the lack of organic cohesion and from the inner weakness inherent in the lack of a unified regional basis. That meant that they sometimes enjoyed an importance exceeding their actual power. Of the great empires, it is truly significant that neither that of the Ptolemies nor that of the Seleucids had a legal name and that the Antigonids were kings of the Macedonians, not kings of Macedon.

We see, then, that the land as such, the territory, important as it was for this kind of state – different, say, from the Polis – did not really form the basis of the state's unity; it was the ruling dynasty that did that. The boundaries of the state's territory were therefore often traced more or less by accident, as the conditions of power at any moment demanded, frequently without regard to natural conditions or historical development; that is why partition of the territory was comparatively easy. The whole history of the Hellenistic age confirms the fact that the attempt, made here for the first time by rulers of western origin, to master large extents of territory – a task destined to become a main theme of European history – succeeded, despite many great achievements, very imperfectly only within the political structure of the various empires. Yet, whether or not a final form was achieved, the mere fact of the large territories was vital to the process by which the state was formed, both in a positive and in a negative sense. The heavy disability implied in the wide stretches of uncultivated and valueless land, the often inadequate development of traffic and trade routes, the necessity of balancing central government against provincial or local administration, the necessarily different forms of settlement, administration, and government in many parts – these and other problems were there to condition the inner structure of the state. On the other hand, the small number of states that counted politically, and the natural consequence that there were few areas of possible friction, made the foreign policy of the great empires comparatively simple. The Aristotelian 'unity of place' seemed reversed, and there was no doctrine in the earlier political theories of the Greeks, no experience in the life of the Polis, that could help to solve the grave problem of ruling large territorial states. Decisive help was rendered by the traditions of Macedon or the East which the new rulers inherited. These made possible a more or less complete administrative unity. Economic unity could hardly be realized; it was most nearly possible in the Ptolemaic empire, though even there the inclusion of the outlying dominions only succeeded partially and temporarily. To all this we may add the 'imponderable' element which has been noted on other occasions; we may describe it as an inner relationship of great political personalities, such as the creative period of the Hellenistic age knew in unusually large numbers, to the tasks that wide spaces and horizons imposed upon the human mind.

Large empires like the Hellenistic, or even the larger among the middle states, could only be governed by division into administrative districts. The satrapies and hyparchies of the Seleucid empire, the Egyptian 'cantons' ($\nu o \mu o \iota$), toparchies, and villages are the best known, though not the only, subdivisions; the nomenclature was not quite uniform, but a similar principle of division existed everywhere. The more urgently did such a state demand a clear and certain centre, such as monarchy undoubtedly offered best. The close connection of the new form of state with land and soil was impressively shown in the decisive importance of the central government and so in the great role played by the 'capital city' – whether the capital of the empire or of large sections of it (such as Sardes in Asia Minor). The capital would sometimes be an old city, but more often a foundation of the new rulers; it was the frequent, if not permanent, residence of the king, the seat of the chief authorities, a trade centre that often ousted older markets or harbours – that is to say, the outcome of the first meeting of the imperial idea with the form of the Polis. Even in later times, the traditional importance of a city like Seleucia in Pieria as πατρίς of the king might be rewarded by the assurance of perpetual freedom (Welles, 71). But the closest connection of the state with the soil lay in the fact that the land was to a great extent the property of the king (βασιλικὴ χώρα, β. γῆ). Following Alexander's example and basing their rule on the right of conquest, the former Macedonian generals, and their heirs after them to the latest times, laid claim to the land 'won by the spear' (δορίκτητος χώρα). They were not, however, kings of a special country, but simply kings; their title was nothing but βασιλεύς. Even in the empire of the 'kings of the Macedonians' all land added to the homeland by conquest, so far as it did not belong to cities or dynasts, seems to have been 'king's land' – in Chalcidice, for example, and then in Thrace and Illyria. Here, as in the Seleucid empire and even more so in Egypt and Pergamum, the king's private ownership of land and soil and the possibility of transferring it in fief or possession (γῆ ἐν ἀφέσει) were the basis of the system of administration and the political economy (see below, pp. 227 ff.).

In this context we must not overlook the great differences between the various states. The Attalids had to buy land before they could give it away (Welles, 62). The Antigonids and Ptolemies never conferred full ownership, but retained the right to take the land back into royal possession. Autonomous in a large degree within the state was the land of the Poleis, dynasts, and temples; in the Seleucid empire and its successor states they played a very different role, and an incomparably more important one than anywhere else. Of the Poleis we shall have to speak later (see section III 3). The dynasts and temples were often fairly independent; but even though some of them might have won their land by conquest – this did happen, though rarely – they still needed the protection of the great empire and therefore placed themselves under the king. The rest of the territory was occasionally called 'the tribes' (τὰ ἔθνη; see OGI. 229, 11), but usually 'the places' or 'the regions' (οἱ τόποι), a parallel to the Egyptian toparchies. The Ptolemies and Seleucids differed in their policy regarding the king's land; the Ptolemies were entirely concerned with grabbing, holding, and managing it like any private owner, the Seleucids rather minded to distribute it in the interest of the Hellenization of their empire and, with that, of the inner strengthening of their rule. Antiochus I, for example, through the intermediary of the provincial governor, gave king's land to a Greek who stood near his person and in this way the land was assigned to a Polis (Welles, 10–13); with it went the villages and their population (λαοί) (cf. also Welles, 18–20). It is interesting to note that land might first be given away, then be found to have been given away before to someone else, and therefore need to be replaced by other land. It is obvious that the central government was not always in the position to control the allotment of land within the empire; it usually left the task to the provincial authorities. Temple states in the Seleucid empire, especially in Asia Minor, seem generally to have their territories increased; apparently, the kings sometimes donated them some land (cf. Welles, 70), but hardly ever took land away. When the kings, on the other hand, left Polis territory alone or even added to it, this can be understood as a tacit recognition of the theoretical autonomy of the Polis. In the medium-sized states, too, as far as we can determine it, there were great variations in the extent, nature, and importance of the royal domains, but all derived from the equally close bond between the monarchy and its territory. It was not the land that made the state; but it is justifiable to say that the state in the person of the king very largely owned and ruled the land.

2. POPULATION

The Hellenistic states, as might be expected from their very varying sizes and densities of population, varied very considerably in numbers of inhabitants; estimates too differ widely. The Seleucid empire with its roughly thirty million was certainly in population as in size the largest state, Egypt, famous for her 'multitude of people' (πολυανθρωπία) (Diod. 1, 31, 6), with six or seven million the most densely populated. Josephus (BJ. II 385) speaks of seven and a half million, not including Alexandria, which like Antioch and Seleucia on the Tigris early grew

to a population of several hundred thousand, and swiftly and steadily
went on growing. Even in the middle states, where the figures of the
population were naturally smaller, there were still almost everywhere
large numbers of the most varied origin. It seems likely that here too –
contrary to the Greek motherland – the population considerably increased. Such vast numbers, like the vast spaces, meant something
unknown to the pre-Hellenistic history of the Greeks.

Alexander had made the Macedonians the ruling people of the
world. His attempt to put the Iranians on equal standing failed; at the
moment when he died there was no longer any talk of Persians sharing
in the imperial government. The Macedonians, though at least their
upper classes shared in Greek culture, were proud of their pure nationality, which neither they nor the Greeks then regarded as Greek; it was
they who now became the rulers of the new empires. The Macedonian
people, however, were most strongly attached to their homeland. Only
as the army, the 'people in arms', could they go out into the world,
and even abroad they did not lose their deep attachment to their home,
as is shown by Alexander's sending back of the veterans. Thus, the
Macedonian element was not very large even in the army of Alexander's last years, nor was it large in the Hellenistic armies, though the
proportion varied; it became definitely small after 300 B.C. We must
only allow for a percentage, at first considerable, in the officer corps.
The Macedonians, therefore, represented no large section of the population of the Hellenistic empires – with the exception, of course, of
that of the Antigonids – even if the sons and grandsons born outside
Macedon are reckoned in, who even after several generations were
clearly proud of their descent. When sometimes tradition records the
recognition of the king by the Macedonian army assembly (we shall
come back to this point later), we must not take that quite literally, at
least as far as the question of nationality goes, and must connect it with
the fact that kingdom and court in general emphasized and treasured
the Macedonian tradition. This is proved, for example, by the official
retention of the Macedonian calendar as late as Antiochus of Commagene (*OGI.* 383, 84); of some of the Ptolemies it is especially recorded
that they had forgotten the Macedonian dialect (Plut. *Ant.* 27, 5). The
Macedonian homeland, on the other hand, in speech as in general
culture, became more and more definitely part of the unified Greek
world, while Greeks in the coastal cities of Macedon usually described
themselves as Macedonians. Occasionally, we find a tenacious retention
of national Macedonian traditions, for example in the Peliganes (a

L

Macedonian word for Council or Gerusia) in the Syrian Laodicea, and probably also in Seleucia on the Tigris (Polyb. 5, 54, 10). Dura too, for a long time a garrison rather than a city, preserved a citizen body of Graeco-Macedonian stock. We find Macedonians as military settlers in Egypt, Asia Minor, northern Syria, Mesopotamia, and their comparatively frequent appearance, especially in the Seleucid empire, may at least partly be explained by the fact that the term 'Macedonians' (Μακεδόνες) increasingly ceased to denote national origin, and came to mean a social group or became a purely technical description in the army. Many of these Macedonians must have been Greeks or sometimes even Hellenized Asiatics, whose military discipline and armour were in the Macedonian tradition. Additions from the home country to the Macedonian element in the population hardly reached any longer either Asia or Egypt, not only because political boundaries and conflicts interfered but also because Macedon, after its heavy losses under Alexander and his successors, suffered from a decisive scarcity of population. Of the Ptolemies we can say with assurance that none of them ever got soldiers direct from Macedon; but much the same is true of the Seleucids as well, although Seleucus I and Antiochus I tried, within certain limits, to pursue a policy of 'Macedonization'; in later years the name of the Macedonians was frequently used for the Seleucids, their army, and eventually even their empire. The mixing of Macedonians and Greeks, on the other hand, set in early and vigorously in all the Hellenistic states; it rested on original ethnic kinship and later common culture. In the course of time it almost obliterated the distinction between them. To what extent it was a case of Greeks becoming Macedonians (cf. FGrH. 80 F 1; 81 F 6) or the reverse can hardly be determined. Many Macedonians, under their veneer of Greek culture, may have found it fairly easy to become absorbed by their Oriental surroundings; in Egypt, on the other hand, we hear of a 'Macedonian' who was persecuted because he was a Greek. It is significant that in spite of the many bearing Macedonian names and the ethnical description Μακεδών, which can be traced in Egypt down to the first century B.C., in spite also of separate settlements of Macedonians which can be demonstrated at least for the third century B.C., not a single papyrus in the Macedonian language survives. To describe the Macedonian military colonies as a 'true Dispersion' is an exaggeration, in spite of Macedonian place-names. The statement is hardly tenable in view of likely ethnic conditions; we do not know how many genuine Macedonians, if any, there were in such a colony after two or three generations. Livy (38, 17, 11) for his part exaggerates in two directions when he makes the Roman consul say in 189 B.C.: 'The Macedonians, who possess Alexandria in Egypt, Seleucia, Babylon, and other colonies scattered over the face of the earth, have degenerated into Syrians, Parthians, and Egyptians.' Outside the immediate surroundings of the king the small number of genuine Macedonians were soon swallowed up, but the name remained in force for the highest stratum in the structure of the army, and the influence of Macedonian organization and tactics continued for long to work in the armies of the Seleucids and Ptolemies.

However small the numbers of Macedonians outside Macedon may have been, the numbers of Greeks were large. The whole development of the Hellenistic age cannot be understood unless we recognize the fact, beyond doubt for the fourth and third centuries B.C., that Greece was very seriously over-populated. If we look closer we may see a proof of this in the great number of exiles from the Poleis, who made the countryside unsafe. The depopulation in the following period was to a large extent caused by the general emigration of earlier years. Many thousands of Greeks, especially in the first decades of the new epoch, to some extent even earlier, went out as mercenaries or merchants, as peasants or labourers, or as plain adventurers. The higher standard of living in the East substantially contributed to Greek emigration during the third century B.C.; the Egyptian fellahin received higher pay than the Greek labourer in Delos. The new courts and states also attracted great numbers of the intelligentsia. Greek scholars and doctors, artists, and engineers gained support and permanent positions; above all, Greeks were mostly taken for officers and officials, and not only for the higher posts. This even happened to some degree in Macedon, where the noble upper class with its Greek culture had suffered a serious shrinkage through the demands made on it by external events and internal strife. The social nature of the Greek emigrants was largely determined by their origin, that it is to say, from which of the various states they came; socially therefore, the Hellenistic age preserved some characteristics of the political division of Greece. To give one example, as late as the second century B.C., there existed in Xoïs in the Nile delta a 'Politeuma' of the Boeotians, which held fast to the gods of its old homeland (*SEG*. II 871, XIV 848; *SlB*. 6664). Everywhere the Greeks, besides the Macedonians, became the special support of the new rulers, and the representatives of that common Hellenistic civilization which rested on the unified Greek

language, the κοινή. One of the main things to be done, then, was to
bind the Greeks to the soil and to the structure of the state; that was
mainly achieved by settlement. This purpose was served by the three
cities and the many country Politeumata of Egypt, by the many cities
and *Katoikiai* of the Seleucid empire or other states of Asia Minor and
the East as well as by the landed estates of high officials, as almost
everywhere either recorded or at least to be assumed. Citizenship in
the cities was a privilege, much striven for by non-Greeks, even by
Macedonians; by acquiring it they became Greeks. Note that citizens
of a Polis, and even non-citizens on Polis territory, only exceptionally
had military obligations. Thus, a Graeco-Macedonian class arose,
under very various forms of settlement and very diverse social conditions, but as the ruling section of the population of increasing unity;
this was the origin of a new bourgeoisie, which at least in the cities was
not unlike the bourgeoisie in the homeland. The Greeks everywhere
found their local centre in the gymnasium; its officials usually stood
under the supervision of the Polis Council (cf. *SEG.* VIII 641). As the
autonomy of the cities weakened (see III 3), the gymnasiarchs came
more and more to be the real representatives of the Greek element in
the cities.

Beside the Macedonians and Greeks, there were in Egypt and Asia
other national groups more or less co-ordinate with them, at least in the
military field, the Cretans, for example, regarded as distinct from the
Greeks, or the Mysians, coming from Hellenized Asia Minor. Special
mention must be made in this context of the 'Persians', settled mostly
in Upper Egypt; this name, like the others, seems to go back to an
original detachment of troops, and subsequently a group of military
settlers – probably, in this case, of the time before Alexander. The first
Ptolemy, it is true, entered Egypt with very few Macedonians and may
therefore have brought Persians with him. Anyway, it was only in
their 'false' use denoting a military group, with no thought of ethnic
origin, that these forms won real importance. We shall have to speak
later (IV 3) of the motley composition of mercenaries and military
settlers, but we may emphasize at once how much the 'Persians', even
before the Hellenistic age, were mixed with Greek mercenaries. How
important these groups were as an army reserve is shown in the Ptolemaic empire by the frequent occurrence of the addition 'of descent'
(τῆς ἐπιγονῆς) to the names of such people; this must mean, even
though details remain disputed, that they were descendants of soldiers
of the people in question or of the corresponding military category.

Thus, we hear of Macedonians τῆς ἐπιγονῆς, which may include two generations of the same family (*P. Cairo Zen.* 54), or again at first sight rather surprisingly of Jews as Persians τῆς ἐπιγονῆς. Jewish communities existed in many places, mostly in the form of a Politeuma. Other descriptions of origin were similarly converted into Persians or Macedonians, whose great numbers can only be explained by such artificial changes. In point of fact not a single one of the Persians τῆς ἐπιγονῆς of whom we know bears an Iranian name. They either were non-Egyptians, born in Egypt, whose fathers had been soldiers, or they may have been Hellenized Egyptians. The institution finally led to rights and duties becoming completely hereditary and, in the case of the Persians, to the creation of a new non-Hellenic class between Greeks and Egyptians. Thus, it appears, the population of Egypt, so far as they were contrasted with the Egyptians, was divided into the 'classes' of Macedonians (and Cretans?), of Greeks and of Persians. Even that solution, however, does not entirely fit the evidence. It is quite obscure why the 'Persians' were excluded from the asylum of the temples; debtors, at any rate, would be designated by their creditors as Πέρσαι τῆς ἐπιγονῆς to prevent them from taking refuge in a sanctuary. It is, after all, more likely that in late Ptolemaic and Roman times the 'Persians' were no more than a legal fiction (cf. *P. Fay.* 12, 6; *P. Mert.* I 10, 4; 14, 3); not only the idea of national descent but even that of a special class had lost its significance. Admittedly, this neither is quite a satisfactory explanation, in particular as the social position of the 'Persians' remains uncertain.

Over against the Macedonian and Greek conquerors and masters stood the native population, without doubt far superior in numbers, but for ages oppressed and often enough ready to fight back; partly, however, they came early under the influence of Greek civilization. The coexistence of Greek and non-Greek elements in the population – except for Macedon where the Thracian and Illyrian sections of the population played no considerable part – was one of the basic facts in the Hellenistic state and was at the same time a grave, nay, insoluble problem for the rulers. This coexistence surely did not imply an absolute separation. Links between the two sides gradually increased, and a considerable mixed population came into being; in Syria or Egypt, for instance, it attained large numbers and great cultural importance. Yet, Alexander's policy of mixing races was abandoned by the realistic policy of his successors. Even so, quite apart from some early attempts by the first Ptolemy, we cannot talk of any discrimination;

there was little in the Seleucid empire against the Iranian upper
class or, occasionally, against other Orientals. It may be significant
that the royal houses often linked themselves by marriage to Eastern
princely families. Force of circumstances made concessions inevitable,
but a share in the government on equal terms was still impossible. The
imperial policy of all Hellenistic rulers was concerned with the supremacy of the Graeco-Macedonian classes, and strove everywhere to
extend the sphere of Greek men and Greek civilization. The Greek
emigration met and fitted in with the tendencies of Hellenistic state
policy.

What we have been saying does certainly not imply any deliberate
oppression of the natives, and it has rightly been contended that the
Ptolemies never pursued a nationalistic or racial policy. But that is not
the whole story, even if we add that the Ptolemies officially appear on
buildings and inscriptions as Pharaohs. In Egypt, the exploiting oppres-
sors were, besides the officials, mainly the rich landowners, either Greek
or Hellenized; Apollonius and Zeno were Hellenized Carians. If it
happened on occasion that Greeks suffered under Greeks, it is yet
significant that from the second century B.C. the 'Hellenes', although
already much intermingled with Egyptians, represented the upper
class. The mere fact that the great majority of the population belonged
to the mass of forced labourers, among whom the native element was
always by far the largest, stamped the rule of the Ptolemies as a foreign
rule and as oppression. This remains true, even though the self-interest
of the king caused him frequently to act as a protector, and he was
appealed to in that quality, for example, in Syria under Philadelphus,
when the 'free natives' (σῶμα λαϊκὸν ἐλεύθερον) were secured against
sale or mortgage of their persons. Peasants and artisans could always
appeal to the self-interest of the state; as they worked for the king (see
also IV 4), it was in his interest that they should not be thrown into
prison or driven to strikes or flight by the oppression of officials and
military settlers. Often enough one interest of the state stood in opposition to another, for example, the cultivation of the soil against the
collection of taxes. The realease of the individual worker from his
traditional attachment to a small piece of land, a release that in the third
century B.C. was frequently permitted or even encouraged by the
administration, became through the economic oppression of the natives
increasingly a flight from his place of work and thus a protest against
the forced labour which the state demanded. Peasants of the king,
tenants, and even officials were among those who escaped from their

intolerable obligations by flight; this often only meant going from one district to the next; often it led to asylum in a temple. Scholars have spoken of an 'internal migration' of the Egyptian population; but the phenomenon is still in need of further study, though it is certain that in later times (from the end of the second century B.C.) it had become a serious threat to the prosperity of the country and to the proper functioning of the administration. The government was bound to try to check it, and this it did partly by punishments, partly by remission of taxes and other reliefs. When the king issued protective letters (πίστεις) or extended the right of asylum, he was not concerned with the protection of the individual in question, but usually with securing the royal rights over that individual as against other rights which indirectly might again be his own. It is doubtful, to say the least, how far we can speak of a deliberate 'welfare' policy. The officials were admonished (*P. Teb.* 703, 41; 60) 'to cheer up everyone and put them in good humour', or 'if anyone is suffering under pressure of taxation or is at the end of his means, you must not let the case go unchecked'. The importance of such exhortations must not be overestimated, still less their actual effects. Yet, the first three Ptolemies did seriously endeavour to rid the native population of the feeling of insecurity and to fight the corruption of the administration (cf. *P. Hib.* II 198, esp. 42–140).

Looked at as a whole, the administrative policy of the Seleucid empire, too, led to a determined reaction on the part of the native peoples, who everywhere, at least in the countryside, maintained their own traditions of kinship and culture, and that despite the impact of Hellenization. In the cities of Asia with the possible exception of Baby-lon whose script and culture were protected by the government, it was mainly Greeks and Hellenized Orientals of whom the social and cultural upper classes were composed, and it was they alone in which the government took a real interest. Nevertheless, the native population kept on gaining ground, and, for instance, with the creation of an Aramaic κοινή, it challenged the Greek language of administration. From the end of the third century B.C. this reaction became more and more manifest, and in Asia after the decisive weakening of Seleucid power by the Peace of Apamea (189 B.C.) it was the predominant factor; it changed the composition of the bureaucracy and army, and could develop (as it did with the Iranians) into a most serious menace to the very existence of the state.

The multitude of native peoples of the most varied origins was confronted in many districts by a Greek element, not weak numerically but strange to the land and divorced from its own national traditions. This situation demanded a policy which in various ways was to give expression to the general and uniform will of the Greeks to keep their power. The Iranian nomads and peasants had to be treated differently from the Semites of Babylon or the Jews or the Hellenized peoples and dynasts of Asia Minor. Antiochus IV refused to pay heed to this demand, which laid on the Seleucids as foreigners a far harder task than that which their Persian predecessors had had to face; for these could count from the first on the support of the large Iranian element in the population. That was perhaps the main reason for Antiochus' failure. The Ptolemaic empire, too, had other peoples to deal with; the Libyans of Cyrenaica sometimes caused difficulties to the Polis of Cyrene no less than to its Ptolemaic overlords. In Egypt itself, uniform though the main body of the population was, members of foreign peoples played their part: Thracians, Celts, Syrians, and, above all, Jews. We know of Jewish and other military settlers from the days of the Persians; but even after that, in connection with the immigration of the Greeks, many non-Greeks changed their place of residence, attracted by the new economic and spiritual possibilities of the Hellenistic states. In the large cities a real hotchpotch of peoples could be found, in Antioch, Seleucia, or Pergamum, but most manifestly in Alexandria. As the nationalistic Egyptian 'Potter's Oracle' puts it, Alexandria was 'the all-nurturing Polis in which every human race (πᾶν γένος ἀνδρῶν) had settled'. In Alexandria, beside the royal government and its foreign soldiers, there was the large Greek Polis, the purely Egyptian village of Rhacotis, a strong Jewish Politeuma, and numerous smaller national groups. Nowhere so clearly as in Egypt but yet visibly in other places as well, we can see the two contrasted developments, caused by the coexistence of several kinds of peoples. It was, above all, Greeks and Egyptians who lived side by side; Greek mercenaries and peasants might marry native women, and so arose a mixed Graeco-Egyptian population whose whole way of life was made up of elements of both civilizations, who combined Greek language with Egyptian religion, both indeed mixed with elements of the other side. These people made up the bourgeoisie of the villages which was of decisive importance for the functioning of the economic system. In this class Egyptian blood and culture slowly but steadily won the upper hand. From about 150 B.C. the linguistic origin of a man's proper name no longer signified anything at all for his ethnic origin. Even the citizens of the Polis of Alexandria, who called themselves Hellenes, belonged, to a considerable extent, to that mixed population, despite the fact that marriage between citizens and natives was forbidden. Yet, as the national Egyptian reaction grew stronger in the second century B.C., it was the Alexandrinians in particular who became champions of the Greek way of life; that is why Polybius says of them (34, 14, 5): 'Although of mixed origin, they were in the first place Greeks and maintained the general Greek customs.' No real union, however, was possible, if only because no government and no ruling class could think of altering the economic system, founded on the work and taxation of the masses. The second consequence of this coexistence of men of different nationality which Polybius emphasizes (and this is essentially true of the other Hellenistic states as well) was that the Greeks, who in the third century B.C. still used the name of their Polis of origin, now passed under one general designation as Hellenes. Free from local attachment, sometimes even from any traditional ethnic loyalty, they mustered round the gymnasium as their cultural centre and the proper symbol of their way of life now partially severed from the Polis. They might occasionally even override all social distinctions, and thus carry on the struggle for the Greek way of life and for Greek civilization. This upper class of men who were Greek by culture gradually extended on the social as well as on the ethnic plane; they eventually became the mainstay of the rule of Rome.

Everywhere inside the Hellenistic population, distinctions of origin and culture helped to determine the character and form of the state; but the distinction between free and non-free had come to signify little, though that cannot generally be said of men's personal feelings. Domestic slavery was still important for the normal way of life, perhaps even more so as time went on. The sacred temple slaves of both sexes, especially in Asia Minor, were only in part actual slaves; but as servants of the god they were not free, though sometimes this condition lasted only for a limited period. In agriculture and manufacture we cannot assume slave labour on any large scale either in Egypt – though there the distinction between slaves and free labourers is often hard to draw – or even at Pergamum, at least outside the cities. The native population, frequently forced into compulsory labour and tied to the soil, Egyptian or Seleucid royal peasants or the λαοί, labouring for the Poleis, temples, or dynasts of Asia Minor, represented a serf class who, we might say, took the place of slaves. They could be sold or given away with the land on which they were settled; but in the Seleucid empire at least, the king saw to it that in such a case they would gain security and often the right to become 'Paroeci' of a Polis (e.g. Welles, 11. 18). On the other hand, we might sometimes find that the word 'slave' was avoided, but not the fact itself; in an Egyptian document (*PSI.* 549) the prohibition that nobody was to sell himself into slavery was evaded that way. It is questionable how far we may generalize from the fact that a Hellenistic ruler, Nicomedes III of Bithynia, delivered slaves to Delphi (*OGI.* 345). On the whole, the small account now paid to the lack of personal freedom in determining a man's political status – in glaring contrast to the old Polis no less than to Rome – may well be explained by the fact that the opposite, individual freedom, had also lost its political significance. The free tenants or labourers, and if we look at the matter rather than the manner, even the citizens of the Greek Poleis, generally possessed freedom in private law only and possibly as members of their local community, whereas in the state they were no better than subjects. The subject population as a whole is often described by a phrase suggesting its complete dependence on the king (οἱ ὑφ᾽ ἡμᾶς τασσόμενοι, or the like); such an expression derives from the military sphere and seems to presuppose absolute obedience. This is quite fundamental. There were no citizens in the Hellenistic states. No part of the population saw in the state their 'fatherland'. No one except the self-sufficient philosopher who had turned his back on the world might in truth still claim that he was free.

CHAPTER THREE

Structure and Nature of the State

I. KINGDOM

The Hellenistic state was a monarchy. It consisted of the king and his subjects; but just because of that, it was no state in the sense of a human community or even of 'common weal' (res publica). The state signified the royal administration, the official affairs of the king (τὰ [βασιλικὰ] πράγματα); the king himself speaks of 'our affairs' (Welles, 22, 8). The subjects were, of course, no uniform group; to a certain extent, Lysimachus' enumeration (Welles, 6) 'We [i.e. the king], our friends (φίλοι), our army (δυνάμεις), and our administration (τὰ πράγματα)', might pass as a description of the king's sphere of power; similarly in an inscription of Antiochus I (OGI. 219), friends and armed forces appear beside the gods as helpers in the fight for the πράγματα and the securing of peace and sovereignty. We shall have to speak in various contexts of the four factors here mentioned; for the moment it is the fact of monarchy that concerns us.

The position of the king was not exactly the same in all states and at all times, but monarchy as such was never called in question. It had become practically necessary because, among other things, there was the task of governing large territories with mixed populations; at the same time, the path had been paved for it in many ways, and thus it had become also a historical necessity. In the first place, it was the Macedonian tradition and the inherited, almost instinctive, acceptance of monarchy by the Macedonians that made kings out of the great men of that people. Evidence can be found that even later Seleucids and Ptolemies described themselves simply as Macedonians (e.g. OGI. 239; IG. VII 4251). The people's monarchy in Macedon found its legality in the recognition by the army assembly; originally it had been the exponent of the people's sovereignty and had the right of free election of the king. Survivals of this original power may be seen in the acclamation of a new king or, it might be, in the appointment of a guardian when the king was a minor. Before the unification of

Macedon, a foreign treaty was sworn to by the king, the dynasts, and selected nobles (*IG²*. I 71). After Philip, that belonged to the past; with him began the gradual inner emancipation of the Macedonian monarchy. An hereditary monarchy had long been taken for granted; it could count on a dynastic sentiment in the nobility, and even more so among the ordinary people, that is to say the foot-soldiers in the army. This dynastic feeling, which after the death of Alexander found tragic expression in the selection of a new-born child and a moron, sometimes served as a mere tool to a monarchy that was strong and sure of itself. When the male line of the dynasty died out, the acclamation by the army assembly again became something more than an expression of dynastic loyalty, though we often find the Diadochi trying to gain dynastic legitimacy by marrying into the royal house or by inventing some legendary connection with it. The original right of the new rulers – satraps who had become kings – rested, as we have said before, on their succession to Alexander and on his right or their own, as victors, to the land 'won by the spear'. It was, however, the Macedonian army assembly which was appealed to again and again during the grave conflicts; there might even exist several such assemblies at the same time, each supposed to confer legitimacy on its king, though it was only in Macedon itself that it could confer the same legitimacy on the Antigonids as on the old royal house. Ptolemies and Seleucids also seem usually to have had an acclamation by the army, though there were very few real Macedonians among the soldiers; the place of the army assembly was taken by the garrison of the capital, with its more or less chance composition, as we find it acting, for example, when Ptolemy VI was declared to be of age (ἀνακλητήρια). Moreover, this form of recognition was only an act of confirmation after the event and little more than an empty formality. No assembly and no army had the right or the power to depose a king. The Antigonids alone had the title of 'king of the Macedonians'; all the other rulers were just plain 'kings'. Yet Cassander first (*Syll.* 332), then the later Macedonian kings (cf. *Syll.* 573–4) and the other Hellenistic rulers put the title before their names; earlier, it had been the other way round (see *IG*. VIII 1355, 7). It is also significant that the dynastic claim was usually based on the king's ancestors (πρόγονοι), including Alexander and the former royal house of Macedon; it was perhaps different with the earlier Seleucids (cf. Welles, 15).

By linking themselves to Alexander, his person, and his empire, the new rulers were necessarily led beyond the Macedonian tradition.

Alexander himself was the successor of Pharaohs and Great kings of Persia, though I feel it is quite inadequate to explain his position as a 'personal union'. It was the Achaemenid empire, above all, whose organization and traditions lived on in the empires of Alexander and the Seleucids. What the East knew was a state that proved itself a state in and through the king only, through monarchy in its absolute form; it was the unrestricted rule of an individual, who, by the special grace of the gods or, as in Egypt, as an incarnation of a god himself, stood on a height unattainable by any stratum of the population, indeed above all human standards. At the same time, the position of this king was by hereditary succession tied to the blood royal. Many centuries of tradition had established a despotism at least semi-theocratic as the one and only possible form of rule in Eastern states, no matter whether they were great empires or smaller territorial states. Only by entering into this tradition could the rule of Hellenized Macedonian kings firmly establish itself over the lands of the East. The West learned from the East the necessity of autocratic monarchy, and to a large extent also what it implied. It was the same process that repeated itself later in the Roman empire.

To make something new out of the union of Macedonian and Oriental forms of rule, that is to say, of two completely different conceptions of monarchy, demanded very strong creative powers. The genius of Alexander made the first breach and sketched the first shape of things to come; but he could never overcome the resistance of his own people, and he did not yet create the new form of state. That was the work of his heirs, a group of Macedonians who by their very greatness put their stamp on the whole epoch. The creation of the new states was a personal achievement of the founders of the various dynasties, and this was true of Macedon just as much as of the other empires. The attempt, sometimes made, to distinguish on principle between 'national' and 'personal' kingship, gives in my opinion a one-sided and oversimplified picture; it is not exactly false nor yet true, but it does not do justice to the origins, still less to the later development. The character of the first, to some extent also of the second, generation of Hellenistic kings not only depended on the unexhausted forces of the Macedonian people but also gave expression to a very special condition of the human mind, which meant in those days the mind of the Greeks. In the evolution of Greek culture, in which these Macedonians had their share, the moment had arrived at which the almost complete disappearance of the Polis from inter-state politics set forces free, both universally and individually, to reach supreme achievement. A prelude may be seen in the passing of the hegemony over Greece into the hand of a single ruler, Philip. That contributed towards establishing the position of Alexander and the older Diadochi, and of the Antigonids after them, over against the Greeks, but it was only the change in the world after Alexander's death that created the framework, within which the will to power of the individual could engage in the actual creation of states. Men whose fame and ambitions were only based on their having been companions of the great king now claimed the right to become the rulers of great states. This was true not only of those Macedonian nobles who from satraps became kings. We find the individual element at work elsewhere, too, when the influence of Greek tradition could be even more obvious. The territorial state of Pergamum grew out of a monarchy that resembled Greek tyranny. In rare instances, as for example in Sicily, tyranny itself as the older form of Greek monarchy passed on into a Hellenistic kingdom, despite all its connection with the Polis. In many places it was individuals of Greek descent or at least of Greek culture who created new states and dynasties. The great personality became the moving and central element in shaping the new form of state. On the other hand, every state, even the empire of the Antigonids so far as it went beyond Macedon, was not bound to any one people; compounded as it was out of more or less accidental sections of the Hellenized human race, it corresponded to the universal tendencies of the age.

The monarch alone embodied the state. Because of that, his power was unlimited, his position an 'office not liable to render account' (ἀνυπεύθυνος ἀρχή). This formula is, of course, one coined by the conceptions of the Greek Polis and does not do justice to the actual nature of the monarchy; but it does allow us to realize that it was not possible to designate the Hellenistic monarchy simply as tyranny or despotism. However, neither the territory as such nor the 'autonomous' Poleis, neither the population as a whole nor any of its parts (not even the *Herrenvolk* of Macedonians and Greeks) possessed any representation or any right that might offer a check to the royal power. This fundamental principle of the Hellenistic state even invaded Macedon, where between Antigonus Gonatas and Philip V the development in the direction of absolutism is quite obvious. Inscriptions and coins of the late third century B.C., it is true, bear the formula 'king Antigonus and the Macedonians' and seem to set king and people on one and the same political level; this remains remarkable, even though it may have indicated no more than an honorary right of the old army assembly. The Poleis, on the other hand, distinguished between kings like the Seleucids or Ptolemies, and kings who could not simply be regarded as absolute rulers. In a number of treaties with Macedon, or even with a city-state such as Sidon in Phoenicia, the king would be acknowledged as the man in power, and therefore as the contracting party; but whenever possible, the Greeks would stress the existence of the people or the citizens beside the monarch. In legal cases, involving life and death, the Macedonian assembly may still have had a word to say (Polybius speaks of Isegoria, 5, 27, 6), but a real limitation of the royal power no longer existed. In spite of some relics of the 'national' monarchy in Macedon, the general rule holds that the Hellenistic king ruled his empire without any obligation to answer for his actions, thereby undertaking a task to which very few rulers were equal. It was a purely personal government. The king received foreign ambassadors, corresponded with provincial governors and other officials as also with 'autonomous' Poleis. He stood at the head of all branches of the administration, his edicts had the force of law, he was master over the life and death of his subjects, lord and beneficiary also of all the revenues of the land. He was the greatest landowner, and owned the greatest treasures of precious metal and other objects of value; the kings, above all the Ptolemies, were rumoured to possess unmeasured wealth. Even if the king could transfer his power in some degree to his highest officials, it was still the will and consideration of the ruler that determined policy; this, therefore, was personal, rational, and almost completely without popular backing. We could also call it 'patrimonial'; in the last resort, the state was the king's property, a fact based on the right of conquest. In varied forms, but essentially as Alexander's legacy, monarchy was not only 'absolute' in the present but also, as a hereditary possession, for the future. This is the explanation for the last wills by which Hellenistic rulers bequeathed their lands to the Romans. Abroad this policy aimed at an equilibrium of the states. The rule of the world was in the hands of a few rulers, closely bound to one another by the similar requirements of their positions although they were ever and again driven to settle their disputes by war.

The king might also be called Great King ($\beta\alpha\sigma\iota\lambda\epsilon\grave{\upsilon}\varsigma$ $\mu\acute{\epsilon}\gamma\alpha\varsigma$) or occasionally later King of Kings ($\beta\alpha\sigma\iota\lambda\epsilon\grave{\upsilon}\varsigma$ $\beta\alpha\sigma\iota\lambda\acute{\epsilon}\omega\nu$), following an Oriental tradition, early acknowledged by the Greeks, which seems to have implied divine descent. The symbol of royal dignity was, above all, the diadem, the white band round the head or round the traditional

Macedonian cap (*kausia*). The diadem was first used by Alexander, probably as part of the Persian royal dress such as the purple robe, perhaps also the sceptre and the signet ring. The traditions of Macedon and Greece saw to it that at least in early times the appearance of the king and of his court in general remained simple. There were royal palaces in several cities, and the king had his secondary residences; the court, but not the heads of the administration, usually accompanied him. More and more there developed a court with an ever-growing number of functionaries (οἱ περὶ τὴν αὐλήν, or similar phrases), with a strict order of rank and elaborate ceremony, and this led to a certain removal of the king from popular contacts; though at the court of the Seleucids, and even more so with the Antigonids at Pella, etiquette was less developed than with the Ptolemies and Attalids. The king's birthday was a public festival, his death an occasion for general mourning; dating was usually by the years of the king's reign, his portrait adorned the coins. Externally the royal court preserved a good deal that was Macedonian; the Macedonian 'uniform' was the generally accepted court costume, there were 'bodyguards' (*somatophylakes*) and the corps of pages, the 'king's boys'. All these things showed a marked attachment to the traditions of Macedon, that is, in the first place, of Alexander and through him, it is true, also of Persia; however, they soon became mere formalities.

Apart from the court of Pella there were few genuine Macedonian noblemen (ἑταῖροι), and even there it disappeared after the original 'companions', through the growing strength of the monarchy, had ceased to be more or less independent chieftains and largely depended on the king. The 'companions' became 'friends' (φίλοι), a group which can already be shown as a permanent institution under Lysimachus (*Syll.* 368 I. Welles, 6); their advice could be sought on important questions, but the title was not bound up with any special functions. It naturally depended on the individual king how to choose his 'friends'; but as far as we can judge, the selection was usually not narrowminded. It is not always certain how far these φίλοι, who are so often quoted in literature, were united in a definite body (συνέδριον, σύνταγμα). Sometimes they were simply personal friends of the king, but in general, formulae like εἷς τῶν φίλων or φίλος ὤν, and the fact that there were grades of rank (πρῶτοι φίλοι, τιμώμενοι φ., ἰσότιμοι τοῖς πρώτοις φίλοις) show that they were an official group of dignitaries. A man could also be φίλος under a number of successive rulers (Welles, 45). There were other descriptions, like that of 'kinsmen' (συγγενεῖς) of the king, a title, highly esteemed and more frequently used from the second century B.C.; it probably went back to Persian tradition. With the Ptolemies, again at least from the second century onwards, a single συγγενής formed the head of a court hierarchy that otherwise would undergo many changes; he might be designated 'brother' by the king (*OGI*. 138), or even 'father and brother' (*SEG.* VII 62, 33). In other places the address 'cousin' was fairly frequent (Welles, 65). Thus with the supreme court nobility of the 'kinsmen', the lower one of the 'friends', and with the 'brotherly' relations between ruler and ruler, there arose a 'family of the kings', which as a monarchical institution continued to operate for centuries.

The Macedonian 'bodyguards' were even before Alexander a purely honorary title, quite separated from the office of the same name; under Alexander the Persian doryphori were amalgamated with the bodyguards. 'Supreme bodyguard' (ἀρχισωματοφύλαξ) was in Egypt at first an individual title, later it became a grade of rank. In the later Ptolemaic empire we find also the 'diadochi', probably candidates for higher titles; that means, they represented the lowest grade. Thus was developed a hierarchy with its different grades, which would include both army officers and administrative officials. But the titles were purely personal, not hereditary; after a change of ruler they might be confirmed, but need not be. It was Ptolemy V Epiphanes, it appears, who brought order into the Egyptian court hierarchy; we shall hardly be wrong in seeing in this a symptom of decline. Only under the later Ptolemies, however, was there something like a court camarilla. Nothing can show better what the external appearance of monarchy was like and how much it was taken for granted, than the fact that it was imitated even by rulers whose position did not really live up to it; the Spartan king Areus (309–264 B.C.) is an early example, to be followed about half a century later by the 'tyrant' Nabis; however, neither of the two had a cult. We may also think of Hiero of Syracuse; as the 'archon of Sicily' he belonged, in spite of the strong traditions of the Polis Syracuse, in more than superficial respects to the same Hellenistic regal type. Probably the strangest effect of the Hellenistic monarchy may be seen in the slave kingship of Eunus in the second century B.C. in Sicily; in court, bodyguard, and coinage he imitated the Seleucid monarchy.

The chief implement with which the government worked was the royal edicts, which were either published as laws or directed as instructions to certain recipients (officials, Poleis). Hardly ever was a

M

royal law called 'Nomos'; that concept remained reserved to the Polis. Monarchy was familiar with various forms of edict, but the nature and aim of each defy definition; our material, which is considerable, shows that the use of these forms was fairly arbitrary. We may distinguish between 'laws' and 'letters', but the ancient descriptions such as διάγραμμα or πρόσταγμα cannot be at once assigned to either group. In general, the 'Diagramma' seems to have been an edict, issued by the king or some other central authority, of a legal or political character; it usually conveyed some general regulation and then, often in the form of a list, detailed a number of separate items. As a royal edict it could be clearly distinguished from the laws of the Polis (e.g. Welles, 3, § 6), and yet it could coincide with them or complete them – as seems to be the case in the constitution dictated to the Polis of Cyrene by Ptolemy I (SEG. IX 1). The descriptive names under which the edicts went out must not be taken too narrowly or too strictly; in particular, there was a great difference between a Diagramma in the internal administration of Egypt and one employed in the relations between states. The form of a letter (ἐπιστολή) was usual in relations with Greek cities, but also with individual governors, and could serve for any purpose. Often there was no difference between ἐπιστολή and πρόσταγμα. The latter was in Egypt the most common form of legislation, but was also used in administrative measures and judicial decisions; in P. Teb. III 703 we read: 'It is not necessary to administer everything by letter.' Rarer expressions such as ἐπίταγμα (Welles, 75) or ἐπιταγή (Welles, 68; OGI. 674), πρόγραμμα or ἐντολή (both only in papyri), διαγράφα (OGI. 8) or διαγραφαί (OGI. 46), prove that there was neither one single nomenclature nor were the various forms used in a uniform manner. Some papyri (e.g. Hib. 198) are collections of a number of royal decrees about all sorts of administrative questions; they were probably put together for the practical use of the officials concerned. As far as style goes, the Diagramma mentioned the ruler in the third person and the directions were mostly in the imperative mood, whereas letters were naturally written in the first person (usually with the plural of majesty, unless the king was acting personally); corresponding to this, the Diagramma had no prescript, whereas Prostagma and letters mentioned both senders and recipients. The personal character of all edicts shows that officials and officers were only executives; a king who took his duties seriously had a vast amount of work to manage.

The decisive problem for every monarchy is the question of the succession; only when that is arranged and secured can monarchy hope to last. In the Hellenistic states the rule, originally won by the power of the strong personality, was, under the influence of both Macedonian and Oriental traditions, transformed into the rule of a dynasty. The hereditary principle was, naturally, only developed by degrees through frequent use, and not at all times nor in all places was it accepted without dispute. The essential principle, however, following the Macedonian usage, was that the firstborn should succeed whether he was born 'in the purple' or not. If the son was a minor the government was taken over by a guardian (ἐπίτροπος) who, as for instance Antigonos Doson, might later make himself king. Such a position as guardian might count for much in politics, but in law its powers were not defined. Neither the widows nor the younger sons (perhaps as part-heirs) had any claim to succession; if there was no son, the nearest male relative took his place. The empire was bequeathed as a whole. Divisions of the inheritance might take place, but only under exceptional circumstances; as a matter of fact, the succession became more and more a question of power and contention. There was no succession in the female line, but here, as in other matters, were deviations from the rule, struggles for the throne, often great influence exercised by women. That was especially true of the Ptolemies, from the great Arsinoe to the last Cleopatra, though sometimes of the Seleucids too. Still, all these things did not affect the principle of succession itself.

To preserve the succession against opposition was a vital task. One method often employed in Macedon, even as late as Alexander, was to put to death all princes who were not entitled to succeed; but that was a very radical measure, only used in particular circumstances. Naturally, every effort was made to strengthen the royal dynasty. We have already spoken of the appeal to one's ancestors; that demonstrated the continuity of the dynasty backwards in time. The assurance of the succession did the same thing for the future and was therefore still more important. Very often the heir was proclaimed co-ruler. This creation of two monarchs instead of one could take various forms; there might be a merely nominal co-rule (as with a child); or a share in the government (for the earliest example, Antigonus I and Demetrius Poliorcetes), combined occasionally with the temporary transfer of part of the empire to the heir (so under Seleucus I); or, finally, actual joint rule, as with Philometor and Euergetes II. In early times at least, the nomination of a second ruler was always confirmed by the army assembly. In many cases it is hard to distinguish between co-rule and joint rule (conceptions which Mommsen coined for the Roman Principate, but which, to some extent, have their meaning in Hellenistic times too). The co-ruler was named βασιλεύς, had as a rule the right to issue coins, and shared sometimes, but by no means always, in the official cult. The duplication of the ruler did not always serve only the succession; the vast extent of the task of government (as with the Seleucids) or internal strife (as with the later Ptolemies) might compel a division of power. Another consideration that might count was that state treaties, which were always concluded in the name of the reigning king, did not need to be renewed at his death, if a co-ruler was named with him.

The principle of monogamy was only very exceptionally violated, though polygamy may have been common practice among earlier kings of Macedon. The two wives of Euergetes II, mother and daughter, were queens at the same time, but that case was without parallel. Are we to think of the queen, the βασίλισσα, as legally sharing in the government – for all her worship, her portrait on the coins, and her diadem? The question remains open. In revolutionary events, of course, strange things might happen: the second Cleopatra was recognized as 'king' by the mob of Alexandria, which represented the Macedonian army assembly; her daughter might be named in the prescripts to documents before her co-ruler, her son Ptolemy IX. In general, however, the fact that the queen stood beside the king simply emphasized, in the royal couple, the principle of dynastic monarchy; the rule of a couple probably went back in the first place to ancient Egyptian practice. All forms of joint rule were fundamentally aimed at preserving and maintaining the dynasty. This was also the reason for the marriages of brother and sister, probably deriving from Oriental models, but repulsive to Greek feeling. Although the queen was frequently described as 'sister' (ἀδελφή), these marriages occurred more frequently, as real marriages, with the Ptolemies only; otherwise, they were mostly fictional. They did, however, contribute towards increasing the inbreeding in the royal families, which must have hastened the degeneration, particularly of the Ptolemies. Moreover, the gulf that separated the royal family from the mass of the subjects, who stood under the ordinary moral laws, widened. The idea of a misalliance was probably unknown; but the rule was to marry women of 'equal rank', that is to say, princesses from royal houses; an exception was the second marriage of Antiochus III. The Hellenistic ruling families thus came to be repeatedly interrelated; marriages played an important part in politics. All this is a confirmation of the fact that the kings were closely bound together and set apart from all ordinary men.

A monarchy that ruled Greeks and Orientals, even though it might aim at the supremacy of the Greeks, was bound to wear a double face. The Macedonian Ptolemies were all genuine Pharaohs, though it was only the fifth of them, Epiphanes, who was crowned in Memphis according to the Egyptian rite; they were sons of Re, they wore the two crowns of Lower and Upper Egypt, they held all the holy names and dignities of the kings of old Egypt. In some aspects, for instance in their active foreign policy and the planned state economy, the Ptolemies seemed to follow the Pharaohs of the eighteenth dynasty rather than those of the later Saïte period. However, this does not alter the fact that they manifestly upheld the traditions of the previous rulers. We can see this phenomenon most clearly with the Lagids, but it also occurred among the Seleucids; they, too, deliberately carried on the tradition of the native kings of their peoples. Naturally, it meant a lot for the general character of the Seleucid kingdom that no one land and no one people had such overriding importance as Egypt and the Egyptians in the Ptolemaic empire. The rulers of the earlier Hellenistic age might show some restraint in the adoption of Oriental forms, and in later times those forms might dominate; but throughout, the union of Graeco-Macedonian with Eastern customs and institutions remains as a vital fact. It is from this standpoint that we can understand a phenomenon in which the position of the individual king no less than the dynastic idea found their strongest expression, the ruler-cult. There, it is true, the stronger emphasis was on the Greek element. It has often been shown how religious worship of great personalities found its place in the development of the Greek mind in general, especially in the anthropomorphic nature of Greek religion and myth. It has been rightly said that the views of Euhemerus, which spread abroad in the Greek world at about the same time as the beginning of ruler-worship, present a perfect parallel to it: if the gods were originally no more than powerful kings, it was equally natural to recognize the great rulers of one's own day as gods. Most of the cults of the kings in the cities were spontaneous creations of the citizen communities; as a local conferment of divinity on great men, they were near the borderline between ordinary honour and religious worship. Often they were expressions of thanks for some special benefit or achievement, often merely a bid for favour. Hardly ever can we think of them as the product of a genuinely religious demand. Still, the worship of rulers by Greek Poleis and Leagues – and its origins can be traced under the last Macedonian kings before Alexander – cannot be understood as mere flattery; it was also the expression of the position that the Greeks naturally adopted towards a changed political world, especially as the effect of the immediate presence of the mighty rulers and the dependence on their will. Thanks and fear were combined in this recognition of human greatness and dignity; but these feelings are natural in the presence of any deity, and it would be rash to deny all evidence of a truly religious side of the ruler-cult. Flattery and vanity and thoughts of political and economic advantage, all played their part. These Polis cults of the rulers would hardly have been as numerous and important as they were, if they had been left entirely to the initiative of the worshippers, if at least the example, everywhere forthcoming as it was, had not induced others to follow. A distinction must be drawn between the official state worship of the ruler and these Polis cults, but the boundary line must not be drawn too sharply, as if one of the two phenomena could be explained without the other. The genealogy of the royal houses, which led back to various Olympian gods or heroes, and finally to Zeus, supplied the necessary framework.

Some influence in this matter was exercised by the cities founded by the rulers and named after them, where they had their cults as founder heroes or founder gods. The worship of the Hellenistic rulers did not as a rule attach itself to Alexander directly; but we always find his figure at the beginning, not so much as a model as a precursor. As the founder of Alexandria he certainly received no more than heroic honours; if in a late document (*SIB*. 6611, A.D. 120) the god Alexander is called 'founder of the city and of its youth groups' (ἡλικεῖαι), the expression may derive from early times and express worship of the guardian hero of the gymnasia, that is to say, of the Greeks in Alexandria. But this founder of cities was more than that. After he had, by way of a prelude, declared himself the son of Ammon, he demanded, in 324 B.C., of the Greek cities his worship as a god. Though this tradition does not occur in our best sources, I believe that we may recognize it as historical; we note, for example, that the ambassadors, who were sent to him soon afterwards, were called 'theoroi', like those sent to the great shrines (Arr. 7, 23, 2). The Alexander of 324 B.C. had grown far beyond any purely Greek sentiment; he felt himself as the successor of Eastern rulers, such as the divine Pharaohs and especially the Babylonian and Persian kings. Taking over their claim to world domination, he also took over their position as a bringer of salvation by the grace of the gods. True enough, the Persian kingship was no divine monarchy; true again, there is no plain line of connection between the god-king of old Babylon and the Hellenistic age; but the historical situation, by itself, will not let us mistake the fact that the worship demanded by Alexander had some roots that were not in Greek soil, that it rather derived from the necessities of the new form of rule and so helped to shape the Hellenistic monarchy.

The demand which during the lifetime of a king could irritate or anger the Greeks and in particular the Macedonians, after his death might become, as it were, natural and necessary. The history of ruler-cult in the Hellenistic state began with the creation by the first Ptolemy of the eponymous worship, throughout his realm, of Alexander; it is certainly no accident that it was Egypt, where the worship of the Pharaohs might serve as a natural model, that made the beginning. The ruler-cult has been called a political religion – quite correctly; but we cannot establish *a priori* any firm and permanent relation between the political and the religious element. Religious forces and political tendencies were combined. It was the ruler-cult that bound the Polis or even the individual Greek to the king's person. The portrait on the coins as much as anything else brought the divinity of the king to the consciousness of the ordinary man, in a way that he could understand; for, with the Greeks, the coin portrait normally showed the god of the state or a symbol sacred to him, and in the Hellenistic states everywhere it showed first of all Alexander as Heracles or Dionysus, that is to say, as a god; later the deified rulers themselves.

We must not overlook the fact that the kings, who were all designated 'gods', were not $\theta\epsilon o i$ in the same sense as the old gods or even as Alexander, who did not need to have their qualifications specially expressed. In Pergamum, king and queen had priests even in their lifetime, but it was only after their death that they were 'translated to the gods' (*OGI.* 308, 4; 338, 4; 339, 16); the same euphemism is occasionally found with the Ptolemies or Seleucids (cf. 2 Macc. 11, 23). A city decree for Attalus III (*OGI.* 332) gives the king the most varied honours of cult, but only calls him 'king, son of the divine king' (l. 22). In these facts scholars have seen, probably rightly, the culmination of that Greek conception which led to homage being paid to a man as 'godlike' ($i\sigma\delta\theta\epsilon os$). It may be paradoxical, but it is a fact, that religious worship did not necessarily mean deification, even though 'heroization' might be out of the question. Men might make a vow to the deified kings, but did not pray to them. The fact that they were born and died – that and general common sense – proved that they were men. Thus, in ruler-cult the divine was blended with the 'godlike', religion with almost irreligious motives. Of the ritual of ruler-cult we know but little. We hear of festivals named after the king in question, of the religious celebration of his birthday (already for Alexander: *OGI*. 222, 5), of months or phylae named after him, of statues in temples of other gods, above all, of priests and priestesses. One of the earliest examples is the cult of Seleucus Nicator in Ilium (*OGI*. 212). Only rarely – though the practice grew – were rulers identified with special gods; sometimes, as later in the Roman empire, male rulers could be identified even with goddesses.

It would, on the other hand, not be correct to conceive of ruler-cult in the Greek states as no more than a means of legal connection between monarch and Polis. What is correct in this view, widely held at least up to recent times, is that the autonomy of the Polis, though retained in theory, could not be reconciled with the dependence on the dominating power of the monarch; the recognition of the divinity of the monarch was held to remove this difficulty. Logically, there is nothing to be said against this explanation; but there is no confirmation of it in our texts. In the many documents in which the interference of the monarch in the affairs of the Polis is revealed, there never is any account taken of the monarch's divinity; the Macedonian kings, who were most directly concerned with the problem of the autonomy of the Polis, only exceptionally enjoyed religious worship. Such worship was, of course, the most impressive form which official gratitude of a Polis could find for a ruler (cf. e.g. Priene and Lysimachus, Welles, 6), and the Seleucids, in dealing with Seleucia, could appeal to their kinship with Apollo (Welles, 22). The most, then, that we can admit is a kind of psychological basis; it was something that was, as it were, latent in that close connection of political and religious life which the Greeks had always taken for granted (cf. also III 3). The close relation of religious and political forces in the ruler-cult found very vivid, though almost grotesque expression in the well-known ithyphallic hymn to Demetrius Poliorcetes.

Without the deification of individual rulers, which had the cult of Alexander as its only forerunner, the official dynastic cult could hardly have arisen. We find it with the Ptolemies, Seleucids, and Attalids, but not in Macedon. Here, we understand, the old popular monarchy did not admit of deification, though we find some hints of it under Philip V, which show that there was a certain assimilation to the common type. We cannot, on the other hand, speak of any close connection of the ruler-cult with the East; neither the Achaemenids nor the Pharaohs supplied the immediate model. There was something actually new which definitely led the Hellenistic monarchy even beyond Alexander. The great personal achievement lay at the root of the matter and that was a very Greek concept; but, as I have already emphasized, there were other roots as well. It is no accident that the worship offered truly or professedly without compulsion, usually started with Greek cities, whereas the official dynastic cult proceeded from the kings, who more and more adapted themselves to the traditions of eastern despotism. In the Ptolemaic empire, after the great Arsinoe had already been deified in her lifetime as θεὰ Φιλάδελφος, a new cult of the successive royal couples (θεοὶ Ἀδελφοί, θεοὶ Εὐεργέται, etc.) was created – for the first time, it seems, as the cult of the Ἀδελφοί, when Arsinoe was still alive. It was attached to the eponymous priesthood of Alexander in Alexandria; this was no mere Polis cult and must be distinguished from the cult of the city founder. It is possible that the 'brother and sister gods' (θεοὶ Ἀδελφοί) at first designated the two first Ptolemies and their wives together; certainly we do not find Ptolemy I and Berenice as 'saviour gods' (θεοὶ Σωτῆρες) before the end of the century, that must be accepted although Ptolemy Soter was probably deified as early as 280/79 B.C., when Philadelphos introduced the festival of the Ptolemaea at Alexandria. Yet, from the first, a direct connection of the dynasty with Alexander himself had been established (see Wilcken, Chrestom. no. 103 ff.). This connection becomes obvious when, in Rhodes for example, the cult of the third Ptolemy and his wife as θεοὶ Εὐεργέται was linked with that of Alexander and a great number of Polis and other gods; but in this case the θεοὶ Ἀδελφοί were omitted, so that it can hardly be regarded as a true dynastic cult. The forms of ruler-cult under the Ptolemies (priesthood, festivals, etc.) were essentially Greek, but the fantastic pomp of the festive procession under the second Ptolemy, as described by Callixenus (Athen. V 196), reveals Egyptian elements beside Greek ones of the Dionysus cult. If we compare the well-known inscriptions of Canopus (238 B.C.), after Raphia (217 B.C.), and Rosetta (196 B.C.) (OGI. 56. SEG. VIII 467; 504a; XVIII 633; OGI. 90), we are compelled to realize how definitely the cult of the Ptolemies within a few decades advanced towards Egyptian ritual and tradition. This cult was, in fact, meant for the Egyptians too, and the divine royal pairs, with the exception of the Σωτῆρες, appeared in the Egyptian temples as 'co-dwellers' (σύνναοι), though they were still distinguished from the native gods, the ἐγχώριοι (e.g. SIB. 5680).

The Seleucid cult, which like the Egyptian was established in the second generation, was never directly connected with Alexander, and it always distinguished between the living king and his ancestors, who could be enumerated back to Apollo. It was divided up into separate cults in every satrapy and in many cities – a contrast here to the strict centralization of the Ptolemies. It was as late as Antiochus III, it seems, that for the first time a high-priest for an imperial dynastic cult in every satrapy was nominated; he also inaugurated a corresponding special cult for his wife Laodice. This shows that the dynastic cult of the Seleucids, that of the king and his ancestors, did not, as in Egypt, as a matter of course include the women; but we find the Koinon of the Ionians sacrificing to king Antiochus I and his queen Stratonice (*OGI.* 222, 8). Even where such cults were Polis cults they were often created by royal decree. As an imperial cult, the cult of the dynasty, both with the Ptolemies and the Seleucids, reflected the main problem of these empires, the relations between Greeks and Orientals. It was at the same time a state cult and, in making the identity of king and state something truly lasting, it showed the absolute monarchy to be independent of the reign, and the length of reign, of any single king. Frequently enough, it is true, especially in the later confusions about the succession in both kingdoms, the ruler-cult served the personal policy and propaganda of individual rulers such as the terrible third Cleopatra.

The 'syncretistic' character of the ruler-cult becomes particularly obvious in certain accompanying cults as we find them at least in Egypt. Ptolemaic documents were dated not only by the year of the reign of the king and the eponymous priest of the dynasty but also by other eponymous priesthoods, the number of which gradually increased. The oldest of these was the 'kanephoros' of Arsinoe Philadelphus, with whose deification the creation of the dynastic cult was most intimately connected. She had her Greek cult as Arsinoe Aphrodite and was also worshipped in all Egyptian temples as σύνναος θεά. She is also found in connection with Isis and Sarapis, making a manifestly syncretistic trinity. Similar connections are found in the official Egyptian oath, the ὅρκος βασιλικός, which was taken by the reigning king, or king and queen; but it included the earlier representatives of the dynasty as well as other gods (cf. *SlB.* 5680; Wilcken, *Chrestom.* 110). An inscription of the Seleucid empire (*OGI.* 229, 60) shows a similar oath by all the gods concerned and by the Tyche of the king; in this widespread formula (cf. Strabo XII 557), just as in the Egyptian oath by the 'daemon' of the living king, the divinity of the royal person is not emphasized.

The dynastic cult in its final form required a distinction of the kings or royal couples by additional secondary names. In origin, meaning, and use they differed widely from one another, but, as a whole, they formed a unified and very characteristic expression of Hellenistic monarchy. Special names of this kind were at first given by Greek states as thanks for particular achievements; but such names were not always identical with the official ones. Titles of honour such as 'benefactor' (*euergetes*) had long been given even to private individuals; but Euergetes became in particular a favourite and very significant name for a king. Ptolemy was celebrated as Soter, Antigonus, and Demetrius as 'the saving and beneficent gods' ($\theta\epsilon o\grave{\iota}$ $\sigma\omega\tau\hat{\eta}\rho\epsilon\varsigma$ $\kappa a\grave{\iota}$ $\epsilon\grave{\upsilon}\epsilon\rho\gamma\acute{\epsilon}\tau a\iota$), Seleucus as Nicator. It was an honest recognition of outstanding personal greatness that produced these epithets in the first place. To what extent the title of 'the Great' ($\acute{o}$ $\mu\acute{\epsilon}\gamma a\varsigma$) was used is disputed; certainly Alexander was never called so, but Demetrius Poliorcetes and Antiochus III perhaps were, though neither really deserved the title. The name Soter ('saviour') was often used in a purely human sense, but on the other hand borne in many places, from early times, by Zeus, Athena, Artemis; more and more definitely it pointed to the divine sphere. The 'salvations' implied in the cult were mainly very real and external events, such as victory in the field; men prayed to the gods for the same things, but these, of course, had not first to earn their names. With the grant of an additional name usually went religious worship; often the new name became the actual name of the god. But there is no good reason for believing that the original ruler-cult was restricted to those who bore such names, and thus explaining it as of pure Greek origin. Other additional names too were found, which might be concerned with family relationships (Philadelphus for Arsinoe, Philopator, Philometor, Eupator, etc.); they emphasized something that seemed often enough doubtful, and certainly served the dynastic idea. In other cases, the names immediately expressed the divinity of their holders (Soter, Theos, Epiphanes), or there were identifications with names of old deities (Seleucus Zeus, Antiochus Apollo). Finally, obvious political reasons produced such names as Philhellen, Philorhomaeus. As some of these names were repeated in the same family, two or more such names came to be used. There were others that can only be described as nicknames, for example Tryphon (perhaps 'the Glutton'). The creation and acceptance of such names usually, later entirely, depended on the will of the ruler; often, but not always, they stood in immediate connection with the dynastic cult. In official documents, for a long time, it was customary to use the additional name only for a dead king, not for the reigning one. Euergetes II and Antiochus IV Epiphanes were the first to designate themselves in this way in their documents; Antiochus most likely meant to emphasize the religious meaning of the name, as 'the god revealed'. Eventually, the names became mere titles and, through their ridiculous accumulation, lost all significance. This development was characteristic of the ruler-cult as a whole; it became ever more exaggerated in the way the kings were honoured. Even the habitual restraint of the Attalids swung round in the opposite direction under Attalus III (cf. *OGI*. 332). The whole development – and with it an increasing tendency towards syncretism – reached, as it were, its climax in the statues and inscriptions of the great tomb of Antiochus I of Commagene; this bombastic monument to a minor king, though ruler of a centre of some importance between East and West, seems to represent the *reductio ad absurdum* of the whole phenomenon.

The state cult of the royal house was one important means among others to awake in the population some kind of dynastic loyalty, or to give a certain unity to existing though different attitudes towards monarchy of the Greeks, Egyptians, Iranians, and peoples of Asia Minor. In diverse ways, sometimes coming down to the tiniest details of daily life, the identity of state and king was forced on men's attention. Thus they learned not only to accept monarchy, but to give positive consent to it. It is significant, for example, that the people of Alexandria, always restless and on occasion revolutionary, yet never thought of overthrowing the dynasty; this dynastic loyalty of the Alexandrians, unaffected by any misgovernment, was something that later Caesar was to experience to his cost. The strength of dynastic feeling varied greatly between various states, and even parts of states; but as awareness of the dynasty took root, it led everywhere to some unity and permanence – the sort of unity and permanence that the indissoluble union of land and people gave to the Egypt of the Pharaohs, that the relation of the royal house to the Iranian ruling people gave to the Persian empire, that Macedon enjoyed through the identity of state and people. The attempt, however, which Mithridates Eupator made, to translate the hostility towards Rome of the Greeks of Asia Minor and even of Greece into a Panhellenic loyalty, serving his own aims of expansion, finally broke down, because no Hellenistic state was strong enough to match itself for any length of time against Rome.

What does all this imply? For the Greeks, monarchy now for the first time left the realms of the heroic past, of barbaric despotism or political degeneration, and became a tangible fact in the 'Greek' reality of the day. The path had been paved by the beginnings of monarchic theory among the Sophists, which gained new and increased importance under the influence of a rule like that of Dionysius I; then came the philosophical conception of the 'regal man' (cf. Plato, *Politicus* 294a) and the ideal of the philosophical individual; moreover, as the Polis declined, there grew the longing for the rule of an ideal monarch. All this meant that the justification of monarchy, the determination of its political and moral purpose, became an urgent task for Greek thought. A picture was now drawn which belonged neither to pure philosophy nor to political reality, but hovered somewhere between the two and brought them into closer connection. It is remarkable how uniform this ideal of the ruler was, how little, if at all, it was influenced by the special character of this or that form of monarchy. Only few of the kings showed any sign of taking such theories as their model. We think, above all, of Antigonus Gonatas, the only Hellenistic ruler who knew how to prevent the worship of his person. Inspired by the Stoic teaching as expressed by Chrysippus that the wise man alone is able to rule, to judge, and to speak, he described his kingship as an 'honourable slavery' (ἔνδοξος δουλεία); he was thinking, it seems, primarily of the heavy burden laid on the ruler, and thus demonstrating the moral right of monarchy. An ideal picture of a monarch was now painted, often in the guise of Heracles; numerous pamphlets περὶ βασιλείας appeared, which were intended, as it were, as textbooks for rulers (*Fürstenspiegel*); unless they remained in the realm of pure theory, they were to serve the education of princes. In the king men saw the benefactor; borrowing from Homer, they called him the shepherd of his people, praised him as deliverer and saviour. The ruler was no despot, he gave his subjects protection and loving care, he possessed certain virtues which were early stereotyped, such as reason (φρόνησις), love of man (φιλανθρωπία), piety (εὐσέβεια), justice (δικαιοσύνη). Above all, goodwill (εὔνοια) was the mutual quality that bound king and subjects together. Note also the amnesties, in Egypt often going under the name of 'philanthropa', various other privileges of individuals or communities, and the king's edicts of grace, the aim of many petitions (ἐντεύξεις). Later on, the concept of the ideal ruler was combined with that of the unity and brotherhood of mankind; but serious philosophical cosmopolitanism is not likely to have existed before the time of the Middle Stoa, that is to say, Panaetius and Poseidonius.

Thus the ideal of the 'true ruler' was sketched, on one side, as an obligation to follow the model; on the other as humble homage. The epithets of the kings and the philosophical basis given to monarchy can be seen to affect one another. Greek thought now probably adopted some ideas that came from the East, particularly from Iran; but it could link up with its own tradition by raising the 'Nomos' to be the governing principle in the monarchic state too. Seleucus I told his Macedonians (App. *Syr.* 61) that he was not minded 'to lay on them the customs of the Persians or other peoples [thus deliberately turning away from Alexander], but the general law, the κοινὸς νόμος, that whatever the king determines is always right!' Taken in its true sense, this meant that the king, as representative of the state, is the embodiment of the Nomos. He could not only be (as in Xen. *Cyrop.* 7, 1, 22) the 'seeing law', but also the 'law alive', the *nomos empsychos*. The latter theory is first found in Philo, but he was not its originator; it will have been considerably older. This metaphysical theory of the new state was an organic growth from Greek political thought; it shared in the religious sanction by which the Nomos was anchored in the Polis; but by this time the impersonal king Nomos, who ruled the Polis as a state of law, had become the Nomos embodied in the person of the king. This doctrine usually remained pure theory; but, as a theory, it provided for the Greek mind the justification of the ruler-cult and, with that, of the whole phenomenon of Hellenistic monarchy. It was harder to justify hereditary monarchy. The question whether it was something natural (φύσει) met with completely opposing views (Letter of Aristeas, 288; Suda, B 147Δ). We easily understand that there were definitely antimonarchic tendencies in the Hellenistic age, such as the one that found very realistic expression in the passage of the Suda, just mentioned. But, at least numerically, the idealizing theory of monarchy seems to have prevailed. Idealization might even end in a complete reversal of the real facts, when kingship was defined 'as the possession of the community, not public property as the possession of the king' (Suda, B 148). In this context, taxes might be condemned as tyrannical that had been demanded 'by arrogance and compulsion' (ἐξ ἀνάγκης καὶ μεθ' ὕβρεως), and only those be recognized as justifiable which were required 'with reasonableness and loving care' (σὺν λόγῳ καὶ φιλανθρωπίᾳ). However, that is no more than abstract theory, deriving entirely from the spirit of the Polis, knowing nothing of the true nature of the Hellenistic state, of its officials, of the position of the Polis in that state or of the economic functions of the king. In this ignorance it was like most Greek thought of the age.

2. ADMINISTRATION

There was no one general scheme under which the Hellenistic states were governed. Only the fact of absolute monarchy was everywhere the initial condition. That monarchy had the task of ruling and main-taining, as a permanent basis of its own power, large territories, varying widely in their soil, their population, and their culture, and this de-manded a steady administration, dependent only on the will of the king.

The administration varied a good deal in different states, and even within a single empire, according to the nature of its parts. Of special importance was the character and position of the upper class, deriving from pre-Hellenistic times. In Macedon the upper classes, whose most powerful members in the fights of the Diadochi either became kings or perished, seems to have fitted without any great difficulty into the new state. That state still preserved the fact of the sovereign people and certain traditions of the national past of Macedon, but with its numer-ous cities, its external possessions, and its kingship ever moving in the direction of greater autocracy, it had become an organic part of the family of Hellenistic states. The nobles, then, filled the offices of the court – still rather a simple organization – or, with some Greeks, the higher posts in the army and foreign service; or they lived on their estates, in part perhaps as feudal holders of royal land. Anyway, they never regained any great political importance. In the Seleucid empire the subjects of the king were officially divided into kings and dynasts, Poleis and peoples (*OGI*. 229, 11; *SEG*. XII 369, 10; Welles, 28; cf. *SEG*. XVI 475). Of the two latter groups we shall have to speak later. The dynasts, some of whom were called 'kings', were as a rule members of the native aristocracies, which had retained a relatively independent position; of the ancient Persian aristocracy of this time our sources have hardly anything to say, but the beginnings of a court nobility can be traced, and have been mentioned before (p. 164). Many of the nobles lived on land assigned to them by the Seleucids; their position in rela-tion to the king was that of feudal vassals, who followed him in war and paid taxes, but in their own regions exercised almost absolute power. Similar in a sense was the position of the many temple states, most of them rather small, often – under various names – sanctuaries of an ancient mother-goddess, which were administered by hereditary priests. Some of these temple states turned into cities, thus probably gaining greater freedom. The attempts of several Seleucids to curb the power of the feudal lords and the priests did in general not weaken their position, and the system of government was no less affected by their existence than it was by the fact of the many Poleis; that is to say, above all, that it was definitely decentralized. Exactly the opposite is true of Egypt; a native aristocracy hardly existed any more, and only the priests had a certain independence, though it had been much restricted by the first Ptolemies. Egypt, and in a lesser degree her external possessions, stood under a system of government in which centralization was carried through with the utmost determination.

It is obvious that even in the Seleucid empire the work of administration proper could not be carried out by feudal lords or by cities, that there was need of royal officials and a regional division of the empire into provinces and districts. It is unlikely that the subdivisions of the Seleucid empire were quite uniform throughout. As a rule, there were satrapies, (eparchies?), hyparchies, and toparchies; here and there, we hear of 'merides' (μερίδες), districts probably intermediate between satrapy and hyparchy. Egypt was divided into cantons (νομοί), districts (τόποι), and villages (κῶμαι); corresponding to them, there were nomarchs, toparchs, and comarchs. Of them and of the part played by strategi, we shall have to speak later.

In Egypt, the Hellenistic rulers inherited a bureaucracy many centuries old, in Asia they succeeded to great empires, admirably organized. For the most part, therefore, they could build on well-prepared ground; but in setting up a professional civil service, they met at the same time tendencies of Greek thought, which had more and more come to demand professional specialization for all departments of life. That may partly explain the fact that in the third century B.C. Macedonians and, above all, Greeks were at hand in sufficient numbers and quality to fill the higher administrative posts, while the lower grades of officials were almost exclusively filled by natives; later, in the second and first centuries B.C., the latter came more and more to fill the higher grades as well. The meaning of this whole development is that the inheritance from the East was extensively transformed, but finally outlasted the imported men and methods. A document like the general instructions of the dioecetes to the 'oeconomi' of the cantons (*P. Teb.* III 703) shows in many points that refinement of administration and finance that derived from the Greeks; but it would have been impossible without the old Egyptian tradition of a state, ruled by officials and organized from the centre. The language of administration was predominantly Greek, but there must have been everywhere a considerable staff of officials who commanded both languages – mostly, we may assume, Hellenized natives. The 'scribes' who were found in all branches of administration have been explained as an inheritance from the East. This is certainly not wrong, but we must not forget that in the Greek Polis too the γραμματεῖς were of special importance; there, however, they were annual officials, whereas in the Hellenistic state it was they who carried on the traditions of the bureaucracy; thus in a way they corresponded rather to the state slaves of the Polis. As for the details of administration, it is only in Egypt that we have any better information, and it is therefore impossible to draw a detailed general picture. Nor can we decide in many cases what was tradition and what new creation. Changes too in the system, in the course of the three Hellenistic centuries, can often be recognized or inferred. In general, we may venture to say that the Ptolemaic system, itself as a whole a continuation and improvement on that of ancient Egypt, did not fail to exercise a certain influence on the practice of other states, of Pergamum for example. Nevertheless, the centralization of the Egyptian administration was unique, and in the Seleucid empire, as mentioned before, almost the exact opposite prevailed. The names given to many officials are instructive, as they show – again most clearly in Egypt – the private character, as it were, of the administration. Just as the land was really no more than the domains of the king, so the officials were supposed to be no more than his servants.

It was in the nature of the case that the administration of the empire, though unified in itself, appears in two parts, provincial and local authorities on the one hand, on the other the highest offices united in the capital, the residence of the king, who himself was the supreme head of all branches of the administration. We must make a clear distinction between the court hierarchy (see above, pp. 164 f.) and the central administration; where one person belonged to both spheres, there may have been a rare instance of accumulation of offices, but mostly it was merely the case of a court title bestowed on an imperial official, binding him more closely to the person of the king. A supreme official without special department did not exist in Egypt, which was most consistently organized as a 'royal household' – any more than such a one had existed in the time of the Pharaohs; but the dioecetes,

N

the supreme financial official, was a true 'second after the king' (see below). With the Seleucids and Attalids, we have evidence at least for the second century B.C. of an ἐπὶ τῶν πραγμάτων who, in accordance with his title, has been assumed to be a 'First Minister' or 'Grand Vizier'; more likely, he was a man nominated by the king to govern for him temporarily. In a similar way in Macedon, in moments of great danger or as a regent when a king was a minor, a strategos could be elected. We might perhaps connect this with the old institution of a 'duke', the leader of the people in war, but what was created now was the special and extraordinary office of a supreme commander who had more than military duties. It is hardly correct to see in this official, whether strategos or ἐπὶ τῶν πραγμάτων, somebody like the chiliarch, an office created by Alexander after a Persian model. Even if the responsibility rested on one man, the same rule held for him which held for all high officials, that legally he held no other position except that of subordination under the king. There was no 'Cabinet', though the heads of departments are now sometimes described as ministers. At the most they, together with the most important members of the royal household and court, might meet as a kind of Council of State (e.g. Welles, 61, 3; Polyb. 5, 41, 6), a Synhedrion summoned *ad hoc*, such as in a similar form Alexander and Dionysius I had already known. As a permanent institution, however, there had to be in every state a royal office, in which the vast work of the central government was done and the official diary, the Ephemerides, as well as written memoranda of official policy (ὑπομνηματισμοί) were issued. It was only natural that in official usage an increasingly stereotyped routine should be developed, though we have only very imperfect knowledge of it even for Egypt; of the royal edicts we have already spoken (pp. 165 f.). The president of the royal chancery was among the most important imperial officials; his title in the Seleucid empire is not known, the Ptolemaic official from the end of the third century B.C. was called ἐπιστολογράφος, with an assistant ὑπομνηματογράφος. But it was the position of the head of the Imperial finances (διοικήτης or ὁ ἐπὶ τῶν προσόδων), with the control of the treasury (τὸ βασιλικόν), that might grow, as suggested before, far beyond the character even of a high office. The wealth, the power, and the courtly establishment of such a dioecetes have been revealed, down to innumerable details, for Apollonius, the minister of the second Ptolemy, by the Zeno papyri. As deputy of the king ('The king and Apollonius have ordered') he was the head of the whole administration, and not only of the finances, both in Egypt and in her foreign possessions. Everything except military and foreign affairs lay within his sphere of action. It is remarkable that there was no real distinction between his official activity and that as a private person – in a sense a repetition of the same fact in the position of the king. The question yet remains, how much in the position of Apollonius was due to his office and how much to his personality. The actual proceedings of this and other central authorities are largely unknown; at the best, something may be inferred from the local administration on which alone the papyri report.

The administration was, of course, everywhere divided into departments. If an edict of a Ptolemy was directed to all officials, whether of the whole land or of a district, they were distinguished both by rank and by department; the priests might be included, and all those not named might be described as 'the rest of those who share in the royal administration' (*UPZ*. I 106). As for the organization of the bureaucracy outside the central offices, it goes without saying that very considerable differences existed between the administration of Egypt, divided up into its country districts, and the Ptolemaic possessions abroad, or between various satrapies of the Seleucid empire. But one feature was common to all Hellenistic states, the appearance of strategi as the leading high officials in the political administration. As representatives of the king they ruled clearly limited territories. The title at once shows that they were Greeks, who held the office in the first place as bearers of military power in a conquered land, the χώρα δορίκτητος, and that the combination of military and civil power was a distinctive mark of the Hellenistic strategi, as it had been – despite all differences of competence – of the strategi of the Polis. The mighty but ephemeral strategi of the early age of the Diadochi were either, as deputies of the king, independent governors of large sections of the empire (thus Antipater under Alexander had been στρατηγὸς τῆς Εὐρώπης), or they were special commissioners of the rulers, in Greece, for example, or in the Upper Satrapies. They were certainly not derived from the strategi of the Polis; they were the products of the military and administrative demands of an age of revolution; nor again was there an unbroken line between them and the provincial strategi of the Hellenistic monarchies. Still, just as in the Hellenistic Leagues the office of strategos derived from the Polis, but had lost its collegiate character and had become a single office of great scope and power, so everywhere the need for a head of the administration who was safely supported by the army led to new tasks and new forms of the office of strategos. In

many points, the connection with the pre-Greek system of administration in the East, especially in the Persian empire, is unmistakable. Undoubtedly, it is significant that the military title of strategos was used so
universally; but we cannot speak of a uniform type of office or even
regard it as belonging exclusively to the territorial monarchy; there
were strategi in the Carthaginian empire.

In Egypt, strategi appeared beside the old officials of the cantons, the
nomarchs, who had been kept in being by Alexander and continued, in
part at least, to be natives. There were nomarchs who were heads of
'districts' too (made up of several τόποι); their duties covered a number
of important agrarian questions, but soon dwindled and finally almost
vanished, as far as civil administration and tax-collection were concerned. Sometimes the two cantonal officials were working together,
later they were combined. From this course of development it is clear
how the Greek military office thrust the Egyptian civil office into the
background. The strategi were at first military commanders; with
other military officials they take precedence of the nomarchs and
other civil officials in the *Revenue Papyrus* (37, 2). The institution of a
single cantonal strategos was probably introduced by Ptolemy III, after
the office had already won increasing importance in the administration,
especially in jurisdiction. By the end of the second century this strategos
had lost all military competence; one of his chief functions was to keep
an eye on the land of the 'catoeci'. By his side stood a royal scribe
(βασιλικὸς γραμματεύς), to whom fell a considerable share of administrative activity (keeping the land register up to date, correspondence,
etc.) as well as an extensive power of control in the interest of the king.
Later, on the other hand, it might happen that the strategos also took
over the office of the cantonal official ἐπὶ τῶν προσόδων, who was in
charge of the royal domains. The cantonal strategos had no right of
command over the Poleis of Egypt, least of all over Alexandria. In the
canton of the Arsinoitis, occasionally in others too, there was more than
one strategos; probably one of them was always chief strategos. The
Thebaid offers its own special problem; in the second century we find
here a strategos, but also an 'epistrategos'. The latter, according to one
view, was the supreme official for the whole country (χώρα), an office
created by Ptolemy V after the great revolt in 187–186 B.C.; according
to another view it was little more than an honorary title, appearing
especially in combination with the strategia of the Thebaid (e.g. *SlB.*
4638). But in the second century B.C. anyway, there was an epistrategos
Hippalus (*OGI.* 103. *P. Teb.* 895. *UPZ.* 110, 163) whose power ex-

tended beyond the Thebaid. Perhaps it can be said that the epistrategia was an extraordinary office, but could sometimes be employed as a mere title of honour. It seems quite certain that there were no regular officials at the head of the two old lands of Upper and Lower Egypt, but there were strategi of the border areas, especially of the 'Red and Indian seas'. Under the cantonal strategi there served, of course, lower officials, above all as political officials the toparch and the comarch, always with the respective scribes and controllers. The village scribe was an especially important representative of the treasury; in political importance the comarch fell behind him although he was a sort of trusted man of the village. Interesting in this connection is the development of the village Elders (πρεσβύτεροι ἐκ τῆς κώμης or πρ. τῶν γεωργῶν). Freely elected by the king's peasants of native stock as their representatives, they were used by the officials in their dealings with them as go-betweens, and so enjoyed the confidence of both sides. Towards the end of the second century B.C. they took over the responsibility for enforcing cultivation, occasionally also police functions; finally, they acted as agents of the treasury, guaranteeing the required taxes. This indeed only happened at a time (first century B.C.) when natives held even the higher offices.

Strategi also governed the foreign possessions of the Ptolemies, where the military character of the office, often combined with the office of admiral (nauarch), was much more important and the independence of the official much greater. The governor of Cyprus, later also granted the priestly dignity of an ἀρχιερεύς, may be described as a kind of viceroy; as the high priest of the ruler-cult, he had also to supervise all temples. As a strategos, he might occasionally be called στρατηγὸς αὐτοκράτωρ and, as he enjoyed extensive financial supremacy and could usually rely on the military and ethnic units of the κοινά, he was well-nigh independent. The ground was thus prepared for the later rule of the second in succession to the throne (secundogeniture). In general, in the outer provinces, the strategi were real deputies of the king; in Cyrene the first Ptolemy, while still satrap, could himself become the chief strategos of the Polis (see also p. 201); the whole province stood under governors like Ophellas and Magas, but later became an independent secundogeniture. In the province of Syria and Phoenicia, too, there was a powerful governor, who probably bore the title of strategos. By him stood provincial oeconomi and local comarchs, and the power of the dioecetes, of Apollonius at least, reached everywhere. On the whole, the important office of strategos, in all parts under the same name and with much the same functions, did a good deal to bridge the many differences between the central part and the dominions and thus to unify the empire.

Just as in the Ptolemaic office of strategos, we find elsewhere tendencies which in part caused its general appearance, in part resulted from it: tendencies to Hellenize, to unite military and civil power, to provide for a government more on lines of military discipline. Above all, it was necessary to have wide territories governed by one powerful official, and in Asia the satrapies of the Persian empire, which more or less survived in the Hellenistic age, were the obvious units of the kind. Under Alexander strategi with purely military functions were installed in those satrapies only which stood under Oriental governors; after his death foreigners were in general excluded from all high office; the division into civil and military offices disappeared, and this led, as we have already observed, to the occasional nomination of strategi. The view once commonly taken that the satraps were replaced at that time by strategi cannot be upheld, though later that was what usually happened. The outlying districts of Macedon, the provinces of Pergamum and maybe of Cappadocia stood under strategi. In the empire of Pergamum there were local dynasts beside the provincial strategi; Poleis, on the other hand, might be placed under such a strategos (*SEG*. II 663). In the city of Pergamum the strategi, nominated by the king, had the right of previous deliberation (probouleutic) and watched over the finances. The coexistence of strategi of Polis and province is remarkable and confirms the view that the two offices should not be completely separated from each other. The king ruled his provinces through his strategi; while the Polis strategi assured his control of the city finances (cf. Welles, 23).

As to the Seleucid empire, there is still a sharp debate going on whether the satraps and strategi existed side by side or only in succession. There were so many different kinds of strategi, from each independent military commander to the provincial governor and the 'Governor General', and that is the reason why so much detail remains obscure; but the gradual disappearance of the title of satrap is unmistakable. It was probably Antiochus III who took the most decisive part in the development that led to the supremacy of the title of strategos. Much earlier than that, however, we find the governor of the Hellespontic satrapy a strategos (*OGI*. 220–1. Welles, 10–12). He may have been, it is true, at the same time governor of Lydia with his residence in Sardes, that is to say, the Viceroy of Asia Minor; the danger of a Celtic invasion (c. 275 B.C.) may have had something to do with that appointment. The rare occurrence of Seleucid strategi, who also held the dignity of an ἀρχιερεύς (cf. OGI. 203), plainly shows that the importance of the office was not purely military; we must remember in this connection that the satrapies formed the framework of the official ruler-cult. The same priestly dignity for the Ptolemaic governor of Cyprus was probably introduced as late as under Ptolemy V; it will have followed the Seleucid model. Even in the Parthian empire there were strategi, for example, a στρατηγὸς Μεσοποταμίας καὶ Παραποταμίας, who was also Ἀραβάρχης. On the other hand, it is not certain whether the chief command in the 'Upper Satrapies', usually held by a princely co-ruler, actually comes under the definition of 'strategia'. The number of satrapies in the Seleucid empire probably amounted to between twenty and twenty-five. When Appian (Syr. 62) mentions seventy-two satrapies, he is either exaggerating wildly or thinking of the smaller districts, the eparchies, which seem to have existed east of the Euphrates, or the hyparchies. Similar to the Ptolemaic system, every satrap or strategos was assisted by a financial officer, the oeconomus, who, it seems (OGI. 225; cf. SEG. XIX 676), received the royal commands through him; under Antiochus III he was supplanted for a short time by the ἐπὶ τῶν προσόδων (OGI. 238). It is impossible to discuss here the numerous and varied evidence for satraps and strategi. There never was a firm distinction of principle between the two offices; but certainly, as heirs of the satraps (for such they really were) the strategi possessed very great power and independence, even though not so great as the satraps in the days of the Persian empire. They reflected the tendency of the Seleucid empire to resist any centralized organization, and it is surely significant that in the structure of the Seleucid empire they ranked with the dependent kings and dynasts (cf. OGI. 272. 277), that is to say, those powers by whom the principle of a purely administrative state was broken in favour of a strong feudal element – still strong, although weakened since the Persian empire. There can be no doubt that a very great part of the Seleucid administration was 'indirect', that is to say, it was left to the local officials and the dependent rulers; as far as possible (and that did not always go very far), they were supervised by the strategi.

The Hellenistic civil service – among whom in this context we must reckon also the army of which we shall come to speak later (see IV 3) – was built up in ever-narrowing circles, till it reached the king, its head; it was divided into numerous departments, which again were locally subdivided and organized. Such an administration was made possible to some extent by a postal system which functioned admirably and was exclusively designed to carry official letters and documents. Of many individual offices we shall have to speak later; here we have to add a few more general points. The strict organization and multi-branched division of a bureaucratic hierarchy, strong in numbers, is best known to us from Egypt, where centralization, carried to its extreme, excluded all opposing factors such as the priests. In strong contrast to the Seleucid empire, it even pushed the military element into the background. Otherwise, a far-reaching similarity of the position of officials may be assumed in the various states. Both higher and lower officials were professionals though, except perhaps for the army, we cannot assume a special preparatory training for them; they learned their profession as they gradually climbed the ladder. They drew a salary, often partly paid in kind or in allotment of land, and their position may have brought them other advantages as well. There were opportunities of making money outside their official activities, and we can often see that the office was regarded as a provision for life. To obtain office, bribery was sometimes employed, or often a man, who had himself 'arrived', brought friends and countrymen with him. In such cases, the new official might stand in a personal dependence on his superior and might even enter his household. Possibly his appointment was not even made in the name of the king, and its official character might sometimes be called in doubt, as in the case of Zeno. As in every bureaucracy, apart from pay, the chances of promotion provided a real attraction; moreover, the official could not be easily transferred, as he usually was bound to the soil by the land allotted to him. On the other hand, every official could be deposed and called to account for any losses caused by him. Above all, he had his 'superior', who was usually more feared than loved; against his authority a man might have the right to appeal to strategos or king, but that right was mostly illusory. The high officials of the central administration, and in the Seleucid empire the provincial governors as well, were mighty lords, whose power might on occasion be painfully felt even by the king. Compulsory office, such as later became the rule in Roman Egypt, was under the circumstances only found for the lower offices which brought more burden than profit, or occasionally as an exceptional measure. What bound the vast majority of these officials, recruited mainly from Macedonians and Greeks of various origins, to office and state, was neither compulsion nor loyalty to king and dynasty (though that might sometimes be found), but ambition and greed. The technical perfection of government by officials might be incredibly good; the bureaucracy, under strict monarchical control, might represent the most successful method of increasing the political and economic capacities of the state; but the danger was always near at hand, that under a weak or corrupt monarchy the political and military authorities might oppress the people beyond endurance or hurl the state into wild adventures. Moreover, the influx of new useful elements gradually ceased in the second century B.C. with the depopulation of Greece; the examples of incapacity and corruption increased accordingly. Again and again, the attempt was made to praise, and by praising to stimulate, the zeal and morale of the officials; the official was to be, as it were, an imitation of the ideal king. Exhaustive instructions dealing with every branch of the administration were issued; they sometimes turned into moralizing commonplaces. The chief duty and at the same time the strongest expression of the authority of the official (τὸ ἡγεμονικώτατον, probably an expression borrowed from philosophy) was to 'administer cleanly and justly' and 'in the country to behave with discipline and sincerity, not to frequent bad company, and to avoid any secret compacts for evil purposes'. This is a clear hint of the prevailing corruption and disloyalty. How decidedly, in the official view, the welfare of the state rested on the harmonious co-operation of king, central administration, and provincial officials is very clearly shown in the letter of an Egyptian strategos to the dioecetes (first century B.C.); there we read that the salvation of the state depends 'on the Tyche of the divine lord and king, on the foresight of the dioecetes, and the fearful [!] and sleepless service of the rest of the officials'. In such utterances, there may be something of Greek moralizing theory; but, far more plainly, we see the actual reality of an imperfect system, striving after greater perfection. Perhaps even more clearly we can realize the fact of an organization the head of which – the king – had become rather weak; that prevented the machine from running smoothly any longer.

We must still say a few words about the general nature of the administration which was carried by the officials. As already emphasized, everywhere the influence of the imperial organizations of the ancient East, especially of Egypt and Persia, can be traced. The Greeks, who for a long time almost monopolized the higher posts, were by nature and tradition no bureaucrats. They had first to learn the methods of an administration that worked entirely in writing. Still, with Greek as the official language, Greek law and Greek enterprise forced their way into the eastern system. Egypt, the one place of which we have a fairly exact knowledge of the administration, was, of course, unique; but it shows traces typical of 'Hellenistic administration'. I am thinking, above all, of the role played by the king as a patrimonial landlord, who assigns estates to his subjects as gifts or in fief. Hellenistic, in general, were also the provincial organization, the postal system, probably also a large part of the practice of the central administration; the kings' letters reveal this plainly. The centralization and fiscal system of Egypt had its forerunners in the times of the Pharaohs; the Greeks introduced a greater subtlety of methods, but also a preponderance of money economy and with it, as equally in their quality of foreign rulers, an increasing harshness. The Ptolemaic system was as far as possible unified and even overcame the dualism of homeland and foreign possessions. With the Seleucids, Antigonids, and Attalids, too, a unified system prevailed that was enforced by the will of the kings to unify. We may assign the greater weight to the legacy of the ancient East, or to Greek achievement; we may regard Egypt as an exception, or we may talk of a κοινή of administration: in any case, the administrative system of the Hellenistic state was an original and remarkable achievement. We can well understand how Greek philosophers could make the administration at least of Ptolemaic Egypt, like monarchy itself, the object of their idealizing and rationalizing thought.

3. STATE AND POLIS

The king and the body of officials were the actual organs of the state, the one identified with the state as its head and heart, the other the functionary in his service; the third active factor, the Polis, was something alien to the nature of the Hellenistic state, a limb not bound to it organically. In spite of this, the state as a whole could not be imagined without the Polis; the reason lies in its historical role as the essential framework of Greek life. In consequence of its changed geographical and political environment, the Hellenistic Polis, it is true, was no longer the same as the old Polis of the motherland or even on colonial soil; but we need not think of any fundamental difference in its nature. It is quite improbable that the political theories which during the fourth century B.C. emerged from the old Polis had any noticeable influence on the new Hellenistic foundations. As for the lack of organic connection between the monarchical territorial state and the Polis, it is confirmed by the lack of uniformity and clarity in the forms of public law that determined their mutual relations. Some historians have supposed that the Hellenistic rulers could be distinguished by the way in which they treated the Polis, whether as an ally or as subject. Some have tried to deny any legal relationship; others again have come to regard the connection of king and Polis as a purely legal relationship. Every such theory has become involved in contradictions; examples could always be found that would not fit into this or that scheme. A general and final settlement of these relations was impracticable even inside a single state; still less was it possible in the whole Hellenistic world of states. Actually, the rulers were not even minded to make the attempt; their policy towards the Polis was opportunist and might use either sweet persuasion or the whip. If the methods actually employed were many and diverse, that was mainly because for the Hellenistic cities there were many possible varieties of political and geographical position and, as a result, many variations in their political and legal relationship with the monarchy. Still, some points can clearly be made that are universally valid. We begin with the statement that the king ruled over the cities lying in his territory, and had to do so, if he was to hold the various territorial units of his empire within the unity of the empire as a whole. On the other hand, it was still true that what determined the nature of the Polis was freedom and autonomy. To maintain them became a primary necessity also for the policy of the kings, however much that might seem theoretically to contradict the fact of a unified empire with a monarch at its head. The result was a number of different ways in which actual dependence on the monarchy was blended with a more or less fictitious autonomy or sometimes, on the other hand, a large amount of autonomy with a purely formal dependence on the king.

The attitude of Alexander towards the Greek cities, old and new, could not fail to influence the policy of the later kings. The cities of the motherland were members of the Corinthian League, of which Alexander was Hegemon (see above, p. 113). The position of the cities of Asia Minor, on the other hand, is disputed. The prevailing view today is that they were, all or most of them, not members of the Corinthian League; but no agreement has been reached as to whether, on being 'liberated', they automatically became free and autonomous allies or whether their freedom and autonomy were expressly granted by Alexander. If modern views differ, the historical situation is partly to blame. Alexander was waging war, and the liberation of the Greek cities was one of the weapons in his hand; he could not simply sacrifice it to Panhellenic ideology. Still, it is going too far to assert that the cities had the same position under him as under the Persian empire, that they 'had merely changed their master'. That would mean forgetting that the liberation of the Greeks of Asia Minor was one of the chief war aims of Alexander. He did indeed come as a liberator, but when he restored the old freedom, it now became a privilege that was expressly granted, that in special cases might not be granted at all, while its extent was always dependent on his will. This is confirmed by the fact that the exemption from taxation is sometimes especially mentioned, that is to say, it is not taken for granted as a part of autonomy. Note also the following: neither Alexander nor his successors would consent to intervene between Eresus and her former tyrants (*OGI.* 8; cf. Welles, 2); there was, on the other hand, no neutrality possible between him and Persia (cf. Arr. I 19, 1). The cities were autonomous bodies within his empire; the general problem of the relations of monarchy and Polis, that was so important in the Hellenistic age, already existed. Of Alexandria and the later foundations by Alexander we shall have to speak later. Cities, which had to maintain their Greek character in a non-Greek environment without the aid of old traditions, or even to fit a non-Greek past to a Greek form of state, were specially bound to depend on royal protection; they might at the same time be important links of the unity of the whole empire. Once again we find that characteristic two-sided position of the Hellenistic Polis which makes it necessary to distinguish between *de iure* and *de facto* relationships; only the latter were historically decisive, but the former too might have some influence on the actual position.

It was the old Poleis of the homeland, the islands, and the coast of Asia Minor, whose attitude remained most independent in face of the new states. There were, however, considerable degrees of independence; only the cities of Asia Minor and, perhaps we should add, of Chalcidice, were surrounded by royal territory and so, from the outset, bound closer to the monarchical state. Rhodes was unique; her independence was assured by her wealth, her commercial and political influence, and her military strength. Special in another sense was the position of the cities of Macedon, or at least of some of them, which had only recently become 'Greek' Poleis. In general, the decree of Antigonus I, proclaiming Greek freedom, made an epoch (Welles, 1). His example was at once copied by Ptolemy I. With this, the policy of Hegemony in the homeland, pursued from Philip down to Polyperchon, was abandoned and, in principle, the freedom of the cities even in foreign affairs was acknowledged. But this principle – adopted also by the Seleucids for the cities of Asia Minor, sometimes with reference to the example of Alexander and Antigonus (Welles, 15) – was a weapon of political propaganda in the struggles of the rulers against one another, and the freedom, the substantial meaning of which depended on the will of the ruler, could only too readily be reversed. The kings attached great value to good relations with the Greek cities – so much is sure; it was partly because the cities could on occasion render military assistance, even more because such relations had a moral value and could be used as propaganda. We must not forget that the Hellenistic kings depended on the ready services of many Greek officials, officers, and soldiers. The actual balance of power, however, was not seriously affected by the endeavour of the kings to show 'good will' (*eunoia*); the autonomy of the Polis was always in a precarious condition. Freedom in foreign relations was left, at the most, to a few states of the homeland, and that only temporarily; as for internal autonomy, it is certain that there were many different shades of meaning. One vital fact remains: Polis and king were very largely dependent upon one another; the guarantee of freedom implied the loyalty of the Polis as much as the military protection by the king.

In general, under whatever protectorate they stood, the cities kept entire the apparatus of their Polis constitution (popular assembly, Council, annual officials, courts of law). Their lack of freedom was seen in their dependence on the king of the day; his wishes or commands were followed by the Polis authorities, though formally their decrees had much the same appearance as they had always had. The king would naturally arrange that his partisans should be in power, increased in numbers, it might be, by new citizens. That, to some extent, explains the often observed changes in allegiance of the Poleis, especially in Asia Minor. Leagues of cities, brought back to new life like the κοινὸν τῶν Ἰώνων, might also play a modest political part. A considerable number of letters and edicts survive in inscriptions (see above, pp. 165 f.) to show how rulers, from Alexander on, communicated their wishes to the Poleis and how the latter carried them out. In their external form the royal communications paid the greatest attention to the autonomy of the Poleis; the language was courteous, and the appearance of a friendly and strictly legal relationship was preserved. But nobody could be in any doubt that to the Poleis the king's wish meant a command which was always obeyed; with the Attalids even the wording very nearly took the form of a command (Welles, 65–7).

It could happen that the king interfered in the administration of justice, and the royal court of law functioned as the regular final court of appeal. Kings often received religious worship, but not all of them or everywhere; this may have made obedience easier to many a citizen. But the ruler-cult in Poleis was very seldom ordered by the king himself; no king, in making a demand, ever appealed to his divinity (cf. above, pp. 171 f.). The payment of tribute, royal garrisons, and other burdens were clear evidence how dependent the Polis was on the rulers, but not a legal expression of the royal rule.

The mutual relations of Polis and monarchy defy as a whole any legal definition or, in fact, any rationalization; they were entirely based on actual conditions of power, though these naturally could be influenced by legal principles and facts. Even when the kings speak of the symmachy that binds them to the Poleis, this alliance is hardly to be thought of as the basis of their relations – except in the case of the Corinthian League, as revived by Antigonus Doson. As a rule, there was no constituent act of law, no organization, no expressed purpose; the symmachy was largely fictitious. Still, it did imply a fairly extensive recognition of autonomy and represented the one and only possible legal link between monarchy and Poleis; it could cover relations that in point of fact varied very widely. In exceptional cases, the conception of symmachy might be expressed in an actual treaty (in the oath of friendship and symmachy between Philip V and Lysimacheia, for example); but much more often, there could be no question at all of a permanent alliance. Occasionally, cities or dynasts were included as partners in a treaty, but the Polis had no longer a real foreign policy of its own. When, as often happened, the king caused a number of Poleis to form a Koinon (the best known is that of the Islanders; see above, pp. 129 f.), that was a method employed to dominate the individual cities through officials of the League, who were nominated by the king or at least entirely dependent on him. The feebleness of the Polis in foreign affairs reached its nadir when the state became a mere pawn in the game of the great powers and might change masters by an agreement in which the Polis itself had no part (cf. Polyb. 22, 8, 10 f.; 25, 2, 7). The political dependence of the Polis found formal expression mainly in the numberless honours paid to the king and his representatives; statues were erected to him, he was named Benefactor and Saviour, golden wreaths were voted to him; this last was a barely concealed tribute, often not paid in the actual form of a wreath. When decrees of the people ordered common sacrifices for king and Demos (a few of these survive), the boundary line between religious worship and legal recognition of his supremacy was almost entirely obliterated. Payments which had to be made went under different names; but, in theory at least, they were held to be consistent with autonomy. That is perhaps why freedom from taxation was given only occasionally as an exceptional privilege (Welles, 15). The presence of royal garrisons, a favourite device especially of the Macedonian kings, was felt as a proof of actual subjection, particularly when a royal strategos or epistates (ἐπὶ τῆς πόλεως, in Alexandria and Pergamum) was made the administrative head. Often, especially in the period when the states were settling down, the title of strategos expressed the fact that he was appointed for one exceptional occasion, even when it was a question not of a single Polis, but of a number of Poleis or of a larger district not ordinarily treated as a province. We may mention the strategos, appointed by Lysimachus for the revived Ionian League (ἐπὶ τῶν πόλεων τῶν Ἰώνων καταστασθείς, Syll. 368), or in the Attalid empire the strategos of the Hellespont (τεταγμένος στρατηγὸς τῶν καθ᾽ Ἑλλήσποντον τόπων, SEG. II 663); in the literary tradition (Diodorus, Plutarch) we find numerous examples of such occurrences, though the designations of office are not necessarily all authentic. The supreme royal official (epistates), usually at first an officer, but often a kind of civil commissioner, was the intermediary between the king, whose deputy he was, and the Polis. The king, however, might lay stress on dealing with the Polis direct, and in that case his officials were simply informed. The right of supervision by the royal official might develop into a share in the regular government of the Polis and might lead to the accumulation of city and royal offices. Quite often the epistates worked with the Polis authorities, above all as proposer of motions in the Ecclesia. The royal official might become a helpful friend of the Polis, and thus, of course, express the policy of his master. Still, he was mostly felt to be simply a representative of the royal power. Even if the ruler had the consideration to have a citizen formally chosen as the royal administrator by his fellow-citizens, as happened in the case of Demetrius of Phalerum, his government, which was peaceful and advantageous for Athens, was regarded as an enslavement, partly, of course, because it was anti-democratic. Apart from such cases as these we may say that, as far as appearances went, the civil life of the Polis in the Aegean was unchanged, though it had less and less to do with politics proper. It is remarkable how in the course of time certain offices of a quite unpolitical character, like the gymnasiarch (see above, p. 152) or the agoranomi, gained in importance, and how in the life of the citizens private associations in increasing measure took the place of the political community.

The king, of course, usually stood outside the Polis constitution, but the Polis had, willy-nilly, to deal with his wishes and demands. In Samos the regulation was that the royal affairs (τὰ βασιλικά), as a point in the agenda, were discussed immediately after the sacred matters (τὰ ἱερά) (Syll. 333, 23; cf. SEG. I 363, 32). The kings, again, were at pains to win the favour of the Polis by guaranteeing its territory (OGI. 228) or by restoring democracy (OGI. 234, 20; 237). The king further concerned himself with two matters of vital importance to the Polis, mostly at its express desire: the introduction of foreign judges and the right of asylum. Of the former we have already spoken (pp. 106 f.); here we may emphasize the fact that the king at the request of the Polis might send a foreign judge (Syll. 426; SEG. I 363) or that an official, nominated by the king (like the Nesiarch in OGI. 43) might call the judges in. Only quite exceptionally did the king arbitrate himself, as Lysimachus did between Samos and Priene (Welles, 7), or as in Dura there might even be a royal court in the Polis. The Polis, as we can well understand, preferred to have judges from another Polis.

The right of asylum was one of the most treasured privileges of autonomous Poleis; it was really all that was left of an independent foreign policy. Asylum was usually centred on single sanctuaries; we know, for example, documents of the Asclepieum in Cos (SEG. XII 368–83; Welles, 25–8), in which king and Polis vie with one another in recognizing the local right of asylum; it is interesting to note the reserve with which one of the kings writes: 'In the future we shall endeavour, as long as we remain at peace, not to disappoint your wishes in this matter.' Often the Polis with the temple in question was declared ἱερὰ καὶ ἄσυλος (e.g. OGI. 228, 5), a position of privilege, which was frequently combined with freedom from taxation and gave security against robbery and plunder (συλᾶν, e.g. Welles, 9). In Magnesia on the Maeander a number of kings recognized a new festival in almost identical words, and promised to get the same recognition from the Poleis dependent on them; only one of the documents speaks expressly of the right of asylum bound up with the festival (Welles, 31–4; cf. Syll. 557–62). The right of asylum of the Poleis – mostly maritime cities which suffered under the pirates, who were often employed by the great powers – was not a question of internal policy; as it seems, it was seldom recognized by the king in whose sphere of interest the Polis lay. The right of asylum implied an 'international' action, the initiative lay with the Polis itself, and the ultimate aim was – at least in a number of cases – to gain a position of some sort of neutrality. Yet, in the last resort the right of asylum, especially of individual sanctuaries (Welles, 70), depended on the rulers; the increase in the number of cases, when the right of asylum was purchased from a weak king, was a symptom of the decay of the monarchical state.

The less tradition a Polis had, the easier might it be to bring it into dependence. This was one reason among many that led the kings to create new cities either by synoecism of earlier settlements (cf. especially Welles, 3–4), or by sympoliteia, or by the transplantation of the inhabitants at will. This brings us to the most important type of Hellenistic Polis, the new foundations first of Alexander, then of his heirs. They owed their origin in the first place to military considerations, secondly to the desire to settle Greeks, whether mercenaries or unemployed, and at the same time to spread Hellenization (which often had immediate political consequences), or possibly to economic motives, when it was a question of harbours or points of intersection on trade routes. We all know how numerous such newly created Poleis were, especially in the empires of Alexander and the Seleucids; but they also occurred in Macedon and in smaller states like Pergamum, Bithynia, and Pontus. Everywhere they gained importance as centres of Greek life in non-Greek surroundings, although some of them were hardly more than 'Macedonian' military settlements. There were great differences in the way in which they originated, in which they were shaped, and what their relation to the monarchy was like. In general we may say that, while the titles of officials and institutions varied, the division into phylae and the 'modern' city plan were universal; but it was more important that the political and legal distinctions between citizens, which had been maintained even in democracy, and any tie of citizenship to social or ethnic origin, had ceased to exist. The dependence on the king was formally less emphasized than with the Poleis of the Aegean, which had often had first to be conquered; but the position of the new foundations, which was nearly always precarious, required a royal garrison and usually a royal administrator, who did not frequently change. This means that the independence of the Polis authorities was severely restricted, and that the actual dependence on the ruler was greater than in the old Poleis of the Aegean. Even in the Aegean the method of new foundations stood its test. The synoecism of Teos and Lebedos, for example (Welles, 3–4), gave Antigonus the chance to

o

interfere in a dictatorial manner in the financial policy of the newly constituted Teos. Most of the new cities were named after their founders; as founder hero or god he enjoyed a special position, which might to some extent be handed down to his successors; but it cannot be proved that the dynastic names of the cities in question automatically insured their autonomy. A special group of these new cities is represented by the capitals, which simply by the local connection with court and imperial government broke the usual framework of the Polis.

In order to get a more vivid picture we need to observe what was the average practice in the different states. The brutal treatment of the Poleis, even some in the Aegean, by Cassander and Lysimachus, and the gentler but hardly less decided treatment by Antigonus I and Demetrius Poliorcetes, may to a considerable extent be explained by the warlike unrest of the age; they are not to be regarded as a normal practice. In the Seleucid empire, as far as we can see, the independence and freedom of the Poleis were comparatively great. The chief reason for this was that the Seleucids saw in the existence of as many and as powerful centres of Greek life as possible the strongest support of their rule and the element of cohesion in their giant motley empire. True, in most of these cities the Greeks were only part of the population, and that fact tended to diminish the independence and importance of the Greek community, of the Polis in its original sense. But whereas Alexander had given new life to Babylon, the ancient capital of the great empires of the East, as an imperial centre, the Seleucids, with their new capitals of Seleucia and Antioch, definitely supported the Greek element and made it count for more, especially in the barely Hellenized East; the view that Antiochus IV intended to make Babylon itself a Greek Polis seems to be refuted by recent finds. In general, the cities of the native peoples retained their old institutions and traditions, although Greeks gradually intruded. The creation of a number of capitals belonged to the same policy which combined decentralization and Hellenization. For the position of the Seleucid Poleis, as we have already stressed, the opposition to any centralized system was essential; it implied the relative independence of numerous smaller areas, those of dynasts, temple states, tribes, and also Poleis, which at the same time formed a counterbalance to the other more feudal elements. The kings, who were exceedingly generous in making gifts out of their vast domains, favoured the transference of landed property to the possession of a Polis. Many a Polis began as a military colony and gradually grew into a Polis proper. We see this, for instance, in a decree of Antioch in the Persis (*OGI.* 233), in which we find displayed the decided Greek patriotism of such a community. Some of the temple states, too, became Poleis. The Seleucid cities, like all others, naturally held fast to autonomy in principle, but it is a matter of debate whether and to what extent, on the ground of the formula πόλιν ἐν τῆι χώραι καὶ συμμαχίαι (Welles, 11, 21; cf. 12, 9; 23), we are entitled to distinguish two groups, to be identified in the main with the new foundations and the old Poleis. Above all, we must stress the fact that autonomy, financial independence, right of asylum, and right of coinage, came more and more to be special privileges, again and again renewed by the kings; they were not matters that could be taken for granted. The official term of symmachy was suited to stress the distinction from other Poleis, which had almost completely been absorbed; but, in point of fact, it remained a euphemism; the word 'protectorate' might perhaps have been better suited to conform with the facts. The cities, often subjected to very oppressive financial burdens, were placed under the governors of the satrapies, or frequently under special royal officials; most of them had 'Macedonian' garrisons. Yet, the dependent condition of the cities dwindled as the kingship weakened; the relative independence of the Poleis in Asia certainly played its part in the internal decay of the Seleucid empire. By then, almost a reversal of the situation could occur when Polis autonomy was fairly secured and the dependence on the ruler had become an empty form.

A word will be in place here on the 'tribes' (ἔθνη), of whom we often hear as subdivisions of the empire; the Jews are the only one among them of which we know a good deal. They were ruled by an aristocracy of priests and elders, which lasted, essentially undisturbed, into Maccabaean times. Afterwards, the High Priest developed into the real head of the state, and thus became the representative with whom the Seleucid government had to deal. We know how much disputed Jewish autonomy after Antiochus IV always was; the analogy with the position of the Poleis can be seen at a glance.

In definite contrast to all this stood the empire of the Ptolemies. When we compare the structures of the two great empires, one of the most striking facts is that the Lagids almost entirely renounced the foundation of cities. Certainly, the lack of arable land played its part here; but more important still was the fact that inside the centralized royal economy free land of the Polis simply could not be tolerated to any considerable extent. In Egypt, apart from the old Greek city of Naucratis which had lost all importance, we find the great Alexandria, which had already been created to be the capital and a place of union for many races. It was at once set in contrast to Memphis, the old Egyptian capital, which had its own Greek community of a kind, the Helleno-memphitae. A similar general situation probably caused Ptolemy I to found Ptolemaïs in contrast to Thebes in Upper Egypt. Ptolemaïs remained a fairly unimportant provincial town, but it retained the pure form of a Greek Polis (*OGI.* 47–9); it was only later, it seems, that it became usual for the Epistrategos of the Thebaid to be also ἀρχι-πρύτανις of Ptolemaïs. In Alexandria, on the other hand, the Greek civic community had only a very restricted autonomy and seems to have lost its Council quite early. The Gerusia, of which we often hear, was only a feeble substitute for it; though, apart from its great social importance, it had a certain influence on the city administration. The passionate endeavours of the Greeks of Alexandria to get their Council back prove clearly how small the political importance of the Gerusia was. At what time the Council was abolished is much disputed. It was certainly under the rule of the Ptolemies; if Octavian and Claudius refused to restore it, we can take that as evidence for its great political importance, which it can only have had as the representative body of the Alexan-drine Greeks. We may suppose that it perished in the struggles between them and some of the Ptolemies, probably in the second century B.C.; the last Ptolemies had little reason to restore it. Alexandria was not simply a Polis, partly because it was the capital and royal residence, and the court, government, and garrison pushed the authorities of the Polis into the background; mainly, however, because beside the Greek civic community there were the Politeumata of other peoples and the large Egyptian community. It was necessary to have a royal officer (ὁ ἐπὶ τῆς πόλεως, later στρατηγὸς τῆς πόλεως) to supervise the whole city. Despite the separation, commonly made in the documents, between the Polis Alexandria and the χώρα, that is the rest of Egypt, despite the political will of the unruly Alexandrine citizens often seen in action, despite its having its own officials and courts, Alexandria was badly off in the matter of autonomy. We cannot even talk of communal freedom, since that only concerned a part of the 'Αλεξανδρεῖς, though, to be sure, the central section. That name, in fact, belonged not only to Greeks of various grades of civic rights but also to privileged Jews and other non-Greeks. Note too that there were no metics here; anyone settled there who was not an 'Αλεξανδρεύς, unless he was an official or a soldier, belonged to a Politeuma. The general unimportance of the Polis within Egypt is at once explained by the system of administration, which aimed at the absolute exploitation of the land and therefore encouraged Greeks to penetrate among the peasant population. The natives and cleruchs lived in villages, and they were settled so thickly that a systematic administration could easily get a complete grasp of the whole population; even the capitals of the cantons seem to have had barely the rudiments of city life. The Greeks were either citizens of one of the three Poleis (though they might not live there) or they had joined together in loose agrarian associations, also called 'Politeumata'; in these we find πολιτικοὶ νόμοι, and that term seems to imply that even then the Greeks felt themselves as citizens.

In the outlying parts of the empire, too, the policy of the Ptolemies showed little regard for the autonomy of the Polis, unless really important cities of the homeland were concerned. Cyprus was in some ways exceptional, being entirely divided into Polis territories; the cities here had their full Polis life, and the Phoenicians became Hellenized with astonishing speed. Although military strongholds under phrourarchs (later also ἐπὶ τῆς πόλεως), the cities, in all matters of politics, stood under the provincial strategos. In Syria and Palestine – occasionally elsewhere too – the cities, founded by the Ptolemies, above all by Philadelphus, were either merely earlier cities renamed or quite unimportant places with perhaps some military significance. For the policy of the Ptolemies, quite apart from a possible wish to advance the Greek part of the population, the absolutism of the monarch was more important than the question of Hellenization. In the peculiar constitution of Cyrene, which Soter gave while he was still satrap (SEG. IX 1; XVIII 726), in which he himself as permanent strategos held the chief office in the Polis, some compromise with the strong urge of the Polis towards autonomy may have been attained, but the office of strategos held by the Egyptian king is built into the whole complex of a clearly organized constitutional document; both facts express the political will and the political power of the new ruler. This constitutional document is in many respects unique, though parallels can be found to many of its arrangements in detail. The autocratic methods of creating citizens, the position of the king as strategos with almost no restrictions on his power (so unlike the eponymous and honorary offices of many rulers), his interference in the jurisdiction, all this shows that the regulations we find here were enforced and ephemeral, the products of a revolutionary situation. Later in Cyrene, Polis and hinterland were separated, but at the same time the autonomy of the Polis was strongly limited; the position was similar to that of Alexandria over against

Egypt. The final form was a protectorate, resting for its legal base on a treaty between the king as protector and the Poleis of the Cyrenaica. In general, there is ample evidence of an extensive interference in the affairs of the Poleis by the Ptolemies and their officials. In cities of Caria we find the Egyptian dioecetes Apollonius behaving almost like an absolute ruler; for example, a Carian can bring to notice an unpaid account of the city of Calyndus and beg Apollonius to demand the money from the Polis with the help of the strategos in question and the oeconomus (*P. Cairo Zen.* 59037, 59341). On the other hand, a city like Aspendus could adopt as citizens two captains of mercenaries with their motley soldiery 'for services rendered to the king and the Polis' – and take money for the gift; that could hardly happen without royal consent. Of course, the Ptolemies could show generosity, if policy seemed to demand it; Ptolemy Philadelphus, for example, presented Miletus with land (Welles, 14). As a rule, however, it is true that the Lagids oppressed the Greek cities of their empire with garrisons and, above all, with heavy taxes; even the liturgy of the trierarchy seems to have been immediately drawn upon to strengthen the Egyptian fleet. Wherever the Ptolemies ruled, the autonomy of the Polis – with certain differences locally – was abolished, if not formally, yet the more decisively so in point of fact.

Similar were the conditions in the empire of Pergamum. Here too we find combined a very strong cultural Philhellenism and an absolutely autocratic policy, directed against the autonomy of the Polis. Here again a distinction was made between Pergamum and its hinterland. The city was an old Polis, but it was now the capital and the residence of the king; at its head stood five strategi, nominated by the king, and royal edicts often interfered immediately and decisively in the life of the Polis (see above, p. 186). The Syracuse of Dionysius, the Halicarnassus of Mausolus were older instances of a similar situation. The excavations, too, make it clear that Pergamum was a royal city. Thus, the autonomy of what was really a purely Greek capital was more severely restricted than in other places, probably just because of the existing Polis tradition. In the χώρα, there seem to have been no Poleis of importance and no new foundations, but both of these are found in the later acquired provinces, where the cities were mostly of decidedly military character and were politically as well as economically dependent on the king. Attalus I can speak of the Poleis which are 'subject to me' and 'obedient to [or 'dependent' on] me' (Welles, 34, ll. 12, 19). Even Aegina, when it became part of the Pergamene empire, had a royal epistates and was entirely subject to the royal edicts (*OGI*. 329). It seems that the Attalids often squeezed their cities dry, and then gave back part of the tax as a royal gift and benefit. Only a few cities, which had expressly been declared free by the Romans, retained their autonomy and were kept attached to the state by a magnanimous and generous policy. Eumenes II, after the humiliating treatment which he had to endure from Rome, found much sympathy in the Ionian Koinon; he reacted to this in a generous spirit, strongly emphasizing his services to the Greeks (Welles, 52).

To sum up, we may say that the Polis in none of the Hellenistic states had any share in the general life of the state, in its actual policy. The cities – if we except the Poleis of the Aegean that had kept their freedom – declined more and more even as champions of social and cultural life. In the satrapies of the East and also in the interior of Asia Minor the Greek Polis, usually no longer purely Greek, was a centre of civilization and trade; in the regions of old culture round the Mediter-ranean and in the great river countries, this was so only in a very limited degree. Still, we must not identify the great Hellenistic city, however important it may have been, with the Polis; where such a city was realized as in some of the imperial capitals, it can only be regarded as the heiress of the Polis in certain external forms. It was in the capitals particularly that the imperial idea had most decidedly overcome and incorporated the Polis form. Alexandria, which never fully belonged to Egypt (*Alexandria ad Aegyptum*) was, before all, a royal city; for cen-turies it had no Council (see above, p. 200; cf. *SEG*. I 161, 8). The radius of influence of these 'world cities' could reach even farther: τῆς γὰρ οἰκουμένης 'Αλεξάνδρεια πόλις ἐστίν. Alexandria and Pergamum might be centres of culture; but they were not so in their capacity as Poleis, but because within their walls were king and court. As for economics, manufacture, and trade, especially in the leading great cities, the non-Greeks and, above all, the monarchy took so large a part that here too the Polis had no decisive role to play – with the exception again of the Aegean (Rhodes and Delos). These facts are plain; but plain too is the other fact, that everywhere, even though under royal control, the urban life of the Greeks, with its Agora and its gymna-sium, was maintained and exercised its influence over the non-Greeks. Furthermore, the military colonies and the Politeumata were new creations that indeed were not Poleis, but could not have existed with-out the Polis as their model. Finally, for a long time, the Greek cities were an almost inexhaustible reservoir from which the kings could draw their officials, officers, technicians, and other experts. The Polis, then, was a kind of counterpoise to the territorial state and its bureaucracy; at the same time, a serious gulf had opened up between the cities with their wealth and their Greek culture on the one hand, and on the other the country population, poor and clinging tenaciously to their ancestral speech and religion. On the whole, however, the positive side may have prevailed. Even the Polis which, deprived of its political nature, had partly changed its form and entirely changed its character, still possessed a certain political importance. When the autonomy of the state was superseded by communal self-government, a way had been found to overcome the inorganic and contradictory nature of the relations between monarchy and Polis. Thus it came about that the Imperium Romanum, in this as in so much else the heir of the Hellenistic age, could be built on the foundations of the *civitates liberae et foederatae* and on the municipal constitution, though the fact of Roman citizenship gave them a different aspect.

CHAPTER FOUR

Functions of the State

King and officials were responsible for government and administration. So far as the activity of the state was concerned with matters essentially political, that is to say, foreign and domestic policy, legislation and executive, we have already said what most needed saying. We have still to speak of the other main functions of the state.

I. RELIGION AND CULT

The close connection between political and religious community which might almost amount to identity, existed, although under very different forms, in both the Greek and the Oriental state, but not in Macedon. The task was to create in the Hellenistic state that unit which the feelings of the great majority of the population demanded, however technical life had become, however much that 'collective piety' which had existed in the old Polis had declined. That task was now set to men who in their hearts were, most of them, alien to it, but who for that very reason confronted it with special clarity. In Alexander a passionate spirit and the inner drive behind his actions were deeply tinged with religious or at least with irrational and mystical feelings; nothing of the kind can be attributed to most of his successors. But many of them had, indeed, a masterly way of catching the religious tendencies and active trends of their age and of making them serve their rule, while they placed themselves at their service. The result was an insoluble union of rational planning and irrational forces.

The political form of the Hellenistic state being what it was, these endeavours centred round the person of the monarch and the fact of the dynasty. The Ptolemies were gods as the Pharaohs had been, and the Seleucids inherited the position of the Achaemenids as 'rulers by the grace of the gods'; but, in both cases, this touched only parts of the population, not the whole state. This is where the ruler-cult came in and played the decisive part of which we have already spoken (pp.

169 ff.). We cannot simply deny that there was a religious force, but the cult was deeply mixed up with the political and economic effects of monarchy. What was missing in it was true belief, the sphere of mystery, which comes from a world outside and above ordinary experience, and so grips men's minds. It was at this time that a mixed array of new beliefs, gods and daemons, cults and mysteries, doctrines and dogmas, began to spread, deriving partly from the ancient piety of the eastern peoples, partly from the passionate longing for a new faith. Both in its inner strength and in its expansion into the world this represents one of the chief movements of the Hellenistic age. Here we need only investigate the matter as far as the state was directly concerned in it.

To arrive at a correct understanding of the problem, we must, however, at least hint at the importance of religion in the Hellenistic period and its importance for the later epoch-making changes in spiritual life. For the upper classes, the intellectual and cultural development of the age had grown to such a power as never before; a modern scholar could even talk of a 'religion of culture'. Yet, at the same time, the conditions necessary for an intensification of truly religious beliefs were present. In Greece proper, the human situation was dominated by a great uncertainty of life and, in increasing measure, by ever-extending impoverishment and desolation. Here was a natural soil in which religious forces might grow. On the other hand, in the lands to which the Greeks emigrated – in all, in fact, except the west of Asia Minor – their own cults were only superficially imposed, and as the comparative security and prosperity of the third century B.C. declined, we can understand how the door was opened ever wider for a fusion with eastern religions. Another influence was that of philosophical speculation which, even in popular consciousness, often substituted an abstraction for the personal gods, or else removed the divine outside the human sphere, by either depriving it of all importance or denying its existence outright. Seen as a whole, the Hellenistic age was creative in the religious sphere; but the most cursory glance reveals that this is far more true of the later times than of the third century B.C., which was so creative in politics. Hellenistic religion had its great phenomena: a certain revival of the old Greek cults which had lost most of their power and significance, but above all the influx of eastern religions, the spread of cults of an emotional and ecstatic character, the intensified belief in miracles, astrology, mysteries, magic – in short, that vast movement which, in even richer and deeper forms, dominated the first centuries of the Roman empire. Still, for all that, it has no right to any large place in a picture of the Hellenistic state. We have, however, to speak of the religious policy of the Hellenistic rulers; we shall see that not only, as a matter of course, it is part of a description of the state and its functions but also that it reveals traces of some of the religious phenomena that later became so important.

The ruler-cult shows most markedly to what an extent religious forces could be made tools of royal policy; but, on the whole, it was a case of mutual relations between politics and religion. The strangest case of this mutual influence of state and cult may be seen in the figure of Sarapis. He seems to have originated in Osiris-Apis, the god of the dead at Memphis; but as a Graeco-Egyptian god, he was a creation of the first Ptolemy, who for this required the help of both a Greek and an Egyptian priest. How this god 'by grace of the king' spread all over the world, how he at the same time gained great internal strength – that is one of the strangest facts in both political and religious history. It had been a more or less general view among modern scholars that Sarapis, though for a long time over-shadowed by the ruler-cult, was the bearer and protector of Ptolemaic imperial policy. More recent research makes it likely that, although his cult was protected and fostered by the Ptolemies, it was at least equally important outside their realm. The worship of an Egyptian god, freed from the features of Egyptian religion that repelled the Greeks, might be directed in the first place to the Greeks inside the Ptolemaic empire, but it also united Greeks and Egyptians as both were combined in the personnel and the rites of the cult. There was, on the other hand, public worship of Sarapis in cities such as Rhodes and Priene. An entirely satisfactory explanation has still to be found, in particular for the importance of the Sarapis cult in Roman Egypt. It seems, however, certain that the cult spread for religious rather than political reasons. An additional cause was that Sarapis became a dominating figure in that circle of gods, who, setting out from Alexandria, conquered the world, though for a long time we cannot prove official propaganda for Sarapis; there is nothing at Delos, for example. In the centre of this circle was the ancient Egyptian Isis, whose temple had at once been securely provided for by Alexander when he was planning the city; her worship had already been known in Greek Poleis for a long time. Beside her now stood Sarapis, who had ousted the purely Egyptian Osiris. This was the divine couple often worshipped beside the kings – for example, when called upon as the special gods of oaths; the two gods together embodied the true divine power. Isis, like Sarapis, though in a much lesser degree, was Hellenized; but there is some justification in the saying that with the worship of Isis and Sarapis it was 'not a case of new gods being added to the old, but of a new religion appearing beside the Hellenistic'. The state might, in the first place, support these deities, but they soon grew beyond the sphere in which it could exercise, or claim to exercise, influence. We find the cult of Isis and Sarapis, for example, in Syrian Laodicea, which is the more surprising because that city in its institutions preserved the old Macedonian traditions (see above, pp. 149 f.). However, this was not before the first century B.C. and, by then, the 'Egyptian gods' were well on the way to becoming universal gods.

In the creation of Sarapis we see one of the means which the monarchy adopted – a very unusual one, be it admitted – to come to terms with the religious feelings and, above all, with the priestly institutions of the native population. Many temples possessed enormous wealth and strong social and spiritual influence. It was obvious that the new rulers had to display great caution in their attitude towards the native cults and their priests. That meant that they tried to avoid everything that might hurt the dignity of the gods and the feelings of the population; but where the priesthood had economic and political power, they did their best to limit it. The right of asylum was usually reduced to a benefit granted by the king; temple land was confiscated, but quite often restored as a sign of particular favour. The decline of the power of the central government in the second century B.C. was accompanied by a renewal of the power of the priests, and gifts and privileges were now given to the temples with a generous hand (cf. e.g. Welles, 70). In both of these phases the policy of the kings had its share in the responsibility for the continuance and for the new missionary drive of the eastern religions.

In Isis the Greeks saw embodied more than one of their own goddesses – Demeter or Aphrodite. The Mother goddess of Syria and Asia Minor, too, with her many names, was equated with her, and her son Attis-Adonis with the Egyptian Horus-Harpocrates or even with Osiris himself. But Isis was also sometimes identified with the great Greek goddess of the third century B.C., Tyche, the goddess of blind fate, mysteriously ruling mankind. It is astonishing how widespread and powerful the belief in this goddess was, with the average citizen as with the philosopher, a fatalism which, in feeling itself dependent on uncontrollable powers, found its consolation in worshipping the arbitrary fate as a personal goddess. The Daemon, again, more and more became a power either for good or for evil, determining the character and life of each individual. Tyche and Daemon had, for some time past, approached one another, and frequently their natures were hardly distinguishable. Every man had his own Daemon, every Polis her own Tyche, as expression of their individual destinies. The Tyche or Daemon of the deified ruler might become a kind of guardian principle of the monarchical state; the deity of the earth, on the other hand, in the form of a snake as 'good luck' (ἀγαθὴ τύχη), or in its older male form as Agathodaemon, became the deity that protected the soil of the Polis and bestowed fertility and blessing. Just as Isis–Tyche and Sarapis–Agathodaemon could be worshipped, thus, in a similar religious and political conception, a new figure arose: Tyche as the goddess of a city. Her special importance was much the same as that of the old state gods as protectors of the city in some of the Poleis of Asia Minor. In the new foundations with their mixed populations, especially in the great cities, there was no traditional protective Polis deity; the new popular goddess, Tyche, filled the vacant place. With this, like other goddesses worshipped on occasion as city goddesses, she also entered into an eastern tradition. The Tyche of Alexandria or Antioch (the latter famous for the statue by Eutychides which became a general model, with her mural crown and the river-god at her feet) was the religious expression of a form of urban community that only became possible in the Hellenistic state.

We have already observed that some rulers bore the names of Olympic gods (p. 175), but only in the case of one god did this identification gain a deeper religious meaning, and that god was Dionysus. In many of his characteristics he answered the tendencies of the age. As the victorious conqueror of the world and founder of cities, he came to be a model for Alexander, whose adventures in India, mostly long after the events, were shaped to correspond to mythical traits of Dionysus. Demetrius Poliorcetes was set on imitating the god of enjoyment and release. Above all, however, it was the god of mystic belief and ecstatic worship who was finding new adherents everywhere, even among the kings. Further, the usual *interpretatio Graeca* had identified Dionysus with Osiris and thus opened the way to a connection with Sarapis; again, Dionysus and the Phrygian Sabazius were regarded as identical. His mysteries, therefore, and those 'orgies' which had developed through earlier centuries, played an important role in Asia Minor, and the great procession of the second Ptolemy was devoted to Dionysus. After him, Ptolemy IV was a particularly zealous servant and initiate of the god. He seems to have created for his cult a special tax (σπονδὴ Διονύσου), and in a remarkable edict he arranged for the registration of the priests of Dionysus and their rendering of accounts. Ptolemaic piety had, as a rule, a very practical basis. One of the latest kings of Egypt, Ptolemy XIII – like Mithradates Eupator (*OGI.* 370) – was called 'the new Dionysus' (Νέος Διόνυσος). With the Attalids, the worship of Dionysus was not merely an affair of individual rulers, but in the form of the 'leader god descended from above' (Διόννσος Καθηγεμών) he was worshipped as one of the protective deities, though perhaps not (as usually assumed) as the ancestor of the royal house; at the same time, he was the centre of a mystery cult. This has been also explained, perhaps rightly, as an expression of the rivalry between Pergamum and Alexandria.

All the cults we have mentioned, whether Greek or non-Greek in origin, share one common characteristic: they threw bridges between Greek and non-Greek beliefs; in this special sense they were 'Hellenistic'. The kings, of course, did show concern also for purely Greek cults. A particularly notable example is that of the great gods in Pergamum. A royal letter (Welles, 24), for example, reports the creation of a priesthood (of Zeus?) to which the yield from certain workshops is allotted, while the priests are required to keep the shops in good order. The worship of Zeus, Athena, and other Olympians by the Attalids was bound up with the traditions of the city of Pergamum; in general, the Greek cults tended to decline. The age of the Olympians was really over, although they continued to exist and were deliberately cared for in the official cults of the Polis. For the Hellenistic empires they had little significance, except in their new Hellenistic syncretistic forms. The mighty ancient deities of the eastern peoples, on the other hand, held their place; only in exceptional cases like that of Isis could belief and worship be so far Hellenized as to free them from their national fetters. Where eastern gods were taken over, a tendency towards monotheism can often be traced; it became common to speak of the 'highest god' (θεὸς ὕψιστος) and to identify him with the Phrygian Sabazius or the Jewish god (Sabaoth). Many of the eastern cults, like those of the 'Syrian Gods' or that of the Phrygian Great Mother, pushed out far beyond their homelands. Asiatic cults were found in the mixed population of Alexandria or in Egypt as a whole, just as in Greece; Hellenized Egyptian cults could be found likewise in Antioch or Athens. Yet, the great majority of Egyptian, Syrian, Asian, and Mesopotamian gods remained set fast in their local and ethnic environment, some for a long time, some for ever. Conditions and methods might vary, but the kings invariably accepted the protection of these cults as an obvious duty which at the same time was politically expedient.

In Egypt, gods and priests were from ancient times a mighty power, organized in a unified system. The Ptolemies, to win the lasting recognition of the priests and to banish the great danger of national resistance, cared for temples and cults on a grand scale; we have plentiful evidence of this. The Ptolemies had some success; they were represented in reliefs and inscriptions on the temple walls like the old Pharaohs, but in the minds of the Egyptians they probably remained strangers. Despite all the honours given to the native gods, despite all their care for the temples, they yet contrived (for a long time, at least) to hold down the power of the priests, whose numbers must have been enormous. One method employed was to bring in the kings as σύνναοι θεοί beside the gods of the temples, and thus let them immediately share in their rights. This gave rise to some strange combinations; for instance, in the Fayyum, in the district renamed after her, Arsinoe Philadelphus stood beside the crocodile god, Suchos. Official inroads like this into the Egyptian religion served to consolidate the monarchy and the ruler-cult, and to enrich the king; sometimes the native cult, too, may have derived some profit from its connection with the royal house. The third Cleopatra introduced a special priest of Isis (ἱερὸς πῶλος) in the series of royal eponymous priests, but that was not repeated after her; she identified herself with 'Isis, the Great Mother of the Gods'. Probably more important than all the cult connections was the fact that the king made the temples economically and administratively dependent on himself. The vast landed possessions of the gods, the ἱερὰ γῆ, was γῆ ἐν ἀφέσει, that is to say, the king legally retained the ownership. The temple land, therefore, stood under state control and taxation, and the same was true of the lively economic activities of the temples (see below, p. 232). The transfer of the important ἀπόμοιρα tax to the worship of Arsinoe probably represented one way in which the revenues of the temples could be secularized. The administration of the temples was partly in the hands of Greek officials, and there were even Greek priests. In all temple affairs the king as the true representative of the god, from whom the priests themselves first obtained their office, had the final say. True, the temples received many privileges and large endowments; true, the kings took over the costly burial of the Apis bull and much else, but in all this they only gave back a part of what they had taken from the priests. As the national movement gained strength and the monarchy decayed, the priests won back a good deal of their power. It is significant of this 'cold war' between kings and temples that into quite late times (e.g. *OGI.* 761) the kings treated the right of asylum, so important for both the temples and the population, as a royal privilege; it was only reluctantly granted, while more and more sanctuaries extorted it from the kings. This involved a renunciation by the state of part of its sovereign rights, and the danger that the priests might generally win an exceptional position for themselves. In their foreign possessions the Ptolemies certainly advanced their chief gods, Sarapis and Isis above all, but they naturally did not interfere with the native cults, for example, in Cyprus or Asia Minor.

In Asia the position was not uniform. Babylon and Judaea were not like Asia Minor, and everywhere, it seems, things were more complex than in Egypt, principally because the majority of the native cults were organized in small independent temple states, which defied bureaucratic control. Land and people belonged to the god; the high priest, usually hereditary, acted as his deputy; under him, as serfs of the god, stood the lower priests, the temple slaves, and the peasants. These temple states were part of that feudal system which in the Seleucid empire and probably also in states like Pontus and Cappadocia was always being fought by the kings, but never quite defeated; contrary to earlier views it is now known (as mentioned before) that the Seleucids even enlarged some of the temple states by donations of land. The kings of Pergamum, however, carried through a very strict supervision of the temples, similar to the Egyptian system. Confidential agents of the king seemed to have been entrusted with the financial administration of the temples (νεωκόροι), and in the city of Pergamum, if nowhere else, a board of officials ἐπὶ τῶν ἱερῶν προσόδων was created. The existence of such a system is not contradicted by the fact that the Attalids negotiated with the high priests of the Great Mother of Pessinus almost as with an equal (Welles, 55–61). For many of the temples in the Seleucid empire, there never was more than a formal acknowledgement of the royal supremacy, though payments in money were always demanded. In Babylon the policy towards the old established gods and their powerful priesthood seems to have varied; in fact, the religious policy of the Seleucids had generally neither the consistency of the Ptolemaic policy nor its success. Moreover, the state hardly carried on any religious propaganda, even for the ruler-cult, let alone for any Hellenized eastern god.

Judaea was a special case. A base of operations for Seleucids and

Ptolemies alike, it stood under Ptolemaic rule in the third century B.C., under Seleucid in the second. For the rulers the community of Jerusalem was hardly different from any other temple state. No government was inclined to concern itself with the character of any native religion; when it did so in Judaea, it was not for the sake of the Jewish religion. A strange decree of Antiochus III which, if genuine, must have been inspired by the priests of Jerusalem (Jos. *AJ.* XII 145) forbade Greek travellers to disregard the Jewish food laws and fixed fines which were to be paid to the priests. There will be few other cases of a king showing so positive an attitude towards a native 'superstition'. Earlier, Ptolemy IV seems to have made an attempt to enlist the Jews for his cult of Dionysus. But the first full-scale interference occurred under Antiochus IV Epiphanes; it was caused by the king's militant attitude towards Egypt, the revolutionary spirit of the lower classes in Judaea, and the violent resistance of most of the Jews to all Hellenization such as the Seleucid king strove to impose on them. The attempt would hardly have been made as it was, if the party in Judaea which inclined towards Greek culture had not misinformed the king. It is well known how his action led to a bloody religious persecution and provoked dangerous insurrections – a confirmation of the fact that for the Hellenistic monarchy toleration was a sheer necessity. Naturally, that did not exclude exploitation of the priests for political and economic purposes.

What is most significant in the relations of state and religion in the Hellenistic age is that we see the first steps made towards creating for the territorial state a new unity of the political and religious spheres. The ruler-cult was the most official form of this endeavour; but the attempt was also made, especially in Egypt, to subordinate the strong religious forces of the East to the political system. A true state religion was not and could not be attained, because there were no citizens of the state, and there could be no demand for any certain belief or cult as a necessary part of civic existence. For all that, we may say that the Hellenistic forms of political religion were a kind of prelude and parallel to those of the Roman empire; we need only think of emperorworship, official recognition of eastern cults, and Christianity as the state religion.

2. LAW

The coexistence of Greeks and Orientals conditioned the legal system as much as it did the religious world. Once again, the ideas and customs of the ruling class of Macedonians and Greeks encountered ancient, firmly established traditions, which up to a certain point had to be respected. Beside Greek law stood the law of the natives, the law of the land (ὁ ἐγχώριος νόμος, or similar terms). They were definitely divided spheres of law, and to some extent the Ptolemies and Seleucids found them already in existence; we need only think of Naucratis and the Greek cities of Asia Minor. But it was only after Alexander that the Greek element gained equal or superior rank to the native. In Egypt, the tradition of the land had long been unified, and in Asia Babylonian law, on the strength of its long unifying cultural tradition, ruled at least a large part of the Seleucid empire. Some of the vassal states might have their own law, especially theocratic states like Judaea, where the development had followed an even more conservative course than in Babylon itself. Greek law, on the other hand, sprang from as many sources as there were Greek states. It is true, there had been before some tendencies to assimilate and unify; the influence of Attic law in particular can be traced in many places. Now, in the new conditions, with foreign law confronting them, the Greeks were the readier to smooth out differences and irregularities. Even in the Hellenistic age the laws of Poleis were not fully assimilated to one another; but it means much that judges were so frequently 'borrowed' by one Polis from the other; the practice must have substantially contributed to unifying Greek law. Further, within each single monarchy at least, the new and most important source of legislation, the king, must have secured an extensive unification. Evidence is very scanty, but I think we can speak of one body of Greek law. As for example the Dicaeomata of Alexandria show, it may be regarded as a mixed interhellenic law, a legal κοινή, which asserted itself in the Poleis as much as in the monarchies; it must in some degree also have led to a class of professional jurists.

The distinction of two spheres of law and the character both of eastern and of Greek law ensured the rule of the personal principle. Every man was to be judged according to the law appropriate to him according to his origin. This principle obviously tended to delay the intermixture of the ethnic groups; but in several points it was weakened. The king, for one thing, represented no one part of the population but the state as a whole. As early as Hammurabi, the royal law was valid for the whole territory of the empire and, now again, royal law and royal justice stood, as it were, under the territorial principle, that is to say, were in force for the whole population of the empire. Further, it appears, in the ancient Mesopotamian empires and then in that of the Seleucids, the law of some regional districts – never, of course, the law of the ruling people – remained tied to their districts, not to the people. Finally, the strong mutual influences exercised by the two legal spheres on one another and the mixing of populations led, not to the abolition of the personal principle, but certainly to its modification; social position often took the place of nationality. If we ask how the Greek and the native law influenced one another, Greek law as the law of the ruler naturally took the more active part; but the native law was usually less receptive. As to the effects of this interchange, they were by no means always good; for example, in family law, which in general kept severely separated on the two sides, it might happen that the Greeks adopted the marriage of brother and sister from the Egyptians, and these the exposure of children from the Greeks! We note with interest that women had full legal capacity. Generally, Greek influences were considerable in Egypt, Asia Minor, and even in Syria, less important, it seems, in Mesopotamia; there, the continuity of the pure native law seems to have been less interrupted than in other places, even though Greek documents have been found and occasional blends of legal conceptions can be pointed out. To be sure, probably nowhere outside the Greek world and Rome could as perfect and advanced a law be found as in Mesopotamia.

In Egypt, where, apart from the central authorities, we know the conditions fairly well, the native law, already codified, it seems, under the Pharaohs, was translated into Greek and then confirmed by the king. In contrast to this, Greek law was composed of the νόμοι πολιτικοί, the laws of the citizens of the three Greek Poleis and the numerous Greek Politeumata. Both spheres of law were subject to the legislation of the king, but this meant naturally a very strong tendency to support Greek law. The effects of the fundamental bipartition of the law can be traced in the positive legal norms, most readily in marriage law and the law of inheritance, far less in the law of property; that was natural, because the gulf between the peoples was much earlier and far more effectively overcome in trade and commerce than where it came to an actual mixture of blood. There was a corresponding division of documents and their language; we have Demotic and Greek deeds with distinct forms of drawing up documents and registering legal

acts. Children of mixed marriages followed the condition of their
father; that, in general, meant a strengthening of the Greek element.
In the same direction worked the fixed terms, prescribed in either
language for the courts. In the administration of justice, too, the
bipartition was the dominant factor, though its fundamental unity
under the king was never abandoned. There were various special
courts. The Laocritae ($\lambda\alpha o\iota$ = natives), mostly priests, formed the
'enchorian' ($\dot{\epsilon}\gamma\chi\dot{\omega}\rho\iota o\iota$) courts, the Chrematistae, who acted as travelling judges in different large areas, the Greek ones. Other Greek courts
were the so-called Court of Ten in the Fayyum and, of course, the
courts of the Poleis. Of the other national groups, the Jews certainly
had their own courts. All these tribunals were corporate bodies; their
members were obviously not officials. Beside these courts there were
also single judges, up to the king himself, who naturally acted in special
cases only; then came the cantonal strategi and, with a competence
varying with the office, most of the administrative officials, from the
dioecetes down to the oeconomus of the canton and the comarch. How
far the jurisdiction of Apollonius was that of the dioecetes, how far
simply that of the owner of the $\gamma\hat{\eta}$ $\dot{\epsilon}\nu$ $\delta\omega\rho\epsilon\hat{a}$, cannot be decided. The
courts of officials, in the third century B.C. at least, seem to have been
mainly concerned with preliminary investigation and provisional verdict, perhaps also with a limited criminal jurisdiction; the papyri
certainly give the impression that the strategos had full competence and
gradually became the court of first instance, with whose decision
people as a rule were satisfied. It follows from *P. Teb.* I 5, 207 that the
royal peasants and other $\dot{\upsilon}\pi o\tau\epsilon\lambda\epsilon\hat{\iota}s$ (tenants, workers in monopolies,
personnel of the state leases, etc.) were subject only to the courts of the
dioecetes and his officials, in the first place the village scribes, that is to
say, of administrative officials. 'Those concerned with royal revenues',
who included also officials, came under the same terms. In these cases,
nationality played no part, and that meant that a very large section of
the population was withdrawn from the ordinary courts of law. It was
beyond doubt the general tendency of the government to usurp as far
as possible all jurisdiction. But even the 'bailiff' Zeno had his own
jurisdiction, and there were private courts of arbitration (some of them
priestly) from whose decisions appeal was of course possible to the
ordinary courts. The picture revealed was manifold, no rigid system,
but one often disposed to compromise. Such compromise may
probably also be found in the practical, if not theoretical, solution of
one of the special difficulties of Egypt with its unified organization; it

was a difficulty, arising out of the division into two spheres of law, in all cases where the two parties to an action had different laws. In the third century B.C., it is true, we find for such cases a *koinodikion*, but we hardly know anything of it but its name, and it obviously had no great importance. The problem of creating a real *ius gentium* was not solved in Ptolemaic Egypt; in fact, it was hardly set about. Jurisdiction seems to have been handled by Greek officials and judges with gross partiality; at the end of the second century a new regulation was introduced in favour of the Egyptians (Mitteis, *Chrestom.* 1), ordering that the language of the documents, on which the charge depended, decided whether a case belonged to the Laocritae or the Chrematistae. Yet, the parties had free choice what court and what law to appeal to in particular cases.

For the rest of the Hellenistic world outside Egypt we have little evidence. In the Seleucid empire, too, the administration of law must have been partly Greek, partly native; the coexistence of documents in Greek and cuneiform confirms this. Here, it seems, the strategi were of decisive importance in settling cases between members of different spheres of law. In Macedon none of these problems existed. Here the whole legal system was certainly closely modelled on Greek law, subject, of course, to such modifications as the monarchy and the social structure of the country demanded. Things seem to have been similar in Pergamum, where the Hellenism of the royal house found a soil already strongly Hellenized to work on. Almost the only evidence of a Pergamene legal system outside the Poleis (Athen. XV 697d) shows an Athenian as a judge nominated by the king over βασιλικοί or βασιλικά in the Aeolis, that is to say, either over king's peasants, who in part at least were non-Greeks, or (more probably) over cases that concerned the king's interests, but equally had to do with both Greeks and non-Greeks. There were royal judges also in Dura (see above, p. 196), and their frequent appearance in the successor states makes it likely that it all goes back to what was originally a Seleucid institution.

Information about the legal executive and the methods used to suppress crime comes only from Egypt; it had a police force, spread over the whole country and mainly organized on military lines, the φυλακῖται. Otherwise we may say that the constant appearance of officials in the task of jurisdiction corresponded to the nature of a state that was ruled by a king and a bureaucracy, a state moreover that exploited justice fiscally by way of special taxes, penalties for breach of contract, and similar devices. This financial bias prevented the creation of a law fit to be compared to the 'classical' Greek law. The officials operated as servants of the king, who in Egypt was the supreme judge and 'justiciary'. In the Poleis that was actually, though not formally, the case; for royal law had precedence of Polis law. Even in the Seleucid empire with its areas of independent law, the king was everywhere the supreme Court of Appeal, and it was he who gave unity to the multifarious system of law.

3. THE ARMED FORCES

Macedonian generals had conquered the world, and in doing so had become kings of great empires. The garrisoning and protection of the empire and its frontiers was a never-ending task; in addition, there was the necessity to have troops ready for battle to meet the wars that never ceased for long. Armies of considerable size were therefore essential, and the great demand for men was often hard to satisfy. The solution was to supplement a regular army of moderate size by reserves that could quickly be mobilized.

It is easily understood that the rulers were inclined, in military matters particularly, to preserve the Macedonian traditions to which in so many ways they clung (see pp. 149 ff., 159 f.). The Macedonian was of a decidedly soldierly cast, for people and army were identical; every man bore his arms, but on the conclusion of peace every man went back to his peaceful work. As the phalanx of heavy-armed troops and the noble corps of cavalry, this people in arms, always ready for an emergency and yet not a standing army, formed the kernel of the army. In the Hellenistic age, it remained for the Antigonids the natural basis of their power. Much the same was in principle true of the other kings, although they, and even the Macedonian kings, could not get through without professional mercenaries; it had been the same with the Poleis since the fourth century B.C. Everywhere there was a guard of hoplites and cavalry, often called by the old Macedonian name of ἄγημα; it consisted in the first place of Macedonians, though their numbers were soon no longer sufficient. The phalanx, too, whatever its composition, continued to be called Macedonian. The Lagids and Seleucids artificially created in their regular army what might seem to be lacking to their rule, the 'people in arms'. This was done as far as possible by the systematic settlement, on a grand scale, of soldiers, including Greek prisoners of war, as cleruchs or catoeci, that is to say, as peasants on the royal land, though in a military organization. This form of settlement is occasionally found in Macedon itself, and Alexander and Antigonus Monophthalmus had created precedents for it; but essentially it was a feature of the new realms. A certain guarantee was thus secured that the men required for military service would always be forthcoming. These settlers served, at the same time, to cultivate the royal land and as garrisons to secure important positions. The size of the lot assigned (κλῆρος) was, in Egypt at least, graded by the kind of troops concerned and by military rank, and to the land was added the lodging (σταθμός), the special right to be quartered in somebody else's house. The kleros, combined with the obligation to serve in the army, was usually hereditary, and the possession of it came very near to being private property; for there was free disposal if by last will, at least for the childless (Welles, 51). The burden of billeting, and at the same time the attempt to reduce its burdensomeness by strict regulations, was characteristic of Ptolemaic rule (apart from many papyri, cf. Welles, 30). Naturally, the cleruchs were liable to taxation, but they might receive the privilege of exemption (Welles, 69), or perhaps provision for old age by the assurance of pay for life (σιταρχία). Quite apart from any special privileges, the prospect of a landed estate alone must have been a vital aid to recruiting. Only very few of the settlers were Macedonians; in the main they were Greeks, who had usually been enlisted as mercenaries, but were so no more after they had accepted the grant of land; they merged very soon in the country and its population. Their numbers were very large; they probably represented the strong majority of the Greek immigrants. Their loyal attachment to the ruler might form a substitute for the traditional devotion of the Macedonians to their dynasty. The honourable name of 'Macedonian' was borne by part of these Greeks, not personally but as a corps. In the Seleucid empire, there may perhaps have been communities of Macedonians, distinct from the troops; they were probably recruiting stations. Apart from this, the recruiting for the royal army was carried out in the catoeciae (κατοικίαι), under direction of the provincial strategi; the organization was essentially the same as in Egypt. When after many intermediate stages the grant of land and, with it, the ethnic title had become hereditary, the analogy with the Macedonian model seemed to be realized as far as possible. The Ptolemies, at the same time, followed rather the precedents of the Pharaohs; that is why the Macedonian analogy was much more definitely true of the Seleucid than of the Ptolemaic army. The military settlements, however, became military strongholds; many of them could hardly be distinguished from new Poleis, and even non-Greek troops (Thracians, Mysians, Persians, and others; cf. pp. 150 f.) could become owners of kleroi; in Egypt they were assembled in Politeumata. In Pergamum the Macedonian tradition, being associated with the Seleucids, was practically banned and the levy of troops from the citizens of the city and the Hellenized inhabitants of the land (χώρα) was organized on purely Greek lines. Only after the battle of Magnesia can there have been in the realm of Pergamum catoeci in any considerable numbers; in 133 B.C. there could be talk of 'the military settlers in Polis and Chora' and of troops once Seleucid, including 'Macedonians' (OGI. 338, 14). In general, then, the Hellenistic kings kept a regular army, which was identical with a large part of the settled Graeco-Macedonian population; in time of peace, the majority of them cultivated the land and thus fulfilled economic functions. Beside the catoeci, the contingents from allied cities or dynasts played but a modest part and were not regularly called up.

From the first, however, there were other troops than the Macedonian phalanx – cavalry and light-armed troops (peltastae); their tactical and strategic importance had grown under Alexander and even more so in the struggles of the Diadochi. When the old cavalry of the hetaeri, though still in existence, declined in numbers and importance in the armies of the Antigonids and Seleucids (cf. Polyb. 5, 53, 4; 30, 25, 7), the light troops were partly supplied by Greeks. Among them, the Cretans represented an especially useful element, always quoted separately in our sources; the kings tried to secure them for themselves by treaties with Cretan cities. Besides these, we find Thracians, and, above all, Asiatics of the most diverse origins. It is clear that it was technical military requirements that led to the introduction of a large number of foreign mercenaries into the Hellenistic armies; they are called either μισθοφόροι or ξένοι, without any clear distinction, and they came from almost all parts of the Mediterranean world. (We have already touched on this point above, II 2.) The military quality of the regular troops deteriorated through their peaceful life as peasants on their lots. Even for the phalanx, the number of Macedonians and Greeks was not always sufficient; there was often no room for new allotments, or no money to pay the costly Greek mercenaries. Mercenaries, as a rule, had each his armour-bearer and, in general, made high demands; the cost of the mercenary armies must have been enormous. That is perhaps the explanation of the appearance of 'mercenary cleruchs' (μισθοφόροι κληροῦχοι); part of the mercenaries may have received, in lieu of full pay, a lot, which they probably let while performing their military service. This often happened, above all in Egypt; the shrewd Ptolemies killed two birds with one stone. The Seleucids, on the other hand, had to sell part of their domains in order to satisfy their catoeci and mercenaries. Even the Antigonids had mercenaries, mostly Celts, who were cheaper; they were partly settled in Macedon. Antigonus Doson wintered 'with his mercenaries', after he had sent his Macedonians home for the winter (Polyb. 2, 54, 14; 55, 1), and the army of Perseus consisted of mercenaries to the extent of almost a third. Likewise there were strong contingents of mercenaries in the army of Pergamum: we have the record of a most instructive text of a treaty between Eumenes I and his mercenaries (OGI. 266), which shows how strict were the conditions to which the king had to submit, even after a mutiny. In numbers the mercenaries were probably everywhere the strongest group in the active army, which was usually not very large; they, before others, were posted in the garrisons, the forts, and camps which were distributed over the cities and the frontiers and, in particular, secured the foreign possessions; their commanders (φρούραρχοι, or the like) were men of importance. Mercenaries were recruited either by diplomatic negotiation with a friendly power or by individual recruitment, carried out by ξενολόγοι; the two methods might be combined on the basis of guarantees, secured by treaty (cf. Syll. 581, VIII). Or, thirdly, a king might take into his pay a 'condottiere' (ξεναγός, ἡγεμών) with his frequently rather brigand-like troops. Even two kings, Demetrius Poliorcetes and Pyrrhus (to say nothing of the kings of Sparta), were notable examples of such commanders of mercenary troops. The royal guards, too, would include, together with Macedonians and Greeks, foreign hired troops. In case of war, mercenaries were naturally recruited according to requirements.

The stronger the motives became for recruiting Greek and, even more so, non-Greek mercenaries, the dearer and harder to find they were. From the end of the third century B.C. it seems to have become increasingly difficult to keep both the regular troops and the mercenaries at the desirable level, either in numbers or in quality; the conditions of which we have been speaking continued to operate. For the hard service in the fleet, at any rate, natives were early called up. Technical difficulties combined with the growing national demands of the native population, of which the governments were naturally much afraid. As early as under Ptolemy III there was a revolt of the native population.

The development could not be held up, and the first result was that independent bodies of native troops were formed. The decisive epoch is usually put in 217 B.C., the year of the battle of Raphia, in which twenty thousand Egyptians and three thousand Libyans took their place in the phalanx (Polyb. 5, 65; 79), thus representing about a third of the whole army; almost half the Seleucid army on that occasion were Asiatics. In Egypt this was not a case of recruiting mercenaries, but of the revival of the old warrior caste of the 'machimi'; hitherto they had been used in the armies of the Ptolemies, if at all, only as non-combatants. Their position in the time of the Pharaohs probably served as a model for the Ptolemaic cleruchs; the machimi now appeared beside these, though with a smaller lot. There was the same division into an active force and the reserve of settlers. The arming of the Egyptian population, which began at this time, added decisive strength to the national movement in later days. An unsolved problem – if we may add this here – is presented by the Mysian catoeciae (κατοικίαι τῶν Μυσῶν) in Asia Minor; they seem in part to have been important garrisons, in part remote villages of Hellenized natives; but we might refer to what was said above about the 'false', purely military, use of this as well as other names of peoples (see pp. 150 f.).

The details of the organization of the three groups, each of which had a part both in the army on a peace footing and in the army at war, is largely unknown; even for the Egyptian cleruchs, of whom we know most, some important questions remain open. In contrast to the Seleucid military settlers they did not form colonies, but were settled individually. The fact that later they bore the name of catoeci (always used in the Seleucid empire) seems to indicate that the name was meant to distinguish them from the native holders of lots. For in the second and first centuries B.C., the Greek and Egyptian soldiers became more and more assimilated and even mixed up; we hear occasionally of Ἕλληνες μάχιμοι (P. Teb. I 120; 139). As for the size of the lands of the soldiers, in the third century B.C. 100, 80, 70, 30 arourae are mentioned (aroura = about two-thirds of an acre); from the second century B.C. on we find also intermediate sizes; while the lots of the machimi were five, later up to ten, and rarely as much as thirty arourae. The problem of who was to look after the lot while its owner was on active service seems to have had no general solution; sometimes the family may have done the work, or the lot might be leased out, or as part of the royal property it might be taken over by neighbouring royal peasants. Naturally, the reliability of the cleruchs as an army reserve depended largely on their economic position (see also IV 4), and where want drove them to run away (e.g. *SIB*. 6746), the financial interest of the king had triumphed over military considerations. The lessee, on the other hand, paid the cleruch when he was absent and, in general, it was not the Greek mercenary who was economically oppressed. As we have said, the lots gradually became hereditary; occasionally a cleruch made his son a 'partner' (σύγκληρος) and thus secured his inheritance. These facts contributed to the stability of the system, but more and more spoilt its military value. The institution of the ἐπιγονή in Egypt (see p. 152 f.), however much disputed among scholars, seems to have insured the military and economic maintenance from generation to generation, while keeping alive the special groups with their originally ethnic and afterwards military character.

The different groups of soldiers were exclusively held together by their common commander-in-chief, the king; the oath of allegiance was taken to every new ruler. There must have been central military authorities, but we hear nothing of them; only for the Seleucid empire have we once the mention of an ἀρχιγραμματεὺς τῆς δυνάμεως (Polyb. 5, 54, 12), who was one of the provincial strategi appointed by Antiochus III after the revolt of Molon; he is unlikely to have been something like a Minister of War before that. The highest officers were always the strategi for the land troops and the nauarchi for the fleet, with the many ranks of the officer corps under their command. A letter of Antiochus III (Welles, 39), dealing with the privileges of a temple, is directed to the 'strategi, hipparchs, leaders of the infantry, soldiers and the rest'; it is probable that 'the rest' (οἱ ἄλλοι) does not mean, as in *UPZ*. 106 (above, p. 183) all the other officials, but only the military officials, connected with the troops in question. How far different nationalities had common commanders is unknown. In the second and first centuries B.C. the garrisons of the capitals took a peculiar turn. Their main contingent was the royal guard, composed of various changing elements. The power that its leaders possessed became manifest fairly early, for example, at the accession of the fifth Ptolemy. The soldiery in Antioch and Alexandria, most of them mercenaries, getting more and more out of hand, amalgamated with the citizens to form an element as unruly as it was powerful; in the end, it exercised a regular tyranny like the praetorian guard in Rome.

We must not, however, take this as the normal form in which army and Polis lived together. We know that the Macedonian garrisons in Greek cities often got on very well with their 'hosts', and many commanders received honours, either from genuine gratitude or from flattery. An important document (*OGI.* 229) shows how Smyrna, acting in the interest of King Seleucus II, concluded a treaty with the catoeci living in Magnesia, the soldiers 'living under canvas' (ὑπαίθριοι), and the rest of the Magnesians, and gave them citizenship. The catoeci were presumably military colonists, the rest of the soldiers mercenaries, while the other Magnesians were civilians, who had to be 'free and Greek' in order to become citizens of Smyrna. This implies that there were non-Greeks among the colonists and mercenaries. They all became citizens of Smyrna, without losing their military position. But the conferment of citizenship on soldiers remained rare; it probably never occurred in Egypt, and billeting was, of course, a burden which hardly ever would make for good human relationship. The discipline too often left much to be desired (cf. *OGI.* 266); Philip V issued strict instructions even to troops in his own country, and in Egypt the courts had often to proceed against the violence of the soldiers. Like the officials, the soldiers received their pay in money (ὀψώνιον) and in kind (μετρήματα), but payment was often in arrears, and then the neighbourhood had to suffer. We can also understand how much the soldiers were concerned for their accumulated property (ἀποσκευή), which, by the way, included wife and children; often its security seemed more important than loyalty to the ruler of the day. If all went well, the soldiers were not so badly off. Many of them were men of property, who after their service did much for their place of residence, especially for the gymnasium and certain cults, the spread of which was frequently due to the army (cf. Wilcken, *Chrestom.* 101). Others went back to Greece, and there they became patrons of the arts – or tyrants.

The Hellenistic armies, composed as they were of many different elements, had both in numbers and organization far outdistanced the armies of the fourth century B.C., even that of Philip. And yet it seems that, in principle, what was retained was the legacy of Philip, not of Alexander, namely the idea of a national Macedonian army. Even the machimi were armed and drilled in the Macedonian style. In fact, however, the army, like practically everything else in the Hellenistic age, was a new creation, made up from Macedonian, Greek, and the most diverse eastern traditions, an instrument that, for all its mixed composition, successfully met the serious new demands of an age that in military affairs as in other things had considerably changed. These new demands were largely due to the vastness of the political scene which asked for strategic combinations, such as even Alexander had never known, above all, war on two or even three fronts. In tactics, too, there were decisive developments, though here along the lines marked out by Alexander: the combination of the most varied kinds of arms (with a strong preference for cavalry, for which the state maintained its own studs), the perfection of weapons and armour, a vast increase in the technical side of the instruments of war, such as elephants, scythe chariots, fortifications, siege engines, large ships. Later, it is true, the Hellenistic armies, far from being uniform, and the slow Macedonian phalanx succumbed to the force and tactical skill of the Roman legions; but we must not forget the great achievements of the Hellenistic armies. It has been shown how a new spirit of concentrated effort and purposefulness determined the conduct of war by many of the rulers. This was possible only because the kings or generals fought at the head of their troops far less frequently than had once been usual; they began to keep mobile reserves, and used them personally to intervene in the battle at a decisive moment, while never quite losing the control of operations as a whole. All in all, it was a strict and rational organization. It shows to what extent the army was a mirror of the state. In particular, it can be said that the ethnic composition and military efficiency of the armies suffered in the second century B.C. precisely those changes and deteriorations that were characteristic of the Hellenistic state as a whole.

4. STATE FINANCES AND POLITICAL ECONOMY

The Hellenistic states, which paid their soldiers and officials and knew nothing of voluntary and unpaid service by public-spirited citizens, were in need of material wealth to an extent the Polis had never known. Without it, they could not hope to maintain their military efficiency and political power. The mere upkeep of army and fleet in time of peace cost a great deal, even though the military settlers then received no pay. Peace, however, did as a rule not last long, and war had become an extremely expensive affair. The administration of the empire, too, was very costly. That meant that economics and finance had a special importance in the whole of the functions of the state. Not only was the political and social structure of the state strongly influencing, and being influenced by, economic forces, but as we have already had occasion to observe, religion, law, and army were all brought into the service of economics and fiscal exploitation. This shows that the Hellenistic states practised a deliberate economic policy. It has often rightly been said that this policy, in its real impulses and aims, was mercantilist and fiscal, that is to say, bent on stepping up production and export to the highest possible point – though with full regard to the agrarian basis – in order to get money for the state and through the state.

Another factor that affected state economy was that the king meant the state. State economy appeared as a formidable private enterprise, most plainly of course in Egypt, where the principle that everything without exception was royal property – land and its yield just as labour and its fruits – was realized in a unique manner. This does not mean that there was an 'absolute' state economy; but even where a certain freedom of activity was left to the individual, the economic power of the king, as the supreme landowner, producer, and merchant, with the whole machinery of administration at his disposal, was so dominant as to make private competition illusory. This peculiar form of the Egyptian state as an all-inclusive business enterprise did not indeed follow any special principle of its own; it was only the most consistent development of a situation common to the whole Hellenistic world. Actually, it could be carried out in this manner in Egypt only; but there were certain signs of similar economic trends in other states as well.

What was vital in the general situation was that first with Alexander, and then with the end of the wars of the Diadochi, economic life underwent a remarkable rise, an extensive strengthening due to geographical expansion, to the discovery and development of new trade routes, to closer internal ties between separate economic areas, to improved technique and methods and thus a general intensification, to increased traffic by land and sea, to cheaper money, to the concentration of men and affairs in the great cities. It was 'a new economic atmosphere' in which the Hellenistic kings built their states. Moreover, up to the middle of the second century B.C., large amounts of capital were assembled in the lands of the eastern Mediterranean, which, in the East, that was poor in capital, gained richer rewards, either by higher rates of interest or by more widespread and fuller use. By about 150 B.C. the movement of capital was reversed and found a new field in Italy. The special position of Egypt within the new economy was also determined by the fact that it had become the chief granary of the Mediterranean world. From all this we see that state finance and general economy in the Hellenistic states formed a unity which admitted of no division. Thus, when everything was most strongly determined by the forces of economic life, it is not desirable to see it in separate items of revenues and expenses.

Agriculture continued to be the basis of Hellenistic economy. From the Greeks it gained improved methods, which were spread everywhere as the kings founded colonies in their empires. Swamps were drained, and new arable land was won, new plants and new domestic animals were introduced, for example in Egypt the camel. Some branches of cultivation (e.g. the vine and fruit) were chiefly in Greek hands, also the keeping of animals and improvement of breeds. In Pergamum scientific studies of agriculture were published; among the authors was one of the kings, and generally a large amount of technical books was produced to teach new methods to the farmers. The close connection of state and agriculture found expression in the fact that the king was the greatest landowner, if not in law the only one. On this presupposition depended the two most profitable sources of agrarian revenue, the royal domains and the land tax. In all states the extent of the royal domains, the $\beta a\sigma\iota\lambda\iota\kappa\dot{\eta}$ $\gamma\hat{\eta}$, was enormous. It included first of all the arable land, tilled by the king's peasants as his tenants; then, there were pastures with herds and breeding stations; stone quarries and mines and large forests (only Egypt had none of these): all this was probably the main source of the king's wealth; the Ptolemies owned forests in Cyprus, and for a time also on the Lebanon. Ownership came in the first place directly from succession to the former kings, and from the fact that the land was regarded as 'won by the spear' (p. 160). In addition, confiscation played a considerable part; it hit especially the estates of the nobles, the temples, or any other big owners. The rest of the land, which was at least not directly royal, had various names and qualities, depending on the recipient or the owner; but in one sense it was a unity, as it was all liable to direct taxation, though the burden fell very variously. This was the second important source of revenue. First of all in direct taxation came the land tax, which in most states meant a general tithe ($\delta\epsilon\kappa\acute{a}\tau\eta$) of the yield; in Egypt there was a system of several taxes varying with the capacity of the soil. Other taxes completed the system; for example, on buildings, cattle, and slaves. There was also a yearly tribute ($\phi\acute{o}\rho os$) from dependent cities or tribes, even from villages on royal lands: the tribute was especially important in the Seleucid empire, and most oppressive, since it was levied without regard to changing economic conditions. Whether there was double taxation is disputed; as the tribute would be mainly taken from the yield of the ground, it is more probable that either tribute or land tax, not both together, had to be paid.

For the Seleucid empire, in Ps.-Aristot., *Oikon.* II 1345b, 31, the domains and the tithe are designated 'satrapal', that is, revenues from the provinces and the main sources of revenue of the empire. They were taken over from the Persian period; in Pergamum they probably retained their place, though the system of the Pergamene land tax is not known for certain. The serfs (λαοί) who cultivated the domains were in both states natives. The two forms of exploitation of agriculture, with the alternative we mentioned concerning the tribute, can probably be found in all states; only sometimes the domains and sometimes the tax were of greater economic importance. In the Seleucid empire the extent of the domains was gradually much reduced by sales and gifts, while the areas subject to land tax did not increase in the same degree, as the growing land of the Poleis remained free. In Macedon there was a land tax; but within the modest setting of this state, financially weak as it was, the domains were far more important; above all, there were the forests that supplied all over the Greek world timber for ships, mines, and buildings. Of quite a different kind were conditions in Sicily, where the famous *lex Hieronica* established the tithe on grain as the only direct tax, while the royal possessions, it seems, took a back seat. With the domains went the mines, mostly worked by slaves, and yielding rich gains in some states, especially in Macedon and Pergamum; the gold of Nubia and the Thebaïd played no big part in the whole economy of the Lagids.

Connections between the legislations of Sicily and Egypt have been established; it was in Egypt that the system of exploitation of soil and men reached its fullest development. Here the royal land was assigned to existing villages, and the unions of the royal peasants (βασιλικοὶ γεωργοί), native tenants, resident in each village and bound to the soil, bore the responsibility for the cultivation of the king's land. As this was almost entirely of the highest grade (γῆ ἐν ἀρετῇ), the yield from the soil must have been very considerable; only so can we explain how it happened that despite taxation and severe official control, the economic condition of these tenants was in general good. However, occasional bad harvests or other disturbances might lead to enforced leasing or to the flight of the peasants. The latter seems to have been most common when too great demands had been made on the working energies of the peasants. It was the king's peasants who were first called on for the great and necessary labours, under the direction of Greek ἀρχιτέκτονες, of the regulation and distribution of the waters of the Nile. The only relief for the utter dependence of the peasants lay in their indispensability (see also above, pp. 154 f.). Under the later Ptolemies, several grave crises of this kind occurred, and from the beginning of the second century B.C., even the upper classes could be drawn into helping – hardly voluntarily – in the cultivation of waste land (*UPZ*. 110), though Greeks and Macedonians were exempted from forced labour. In all this the Ptolemies were carrying on the tradition of the Pharaohs, albeit with some Greek improvements; similar traditions must have continued to work in Mesopotamia. These and other public works must have formed a main item in the state's expenses. What fraction of the whole land the royal land represented is unknown; in one village in the Fayyum it amounted to more than half. The rest of the land, the γῆ ἐν ἀφέσει, was divided generally into temple land (ἱερὰ γῆ), assigned land (κληρουχικὴ γῆ and γῆ ἐν δωρεᾷ, that is to say, the land of the cleruchs or catoeci and the estates of the high functionaries), and private land (ἰδιόκτητος γῆ). As land 'given' by the king, all these classes of land were liable to tax, though at different levels. The temple land was mostly let out on lease and then treated much like the royal land; it was also under the state authorities (cf. above, pp. 210 f.). The land of the cleruchs was, to a large extent, allotted with the obligation of improving the land, or even, as in the Fayyum, of creating new arable ground for cultivation; for that reason quite apart from military considerations, it was usually assigned to soldiers. It was in the main poor land (ὑπόλογον), and its importance for the general economic system and long-term policy was greater than any immediate financial advantage. The 'gift estates', though they remained formally in royal possession, usually carried privileges, ensuring far-reaching independence to the owners, but also putting them under a lasting obligation to the king. That was the main importance of the δωρεαί; but as they were cultivated on the grand scale, they also led to an intensification of the economic effort. Private property, on the other hand, always on a small scale, consisting of houses, vineyards, and gardens, or else emerging from the hereditary lease to royal peasants, was, it seems, in principle liable to taxation; only it often received special privileges. By itself stood the land of the Poleis, which was not royal property; in Egypt it was by no means extensive.

In manufacture, as in agriculture, the Greek influence brought an intensification; new aims and new methods appeared, although, it seems, only comparatively few Greeks were active in manufacture. Certainly, the prevailing method was still to work in a man's own home; but for certain branches of production, at least in the large cities,

Q

there must have been bigger workshops with paid free workers or with slaves. All manufacture, too, was subject to direct taxation, sometimes in the form of a licence to practise a handicraft or to found a workshop, sometimes as a percentage on the earnings. Just as the king was the largest landowner, so he was, at least in Egypt and Pergamum, also the most important manufacturer and merchant. To the royal domains corresponded the monopolies, which were not restricted to sales, as the name might imply. By such monopolies or by taking at least a dominating part in the single branches of trade – it might be by having workshops (ἐργαστήρια) of their own – the kings simply kept production and sale in their own hands, or at the least, they exercised an exact control and had the main share in the profits. We should not call this a capitalist enterprise; rather, it meant the exclusion of private competition, imposed for purely fiscal reasons. It thus became possible to fix prices beforehand. In the Seleucid empire, in spite of the general decentralization, there seems to have been a sales monopoly of salt, and the same seems true of the successor states and in Egypt. In the case of many monopolies, production and sale seem to have been combined; in fact, generally manufacture and trade were closely linked. In Egypt the import of raw materials, the export of agrarian and manufactured produce, and the replacement of imported goods by home production (wine, oil, wool), all helped to secure a positive trade balance. That was the aim of the royal trade policy, and the customs duties alongside the monopolies served its ends. In the other states, too, so far as we can trace their trade policy, the customs were one of the main sources of revenue. The customs included both import and export duties, especially at the great Mediterranean ports. They thus served to protect home production, agricultural as well as manufactured, and prevented the cutting of prices. Even when the customs served mainly fiscal purposes as they often did, and might amount to 50 per cent of the value, the Polis system of one unvarying percentage had been abandoned and a determined trade policy established. Of great importance were also the internal customs duties and the city tolls which, especially in the Seleucid empire though also in Egypt, covered the transit trade, which the kings much encouraged. On old and new trade routes from east and south-east to the Mediterranean and back, it passed through the new empires. In the Seleucid empire the road linking Seleucia on the Tigris to Antioch was the life vein in the vast economic body; in Egypt the caravan track, first used by Philadelphus, from Coptos to Berenice on the Red Sea was a necessary condition for the flourishing trade with Arabia and India. Finally, important factors in state economy were the foreign possessions, which could supply raw materials lacking in the home lands (for Egypt, for example, timber and metals) or could supply supporting stations or trade terminals on the grand scale; Syria by its ports, so much disputed between Lagids and Seleucids, gained greatly in economic importance.

Of the Ptolemaic monopolies one, that of oil, is very familiar to us (from the *Revenue Papyrus* and *P. Teb.* 703). Apart from a certain privilege belonging to the temples – though a mere vestigial relic of a much more extensive activity in earlier times – both production and sale were entirely in the hands of the king. The monopoly, it is true, was always leased out for the area of one canton, but the lessees had hardly any opportunity of making a profit. The whole business stood under strict control by royal officials, the extent of the land under oil, the sowing and harvesting, no less than the actual production of oil in the royal workshops or in private establishments; the workmen, for instance, were forbidden to change their place of residence. It seems, however, that, to heighten their efforts, they were allowed a share in the profits. Finally, the retail sale was leased out under yearly renewed fixed prices. Import of oil from abroad (Greek olive oil, for instance, that generally was of superior quality) was forbidden; that meant practically the exclusion of any competition with the royal monopoly. Papyrus, too, was a monopoly, also with great importance for foreign trade; it only grew in Egypt, and the itch for the pen that possessed the age made it an article of mass export. The king took a large part in its production, sale, and export, and made great profits thereby; we know of a special official, charged 'with the distribution of the royal papyrus' (ὁ πρὸς διαθέσει τῶν βασιλικῶν χαρτῶν; *P. Teb.* III 709). Here and otherwise when we speak of monopolies, it should be understood that many of them were partial monopolies only, and that the king often simply shared them by special taxation and by strict control. Important above most other things was the regulation of the grain production and trade. The fiscal exploitation and control of the royal land and the γῆ ἐν δωρεᾶι led to a great enrichment of the king, to good profits for the owners of the δωρεαί, and, at the best, some trivial gains for the peasants. The king again was the greatest dealer in grain, and so it was most to his advantage that all grain not needed at home should immediately be sent under safeguard from every district to Alexandria, where large quantities were needed to feed the growing population; at the same time, the selling price there was higher, and even higher prices could be obtained by export to Greece. The royal income from growing and trading again amounted, according to a modern estimate, to about one-third of the total production. The Ptolemaic monopolies, as a whole, covering different grades of royal partnership, embraced especially the necessary food of the poorer classes (oil, honey, salt, fish, flour) and many articles of utility, particularly linen and woollen material, and in addition glass and all manner of luxury goods. The temples, which in earlier times had taken a large part in production and trade, were now, in the production of oil and the making of linen, as in other economic branches, almost entirely restricted to covering their own requirements only. When apparent concessions were made, they meant as a rule the cancelling of older monopolies of the temples. The transference of the ἀπόμοιρα tax, a sixth of the yield of vineyards and gardens, from the temples to the worship of Arsinoe Philadelphus and so to the state, was a masterpiece of royal fiscalism which did not stop before the temples; but from the second century, as we have mentioned, the position changed in favour of the priests. It is perhaps surprising that the extensive abolition of all competition in the whole of economic life did not result in any perceptible decline in economic efficiency. Everything was directed with a magnificent consistency towards the profit of the king; any intention, such as we might have imagined could exist, to make the necessaries of life cheaper, was remote from the system.

Beside the revenues that we have mentioned, which were so deeply involved in the economic structure of the state, there were taxes of a purely fiscal character, taxes on sales and traffic like the Egyptian ἐγκύκλιον, taxes, also found in the Seleucid empire, on the sale of slaves and other articles (ἀνδραποδικόν, ἐπώνιον, κηρύκειον), all hitting trade as well as production; above all there was the poll tax (ἐπικεφάλειον, Ptolemaic σύνταξις, the prelude to the later λαογραφία). It was only levied on the non-Greek population and thus, as before in the Persian empire, it was a tool of political domination. Other revenues consisted of legal fines which could go as far as the confiscation of property, of the sale of priesthoods, and taxation of river transport on Nile and Euphrates. Here we may also mention the compulsory labour, demanded almost exclusively from the natives, which in Egypt was intended to facilitate the travelling of the king and his high officials in the country. Everywhere we see how state economy was ruled not by social, but exclusively by fiscal motives.

We get the same impression from the state expenses; the main items, as we have briefly mentioned, were army and fleet, fortifications, and the foundations of colonies as well as the internal administration, including cult and public works; among the latter as a main item were the dams, ditches, and canals, that served to regulate the rivers both in Egypt and Mesopotamia. In general, we may say that some officials were certainly not paid directly by the king and that the cult sometimes brought in a profit; yet, the expenditure increased steadily everywhere, and not only on account of the inflation prevailing at least in Egypt if not elsewhere. Apart from these expenses, the costs of the court played a very big part; the expenses, in Egypt and Pergamum, for science, art, and education, though not inconsiderable, were small in comparison with the rest. It is impossible to make even an approximate estimate of the expenditure of any of the Hellenistic states.

Every system of taxation that rested on the land tax, especially the Egyptian, required a very exact method of tax assessment, particularly a system of land registration. It existed also under the Seleucids in Asia Minor, though it was less elaborate than in Egypt. A vast apparatus of tax collection was also required, and if in this the practice of leasing out was largely followed, the unheard-of strictness of control reduced the lessees increasingly to mere agents of the state (how unlike Rome!); they made little out of it and, it seems, had often to be kept at their duties by force. Such were the methods employed in Egypt; how far they were employed elsewhere is not known. The official apparatus necessary for the administration of finance was always very considerable; the general importance of economic considerations explains the great power held by the chief financial official in Egypt, the dioecetes, yet in name he was no more than the administrator of the king's household. There was no clear line of division, in principle, between the profit of the king and the revenues of the state, though in practice it existed often enough. The special treasury of the *Idios Logos*, created late beside the state treasury of the *Basilikon*, was not devoted to any kind of private income, but to extraordinary public revenues. Quite another matter was the personal greed of the high officials, who were hardly inferior to the king in the manifold variety and grand scale of their economic enterprises. In the documents of the Zeno archive, we can often not determine whether the agents of Apollonius were acting in official or private commission. The system of strict state economics, then, was broken by some of its highest representatives, and some tendencies to private enterprise could flourish under the very protection of the state. This applies even more to the strategi and other dignitaries in other states; as landowners on the grand scale, they had almost complete economic independence. Lastly, even the merchants and artisans of the Greek cities enjoyed great economic freedom. When there was no monopoly, farmers and artisans could sell the surplus of their goods; that is confirmed by a large number of papyri, and native as well as foreign traders played an important part. Yet, the statement we have made before still stands, that there was no question of an essentially free economy of private competition. Any official permission for a limited private competition, granted in some branches of the monopoly system (for example, in the grain trade in Egypt) kept the recipients of such favours personally dependent on the state; it did not alter the main fact that the monarchy was in a position to organize and direct economic life.

If we consider the special character of the tax regulations and the economic situation as a whole, we realize that the Hellenistic age everywhere demonstrated the triumphant advance of money economy as opposed to an economy in kind, though the latter still retained considerable importance. As is well known, it was Alexander who by turning into coins the precious metals of the Persian treasury gave such a vehement impulse to money economy. Actually, the Persian darics had even before shown some tendency to become an international currency. In Egypt, that 'model country of the economy in kind', it was the financial tricks of the governor Cleomenes of Naucratis after the Persian era that opened the way to money economy; the treasure of eight thousand talents that he left behind was the foundation on which the Ptolemies built. Linking their systems to various standards and often ousting the coinage of the Poleis, the Hellenistic dynasties issued money in vast quantities, aiming at unification first within the territory of each single empire. These coins of the various empires naturally spread and had influence beyond their own borders. An economic war developed which, like the political struggle, led to a sort of balance between Seleucids and Ptolemies. No one coinage gained universal supremacy. Still, the Attic standard which, ever since Alexander used it for his silver coinage, was generally accepted in Hither Asia, did facilitate exchange between Asia Minor, Mesopotamia, and Syria, thus creating under Seleucid rule a more or less unified economic area. On the other hand, the Phoenician standard, shared by the ports of Phoenicia and by Egypt, bound these two together. Within the several empires money economy steadily advanced; the Greeks, wherever they went, carried it with them. Everywhere it led to the evils of loans and usury, due at first to scarcity of money. Even the legal rate of interest was 2 per cent per month, and that, although mostly accepted, was often exceeded. Foreign trade with some peoples of the South and East continued to be by barter; for the trade with India and Inner Asia both Ptolemies and Seleucids struck gold coins. For a long time silver coinage predominated, but from the late third century B.C. onwards the alloy worsened, and gradually the bronze coins, used in local trade and struck by many cities in the Seleucid empire, became more important than silver; in Egypt, where silver had to be imported, silver coins entirely disappeared, and towards the end of the third century B.C., copper currency was officially introduced. The revenues of the state came in almost entirely in money; only a part of the land tax, though not a small one, was paid in kind, namely all taxes on grain-growing land; and this grain was then used for payment of salaries and similar purposes. For this residue of the economy in kind (we should more properly call it a money economy, with kind as money), there was a special system of administration, which we know at least for Egypt. Here the state built magazines ($\theta\eta\sigma\alpha\nu\rho\sigma\iota$) in all parts and, round them, organized the transport of the grain and the banking of the corn deposits. For the 'grain money', these $\theta\eta\sigma\alpha\nu\rho\sigma\iota$ were what the public pay-offices ($\beta\alpha\sigma\iota\lambda\iota\kappa\alpha\iota$ $\tau\rho\alpha\pi\epsilon\zeta\alpha\iota$), spread over the whole country, were for loans of money; they were, in fact, banks. Under these two forms, a banking system was created, on Greek models, with transferable accounts. This system was mono-polized in the hands of the king through its public pay-offices and their official heads ($\tau\rho\alpha\pi\epsilon\zeta\iota\tau\eta\varsigma$, $\sigma\iota\tau\sigma\lambda\acute{o}\gamma\sigma\varsigma$). A central state bank existed in Alexandria; it had branches in the provinces, and everywhere it was used for private deposits; the king received some special revenue from that form of business. In a sense, the whole system of Ptolemaic economy found its crowning success in the state bank; in other states this kind of business was chiefly in the hands of temples, cities, or private people.

Much light has been thrown on the economic system of Egypt by the activities of Apollonius, that powerful minister who himself in the first place was responsible for the functioning of the administration. The system naturally repeated itself in his own sphere. The picture that we get from the Zeno papyri (see pp. 181 f.) is one of a selfish capital-ism, which exploited the workers and made them enemies of the system. Here we do not even find any hint that the self-interest of the master demanded a certain degree of welfare for the workers, while the royal government often enough recognized that principle. We notice too that the whole complicated economic system was not based on any theoretical principle, unless it be called a principle to take as much as possible and spend as little. Out of the tradition of pre-Greek times as well as immediate experience grew a system that could only continue to exist by compulsion and excessive taxation. In different ways and in a different degree, this was true of all the Hellenistic states. Everywhere, too, the right of asylum was one of the few possible escapes for the oppressed population. The officials who had to carry out the system in practice found themselves in a permanent dilemma; the official actions that they took under higher authority came up against counter-actions which could be very dangerous economically. Moreover, these officials were only human beings, sadly rushed and overworked men at that, without the freedom of individual initiative, who often tried to overcome their difficulties by brutality and injustice (e.g. *BGU*. VIII 1730). In this all-embracing and controlling system there was one guiding principle, expressed in the often quoted *P. Teb.* III 703, with an optimism that may have been genuine, but was far from justified (230): 'No one has the right to do what he wants to do, but everything is regulated for the best.'

Hellenistic political economy on the whole succeeded well in its main purpose, the procuring of money – most successfully where it has carried to its logical conclusions; the Ptolemies were the richest rulers in the world and could grant or refuse loans to states like Rome or even Carthage. The wealth, then, served above all king and court and the maintenance of power abroad. The people were as poor as the land was rich. No attempt was made to raise the general standard of living. Everywhere the imports, in which slaves and luxury goods played a large part, mainly contributed to the welfare of the upper classes. In Egypt, internal trade moved almost entirely in one direction, from the country to Alexandria, from the numerous agricultural and manufacturing units to the city, which was the centre of money and administration. The land did the producing, government and city did the trading and pocketed the profits. Yet, personal enrichment was not the only aim of Ptolemaic policy. The real aim of the best of the rulers and of the creators of the system in particular was that of all Hellenistic dynasties: the creation of a strong and independent state. There is no doubt that human beings came off badly in the process. That had its effects on the state. We are not speaking so much of the material side. A considerable part of the population found itself, like its state, in a not intolerable economic position. Everyone, it is true, groaned under the pressure of taxation, and there was not a sign of any social policy; yet, in contrast to the Hellenistic Polis of the homeland, there was no 'social question' in any Hellenistic state, if only because all suffered under the same burden. But it is true that this autocratic and bureaucratic system, which kept economy and life under control and tutelage down to the tiniest details of everyday life, crippled the spirit and will of the subjects – just because they were no more than subjects. The great problems of politics and economics remained unsolved. The Greeks, who for a long time stood especially to profit by the system, were just the ones who changed sadly under these conditions. The Orientals had their traditional fatalism, which in no way affected their forms of life, rooted in religion; but with the Greeks, divorced from their own land and their traditional social and moral bonds and largely blended with the native population, it led to a shrinking of their political and moral powers. The ζῷον πολιτικόν once again became a ζῷον οἰκονομικόν. The special servants of the state, the officials, were by no means exempt from this development; on the contrary, bureaucracy became ever more fussy and more lifeless, and its work threatened to degenerate into an empty and senseless routine. Moreover, it had its sad effects that, beyond the decay of the internal life of the Polis, even its constitutional forms were degraded. To sum up, the Hellenistic state from the first had no strong support in the minds of the Greek as well as the non-Greek population. It found its secret enemy in its own economic and administrative system, and only a strong monarchy could prevent that enemy from coming into the open. The more consistently the centralization, bureaucracy, and state economy developed, the worse did things become. Egypt maintained its independence longest, the reason being its firm framework, together with the foreign policy of Rome; but in the sense of a state's own dignity and self-assertion it was the first to lay down its arms. The lack of political interest in the population, due not only to the absence of political rights but also to economy and the general conditions of life, was largely responsible for the fact that the national strength of the Roman citizens destroyed the Hellenistic world of states. Still, while admitting this, we should not forget that the Hellenistic state exercised on the Roman empire an influence that gradually gathered fresh strength, and that the culture of the Hellenistic centuries, which cannot be imagined without its world of states, laid the foundations for the higher education of Rome.

CONCLUSION

State and Civilization in Hellenic and Hellenistic Times

State and Civilization in Hellenic and Hellenistic Times

To sum up, a few remarks about the impact which the various forms of state exerted on Greek civilization seem appropriate. They cannot be in any way complete, but they can perhaps help to strengthen the bridge between political history and the history of civilization. To combine these two branches of historical writing in a new and, as far as possible, complete unity is one of the major tasks set to our generation. It does not imply a widening of the historical outlook, as does the challenge presented by the idea of a 'history of mankind', which forces the historian to emerge from the narrow concept of 'European' history. Professor Arnold Toynbee has tried to tackle that task, titanic for any single writer; but even for his vitality and knowledge it has proved too big. Others are trying to find a possible approach, or to see the concept in its innate dubious and contradictory nature. Our problem is different, one of intensifying rather than widening the picture. We are tired today of those special chapters within the frame of general history, chapters on art, literature, religion, and the rest. Attempts at a synthesis have frequently been made, especially in what in German is called *Geistesgeschichte*, and in America the History of Ideas. No doubt, these are fertile methods, though there frequently looms the danger of losing contact with the political and social realities, and thus with historical reality itself. The opposite is true of Marxist historiography which, in its strong dogmatism, practically denies any but the economic-social point of view.

Civilization is, and always has been, the offspring of society. Its achievements, however, were reached by individuals who were both free and creative – we would call them 'civilized'. We take 'civilization' not as contrasted with 'culture', but regard the one as the *alter ego* of the other; at the bottom is always the interconnection of society and individuals. That means that the framework of a community is needed, and that is normally the state. Thus, Aristotle could pronounce the paradox that the state is older than man. We ask what is the part of the state in the shaping of a civilization, that is to say, to what extent is civilization really a matter of the *civis*, the political animal? There is no general answer to that question; for the character of the state differs at different times and with different peoples. Between the extremes of deliberate direction by the state and complete freedom of cultural life, there have been innumerable varieties. Instead of discussing general principles it seems safer, and also more hopeful for valuable results, to deal with the question within a limited historical period. In this book we have frequently been concerned with the mutual relations between state and civilization; it remains to summarize that theme, taking the risk of some repetition.

About the time when the Polis emerged as a special form of state, in the eighth century B.C., Homer, the poet of the *Iliad* and perhaps the *Odyssey* too, composed his poetry. He was the summit of a long oral tradition going back to Mycenaean times. He was the greatest of the *aoidoi*, the bards, who sang about heroic deeds for an audience of aristocratic warriors. He was, at the same time, more or less a contemporary of the invention of the Greek alphabet and also the abstract geometric style of vase-painting; he was soon to be succeeded by the *rhapsodoi*, the 'reciters' of epic poetry. The oral tradition came to an end, whether Homer himself wrote or not. The analogy, for example, of the Yugoslav popular poetry has rightly been stressed. With Homer epic poetry began to be written down. A new society was being formed, emerging from the decline and final destruction of the Mycenaean civilization, and from the last great migrations. The new society was able, due to the innate genius of the Greek people, to combine the epic heritage with new creative forces. We find its beginnings in the *Odyssey* and especially in Hesiod; it was a society, a ruling aristocracy, within a state which more and more centred on a single urban settlement. This type of state, the Polis, was brought to most parts of the Mediterranean by the Greek colonization, not least to the West where Greek cities spread along the shores of Sicily and Southern Italy. Each place was an independent community, creating its own way of civilized life. Agriculture, trade, manufacture, different in strength and distribution, provided the economic and social foundations of cultural development. That development could be intense or weak; some cities led in one field and some in another, but they all contributed to a common Greek civilization. Everywhere, however, civilization was the product of a developing society, in a process by which the ruling nobility learned to merge in the Polis community and gradually to make concessions to the free non-nobles. The state itself did not guide or enforce any way of life, whether economic or cultural. This was even true of the tyrants, although they might favour a certain class among the citizens or certain economic activities, or be particularly interested in some field of religious or intellectual life. The state, however, without guiding or ordering, was the necessary basis, not least by means of the cults and festivals of the community, for which the artists and poets worked. Without the Polis, there would have been no Greek society or Greek culture, and the wealth of archaic Greek civilization is largely due to the number of independent communities.

We have mentioned two essential factors for the birth of Greek civilization, the genius of the people, and the large number of political centres. A third factor can be added, the *kairos*, the grace of the historical moment. For the first time in human history, the individual was to challenge society, in the political as well as the cultural field. The centuries from the late eighth to the sixth were the age of emerging individuals, of tyrants and lawgivers, that is to say, of social reform, economic progress, and cultural splendour. Those centuries also were the age of the great lyric poets who expressed their own personal feelings, as lyric poetry has done ever since. There was also a wonderful development in architecture and art, when the grandeur of the Doric temple was created, and the beauty of the nude male body was discovered as well as that of the draped female figure. Vase-painting proceeded from the abstract rhythm of the Dipylon style to the baroque wealth of the orientalizing vases and further to the magnificent or charming simplicity of the Attic black- and red-figured styles. Thought and religion began to explore new depths from where ways to a great future of the human mind opened up, both in the rational and in the irrational spheres. The individual developed his mind in a stormy rise, though always within state and society; that is even true of those who were rebels like Archilochus, or of the tyrants who despite their arbitrary and egotistic ways never put cultural life into a strait-jacket. Among the leading city-states which took part in that process of general development with particular strength, we may think of Corinth and Athens, of Syracuse and Selinus, of Miletus and Samos; but others followed. The Panhellenic festivals at Olympia or Delphi or on the Isthmus offered the opportunity for the agonistic and spiritual competition of the Greek states; but Panhellenic unity remained weak as compared with the unity of cultural life in each individual Polis.

In one man, Solon of Athens, this unity was particularly strong, as it is obvious from his poetry. Son of an old noble family, but 'modern' enough to engage in sea-trade, a social and political reformer, but no revolutionary or ambitious tyrant, he was at the same time politician and patriot, poet and pamphleteer, a statesman of wisdom and moderation, driven by his sense of ethical duty, but granted the gift of practical action. A man of the middle line and therefore never a complete success, he yet ranked among the Seven Sages. He reduced the power of the noble clans and gave even the poorest citizens a share in the state; he laid the foundations of what was to become Athenian democracy. He abolished slavery for debt, and made life at least tolerable for the small peasants and the growing numbers of artisans and traders; thus he opened the way to the economic and cultural greatness of Athens. He produced a new code of law, and made it possible for a society that was in the process of being reshaped to be subjected to the rule of a state based on justice. It needed the enlightened absolutism of Peisistratus and the new democratic order of Cleisthenes to complete the work of Solon; but without him, the true glory of Athens, the full unity of state and culture would never have come into being.

It is almost ironical that Solon should have called his state *Eunomia*, the well-ordered community, and that his Spartan near-contemporary Tyrtaeus should have used the same word for his state; but the fact is significant. During the eighth to the sixth centuries Sparta, with all her special features, was one of the leading Greek states. While retaining some characteristics of the primitive community of warriors and conquerors, Sparta took part in the general Greek development and opened her doors to poets and artists. At that time Spartan life was free and rich. It was, of course, the state of the ruling people who had their land tilled by serfs, the Helots, and lived on their labour. When the number of citizens increased, new land was needed, and Sparta conquered the rich plains of Messenia and turned their inhabitants into helots. However, the two Messenian wars proved almost too much for the Spartiates; the songs of Tyrtaeus during the second war towards the end of the seventh century show that the vigour and the patriotism of the citizens were in need of being revived. It was then that Spartan society was gradually reshaped in a process of reform, called after the mythical lawgiver Lycurgus; Sparta became a rigid, well-disciplined community of soldiers, politically powerful and culturally dead. Athens and Sparta were both reshaped into a new order by the will of individual leaders under divine guidance; that is why they could both be called by the name of *eunomia*, although it meant different things. In the course of the next century Athenian *eunomia* changed into *isonomia*, an order based on equality, while Sparta's *eunomia* became the symbol of oligarchic rule and cultural barrenness. Sparta is not the only example in history of the fact that authoritarian states may be able to do heroic deeds, but are unable to create a lasting culture of their own.

At Marathon victory was due to the citizen hoplites of Athens, at Thermopylae Leonidas died with three hundred Spartiates and seven hundred men from Thespiae in Boeotia, the latter the greater heroes, as they were not subject to the severe law of Sparta; at Salamis the Greek navy was victorious, by far its largest contingent being Athenian; at Plataeae the Greek army under Spartan leadership defeated the Persians, and the Spartiates were bearing the brunt of the battle. In the West, at Himera, the Sicilian Greeks under their powerful tyrant Gelon conquered the Carthaginians who were acting in conformity with Persia. Greece had defended herself against the eastern empire – but was it Greece? Gelon had refused to help the motherland by asking for unacceptable conditions. Thebes, Argos, Thessaly, also Delphi, had remained neutral or even joined the enemy. They had no share in the victory, but they could enjoy its results, that is to say, they too were saved from the fate of the Asiatic Greeks to be ruled as part of a Persian province by satraps or obedient tyrants. The Greeks had won freedom, and it was the freedom of all the states in the motherland, and soon of those on the islands and in Asia Minor as well.

Freedom made possible the startling progress, the economic prosperity, the artistic grandeur of the following half century. That happened in many centres, but at Athens all the trends united most clearly. This was really to be the Athenian century. Head of an Aegean alliance, and thus the dominating leader of a large number of states; led by aristocrats such as Cimon and Pericles, yet building up the rule of the people; an economic centre where the goods of most of the known world traded, where the tributes of the allies were soon to accumulate; the place of the Dionysus festivals and therefore the home of tragedy and comedy; the city of Athena, the goddess of wisdom and craftsmanship. the city of homely piety, but also of passion, wit, and irony, of the growing secularization of thought, of the teaching of the Sophists who came to Athens from all parts of the Greek world; the city, finally, of Ictinus, Pheidias, Polygnotus. *ΕΛΛΑΣ ΕΛΛΑΔΟΣ ΑΘΗΝΑΙ.*

The freedom from any overruling power, and the freedom of each Polis, were in full contrast to the situation of the 'barbarians' who had

R

no freedom, neither political nor individual. Down to the end of the fifth century the Greeks had an almost undisturbed superiority complex towards all non-Greeks. It could only add to their feelings that most of their slaves were of barbarian origin. The institution of slavery came natural to the Greeks. It hardly ever was a serious problem, although the serfs in some states, such as the helots at Sparta, could become a real danger. The freedom of the Greek citizens, and everything it involved, could never have existed without the suppression of others. Moreover, the freedom of one Polis stood up to and against the freedom of every other Polis. These, as it were, innate obstacles to general freedom were largely responsible for the fact that the Greeks never reached political unity. Their ideas about barbarians and slaves, however, changed from the age of the Sophists. The decisive new idea was the contrast between *Nomos* and *Physis*, between Polis tradition, law, and custom on the one hand, human nature on the other. The idea could be differently understood; but the belief that some people were slaves by nature could eventually not last against the idea of at least a minority (though not of Aristotle) that all men were born free and equal.

The free Polis often followed up imperialist dreams, and in turn tried to suppress the autonomy of other Poleis. Again the Athenians were leading. In their 'empire', they treated independent allies with harshness, interfered with their local politics, and used their tribute not only for the war against Persia or its prevention but also for the embellishment of their own city. It was also Athens that mainly created the lasting and fateful dualism in the Greek world which ultimately led to internecine war and her own catastrophe. Even during the years of danger and defeat, however, even under banausic middle-class leaders, the Athenians never lost their vitality and creative power. The Erechtheion, artistically the richest, if not the most perfect, of the buildings on the Acropolis, was erected during the later years of the Peloponnesian War. That was also the time of Socrates' teaching; he suffered death for his loyalty to his Polis and the freedom of his thought, and it was the democratic politicians who accused him, and the people who killed him.

There were beautiful temples, prospering schools of sculpture, poets, and thinkers, at many other Greek centres, in Ionia, in the Peloponnese, in Italy. But with Athens as its centre, Greek civilization in the fifth and fourth centuries displayed a far-reaching unity, while at the same time it was rich, multifarious, and very much alive. Politically, the tendency among the larger states grew to deprive the smaller ones of their independence, while even in the most important states the citizens slowly began to lose interest in politics; the bourgeoisie began to concentrate on their private, mostly material aims, and left the running of political affairs to the professional orators. More and more Greeks served as mercenaries abroad, often with Spartan kings or Athenian strategi as their commanders, while the citizens' armies at home no longer found enough soldiers. The Polis was still to live for a long time, but its role changed in a changing world, and destruction or at least disorganization threatened from inside as well as from outside. Art, philosophy, literature, though increasingly matters of purely private concern or pure theory, were still flourishing; partly they even gained new strength and new forms of expression from the very changes in political consciousness and public spirit. It can be said that such different minds as Plato, Isocrates, and Menander, all in their different ways, reacted to the experience of the decline of Polis life.

Aristotle and Alexander finally shaped the world into something new. The personality of the universal genius burst the walls of the Polis, and in the Hellenistic world, state as well as civilization took on a new face. Aristotle, although as a political philosopher completely bound to the Polis, was no longer a *polites*; he belonged neither to Stagira where he was born, nor to Athens. He lived for many years at the courts of Hermias, an enlightened Asiatic ruler, or of the Macedonian king. With his philosophical school of the Peripatetics, which like all philosophy then could exist nowhere but at Athens, he became the great systematizer who led the human mind into the new world of scholarship and science, no longer tied to any frontiers. Alexander, on the other hand, with the unheard-of force of his will-to-power and his world-wide imagination, not only conquered the realm of the Persians but also destroyed the existing norms of Greek political concepts. He founded the first universal empire based on Europe, which when disrupted turned into the world of Hellenistic states, all of them territorial monarchies. He founded the first and greatest universal city, Alexandria. He made his Macedonians the ruling people of the world, and the Greeks the people to carry on the civilization of this world. Universalism, in its occidental shape, although mixed up with ideas of the East, was victorious, and it became the ancestor of the Imperium Romanum, and in the spiritual world one of the foundations of Christianity.

The old type of the Greek state, the Polis, was left with an essentially cultural task. Political action and political rule were now something to be dealt with by the large states and their kings, and they naturally dominated economic life as well. The Greeks, in their thousands leaving their impoverished homeland, were cast for a new though highly important role. They filled the posts of officials and officers in the new administrations and armies, they acted as merchants and artisans, as physicians and teachers, as artists and engineers, as colonists and farmers. They set their stamp on the society of the new states. Most of the Greeks gathered again in cities, either in the ancient Poleis of the Aegean and in Asia Minor, or in the new royal foundations deep into the East. Everywhere the old Polis institutions survived or were recreated, usually as a merely municipal structure; everywhere the Greek way of life was revived and preserved. There was instruction for the young, and the gymnasium was a social and cultural centre around which a closely knit community existed. There were non-Greeks as well who, on the basis of the common language of the *Koine*, were educated to be Greeks. The old Isocratean thesis was generally accepted that a Greek was a man who could speak and think in Greek, who shared the Greek way of life; he was Greek, regardless of his descent. The Gospel of St Mark (7, 26) speaks of a woman who was 'Greek, by descent ($\gamma \acute{\epsilon} \nu \epsilon \iota$) a Syro-Phoenician'. The educated became Greek, though not only they, and the Greeks, especially the philosophers, though not only they, became cosmopolitan. Many Greeks, above all those who had married foreign women, accepted a great deal from their eastern surroundings; nothing influenced them more than the gods and cults of the East, its beliefs and superstitions.

In the later centuries of the Hellenistic age and the earlier of the Roman empire the intermixture and fusion between East and West was the decisive general element; in that process the Greek Polis played an active part. With the geographical shifting of economy and culture, certain city-states, such as Rhodes and later Delos, were busy trade as well as cultural centres; the Rhodian school of sculpture held first place for a time. Rhodes was even a political power which could raise its voice, along with Pergamum, as a kind of buffer state between the Seleucid empire and Rome. Athens and Sparta made a few rather unfortunate attempts at displaying some political independence. Eventually, the latter was little more than a musuem of her own past, while Athens served as the city of philosophers and teachers of rhetoric, as the university, which transmitted the legacy of Greek thought and knowledge to the sons of the Roman upper classes.

The federal states in Greece, on the other hand, which for a time played an important part in inter-state politics and, above all, in the struggle against Rome, displayed little cultural activity of significance, though we must not forget the Achaean partisan Polybius. A few of the old cities in Asia Minor, for example Ephesus, without any say in politics, had a share in the general economic and cultural movements. Within the widespread mixture of Greeks and Orientals, the relations between Greeks and Jews deserve special mentioning. There is a danger of over-estimating their importance because of their historical role in the formation of Christianity. Influence was at first small and one-sided, from the Greeks upon the Jews; of the latter the upper classes were Hellenized. Influence the other way round cannot be denied, though Jewish and later Christian universalism largely grew from Greek roots. The attempt by Antiochus Epiphanes and a group of Hellenized Jews to turn Jerusalem into a Greek Polis failed completely. The new Jewish state, on the other hand, which had been started by the Maccabees, eventually – under Herod – became a Hellenistic monarchy.

Centres of real Hellenistic life and far-reaching influence were the capital cities of the large territorial states, such as Alexandria, Antioch, and Pergamum. In all these cities life was powerful, sometimes stormy. It is known in incidental features only, but they show that here was really new life. Manufacture and trade were flourishing, art expressed itself even in the small matters of life and worship, and at least at Alexandria and Antioch a mixture of peoples and races prevailed, among them strong and self-contained Jewish communities; thus the cities were the focus of many material and spiritual movements. Moreover, through the munificence and the vaingloriousness, sometimes even the real intellectual interest, of the kings, culture received patronage on a large scale; Alexandria was given the Museion and its famous library to become a centre of scholarship and science. In the latter field, great discoveries were made, though owing to the lack of technical knowledge, they remained unproved and unpractised for many centuries. We are used to speaking with some contempt of the learned Alexandrinians, especially the literary scholars, but whatever their shortcomings, they were the ancestors of all later scholarship and science, and the true predecessors of our universities. Learned poetry too, like that of Callimachus, grew on this soil. The mixed population was the bearer of an intense religious life which to some extent was protected and even fostered by the government; it displayed more clearly than anything else the union of East and West. In Pergamum, the most notable feature was the magnificent planning of the Acropolis with its terraces, temples, and palaces. The Great Altar with its frieze bears witness to the power and the skill of its Greek artists; in its baroque passion and intensity, the classical tradition is mixed up with a certain barbarization. The Pergamene kings were also patrons of scholarship; a great library was created, and the place of the Egyptian papyrus was taken here by the use of parchment which from the name of the city received its name for all times.

The capital cities were part of territorial empires. The question arises to what extent these monarchies outside their capitals influenced the civilization of the age. There is no simple answer to that question, but in a sense, the mere organization and administration of large territories was an act, indeed a continuous action, of civilizing. Progressive methods were introduced in almost all branches of professional activity. Trade was extended by the discovery of new and secure trade routes and of new raw materials; the Mediterranean world was in contact with Iran, India, and even China. An unavoidable part of economic activity was a much increased slave trade, in which Rome soon provided most of the buyers. The governments did much for promoting economic life; that meant partly, however, the exploitation of land and people for the advantage of the rulers and their officials. Whatever they spent on temples, libraries, agricultural, or military improvements, returned to them hundredfold in taxes and tributes; nowhere the system worked as effectively as in Ptolemaic Egypt. It could be a blessing for the population under a strong king and an incorruptible administration; but both were rare, and generally the Egyptian fellaheen, the peasants in Mesopotamia, the serfs of temples and dynasts in Asia Minor, gained little or nothing from the prosperity around them. The lower classes naturally tried to shun bureaucratic control or feudal mastery; wherever possible, they aimed at being incorporated into Polis territory. If they sometimes found help with the kings, who were acting in their own interest as well, that help more likely than not remained a theoretical expression of goodwill.

It can easily be understood that many people set their hopes increasingly on a reward in a better afterlife, as it was promised by most of the eastern religions. Neither the worship of the deified kings nor the ancient Greek deities could satisfy the needs of people who longed for personal contact with the divine world. Thus, Egyptian, Syrian, Asian gods entered the Greek Pantheon. They brought with them individual redemption through initiation in certain mysteries, ecstatic transformations and orgies, astrology, and all the other paraphernalia of such forms of worship. People flocked to join the new cults; with or without state help, these religions, some of them real church organizations, spread, making proselytes far and wide. The whole development, still strong during the first two centuries A.D., culminated in the expansion of Christianity. By then, the Hellenistic states had disappeared; the early church learned from the organization of the Roman empire.

The most important after-affects of Hellenistic civilization, whether on Christianity or Rome, were ultimately the work of the cities. It was in the urban centres of the Dispersion with their Greek and Jewish communities that Christianity changed from a Palestinian sect to a universal religion – as St Paul says: 'where there is neither Greek or Jew, barbarian, Scythian, bond or free'. As for Rome, the full force of Hellenization belonged to the second and first centuries B.C. Rome was Hellenized at the very time when she fought and destroyed, one by one, the Hellenistic kingdoms. Their influence was negligible, compared with the traditions preserved in the Greek cities. It was no longer the old Polis culture but a cosmopolitan Greek civilization, the Greece of the Stoics and Epicureans, but also of New Comedy, and always the Greece of Homer. It was the culture of the Hellenistic Polis, whether capital city or not; that is to say, of the heir to the ancient Greek state.

Abbreviations

AfP.	Archiv für Papyrusforschung
AHDO.	Archive d'histoire du droit oriental
AJA.	American Journal of Archaeology
AJhb.	Jahrbuch des deutschen archaeologischen Instituts
AJP.	American Journal of Philology
ASAI.	*Ancient Society and Institutions.* Studies presented to Victor Ehrenberg (1966)
ATL.	B. D. Meritt, H. T. Wade-Gery, and M. F. McGregor, *The Athenian Tribute Lists* (1934–53)
BCH.	Bulletin de correspondence hellénique
BICS.	Bulletin of the Institute of Classical Studies, London
BSA.	Annual of the British School at Athens
Chr.d'Ég.	Chronique d'Égypte
CIG.	Corpus Inscriptionum Graecarum
ClW.	Classical Weekly
CP.	Classical Philology
CQ.	Classical Quarterly
CR.	Classical Review
DLZ.	Deutsche Literatur-Zeitung
DSDA.	H. Bengtson, *Die Staatsverträge des Altertums* II (1962)
FGrH.	F. Jacoby, *Die Fragmente der griechischen Historiker*
GGA.	Göttingische Gelehrte Anzeigen
Harv.St.	Harvard Studies in Classical Philology
Herm.	Hermes
HThR.	Harvard Theological Review
HZ.	Historische Zeitschrift
IG.	Inscriptiones Graecae
JdS.	Journal des Savants
JEA.	Journal of Egyptian Archaeology
JHS.	Journal of Hellenic Studies
JRS.	Journal of Roman Studies
Kaibel	G. Kaibel, *Epigrammata Graeca ex lapidibus conlecta* (1878)
NGG.	Nachrichten der Göttinger Gesellschaft der Wissenschaften
NJhb.	Neue Jahrbücher
OGI.	Orientis Graecae Inscriptiones Selectae, ed. W. Dittenberger (1903–5)
ÖJh.	Jahreshefte des österreich. archaeologischen Instituts
P.	Papyrus

P. u. I.	Victor Ehrenberg, *Polis und Imperium* (1965)
Philol.	Philologus
PhW.	Philologische Wochenschrift
Proc.	Proceedings
PSI.	Papiri greci e latini (Pubbl. della Società Italiana)
RE.	Realencyclopädie der klassischen Altertumswissenschaft (Pauly-Wissowa)
REA.	Revue des études anciennes
REG.	Revue des études grecques
REJ.	Revue des études juives
Rfil.	Rivista di filologia e d'istruzione classica
Rhist.	Revue historique
RhM.	Rheinisches Museum
RHD.	Revue historique de droit français et étranger
RIDA.	Revue internationale des droits de l'antiquité
RPh.	Revue de philologie
Sav.-Ztschr.	Zeitschrift der Savigny-Stiftung für Rechtsgeschichte, romanistische Abteilung
SB.	Sitzungsberichte
SEG.	Supplementum Epigraphicum Graecum
SGDI.	Sammlung der griechischen Dialektinschriften (Collitz-Bechtel)
SlB.	Preisigke und Bilabel, Sammelbuch griechischer Urkunden
S. to S.	V. Ehrenberg, *From Solon to Socrates* (1968)
Syll.	Sylloge Inscriptionum Graecarum, ed. tertia, ed. W. Dittenberger (1915–24)
TAPA.	Transactions of the American Philological Association
Tod	M. N. Tod, *Greek Historical Inscriptions* I² 1946, II (1948)
UPZ.	Urkunden der Ptolemäerzeit, ed. U. Wilcken, Bd. I (1922–7)
Welles	C. B. Welles, *Royal Correspondence in the Hellenistic World* (1934
WSt.	Wiener Studien
ZfN.	Zeitschrift für Numismatik

Notes

I

Our sources for the knowledge of the Greek state are the same as for Greek history and Greek culture in general: literary and non-literary written sources and archaeological evidence. For constitutional history, the documents of public law are, of course, specially important; we read them occasionally in literature, but far more often in inscriptions. Coins too have the quality of official documents. In the last decades this primary material has vastly increased; here, apart from mere quantity, we grasp the life of the state in its immediate activities. For epigraphy in general see G. Klaffenbach, *Griech. Epigraphik* (1957). A. G. Woodhead, *The Study of Greek Inscriptions* (1959). About new epigraphical material and its historical implications, we get help, above all, from the reports of J. and L. Robert in *REG.*; publication year by year of new material is now found in *SEG*. The most important selections are mentioned in the list of abbreviations under *OGI.*, *Syll.*, and Tod. For coins, see B. V. Head, *Historia Nummorum* (1911²) (HN²), and separate publications such as the Catalogues of the British Museum (*BMC.*).

These documents are the more important because Greek writers very seldom discuss the real form and content of state activity. Scientific investigation of the state began with Aristotle, who produced descriptions of 158 states, that served him and his school as a material for theoretical discussion. The only one that survives is the 'Αθηναίων πολιτεία, known since 1891 from a papyrus in London. The doubts about Aristotle's authorship, often expressed and recently revived by C. Hignett, *A History of the Athenian Constitution* (1952), can scarcely be justified; cf., e.g., J. Day and M. Chambers, *Aristotle's History of Athenian Democracy* (1962), also J. H. Schreiner, *Aristotle and Perikles* (1968) (of wider relevance than the title suggests). Despite the difference of its scientific level from the *Politics*, the work must be assigned at least to the school of Aristotle in his lifetime, and cannot be taken out of the literature over which he had personal supervision; it was probably published after his death (cf. Hommel, *Festschrift f. F. Zucker* [1954], 195). The book must certainly still be quoted under his name. It displays weaknesses which do not allow us to assess its historical worth – great as it is – as high as did such an outstanding scholar as U. v. Wilamowitz-Moellendorf in his fundamental work *Aristoteles und Athen* (1893). The 'Αθηναίων πολιτεία (*Ath. pol.*), which shows the unmistakable influence of oligarchic views, but also many inconsistencies (perhaps on account of

different sources), is divided into two parts, unconnected but set side by side, a
history of the constitution and a systematic survey of the various elements in the
state at the time of Aristotle. Presumably, the other πολιτεῖαι of Aristotle were
arranged after a similar scheme. Both forms of treatment will have had their
predecessors, especially local historians like the writers of the *Atthides*; on
them, cf. F. Jacoby, *Atthis* (1949); FGrH. III B and b, Suppl. I. II (1950–4).
Jacoby has set our source criticism of Athenian constitutional history on a new
basis and given us a problem which in many ways is like that of the Roman
annalists. Aristotle further used collections of laws, sketches of constitutions, and
probably summaries for practical use, such as we know from the Alexandrian
Dikaiomata. Besides all this, the writings of the political philosophers are of
special significance, though they always envisaged the problems of the state
from the point of view of the ideal, of the 'best' state. This led to a very intensive
occupation with constitutional questions, and the idea of a written constitution
played a great part, for instance, in the constitutional struggles at Athens
towards the close of the fifth century B.C. Such a constitution, whether it
remained pure theory or not, was no organic growth and not a reproduction
of real conditions, but a scheme into which the Polis might develop. To such
theoretical writings as survive belong Xenophon's Λακεδαιμονίων πολιτεία
– though that goes half-way to considering the state as it really was – and, as a
kind of contrast, the oligarchic pamphlet, the pseudo-Xenophontic 'Αθηναίων
πολιτεία, the 'Old Oligarch'. In this class fall, above all, the political writings
of the philosophers, first the Sophists, then Plato and Aristotle. Not only are
they important sources for our knowledge of the Greek state as it really was, but
they could reveal the idea of the state even more clearly than it can be traced in
the evidence of the real facts. On the other hand, these works are philosophy and
not history; that is also true of Aristotle's *Politics*; cf. R. Weil, *Aristotle et
l'histoire* (1960). Philosophic interest equally explains the many books from the
Hellenistic age περὶ πολιτείας or περὶ νόμων, of which we have a fragment
here and there, but usually only know author and title. The prominence of
Sparta in this literature as the creation of 'Lycurgus' only proves that the theme
was the ideal state. Much of this literature has found an echo in later authors,
especially Plutarch. For the rest, the erudition of the Peripatetics and the
Alexandrians was brought through channels, mostly untraceable for us, into the
scholia and lexicons of late antiquity; though frequently thinned down and
excerpted, they have still much to teach us.

2

On the development of modern research into the Greek state, good general
surveys may be found in most of the textbooks. Apart from that, cf. A. J.
Neumann, *Entwicklung und Aufgaben der alten Geschichte* (1910), and H. Bengtson, *Einführung in die alte Geschichte* (1959³).

Modern scholarly study of Greek 'Political Antiquities' goes back to the seventeenth century (Ubbo Emmius). This earlier period was marked by a number of learned works which devoted themselves to the collection of anti-quarian material but are barely readable. Later, true research into the Greek state went hand in hand with the first Greek histories which deserve that name; they belong to the last decades of the eighteenth century. Research, then, in our field drew its strength partly from the beginnings of critical classical scholarship (F. A. Wolf), partly from the swifter advances in the fields of Roman history and the Roman state (Montesquieu, Gibbon, Niebuhr). It was A. Boeckh (1785–1867) whom we may justly regard as the real founder of the study of Greek political institutions, for his *Staatshaushaltung der Athener* (1817, 1886³) and the *CIG*. (from 1825). His penetration into the real factors of public life, and his opening-up of new sources, have decisively influenced later research on our subject.

A special position must be reserved for K. O. Müller's brilliant attempt to show that the Greek state was a product of the history of the Greek tribes: *Geschichten hellenischer Stämme und Städte*. I. *Orchomenos und die Minyer* (1820), II. *Die Dorier* (1824; 1844²). Following him, tribal differences have sometimes been over-emphasized as, for example, by H. Berve, *Griech. Geschichte* (1951–3²); they have been exploited by racial doctrines that have nothing to do with scholarship and, in fact, contradict it; against them see E. Will, *Doriens et Ioniens* (1956). At the same time, the antiquarian approach went on. New material, as it grew, was collected, and a whole series of learned textbooks came into being; they are now very much out of date.

Under the leadership of Mommsen, and later of Wilamowitz, the study of antiquity leapt forward. The publication of *IG*. began in 1873; Grote first, and then above all Ed. Meyer and Beloch, published works on Greek history that got beyond the aesthetic classicism of E. Curtius; the *Römisches Staatsrecht* of Mommsen appeared; the Ἀθηναίων πολιτεία of Aristotle was discovered. All this led to an advance and deepening of our knowledge of the Greek state. There are many monographs which will mostly be cited in their proper places, but there are a few other works in which antiquarian research finds its culmina-tion and at the same time becomes something more. B. Keil, *Griech. Staatsalter-tümer*, in the first and second editions of A. Gercke and E. Norden, *Einleitung in die Altertumswissenschaft* (1914²) is an admirable work, rather overcrowded with detail, but acute, constructive, and directed towards a discussion of public law. H. Swoboda has a very good historical treatment of the general development and of the federal states (1913) in K. F. Herrmann's *Lehrbuch der griech. Staatsalter-thümer* (I 3). Finally, there is G. Busolt, *Griech. Staatskunde* I. II (1920–6, com-pleted by H. Swoboda) with masses of material and at least partly deeper historical insight. Beside these works of a wide scope, we may place H. Fran-cotte, *La Polis grecque* (1907), a number of useful essays, bundled together rather unorganically. The works of Keil, Swoboda, and Busolt-Swoboda are suitable to serve as the basis for further detailed research; they contain ample references to sources and literature. In the last decades much work has been done on single questions, to which reference will be made as needed; no comprehensive work on the subject has appeared. A useful, if uneven, survey which includes the Hellenistic age, is *The Greek Political Experience* (*Studies in honour of W. K. Prentice*) (1941) [by a number of authors]. The book of Hignett quoted above has its interest as an attempt at a detailed constitutional history of Athens; it is often brilliant, but he is over-critical of the sources and the views of others, and not critical enough of his own hypotheses; cf. also Berve, *Gnomon* (1955), 225. G. de Sanctis, *ATΘIΣ*, *Storia della repubblica ateniese* (1912²) is still the best critical constitutional history of Athens; but see what I have said above about Jacoby. A short sound survey: A. Aymard, *Les cités grecques à l'époque classique. Rec. soc. J. Bodin* VI (1954), VII (1955) (= *Études d'histoire ancienne* [1967], 273, 285).

Away from antiquarian research, we have U. v. Wilamowitz-Moellendorf's *Staat und Gesellschaft der Griechen.* (*Kultur der Gegenwart* II 4, 1923²), on the grand scale and full of insight, though rather unsystematic; also A. Zimmern's very lively picture of the politics and economy of Athens in *The Greek Commonwealth* (1931⁵). On the first edition of the present book (in Gercke-Norden, *Einleitung in die Altertumswissenschaft*³ III, 1932) and its place in scholarship, see F. Heichelheim, *Griech. Staatskunde* 1902–32 (*Bursians Jahresberichte* 250, Suppl. 1935). In addition, we refer to recent works on Greek history; G. Glotz, *Histoire grecque* I–IV 1 (1925–38); G. de Sanctis, *Storia dei Greci* (1939); J. B. Bury, *A History of Greece* (third edition by R. Meiggs, 1951); A. Aymard, *L'Orient et la Grèce* (1953); F. Taeger, *Das Altertum* I (1958⁶); H. Bengtson, *Griech. Geschichte* (1969⁴); F. Schachermeyr, *Griech. Geschichte* (1961) ('kulturmorphologisch'). – Economic history: F. M. Heichelheim, *An Ancient Economic History*, vols I, II (1961–4). A good special study: A. French, *The Growth of Athenian Economy* (1964).

Along a path, separate from the track of critical scholarship, moves Fustel de Coulanges, *La cité antique* (1864; many editions) [in substance and in method fanciful, but a great concept, showing a deep realization of the importance of religion and of kinship groups for the state]. Jacob Burckhardt's picture of the Polis in the first volume of his *Griech. Kulturgeschichte*, is also off the track of strict scholarship. His conception of the Polis as an all-powerful instrument of compulsion (*città dolente*) was strongly influenced by contemporary philosophy, and lastly by the political ideals of the ancient philosophers. The sources are handled uncritically, and yet the work is of great importance because it views Greek life and spirit really as a whole. Important especially as an advance of modern French scholarship beyond Fustel de Coulanges, though at the same time a considerable independent achievement is: G. Glotz, *La cité grecque* (1928, reprint with brief appendix of little value, 1954) (in English: *The Greek City* 1930); cf. Ehrenberg, *Gnomon* 1929, 1. A critical continuation of Burckhardt's views, with a penetrating picture of the Polis in general, is contained in

J. Kaerst, *Gesch. des Hellenismus* I (1927³); an idealizing account without evidence, but correctly emphasizing some important features, is given by B. Knauss, *Staat und Mensch in Hellas* (1940, reprint 1949). Of some interest are the discussions at the *IX Congrès internat. des sciences historiques* 1950 (I 261; 325; 385; II 119; 153; 179).

Most of the books we have quoted may be regarded as attempts to deepen our historical knowledge of the Greek state. The path of legal systematization, as Mommsen had indicated for Rome, could hardly be applied to the Greeks; still, it was taken by U. Kahrstedt, *Griech. Staatsrecht* I: *Sparta und seine Symmachie* (1922); but cf. Ehrenberg, *Hermes* 59 (1924), 60 (=*P. u. I.* 192). The work was carried on in sections: *Staatsgebiet und Staatsangehörige in Athen* (1934); *Untersuchungen zur Magistratur in Athen* (1936); for a criticism, see Ferguson, *AJP.* 1938, 229. If we ask whether there ever was one kind of Greek constitutional law, the answer is, of course, in the negative. No scholar so far has tried to write a Greek constitutional history, though attempts have been made to take the ancient state, in both its Greek and its Roman form, as the same constitutional type, for example in the survey of 'Constitution and Administration' by L. Wenger in *Kultur der Gegenwart* II 2 (1910), and A. Rosenberg, *RE.* I A, s.v. *Res publica*; both writers hardly touch the problem of the difference between Greek and Roman legal thought. Finally, I refer to two outstanding critical reviews of the German edition of this book, one by H. Schaefer, *Sav. Ztschr.* 1960, 422 (= *Probleme d. alten Gesch.* 384), the other by D. Nörr, *Der Staat* 5 (1966), 353.

3

In dealing with the special literature, I shall confine myself mainly to mentioning important writings, and only now and then discuss their problems. I make no attempt at completeness, nor have I always indicated where I do not share the view of the author concerned. For the Introduction, cf. F. Schachermeyr, *Diogenes* I (1954), 435. On the 'ideal type', see the clear and judicious book by H.-I. Marrou, *De la connaissance historique* (1955²), especially ch. 6, also A. Heuss, *Zur Theorie der Weltgeschichte* (1968), 64 – I have tried to defend the view that the Polis is the essential form of the Greek state in 'Von den Grundformen griechischer Staatsordnung' (*SB. Heidelbg. Ak.* 1961 (=*P. u. I.* 105), in parts opposed by F. Gschnitzer, *Sav. Ztschr.* 80 (1963), 400.

Chapter One

SECTION I (p. 3). Geography and history: J. L. Myres, *Geographical History in Greek Lands* (1953). [On pp. 114 ff. there are several maps, showing Greece as the centre. Myres's assumption that the Adriatic Sea was not colonized is refuted by Gitti, *La Parola del Passato*, 1952, 161.] M. Cary, *The Geographical Background*

of Greek and Roman History (1949), good general survey. – Mediterranean and
Aegean: A. Philippson, *Das Mittelmeergebiet* (1922⁴). *Land und See der Griechen*
(1947). O. Maull, *Das griech. Mittelmeergebiet* (1922). On the Greeks and their
relation to the sea: A. Lesky, *Thalatta* (1947). For the geography of Greece, cf.
the posthumous work by A. Philippson, *Die griechischen Landschaften*, with
important 'Beiträgen zur historischen Landeskunde' by E. Kirsten I–IV (1947–
59). Kirsten, *Die griechische Polis als historisch-geographisches Problem des Mittel-
meerraums* (1956); for criticism, cf. *JHS*. 1958, 155. To Kirsten (pp. 43, 48) I
owe the two forms of Polis settlement mentioned in the text. – Summaries by
and for non-specialists: F. Bölte, *Grundlinien altgriechischer Landeskunde. Jahrb.
d. Freien Deutschen Hochstifts Frankfurt*, 1910. Ehrenberg, *Griech. Land und griech.
Staat. Die Antike*, 1927 (=*P. u. I.* 63), in English: *Aspects of the Ancient World*
(1946), ch. 3. – Colonization: in general: A. Gwynn, *JHS*. 1918, 88. H. Schaefer,
Hdlbg. Jahrbücher 1960, 77 = *Probl. d. alt. Gesch.*, 362. A. J. Graham, *Colony and
Mother City in Ancient Greece* (1964). West: Blakeway, *BSA*. 1932–3. *JRS*.
1935, 129. T. J. Dunbabin, *The Western Greeks* (1948). East: F. Bilabel, *Die ion.
Kolonisation* (*Philol.* Suppl. XIV, 1920). M. B. Sakellariou, *La migration grecque
en Ionie* (1958); cf. Picard, *JdS*. 1959, 49. C. Roebuck, *Ionian Trade and Colonisa-
tion* (1959). H. Gallet de Santerre, *REA*. 1962, 20. Black Sea: Graham, *BICS*.
1958, 25. Danoff, *RE*. Suppl. IX 866, esp. 1046 ff. Atlas: H. Bengtson and
V. Milojčić, *Grosser historischer Weltatlas* I (1954²). Westermann's *Atlas zur
Weltgeschichte* I (1956).

SECTION 2 (p. 7). Research into the problems of the Greek migrations, which
are indissolubly connected with those of Crete, the Aegean, and Asia Minor, is
slowly reaching agreement on a few points; but much remains quite uncertain.
The second view mentioned in the text is expressed by J. Chadwick, *Cambr. Anc.
Hist.* (revised edition), vol. 2, ch. 39. The decipherment of Linear B has produced many new problems; the amount of literature is enormous. I refer to
the reports by Schachermeyr in *Anzeiger f. d. Altertumswissensch.*, the news-
sheets *Nestor*, edited by E. L. Bennett, and the *Minutes* of the Mycenaean
Seminar, London Inst. of Classical Studies. – For the general importance of the
eighth century, cf. W. Schadewaldt, *Von Homers Welt und Werk* (1959³), and
my *S. to S.* 8. – Origin of the Polis: Ehrenberg, *JHS*. 1937, 147 (=*P. u. I.* 83).
Kirsten (see I 1), p. 100, has maps, showing the connection between the dispersion of the Polis and Mycenaean settlements. As early as the seventh century
B.C. there were precursors of the later rectangular scheme of town planning,
above all in Sicily; cf. R. Martin, *L'urbanisme dans la Grèce antique* (1956), esp.
pp. 82 ff. A city of early Ionia seems to some extent to have been recovered by
the excavation of Smyrna (*c.* 700 B.C.); cf. Cook and Nicholls, *BSA*. LIII
(1958). Some deeper truth may be reflected in Christopher Dawson's statement
(*Dynamics of World History*, 1957, 152): 'The city state . . . owed its existence to
the marriage of the oriental sacred city with the Indo-European warrior tribe.' –
Primitive tribal organization: Nilsson, *Klio* 1912, 308. G. Thomson, *Studies in*

Anc. Greek Society I (1954²). R. F. Willets, *Aristocratic Society in Anc. Crete* (1955). Cf. also Finley (see I 4) and section 5. The πάτρα is perhaps to be recognized, in early inscriptions from Thasos and Paros, in the τοῦ δεῖνα παῖδες; cf. Pouilloux, *BCH.* 1955, 75. It is possible that the φρατέρες never were real brothers, rather sons of one whole generation of 'fathers', the words being understood in the meaning of the 'classificatory system'. Among classical scholars it is in particular G. Thomson who has worked with such anthropological concepts. – On the clan cf. the 'Salaminioi': Ferguson, *Hesperia* 1938, 1. Nilsson, *AJP.* 1938, 385. Guarducci, *Rfil.* 1948, 223. Jacoby, *FGrH.* 328 F 14–16. – *Hetairiai*: Code of Gortyn X 38, cf. Willets, *The Law Code of Gortyn* (*Kadmos*, Suppl. 1) (1967). – Phratries: *Syll.* 921. *IG*², II 2, 2343 ff. M. Guarducci, *Mem. Acc. dei Lincei*, Ser. VI, vol. 6 (1937); 8 (1938). Seyfarth, *Aegyptus*, 1955, 3. Andrewes, *Herm.* 1961, 139. *JHS.* 1961, 1. N. G. L. Hammond, *JHS.* 1961, 76. *S. to S.* 52 f. – Rhodes: Hiller v. Gaertringen, *GGA.* 1934, 195. – Phylae: E. Szanto, *Ausgewählte Abhdlgn.* (1906), 216 [a basic study, despite some over-rationalistic explanations]. Latte, *RE.* XX 994. – Fifth Athenian phyle: W. K. Pritchett, *The Five Attic Tribes after Cleisthenes* (1943). – Erythrae: Larsen, *Repres. Govt.* (see III 4), 496. – On kingship in early Greece: M. P. Nilsson, *Das homerische Königtum. SB. Berl. Ak.* 1927. G. Jachmann, *Maia* 1953, 241. F. E. Adcock, *Greek and Macedonian Kingship* (*Proc. Brit. Acad.* 1954). P. Oliva, *Graecolatina Pragensia* II (Festschrift, G. Thomson) (1963), 171. Some revision of our ideas of Homeric kingship will be necessary on account of the documents in Linear script B; but research on these matters is still quite fluid. Cf. T. B. L. Webster, *From Mycenae to Homer* (1958) [imaginative, but over-bold]. – Tyranny and Oriental kingship: Gallavotti, *Parola del Passato* 1949, 69. – For the division of land and the distinction between common pasture land and private fields, cf. the Locrian law of settlement: Wilamowitz, *SB. Berl. Ak.* 1927.

SECTION 3 (p. 14). The three groups of Olympian, chthonic, and Polis gods appear in Plato, *Laws* 717a. – The connections between religion and state are usually not discussed in works on history of religion, but cf. Nilsson, *Cults*, etc. (see section 2). Further, see Nilsson, *Geschichte d. griech. Religion* (I² 1955, II² 1962). W. K. C. Guthrie, *The Greeks and their Gods* (1950). – On the relations to the Mycenaean age, important for the Polis cult, see: M. P. Nilsson, *The Minoan-Mycenaean Religion and its Survival in Greek Religion* (1950²). Lehmann-Hartleben, *Die Antike* 1931; 1932. – Zeus in Sparta: Schaefer, *X Congresso internat. d. scienze stor.* VI 693.

SECTION 4 (p. 17). On aristocratic civilization: M. I. Finley, *The World of Odysseus* (1956). *Historia* 1957, 133. – Aristocracy and colonization: Schaefer (see I 1). – Noblemen and state: Hoffman, *Festschrift B. Snell* (1956), 153. – On the change from the state of the aristocracy to the Polis in Athens: G. de Sanctis, *Atthis* (1912), chs 4–8. Ehrenberg, *Neugründer des Staates* (1925), ch. 2. – For the interesting conditions in Thessaly, cf. Kahrstedt, *NGG.* 1924. Momigliano, *Athenaeum* 1932, 47. Gschnitzer, *Herm.* 1954, 451, also see below, III 4. – Sparta:

S

de Sanctis, *Rfil.* 1932, 425. H. Michell, *Sparta* (1952). F. Kiechle, *Lakonien und Sparta* (1963); cf. Ehrenberg and Neumann, *Gnomon* 1964, 604. *S. to S.*, ch. 2. The decline of the tribal kingship is very clearly indicated in what Thucydides (II 80) reports of the Epirote tribes. Molossian dyarchy inside the royal family: Accame, *Rfil.* 1934, 522. – On social and economic history in general: M. Weber, *Ges. Aufsätze* (1924) [important, though partly out of date]. J. Hasebroek, *Trade and Politics in Ancient Greece* (1933) and *Griech. Wirtschafts- und Gesellschaftsgesch. bis zur Perserzeit* (1931) [simplifies too much, but gets rid of the tendency to modernize]. F. Heichelheim, see above, p. 258. – On orgeones, etc.: Guarducci, *Rfil.* 1935, 332. Ferguson and Nock, *HThR.* 1944, 61, 141; Ferguson, *Hesperia*, Suppl. VIII (1949), 130. Jacoby, *FGrH.* 328 F 35. Andrewes, *JHS.* 1961, 1.

SECTION 5 (p. 22). Gschnitzer, *WSt.* 1955, 210. Cf. also H. Swoboda, *RE* Suppl. IV 950. – For the early history of the more important Poleis, cf. A. R. Burn, *The World of Hesiod* (1936), ch. 6. F. Sartori, *Problemi di storia costiz. italiota* (1953). – Halicarnassus and Salmacis: Gschnitzer, *RhM.* 1961, 237. – Synoecism of Rhodes: Pugliesi-Carratelli, *Studi Class. e oriental.* 1951, 77. – *synoikia* for *synoikismos*: *DSDA.* II, no. 297 (cf. Gschnitzer, *Anz. f. d. Altertumswiss.* 1965, 73). – Concept of Polis: *P. u. I.* 105, also Schaefer, *Historia* 1961, 387 (= *Probl.* 428).

Chapter Two

SECTION 1a (p. 26). In general: E. Kornemann, *Stadtstaat u. Flächenstaat, NJhb.* 1908. – F. Hampl, *Klio* 1939, 1, has drawn a sharp distinction between the state territory and the land of the citizens, and speaks of 'Poleis without territory'. I believe this is the result of an exaggeratedly legal point of view which does not fit Greek conditions; cf. also Bengtson, *SB. Bayr. Ak.* 1939, 65. Recently F. Gschnitzer, *Abhängige Orte im griech. Altertum* (*Zetemata* XVII, 1958) has made a stronger case of Hampl's theory. He has pointed to relations not sufficiently taken into consideration; but even he sometimes regards as a question of law what really is one of power; cf. Habicht, *Gnomon* 1959, 704, and *P. u. I.* 105. – Peraea: P. M. Fraser and G. E. Bean, *The Rhodian Peraea* (1954). – Basic for determination of areas, though in need of correction: J. Beloch, *Die Bevölkerung der griech.-röm. Welt* (1886); cf. also H. Hommel, *Philol.* 1958, 84. – Naucraries: A. Ledl, *Studien z. älteren athen. Verfassungsgesch.* (1914), 393; a different view in J. Hasebroek, *Wirtsch.- u. Ges.gesch.* 56. Cf. Hommel, *RE.* XVI 1941. Jacoby, *FGrH.* 323 F 8. Wüst, *Historia* 1957, 176 (Prytans = Archons?). – Old trittyes: Ferguson, *Class. Studies presented to E. Capps* (1936), 151. Hommel, *RE.* VII A, 330. Jacoby, *FGrH.* 328 F 94. Wüst, *op. cit.* 182. – Interesting discussion of the three Attic 'parties': R. J. Hopper, *BSA.* 56 (1961), 189. – The trittyes and demes of Cleisthenes: Hommel, *Klio* 1940, 181. Bradeen, *TAPA.* 1955, 22. Important recently: D. M. Lewis, *Historia* 1963, 22. W. E. Thompson, *Historia* 1966, 1. C. W. J. Eliot, *The Coastal Demes of Attica*, *Phoenix*, Suppl. 5 (1962). *Phoenix* 1967, 79. 1968, 3. – *Κτοῖναι* in Rhodes: *Syll.* 339. Momigliano, *Rfil.* 1936, 57. Pugliese-Caratelli (s. I 5). – Obae in Sparta: Ehrenberg, *RE*. XVII 1693. Wade-Gery, *CQ*. 1944, 16 (= *Essays in Greek History* [1958], 75). W. den Boer, *Laconian Studies* (1954), 171. – Alexandria: Seyfarth (see I 2).

SECTION I b (p. 30). Figures of population: Beloch, *Bevölkerung* (see I a). *Griech. Gesch.*² III 1, 263. Higher figures in Ed. Meyer, *Forschungen* II 149. A. W. Gomme, *The Population of Athens* etc. (1933), also Finkelstein, *ClW*. 1935, 87; 161. Gomme, *JHS*. 1946, 127. Jacoby, *FGrH*. 328 F 119; E. Kirsten, *Raum und Bevölkerung in der Weltgeschichte* I (1956), 186. The difficulties of all attempts at tracing the figures of population have been well stressed by A. H. M. Jones, *Athenian Democracy* (1957), ch. 4 and Appendix. In comparison to the figures given in the text, he believes in a far greater increase of population between the Persian and the Peloponnesian Wars, at the same time in a much smaller number of slaves; cf. Gomme, *JHS*. 1959, 61. – πόλις μυρίανδρος: Ehrenberg, *RE*. XVI 1097. Schaefer, *Historia* 1961, 292 = *Probleme d. alt. Gesch.*, 401. – Ziehen, *Herm.* 1933, 218 [Earthquake and Spartan decline of the birthrate]. – There is plenty of literature on the various groups of the population. See in general: Ehrenberg, *The People of Aristophanes* (1962³), chs 3–6. – Slavery: Ed. Meyer, *Die Sklaverei im Altertum* (= *Kl. Schriften* I 171). W. L. Westermann, *RE*. Suppl. VI 894. *Slave Systems of Greeks and Romans* (1955); cf. de Ste Croix, *CR*. 1957, 54 [Slaves in Attica in 431 B.C. assessed at only 60–80,000; a similar result in Jones, op. cit., ch. 1]. Lauffer, *Abh. Ak. Mainz*, 1955; 1957 [slaves in Laurion mines]. *Gymnasium*, 1961, 370. M. I. Finley (ed.), *Slavery in Class. Antiquity* (1960), also Heichelheim, *Gnomon* 1960, 133. Chios: A. Fuks, *Athenaeum* 1968, 102. Slaves and serfs: D. Lotze, Μεταξὺ ἐλευθέρων καὶ δούλων (1959) (excellent, though his expression 'Kollektivsklaverei' is hardly helpful); cf. Wolff, *Sav. Ztschr.* 1960, 438. Beringer, *Gnomon* 1960, 452. M. I. Finley, *Comparative Studies in Society and History* VI 1964, 233. The view that various intermediate stages existed both of freedom and of the lack of it, and that the Greeks never devised a systematic scheme for them, is shared by Finley, *RIDA*. 1960, 45 (important his stress on παραμονή, that is, temporary slavery). F. Gschnitzer, *Abh. Ak. Mainz* 1963. – Slaves at Argos, sometimes acting as masters: Kiechle, *Philol.* 1960, 181. – Sparta: Ehrenberg, *Herm.* 1924, 39 = *P. u. I.* 161. F. Bölte, *RE*. III A, 1303. Larsen, *RE*. XIX 816. A critical survey of modern views on the helots, written from a Marxist point of view: P. Oliva, *Historica* III (Prague 1961), also *Acta Antiqua Philippopolitica* 1963 (in general following Lotze's line of thought). – Crete: H. van Effenterre, *La Crète et le monde grecque* (1948). R. F. Willets, *Cretan Cults and Festivals* (1962), esp. ch. 1, also ΓΕΡΑΣ, *Studies pres. to G. Thomson* (1963), 25. Beringer, *Historia* 1964, 11. – Perioeci: in general Larsen *l.c.* Hampl, *Herm.* 1937, 1. Parke, *Hermathena* 1931, 31 (harmosts in Laconia). Momigliano, *Athenaeum* 1934, 255.

Gschnitzer, *Abhängige Orte*, 141. Aymard, *Etudes d'hist. anc.* (1967), 300. – Proxeny decree for Lacedaemonian perioecus: Charneux, *BCH*. 1953, 395; cf. also *FGrH*. 324 F 49. Perioeci in Crete: Larsen, *CP*. 1936, 11. Guarducci, *Rfil*. 1936, 356. Elis: Kiechle, *RhM*. 1960, 336 (linguistic arguments). – Athens: de Sanctis, *Atthis* 127; 195. Hommel, *RE*. XV 1413. Finley, *Studies in Land and Credit* (1951), 76. Hectemorri: Lotze, *Philol*. 1958, 1. *S. to S*. 57. Servitude for debts generally: Finley, *RHD*. 1965, 11. – Paroeci: Pouilloux, *BCH* 1946, 488. SECTION 2 a (p. 38). 'Politeia' cannot be translated; it had several meanings. In the passage from Plutarch, quoted in the text, a different meaning of *politeia* is mentioned as βίος ἀνδρὸς πολιτικοῦ. – At least from the second century A.D. πόλις and πολιτεία can indicate town and municipal district respectively; cf. F. Papazoglou, *REG*. 1959, 100. Fundamental for citizenship: E. Szanto, *Griech. Bürgerrecht* (1892). – Agoge and age groups at Sparta: Marrou, *REA*. 1946, 216. Billheimer, *TAPA*. 1947, 99. K. M. T. Chrimes, *Ancient Sparta* (1949), 84; 205. *mothakes, nothoi, trophimoi*: Ehrenberg, *RE*. XVI 382; 385. VII A, 675. Lotze, *Historia* 1962, 427. – Neodamodeis: Ehrenberg, *RE*. XVI 2396. Willets, *CP*. 1954, 27. – Cleisthenes' new citizens: against Oliva, *Historia* 1960, 503, see Kagan, *Historia* 1963, 41. – Rhodes: Pugliese-Carratelli, *Studi in onore di Arangio-Ruiz* IV 485. – Cretan mercenaries as citizens of Miletus: M. Launey, *Recherches sur les armées hellenist*. II (1950), 660; 680. – γραφαὶ ξενίας: the officials in question seem to have been in the first place the ξενοδίκαι, later the ναυτοδίκαι; cf. Körte, *Herm*. 1933, 238. – διαψηφισμός: Jacoby, *FGrH*. 324 F 52; 328 F 119. Welwei, *Gymnasium* 1967, 423. – Oath of the Ephebi: L. Robert, *Études épigr. et philol.* (1938), 296. – Atimia: E. Weiss, *Griech. Privatrecht* I (1923), 165. – Aristotle's narrowing down of citizenship to the fully privileged citizens, which Szanto takes over from him, has lately been refuted by documents as, for example, the constitution of Cyrene (*SEG*. IX 1); cf. Taeger, *Herm*. 1929, 440.

SECTION 2 b (p. 43). The clear recognition that oligarchy and democracy are only variants of the same type of state, and that that state is characterized by the 'sovereignty' of the citizens with full rights, is due to Wilamowitz. Cf. also Rosenberg, *RE*. I A 650. The arguments brought against this view prove that there was no rigid principle, but qualifications only confirm the essential aspect. – Origin of the word δημοκρατία: Ehrenberg, *Historia* I (1950–2), 515 [with further literature; the early date there assumed for Aeschylus' *Suppliants* has been put in question by a *didaskalia* in an Oxyrhynchus papyrus; cf. Lesky, *Herm*. 1954, 10. Turner, *CR*. 1954, 21. Ehrenberg, *Sophokles und Perikles* (1956), 4, 2. – On (iso)nomia, (olig)archia, (demo)kratia, see Chr. Meier, 'Discordia concors', *Festschrift E. Bonjour* (1968), 3. – Office of βασιλεύς, for example, in Mantinea: Waisglass, *AJP*. 1956, 167. – The question of the origin of the double kingship in Sparta is still unanswered, in spite of the bold hypotheses of Giarrizzo, *Parola del Passato* 1950, 192. – Archilochus: Gallavotti, *Parola del Passato* 1949, 69; 130. – On tyranny in general, besides Burckhardt's impressive description in his *Griech. Kulturgeschichte*, vol. 1. Berve, *HZ.* 177 (1954), 1, and recently a comprehensive survey *Die Tyrannis bei den Griechen* (1967); cf. Gnomon 1969. Also: A. Andrewes, *The Greek Tyrants* (1956). P. N. Ure, *The Origin of Tyranny* (1922) [excellent on archaeological evidence; but in turning the tyrants into big businessmen, he gives a one-sided and too modernizing picture]. Laws against tyranny: cf. *OGI.* 218 (on this, cf. Wilhelm, *Symb. Osloenses* 1949, 28); as to Athens: Meritt, *Hesperia* 1952, 355. Ostwald, *TAPA.* 1955, 103. – Athenian democracy: A. H. M. Jones (see II 1 b) [reprint of earlier articles; additional ch. 5: 'How did the Athenian democracy work?']. – Great Rhetra: new theories with discussion of many earlier writers, e.g. in Hammond, *JHS.* 1950, 42. Tsopanakis, Ἑλληνικά, παρατ. 6 (1954). W. den Boer (see II 1 a), 153; J. H. Oliver, *Demokratia, the Gods, and the Free World* (1960). Butler, *Historia* 1962, 385. *S. to S.* 32. – Constitution of the 5000: de Ste Croix, *Historia* 1956, 1. – Hetaeriae: F. Sartori, *Le eterie nella vita politica ateniese del VI e V secolo A.C.* (1957); but cf. Raubitschek, *AJP.* 1959, 81. – Codification at Athens: S. Dow, (provisionally) *Proc. Massach. Hist. Soc.* 71 (1953–7). – On law, equality and freedom, Eunomia and Isonomia, cf. Ehrenberg, *Rechtsidee im frühen Griechentum* (1921). *RE.* Suppl. VII 293. *Aspects of the Anc. World* (1946), ch. 6. *Historia* I 515. *WSt.* 1956, 57. G. Vlastos, *AJP.* 1953, 337. Ἰσονομία πολιτική in: *Isonomia* (ed. J. Man and E. G. Schmidt, 1964), 1. E. Will, *Korinthiaka* (1955), 613. In general, cf. E. Wolff (see II 5). M. Pohlenz, *Griech. Freiheit* (1954). A. A. T. Ehrhardt, *Politische Metaphysik von Solon bis Augustin* I (1959), esp. ch. 2; cf. *Sav. Ztschr.* 1962, 369. The transition from θεσμός to νόμος is the first crucial problem in M. Ostwald's new important book *Nomos* (1969).

SECTION 3 (p. 52). In my opinion it is one of the few serious errors of B. Keil that, in precise contradiction of the view here represented, he declares (p. 346): 'Our extremely imperfect tradition easily makes the enlarged Council appear as an oligarchic assembly, and conjures up the false idea of constitutions with only an Ecclesia, but not a Council. Yet, a Greek "Politeia" without an Ecclesia is conceivable, but not one without a Council.' With this is connected Keil's curious explanation of the ἐκκλησία as formed by co-option of ἔκκλητοι by the oligarchic Council, and as a court of arbitration at the same time; against this, see Busolt, *Staatskde.* 443, 2, who himself thinks that the nobles continued to be summoned by the king, thus, like Keil, neglecting the inner connection between the tribal 'people in arms', the oligarchic citizen assembly, and the democratic Ecclesia. On our attitude to this fundamental question it largely depends how far we can believe in a possible representative system in the Polis and, later, in the federal states (cf. the works of A. Aymard and J. A. O. Larsen, section III 4). – ἄρχοντες in the prescripts of Hellenistic letters: Welles, *Royal Correspondence*, nos. 43. 45. 72. 75. – Athens in the Roman empire: D. J. Geagan, *The Athenian Constitution after Sulla* (*Hesperia*, Suppl. XII 1967).

SECTION 3 a (p. 52). Damos in Sparta: Ehrenberg, *Herm.* 1933, 288 = *P. u. I.*

202. – For the use of the name 'Apella', see *S. to S.* 383, 14. On the power of the assembly: Andrewes, *ASAI.* 2f. – Places of meeting: W. A. MacDonald, *The Political Meeting-Places of the Greeks* (1948). – On Arist. *Pol.* 1298a, 40, cf. Larsen, *CP.* 1950, 180. – Open and secret voting: Larsen, *CP.* 1949, 164 [his attempt to throw light on the obscure origins of the methods of voting remains hypothetical]. – σύγκλητος and similar names: F. Ghinati, *La Parola del Passato* 1960, 353. – *isegoria*: Griffith, *ASAI.* 115. – Nomos and Psephisma: Busolt, *Staatskunde* I 458. E. Weiss, *Griech. Privatrecht* I 86. Cf. also (with special emphasis on the institution of the νομοθέται) Kahrstedt, *Klio* 1938, 1. Atkinson, *Bull. J. Rylands Libr.* 1939, 1. Harrison, *JHS.* 1955, 26. – Demagogues: M. I. Finley, *Past and Present* 1962, 3. – Mantineia: Larsen, *CP.* 1950, 180. – ἀναψηφίζειν: Dover, *JHS.* 1955, 17. – Deification of Demos and Demokratia: Oliver (see II 2 b). Raubitschek, *Hesperia* 1962, 238. – Ostracism: (later date?) Schaefer, *Probl. d. alten Gesch.* 144. Raubitschek, *AJA.* 1951, 221. Jacoby, *FGrH.* 324 F 6. F. Willemsen, *Ath. Mitt.* 1965, 101.

SECTION 3 b (p. 59). Gerusia, originally γερωχία?. Cf. Busolt, *Staatskde.* 679, 4. The only evidence is a joke in Aristoph. *Lys.* 980. Recently a γεροντία has with some probability been recognized in the Linear B tablets from Pylos. However, there was in Cos a γερεαφόρος βασιλέων (Herzog, *Abh. Berl. Ak.* 1928, 6, 45), a 'legal successor of the βασιλεῖς' (?). – Probuloi, for example, in Corinth (E. Will [see 2 b], 609) and Cnidus (Plut., *qu. graec.* 292A); cf. above all, Schaefer, *RE.* XXIII 1221. – The view expressed in earlier editions (cf. also Swoboda, *Staatsaltertümer* 63, 6) that the 'Thousand' at Acragas were elected for three years, is based on a misunderstanding; in our source (Diog. Laert. VIII 66) it is probably said that this Council lasted for only three years (correction due to Momigliano). We may admit that the Spartan Gerusia had a certain power of preliminary deliberation, but it can hardly be proved that a definite technique of government can be inferred from the text of the Great Rhetra (A. Andrewes, *Probouleusis*, Inaugural Speech, 1954). Cf. in general Schaefer, *RE.* XXIII 48. The (sacred) Gerusia of Hellenistic and Roman times (for example, in Ephesus, later also in Athens) was a purely social and economic body, which had nothing to do with the Council; cf. Oliver, *Hesperia*, Suppl. VI (1941). *Historia* VII (1958), 472. Similar, it appears, was the character of the Gerusia of Alexandria (P. bibl. Giss. 46), which certainly existed, whether or not there was a *boulé* in Alexandria (see Part II, section III 3). – Chios: improved text of Tod, no. 1, in: Jeffery, *BSA.* 1956, 157; cf. Wade-Gery, *Essays in Greek Hist.*, 198. Oliver, *AJP.* 1959, 296. – Constitution of Dreros: Ehrenberg, *CQ.* 1943, 14 = *P. u. I.* 98; Willets (see I 2) takes a different view. On ἔδοξε τῶι δήμωι and similar formulae, see *JHS.* 1937, 150. *CQ.* 1943, 14 = *P. u. I.* 86, 99). I cannot believe that the early formula ἔδοξε τῶι δήμωι only meant an 'abbreviated decree' without further significance (G. Klaffenbach, *Griech. Epigr.* 69). Later, too, but rare: ἔδοξε τῆι ἐκκλησίαι; cf. L. Robert, *Hellenica* V 5. – Against the Council of 400 under Solon: Hignett (see p. 255), 92. – *IG.* I², 114; cf. *SEG.* X

119. Larsen, *Repres. Govt.* (see III 4), 15. – Jurisdiction by the Athenian βουλή: see the discussion in *Les Études class.* 1941, 193; 329; 1943, 114. – Later, councillors could be elected for six months, for example in Argos, Rhodes, and elsewhere (Busolt-Swoboda, I 420, 0). – Council and the principle of representation: Larsen goes further than I do (op. cit. 4): 'Even the fully developed Greek democracy contained so much representative machinery that little more than a shift in the emphasis on the various organs was needed to transform it into a representative government.' The numbers of councillors from each deme varied; cf. Larsen, *CP.* 1962, 104.

SECTION 3 c (p. 65). On the character of officialdom in Greek, Roman, and modern times, cf. F. Leifer, *Studien zum antiken Ämterwesen (Klio*, Beiheft 23, 1931). – δαμιουργός: Murakawa, *Historia* 1957, 385 [he tries to connect historically the two different meanings of the word]. – Tagos: Momigliano, *Athenaeum* 1932, 52. Gschnitzer, *Anzeiger f. d. Altertumswiss.* 1954, 191. – μόναρχος as an official in Cos: R. Herzog, *Koische Forschungen* (1892), 191. – For eponymity in Greece, cf. K. Hanell, *Das altrömische eponyme Amt* (1945), chs 5–7. – That the polemarch in virtue of his title must be later than the archon (de Sanctis, *Atthis*, 124. Hignett, 42), seems doubtful, and the analogy of Sparta proves nothing. Cf. Schaefer, *RE.* Suppl. VIII 1101 ff. – The ten archons of 580 B.C.: denied by Gernet, *RPh.* 1938, 116. – ephors: see recently Andrewes, *ASAI.* 8. – Prohibition of re-election within ten years in Dreros, within three in Gortyn (*SGDI.* 4979, 2). – *dokimasia*: apart from officials and new citizens, there was also a test for the young men and their horses when entering the cavalry service (Lys. XIV, XV, XVI); rhetors: Aesch. 1, 28 ff., 186. – Unwritten commandments of Polis ethics: Ehrenberg, *Sophocles and Pericles* (1954), ch. 2 and Appendix A. – ὑπογραμματεύς: Busolt-Swoboda, 1058. For the γραμματεῖς of the fourth century B.C., cf., for example, S. Dow, *Prytaneis, Hesperia*, Suppl. I (1937), no. 1. Kirchner, *Gnomon* 1938, 459. – Appointment by lot: W. Headlam, *Election by Lot in Athens* (1933²). Ehrenberg, *RE.* XIII 1467. Lot machines: S. Dow, loc. cit. 198. *Harv. St.* 1939, 1. – Polemarch in Chios: Robert, *BCH.* 1933, 517. Schaefer, loc. cit. – Strategi with full authority: M. Schede, Στρατηγὸς αὐτοκράτωρ. Diss. Leipzig 1932. – On the position of Pericles: Ehrenberg, *Sophocles and Pericles*, especially chs 4 and 5. Vogt, *HZ.* 182 (1956), 249. – στρατηγὸς ἐξ ἁπάντων: Jameson, *TAPA.* 1955, 63. Staveley, *ASAI.* 275.

SECTION 3 d (p. 72). On the people's courts: H. Hommel, *Heliaia* (1927). On the names of the Athenian courts of law: Jacoby, *FGrH.* 324 F 59. – γραφὴ παρανόμων, etc.: Cloché, *REA.* 1936, 401, and especially Ruschenbusch, *Historia* 1957, 257. Homicide: Ruschenbusch, *Historia* 1960, 129. D. M. MacDowell, *Athenian Homicide Law* (1963). – On the functioning of democracy, cf. Gomme, *History* 1951, 12. A. H. M. Jones (see II 1 b), ch. 5.

SECTION 4 (p. 74). A fuller treatment of the administration will be found in Busolt's *Staatskunde*. The limitation that I make here to religion, law, army, and finance is for Busolt no recognizable problem. My own justification is not fully set out in the text, but is at least alluded to.

SECTION 4 a (p. 74). Generally Pfister, *RE*. XI 2106. – Sacrificial calendars: S. Dow (see II 2 b). *Historia* 1960, 270. – On the *leges sacrae*: edition by Ziehen-Prott; also F. Sokolowski, *Lois sacrées de l'Asie Mineure* (1955); the important inscription from Cyrene: *SEG*. IX 72; cf. Wilamowitz, *SB. Berl. Ak.* 1927. G. Oliverio, *Documenti antichi dell' Africa ital.* II 1 (1933).

SECTION 4 b (p. 77). A fairly comprehensive and systematic survey of the legal system of the Polis exists for Athens only: J. H. Lipsius, *Das attische Recht und Rechtsverfahren* (1905–15). Cf. also E. Weiss (see II 2 a). An historical survey: R. J. Bonner and G. Smith, *The Administration of Justice from Homer to Aristotle* I. II (1930–8). On the question of legal differences among Greek states: M. I. Finley in: *La storia del diritto nel quadro delle science storiche* (1966), 129. – Not without interest in our context, though largely legalistic and philosophical: J. W. Jones, *The Law and Legal Theory of the Greeks* (1956). Important questions are discussed by H. J. Wolff, *Beiträge zur Rechtsgeschichte Altgriechenlands* (1961). – On jurisdiction being taken over by the Polis: Paoli, *RIDA*. 1948, 153. – Arbitrators: L. Gernet, *Droit et société dans la Grèce ancienne* (1955), 103 (= *REG*. 1939, 389). – Forms of sacred law: K. Latte, *Heiliges Recht* (1920). – Penal law: Paoli, *Sav. Ztschr.* 1959, 97. – Torture: E. W. Bushala, *Greek, Rom. and Byz. Studies* 1968, 61. – Prison: Barkan, *CP.* 1936, 338. – Areopagus and Ephetae: Kahrstedt, *Klio* 1937, 10.

SECTION 4 c (p. 80). In general: J. Kromayer und G. Veith, *Heerwesen und Kriegführung der Griechen u. Römer* (1928). – On the 'Hoplite Polis': M. Weber, *Wirtschaft u. Gesellschaft* (1922), 595. Nilsson, *Klio* 1929, 240. J. Hasebroek, *Griech. Wirtschafts- u. Gesellschaftsgesch.* (1931), 158. A. Andrewes, *The Greek Tyrants* (1956), ch. 3. – Ephebia: C. Pélékidès, *Histoire de l'éphébie attique* (1962).

SECTION 4 d (p. 83). The problems of Greek financial administration were, at least for Athens, first and fundamentally handled by A. Boeckh in his *Staats-haushaltung der Athener* (see p. 257). More recent treatments: A. Andreades, *A History of Greek Public Finance* I (1933); C. D. Sterghiopoulos, *Les finances grecques au Ve siècle* (1949) [useful but often uncritical]. – Early coinage: for example, E. S. G. Robinson, *NumChr.* 1956, 1. R. M. Cook, *Historia* 1958, 257. C. M. Kraay, *JHS.* 1964, 76. Important: Heichelheim, 'Die Ausbreitung der Münzwirtschaft' etc. *Schmollers Jhb.* 1931. – Temple treasures: Laum, *RE.* Suppl. IV 71; banking: R. Bogaert, *Banques et banquers dans les cités grecques* (1968). – Distributions to the citizens: Latte, *NGG.* 1946–7, 64. Bengtson, *Historia* 1954, 485 (Thasos). J. and L. Robert, *Hellenica* II (1953), 333 (Sardes, time of Augustus). J. Labarbe, *La loi navale de Thémistocle* (1957). – The state treasure of Pericles (amount disputed): Thuc. II 13, 3. Schol. Aristoph. *Plut.* 1139; cf. Gomme, *Historia* II (1953), 1; III (1955), 333. *Hist. Comm.* II (1956), 16–33. Meritt, *Hesperia* 1954, 185. Wade-Gery and Meritt, *Hesperia* 1957, 163. On the decree of Callias: W. Kolbe, *Thukydides im Lichte der Urkunden* (1930),

68. *ATL.* III *passim.* – On the financial policy of the fourth and third centuries B.C.: K. Riezler, *Über Finanzen und Monopole im alten Griechenland* (1907). E. v. Stern, *Herm.* 1916, 422. Schwahn, *Herm.* 1931, 337 [Boeotian state-loans]. A. H. M. Jones, *Athenian Democracy* (1957), ch. 2. de Ste Croix, *Classica et Mediaevalia* 1953, 30. The fact of a common tithe, attested for Cretan states of the third century B.C. (Guarducci and de Sanctis, *Rfil.* 1930, 471), is probably to be traced to the influence of the great monarchies or is connected with the ἀνδρεῖα, the common meals (Guarducci, *Rfil.* 1933, 488). – I owe references to Aeneas Tacticus to a paper by H. Bengtson, *Historia* 1962, 459. – Agis and Cleomenes: for example Fuks, *CP.* 1962, 161. Walbank, *ASAI.* 303.

SECTION 5 (p. 88). Since the days of Hegel a vast amount has been written about the nature of the Polis. It is sufficient to refer here to the general literature (above, pp. 256 ff.). – State and society in Sparta and Athens: Ehrenberg, *Neugründer des Staates* (1925), 105. Strata of society: Lauffer, *HZ.* 185 (1958), 497 – Socrates and the nobility: K. Reinhardt, *Vermächtnis der Antike* (1960), 228. – An attempt to outline the history of the Athenian 'parties' and to investigate their nature has been made by K. D. Sterghiopoulos, Τὰ πολιτικὰ κόμματα τῶν ἀρχαίων Ἀθηνῶν I, II (1955–8). – Individual and state: Strasburger, *HZ.* 177 (1954), 227. Schaefer, *HZ.* 183 (1957), 5. Cf. also C. M. Bowra, *The Greek Experience* (1957), ch. 4. – ἄριστος Ἑλλήνων: Robert, *REA.* 1929, 13; cf. with application to Rome: Vogt, *Herm.* 1933, 87. – Alcibiades and *tyrannis*: R. Seager, *Historia* 1967, 6. Berve, *l.c.* 208. – On ἐλευθερία and αὐτονομία: H. Schaefer, *Staatsform u. Politik* (1932). G. Tenekides, *La notion juridique de l'indépendance et la trad. hell. (Coll. de l'Inst. franç. d'Athènes)* (1954). Bickerman, *RIDA.* 1958, 22. Ehrenberg in: *The Living Heritage of Greek Antiquity* (1967), 132. – Festival of the Eleutheria: *ATL.* III 101. – On ἀποικία and κληρουχία: Bengtson, *SB. Bayr. Ak.* 1939, 42. Ehrenberg, *Aspects of the Anc. World* (1946), 128; *CP.* 1952, 143 = *P. u. I.* 245. E. Will, *La Nouvelle Clio* 1954, 413. Brunt, *ASAI.* 71. – On economic self-sufficiency, cf. the works of Hasebroek (see I 4). Economics and society: H. J. Diesner, *Wirtschaft und Gesellschaft bei Thukydides* (1956). – Slavery and humanity: Vogt, *SB. Ak. Mainz* 1953. – On the development of the Polis in Hellenistic and later times: W. S. Ferguson, *Hellenistic Athens* (1911). A. H. M. Jones, *The Greek City from Alexander to Justinian* (1940). Préaux, *Rec. Soc. J. Bodin* VI (1954). The epigraphical literature is especially important (see above, p. 255). See Part II, III 3. – On the Nomos of the Polis: Stier, Νόμος βασιλεύς. *Philol.* 1928: E. Wolf, *Griech. Rechtsdenken,* I–III 2 (1950–6). M. Gigante, *Nomos Basileus* (1956). W. Theiler, *Mus. Helv.* 1965, 69. – Paideia: W. Jaeger, *Paideia* I–III (Engl. edition, 1939–45). H.-I. Marrou, *Hist. de l'éducation dans l'antiquité* (1950²). P. Treves, *Atene e Roma* 1967, 2. – Kalokagathia: Jüthner, *Charisteria f. A. Rzach* (1930), 99. Ehrenberg, *People of Aristophanes* (1962³), *passim.* – State and nation: explained as a struggle between particularism and the national state, according to nineteenth-century ideas, a view shared by many scholars down to Ed. Meyer and Beloch. Comparison with Europe and

the European states: H. E. Stier, *Grundlagen u. Sinn d. griech. Geschichte* (1945);
his arguments are not strengthened by his interpretation of Isocrates, *Paneg.*
50 and Ephorus, *FGrH.* 70 F 20 (*X Congr. internaz. di scienze stor.* VII 143; *Atti*
(1957), 230; 276). Cf. also III 3. For Herodotus, cf. A. Heubeck, *National-
bewusstsein bei Her.* Diss. Erlangen 1936. In general cf. Bengtson, *Festschrift F.
Lammert* (1954), 31. Schaefer, *X Congr. intern. di scienze stor.* VI 677 = *Probl. d.
alten Gesch.*, 269, also my early attempt: *HZ.* 127 (1923), 377. – Greeks and
barbarians: Jüthner, *Hellenen u. Barbaren* (1923). *Entretiens Hardt* VIII (1961).
S. to S. 173. I. Weiler, *Gr., Rom. and Byz. Stud.* 1968, 21. – On the developments of the fourth century B.C. (economic, political, theory), see A. Mossé, *La
fin de la démocratie athénienne* (1962). – Later bourgeoisie: M. Rostovtzeff, *Soc.
and Econ. Hist. of the Hellenistic World (SEHHW.)* (1941), II 1115; cf. Walbank,
CR. 1942, 81. – On the connections between the real state and political theory:
E. Barker, *Greek Political Theory* (1918). M. Pohlenz, *Staatsgedanke und Staats-
lehre der Griechen* (1923). T. A. Sinclair, *History of Greek Political Thought* (1951).
M. Hammond, *City-State and World State* (1951), chs 1 and 2. – Changes of the
constitutions: H. Ryffel, Μεταβολὴ πολιτειῶν (1949). Cf. also the literature on
Polyb. VI, especially: Brink and Walbank, *CQ.* 1954, 97. K. v. Fritz, *The Theory
of the Mixed Constitution* (1954). Walbank, *Hist. Comm. on Polyb.* I (1957). –
Crete and Plato: H. van Effenterre (see II 1 b). – Theory and Utopy: H.
Braunert, *Geschichte in Wissensch. u. Unterricht* 1963, 145.

Chapter Three

Any system of constitutional forms between or above the individual states is
made difficult by the fact that their divisions tend to melt into one another. The
very complicated concepts with which Busolt (*Staatskunde* II) tries to meet all
possibilities are only confusing. Nor do I regard the very general use of the
expression συμπολιτεία – ancient, but mainly literary – as very happy; like
ἰσοπολιτεία, it really denotes a process in public law, not a special form of
state. This view is confirmed by the inscription published by Bean, *JHS.* 1948, 46,
ll. 54 ff., where a city is admitted εἰς τὴν τοῦ Λυκίων ἔθνους συμπολιτείαν,
while the League as such is called κοινὸν τῶν Λυκίων. Note also the renewal of
ὁμοπολιτεία between Cos and Calymnus, by which the latter became a
deme of the Polis of Cos (M. Segre, *Tituli Calymnii* (1952), Test. XII, cf.
Klaffenbach, *Gnomon* 1953, 455). – In my arrangement of the text I tried to
stress in the first place the historical and political sides, which are more obvious
to see, and the legal features in the second place only. – Inter-state treaties:
DSDA. General literature (besides the books of Busolt, Keil, and Swoboda):
V. Martin, *La vie internationale dans la Grèce des cités* (1940) [cf. *JHS.* 1950, 100].
I. Calabi, *Ricerche sui rapporti fra le poleis* (1953) [but cf. Larsen, *CP.* 1955, 79.
Brunt. *JHS.* 1955, 193].

SECTION I (p. 103). Giving of gifts: Finley (see I 4). – δίκαι ἐμπορικαί: Schwahn, *RE*. XVI 2053. – Proxeny: Busolt-Swoboda, 1246. Schwahn, *Herm.* 1931, 108. L. Robert, *Études de numism. grecque* (1951), 178. Gavazzi, *Epigraphica* XIII (1951), 50. On the later degradation of the proxeny, cf. A. Wilhelm, *Att. Urkunden* V (*SB. Ak. Wien* 1942) and, on the other side, G. Klaffenbach, *Griech. Epigraphik* (1957), 81. – Diplomacy: Adcock, *L'antiquité class.* 1948, 1. – Asylum: Tod, no. 34. In general: E. Schlesinger, *Die griech. Asylie* (1933) [His thesis that all secular right of asylum derived from the religious asylum needs some restriction]. – Armistice and conclusion of peace: Bickerman, *AHDO.* + *RIDA.* I (1952), 199. – Forms of ancient treaties: Heuss, *Klio* 1934, 14. 218. Cf. also M. Treu, *Historia* 1968, 129. Arbitration: A. Raeder, *L'arbitrage internat. chez les Hellènes* (1912). M. N. Tod, *Internat. Arbitration amongst the Greeks* (1913). *Sidelights on Greek History* (1932), ch. 2. Early example: *DSDA.* no. 148; frequent in the Hellenistic age, also decrees of honour for foreign judges (cf. L. Robert, *Hellenica* VII 171); a complicated procedure between two Boeotian cities: Robert, *BCH.* 1929, 156. – Isopoliteia: E. Szanto, *Griech. Bürgerrecht* 67. Sympoliteia: see above. – Alliance of 481 B.C.: *ATL.* III 95; 183. Brunt, *Historia* II (1953), 135 [I cannot accept either Larsen's view that the Hellenic League was refounded in 479 B.C. (see III 3) or Brunt's that the military League of 481 B.C. was the model of the Delian Confederacy]. Cf. *S. to S.* 147. – Panhellenism of Pericles: cf. the literature on state and nation under II 5; on the Athenian League as οἱ Ἕλληνες, see III 3. Panhellenism in fourth century: Ehrenberg, *P. u. I.* 35 ff. G. Dobesch, *Der panhellen. Gedanke im 4. Jh. und der 'Philippos' des Isokrates* (1968). – κοινὴ εἰρήνη: Momigliano, *Rfil.* 1934, 482. *Athenaeum* 1936, 1. Larsen, *CP.* 1944, 145. T. T. B. Ryder, *Koine Eirene* (1966). See also III 3. – The King's Peace: Cf. Wilcken, *Abh. Berl. Ak.* 1941; against him: Martin, *Mus. Helv.* 1949, 127. – I shall not go further into the history of the congresses and treaties of the fourth century. Recent writings are plentiful; I refer to: F. Hampl, *Die griech. Staatsverträge des 4. Jahrh.* (1938) (cf. Wüst, *Gnomon* 1938, 367. Meyer, *Sav. Ztschr.* 1939, 598. Larsen, *CP.* 1939, 375) and Accame (s. III 3), where further literature is mentioned.

SECTION 2 (p. 108). For the name and conception of Amphictyony cf. Calabi (see above), ch. 2. Wüst, *Historia* III (1954), 129 [much is hypothetical]. – Calauria: Strab. VIII 6, 14. Wilamowitz, *NGG.* 1896, 160. Harland, *AJA.* 1925, 160. Kelly, *AJA.* 1966, 113. – Delos: Tod, nos. 99. 215. Groh, *Athenaeum* 1932, 148. W. Laidlaw, *Hist. of Delos* (1933), 75. Coupry, *REA.* 1947, 78. Whether the Delian Amphictyony was really responsible for an alleged assimilation of the political structure in Ionian Samos and Dorian Cos (cf. Herzog, *Abh. Berl. Ak.* 1928, 42), remains doubtful. – Delphi: U. Kahrstedt, *Griech. Staatsrecht* I (1922), 383. H. W. Parke and D. E. W. Wormell, *A History of the Delphic Oracle* (1957²), *passim.* J. Defradas, *Les thèmes de la propagande delphique* (1954). Forthcoming: G. Daux, *L'amphictionie delphique* (Sather Class. Lectures). – Delphic Panhellenism as different from that behind the congresses of the fourth century: Sordi, *BCH.* 1957, 38. – On Sparta's position in the Council of the Amphictyony: Daux, *BCH.* 1957, 104. – Jurisdiction: Bonner and Smith, *CP.* 1943, 1. International policy: Calabi, *Parola del Passato* 1949, 250. – Oath: Larsen, *CP.* 1944, 146. Parke, *Hermathena* 1948, 106. Daux, *Studies presented to D. M. Robinson* II (1953), 775 [various oaths reconstructed]. Important is *Syll.* 145.

SECTION 3 (p. 111). The concept, coined in the first ancestor of this book (1932), of the 'hegemonial alliance' (alliance under a hegemon) has been generally accepted; but there has been criticism of details and, in particular, it has been disputed whether the League of Corinth belongs to the same type. I still maintain that in principle this is the case, but I have tried to take account of criticism and recent discussions. Symmachy: Schwahn, *RE.* IV A, 1102. – Symmachy and Hegemony: Bickerman, *RIDA.* 1950, 99. In general, see the ingenious speculations of H. Schaefer, *Staatsform u. Politik* (1932) [cf. *Sav. Ztschr.* 1933, 533] and the comprehensive legal description given by H. Triepel, *Die Hegemonie* (1938) [important review by Schaefer, *Sav. Ztschr.* 1943, 368]. – On the separate Leagues (apart from the general works): Peloponnesian League: Larsen, *CP.* 1932, 136; 1933, 257; 1934, 1; 1944, 145. K. Wickert, *Der peloponnes. Bund v. seiner Entstehung bis z. Ende des archidam. Kriegs.* Diss. Erlangen 1962. Harmosts: cf. G. Bockisch, *Klio* 46 (1965), 129. The treaty of Sparta with Tegea: Jacoby, *CQ.* 1944, 15. The dating to the sixth century is practically certain, because of the phrase χρηστοὺς ποιεῖν meaning 'to make citizens', which Aristotle could no longer understand. – Delian confederacy and Athenian empire: H. Nesselhauf, *Untersuchungen zur Gesch. der del.-att. Symmachie* (*Klio*, Beiheft 30, 1933). L. I. Highby, *The Erythrae Decree* (*Klio*, Beih. 36, 1936). Schaefer, *Herm.* 1936, 129; 1939, 225 = *Probleme d. alt. Gesch.*, II. 41. Larsen, *HarvSt.* 1940, 175. *ATL.* I–IV (1939–52) (bibliography in IV). R. Meiggs, *JHS.* 1943, 21. *HarvSt.* 1963, 1. A. S. Nease, *Phoenix* 1949, 112. de Ste Croix, *Historia* 1954, 1. Bradeen, *Historia* 1960, 257. Pleket, *Historia* 1963, 70. Popp, *Historia* 1968, 425. Larsen's articles on the two earlier Leagues are important, but in my view too legalistic. The opinion frequently expressed that the Delian League was officially called οἱ Ἕλληνες seems also to find support in Thucydides, especially in the speech of the Mytileneans (III 10, 3; 13, 1); but here we have to do with the somewhat artificial construction of Mitylene's διπλῆ ἀπόστασις, and of Ἕλληνες does not describe the League as such, but the Greeks as enemies of the Persians. On the other hand, in Ephorus (*FGrH.* 70 F 20), when he takes as normal the description of the Lacedaemonians as Peloponnesians and that of the Athenians as Hellenes there is, in my opinion, a reminiscence of the fifth century B.C., which confirms the (unofficial) claim of Athens. – Second Athenian League: Tod, no. 123. S. Accame, *La Lega ateniese del sec.* IV (1941). Burnett, *Historia* 1962, 1. – ἔδοξε τοῖς συμμάχοις: see the inscription, Accame, 230. Cleruchies: Schweigert, *AJP.* 1940, 194. F. Gschnitzer, *Abhängige Orte im griech. Altertum* (1958), 98. – League of Corinth:

the legal character of this creation of Philip is one of the most hotly debated questions. Wilcken, in several articles (latest in *SB. Berl. Ak.* 1929, 297), described the League definitely as a Symmachy; but many scholars have seen in the League simply the realization of the κοινὴ εἰρήνη (literature: Tod, no. 177. Heuss, *Herm.* 1938, 133. Roebuck, *CP.* 1948, 73. Calabi, *Rfil.* 1950, 630. Ryder [see III 1]). But, as Larsen observes (*CP.* 1939, 378), this has become 'a regular obsession in recent years'. Far too exact deductions have been drawn from the texts of our sources. The real nature of the League of Corinth, in my view, is seen precisely in the combination of κοινὴ εἰρήνη and συμμαχία [so also Berve, Bickerman, Triepel, and, with an attempt at a more exact interpretation: Dienelt, *ÖJh.* 1956 (Beiblatt), 247]. The League had a Synhedrion, and, even if the idea of the κοινὴ εἰρήνη had its origin in the Amphictyonic peace (which is possible, but not certain), yet the Synhedrion was no Amphictyonic Council (Momigliano takes a different view, *Rfil.* 1934, 482). The fact (first established by Larsen, *CP.* 1925, 319) that the number of votes depended on the strength of the military contingents, proves that it really was a Symmachy. The existence and the composition of the Synhedrion prove that something more than securing of the peace was aimed at; it was only the League as directed by the Synhedrion that gave Philip the Hegemony which he claimed – quite apart from the expedition planned against Persia. The further question whether this arrangement was accomplished in one or two treaties is less important; I am inclined to believe in a single treaty. The combination of κοινὴ εἰρήνη and συμμαχία had its precursors in the treaties of the fourth century, in which it took more and more definite shape; here, too, details are disputed (see above, p. 116 f.). – On the League of 302: *IG*², IV 1, 68. Wilcken, *SB. Berl. Ak.* 1927, 277. L. Robert, *Hellenika* II (1946), 15. Daux, ᾿Αρχ. ᾿Εφημερίς 1953–4, 245. – Renewal of the League in 224: Larsen, *CP.* 1926, 67. Bickerman, *RPh.* 1935, 65. A. Heuss, *Stadt und Herrscher des Hellenismus* (1937), 158.

SECTION 4 (p. 120). In general: after E. A. Freeman, *History of Federal Government* I (1863), cf. Schwahn, *RE.* IV a, 1171, and above all, J. A. O. Larsen, *Representative Government in Greek and Roman History* (1955). *Greek Federal States* (1968) (important for all questions in this section). Cf. also L. Moretti, *Ricerche sulle leghe greche* (1962). – About the beginnings of most Leagues we are very poorly informed; see, for example, as to the possibility of an Arcadian League about 490: Wallace, *JHS.* 1954, 32. It is improbable, though not quite out of the question, that the Αἰτωλῶν τὸ κοινόν which occurs in an inscription of 367–366 B.C. (Schweigert, *Hesperia* 1938, 8) was still the old closely coherent tribal state, and not the federal state, the creation of which would then belong to the last quarter of the fourth century (Sordi, *Acme* 1953, 419). – On the early development of Arcadian unity: C. Callmer, *Studien zur Geschichte Arkadiens* (1943). Larsen, *Studies pres. to D. M. Robinson* II 797. – Cult of Zeus Homarius: Aymard, *Mél. Cumont* (1936) I, 1. – Acarnania: *IG*². IX 1, 2, no. 583; cf. Habicht, *Herm.* 1957, 86. Gschnitzer, *Herm.* 1964, 378. – Panionion: Wilamowitz,

SB. Berl. Ak. 1906. Caspari (= Cary), *JHS.* 1915, 173. Judeich, *RhM.* 1933, 305. Ziehen, *RE.* XVIII 601. Roebuck, *CP.* 1955, 26. Larsen, loc. cit. 29, in my view, exaggerates the possibility that a united state could have arisen here. – Thessaly: M. Sordi, *La lega tessala fino al Aless. Magno* (1958); but cf. Larsen, *CP.* 1960, 229. Inscription: Daux, *BCH.* 1958, 329. Cf. also I 4. – Epirus: G. N. Cross, *Epirus* (1932). P. R. Franke, *Alt-Epirus u. d. Königtum der Molosser* (1955), concludes (63 ff.) from the appearance side by side of king and Epirotes (or Macedons) in *Syll.* 392 and 518 that there was a Symmachy under a Hegemon or that there was a concession to the κοινὸν τῶν Μακεδόνων; this can hardly be right, rather is it a case of the personal kingship that had grown beyond the older popular kingship (cf. also Walbank, *CR.* 1957, 59). – Crete: M. van der Mijnsbrugge, *The Cretan Koinon* (1931). Guarducci, *Rfil.* 1950, 142. van Effenterre (see II 1 b), 127. Willets (see I 2), 225. – Boeotia: Larsen, *TAPA.* 1955, 40. In *CP.* 1960, he discusses the importance of Orchomenus. Cf. also A. J. Graham, *Colony and Mother City* (1964), 126. – Chalcidice: The nature and history of the political union founded by Olynthus are disputed. Literature in Hampl, *Herm.* 1935, 177, whose own theory of the identity of οἱ Ὀλύνθιοι and οἱ Χαλκιδεῖς is not convincing. L. de Salva, *Athenaeum* 1968, 47, believes in an even earlier origin. – Island League: A. T. Guggenmos, *Die Gesch. des Nesiotenbundes.* Diss. Würzburg, 1929. – On the much discussed questions of the constitutions of the Achaean and Aetolian Leagues, cf. A. Aymard, *Les assemblées de la confédération achéenne* (1938) [cf. the reviews by Gelzer, *Gnomon* 1939, 614. Larsen, *CP.* 1941, 408. Laistner, *AJP.* 1941, 507], also earlier in *Mél. Glotz* (1932), I 49; *Mél. Jorga* (1933), 71. Larsen, *TAPA.* 1952, 1. *Stud. to Robinson* (see above). *Greek Fed. States,* 195. 203. My view of σύνοδοι and σύγκλητοι is essentially the same as Larsen's. – Lycian League: A. H. M. Jones, *The Cities of the Eastern Roman Provinces* (1937), ch. 3. Larsen, *CP.* 1943, 177; 246; 1945, 65; 1956, 151. *Symb. Osloenses* 1957, 5 [important because of the possible limitation of federal citizenship, but the case is not yet proved; cf. also J. and L. Robert, *REG.* 1958, 196]. Araxa inscription (*SEG.* XVIII 570): Bean, *JHS.* 1948, 46. Robert, *REG.* 1950, 185. Here one ruling body only is mentioned and called *ekklesia*. – Macedon: Larsen, *CP.* 1949, 73. Aymard, *CP.* 1950, 96. The translation of Polyb. 31, 2, 12 given in the text goes back to Thirlwall and was adopted by Larsen (*Repr. Govt.* 104. *Fed. States,* 297); in fact, the mention of the συνέδριον can hardly mean anything else than that 'democracy' had its chief organ of government in a 'representative' Council. – Aetolian πολίτευμα: Klaffenbach, *SB. Dtsch. Ak.* 1954. Further discussion of the treaty between Rome and Aetolia: McDonald, *JRS.* 1956, 153. Badian, *Latomus* 1958, 197.

PART II: THE HELLENISTIC STATE

I

The Hellenistic state and its political character were never really understood by the ancient world. It is even more true of it than of the Polis, that the sources for our knowledge of the state are the same as for general history. Our material varies completely from place to place and from subject to subject, both in quality and in quantity; our literary sources are extremely poor, even more so than for general history (cf. F. Jacoby, *FGrH.* II D, p. 543). In Polybius we do find a number of statements that throw light on the facts of political law and state policy; on him cf. especially F. W. Walbank, *A Histor. Commentary on Polybius* I (1957), II (1967). The primary sources, on the other hand, are of vastly superior importance. In the first place come inscriptions and papyri, after them coins and ostraca; the internal social and economic life of Egypt is better illuminated by the papyri than any other part of political life in the Hellenistic age. Inscriptions are usually quoted here from the most important selections; on them, see p. 255. We must add: C. B. Welles, *Royal Correspondence in the Hellenistic Period* (1934) [extremely useful]. Of special value are all the writings of L. Robert. For recent finds in the American excavations, especially those on the Athenian Agora, cf. the reports of Meritt and others in *Hesperia*. – Papyri: Mitteis-Wilcken (see below). Preisigke and Bilabel, *SlB.* Most editions (like the many volumes of the *Oxyrhynchus Pap.*) contain a mixture of records, letters, literary texts, etc. Important single papyri: *Dikaiomata* (*P.Hal.* 1913). *Revenue Laws*, ed. by J. Bingen, *SlB.* Beiheft 1 (1952). *Tebtunis Pap.* III (1933). *Hibeh Pap.* I (1906), II (1956). The largest coherent and therefore most instructive body of papyri comes from the archives of Zeno, the bailiff of the dioecetes Apollonius (time of Philadelphus); for literature, see III 2. A unity of a special kind is represented by the *Corpus Papyrorum Judaicorum*, ed. by V. Tcherikover and A. Fuks (*C.P.J.*) I–III (1957–64).

Modern literature on the Hellenistic state, still rather rare, has increased in recent times, partly in agreement with, and partly critical of, the present book in its earlier editions. The valuable antiquarian collections of material (see above, p. 257) do not exist for the Hellenistic state. Droysen's inspired insight into the creative quality of the Hellenistic age has taken time to spread; the material, too, has only reached considerable proportions through discoveries of the last seven or eight decades. It has revealed at least some of the relations between the different political factors. No book on 'Hellenistic Public Law' has yet appeared, though now and again it has been promised. The general histories of the Hellenistic period are therefore of particular importance, above all the following: J. G. Droysen, *Gesch. des Hellenismus* I–III (1833–43. ³1877–8). K. J. Beloch, *Griech. Gesch.*² IV 1 and 2 (1925–7). J. Kaerst, *Geschichte des Hellenismus* I³, II² (1926–7). P. Jouguet, *L'impérialisme macédonien et l'hellénisation de l'Orient* (1926). *Cambridge Ancient History* VII, VIII (1928–30). M. Cary,

A History of the Greek World from 323 to 146 B.C. (1963³). H. Bengtson, *Griech. Geschichte* (1965³), esp. pp. 415–43. A. Aymard, *L'Orient et la Grèce* (1953), 2ᵉ partie, livre III. Ehrenberg, 'The Hellenistic Age' (*Encyclopaedia Britannica*) (1965). C. Schneider, *Kulturgeschichte des Hellenismus* I (1967). For the earlier times down to 280, see also P. Roussel in G. Glotz, *Histoire grecque* IV 1 (1945²). The picture of the Hellenistic state is in general either set in the course of political history or divided into the various forms of the separate empires. The second method is certainly suggested by the great differences of organization in the various realms, and by the even greater differences in our knowledge, based on the surviving sources. The Ptolemaic or Lagid empire has in that respect a remarkable advantage through the papyri; far behind them comes the evidence of the inscriptions, especially from Asia Minor – to say nothing of the coins, which for some regions, as, for example, Bactria, are almost the only evidence; cf. W. W. Tarn, *The Greeks in Bactria and India* (1951²). A. K. Narain, *The Indo-Greeks* (1957). The division of the material according to the separate states is also maintained in the excellent systematic work of W. W. Tarn and G. T. Griffith, *Hellenistic Civilization* (1952³), or in the book, written from a Marxist point of view, by A. B. Ranowitch, *Der Hellenismus u. seine geschichtl. Rolle* (1958). There is no lack of studies of the various empires, especially of the Ptolemaic. Cf. the admirable chapters by M. Rostovtzeff in the *Cambridge Ancient History* (VII 4 and 5; VIII 19). Ptolemaic empire: A. Bouché-Leclerq, *Hist. des Lagides* III, IV (1906–7) [very detailed and sensible, but, of course, largely out of date]. W. Schubart, *Verfassung u. Verwaltung des Ptolemäerreichs* (Der Alte Orient 35, 4) (1937). Préaux, see IV 4. H. Volkmann, *RE.* XXIII, esp. 1602 ff. It is interesting and instructive to see how the actual institutions and conditions were reflected in the Hermetic literature; cf. F. Cumont, *L'Égypte des astrologues* (1937). – Chronology of Ptolemies: Skeat, *The Reigns of the Ptolemies* (1954). A. E. Samuel, *Ptolemaic Chronology* (1962). – Seleucid empire: E. Bickerman, *Institutions des Séleucides* (1938). H. Bengtson, *Strategie* (see III 2), Bd. 2. – The East as a whole: Ed. Meyer, *Blüte u. Niedergang d. Hellenismus in Asien* (1925). – Macedon: W. W. Tarn, *Antigonus Gonatas* (1913), esp. ch. 7. – Pergamum: F. Cardinali, *Il regno di Pergamo* (1906). E. V. Hansen, *The Attalids of Pergamon* (1947). R. B. McShane, *The Foreign Policy of the Attalids* (1964). – Judaea: W. Otto, *Herodes. RE.* Suppl. II 54. Ed. Meyer, *Ursprung u. Anfänge d. Christentums* II (1922). A. H. M. Jones, *The Herods of Judaea* (1938). E. Bickerman, *The Maccabees* (1962). – Syracuse: J. Carcopino, *La loi de Hiéron et les Romains* (1919). A. Schenk v. Stauffenberg, *König Hieron II.* (1933) [cf. *HZ.* 149 (1934), 313. H. Berve, 'König Hieron II'. *Abh. Bayr. Akad.* 1959. *Die Tyrannis bei d. Griechen* (1967), 462]. – For the social and economic history of the Hellenistic age, see the extensive and fundamental work by M. Rostovtzeff, *A Social and Economic History of the Hellenistic World (SEHHW.)*, I–III (1941), with its ample *bibliographies raisonnées* in Vol. III [Cf. Momigliano, *JHS.* 1943, 116. Bengtson, *HZ.* 185 (1958), 88]. – For Egypt, the well-known works of introduction to the papyri are fundamental: Mitteis-Wilcken, *Grundlagen und Chrestomatie der Papyruskunde* I. II (1912). W. Schubart, *Einführung in die Papyruskunde* (1918), and recently E. G. Turner, *Greek Papyri* (1968). Reports on documents and bibliographies in *AfP.*, *JEA.*, *Aegyptus*, and *Chr. d'Ég.* – U. v. Wilamowitz-Moellendorff has tried to represent the Hellenistic type of state as a general cultural phenomenon: *Staat und Gesellschaft der Griechen* (1923²), 153; as always, he offers illuminating questions and answers; cf. also the first section of his *Hellenist. Dichtung in d. Zeit d. Kallimachos* (1924).

When I first endeavoured to present an account of the Hellenistic state, I found very little in modern literature to help me. Meanwhile, things may have improved, but the sources have increased enormously, and the epigraphic and papyrological material can no longer be covered except by the specialist. I can only repeat what I wrote thirty-eight years ago, that my attempt must be taken for what it is. The hope I then expressed that my book would soon be replaced by something better has been fulfilled for partial areas and questions only, not by the issue of an exhaustive general survey. Perhaps this was inevitable, but I should like to express the same hope again.

Obviously, the multitude of individual states could not find room in the modest framework of this book. Welles, *CP.* 1960, 136, is quite right in regretting that fact, but I cannot accept his statement that I looked 'almost exclusively at the two states of the Seleucids and the Ptolemies'. Macedon, Pergamum, and others have been included, though some restrictions were necessary. Not only Rome and Carthage must be left out but also other states not founded by Macedonians or Greeks, for example Parthia. The essential aim was to describe what is specifically Hellenistic in the world of states during the three last centuries B.C. Until that extensive work is written which will provide a more complete picture, the present revised and enlarged edition may remain of some use.

2

All the references given here to special literature presuppose a knowledge of the general works, quoted in the first section; I only refer to them again in a few exceptional cases.

Chapter One

On the concept of the 'Hellenistic age', cf. the penetrating article by A. Momigliano, *Contributo alla storia degli studi classici* (1955), 165. – The Hellenistic monarchy as 'a Greek fact': A. Aymard, *Études d'hist. anc.* (1967), 123. C. B. Welles, *Studi in onore di A. Calderini e R. Paribeni* (1956), 81, makes writers like Isocrates responsible for the creation of the Hellenistic monarchy! Though some people may think more highly of the effects of monarchical theory on the early Hellenistic monarchy than I am prepared to do, Welles' statement remains a paradox which few will like to accept. On the interpretation of the

T

relevant passages in Isocrates, see E. Buchner, *Herm.* 1954, 378, who however goes much too far in identifying Isocrates' and Aristotle's views on Greeks and barbarians; the former thinks of it as a cultural 'mission', the latter speaks in terms of power politics. – From the large literature on Alexander's empire, cf. especially H. Berve, *Das Alexanderreich auf prosopographischer Grundlage* (1926). R. Andreotti, *Il problemo politico di Aless. Magno* (1933), also *Historia* 1950–2, 583. G. Walser, *Schweizer Beiträge z. allg. Geschichte* 1956, 156. – Aristotle and Alexander's empire: Ehrenberg, *Alexander and the Greeks* (1938), ch. 3. – 'Throwing the spear' and χώρα δορίκτητος: W. Schmitthenner, *Saeculum* 1968, 31. – Alexander's last plans: F. Schachermeyr, *ÖJh.* 1954, 118. Badian, *HarvSt.* 1968, 183. – Universal monarchy: Andreotti, *Saeculum* 1957, 120. – Carthage: Ehrenberg, *Karthago* (1927) = P. u. I. 549. – Dionysius I: F. K. Stroheker, *Dionysios I* (1958). Berve, *Tyrannis bei d. Gr.* 222. – Agathocles: Berve, *SB. Bayr. Akad.* 1952. *Tyrannis* 441. – Alexander's 'first empire', and the different relations of the successor states to him: Ehrenberg, *Alexander u. Ägypten* (1926) = P. u. I. 399. Schachermeyr, *Alexander d. Gr.* (1949), 212. – On Antigonus I much has been written, though there still is no comprehensive work. Demetrius: G. Elkeles, *Demetrios der Städtebelagerer.* Diss. Breslau 1941. E. Manni, *Demetrio Poliorcete* (1952). Lysimachus: W. Hünerwadel, *Forschungen zur Gesch. d. Königs Lysimachos.* Diss. Zürich 1900. Geyer, *RE.* XIV 1. Saita, *ΚΩΚΑΛΟΣ* (1955), 62, esp. 97.

Chapter Two

SECTION I (p. 142). General and fundamental for the significance of the great territories and wide spaces: F. Ratzel, *Politische Geographie* (1923[3]), section 5, ch. 13, where attention is called to the connection between great territories and great personalities. On the approximate areas of the Hellenistic states something may be found in Beloch IV 1, 328, also his *Bevölkerung* (see p. 262), *passim.* All figures give only very rough measures. – Against the concept of a 'balance of power' such as I use it like others (e.g. Bengtson, *Griech. Gesch.*[3], 388), to describe the Hellenistic situation cf. Braunert, *Historia* 1964, 80 (see also III 3). – Frontiers: E. Meyer, *Die Grenzen der hellenist. Staaten in Kleinasien* (1925). U. Kahrstedt, *Syrische Territorien* (*Abh. Gött. Ges. d. Wiss.*, 1926) [in parts very hypothetical]. – For political nomenclature is specially significant: *SEG.* III 378, B 9: [τὸν βασιλέα τὸν ἐν Ἀλεξ]ανδρείαι καὶ Αἰγύπτωι βασιλεύοντα καὶ . . . τοὺς βασιλεῖς τοὺς ἐν Συρίαι βασιλεύοντας. Titles like 'king of Syria', 'king of Asia' in our literary sources are unofficial. – 'Uniqueness' (originality) of Egypt: Préaux, *Mus. Helv.* 1953, 203. – Royal land, etc.: M. Rostovtzeff, *Studien zur Gesch. des röm. Kolonats* (1910); the objection raised by Beloch, *Gr. Gesch.* IV 1, 337, 3, who denies that γῆ ἐν ἀφέσει legally belonged to the king, confuses practical effects and theoretical basis; there was certainly private property in land. – Estates: βασιλικαὶ γραφαί in Sardes:

Welles, 18. περιορισμοί: Welles, 41. – Provinces: O. Leuze, *Die Satra-pieneinteilung in Syrien u. im Zweistromland* (1935); cf. Bengtson, *Gnomon* 1937, 113. – Temple states: A. H. M. Jones, *The Greek City* (1940), 309. Broughton, *Studies pres. to A. C. Johnson*, (1951), 236.

SECTION 2 (p. 148). Peliganes: Roussel, *Syria* 1942–3, 21. Klaffenbach, *Philol.* 1948, 376. On Polybius 5, 54, 10, where Ἀδείγανες is recorded, see Bengtson, *Strategie* II 402. Macedonian Diaspora: M. Launey (see IV 3) I (1949), 292; cf. Jones, *l.c.* 23 (he believes that there were very many Macedonians as military colonists in Egypt and Asia, but by a simple calculation asserts that their total number cannot have been large. C. Edson, *CP.* 1958, 158, collects a great deal of late evidence on the *Imperium Macedonicum* (the Seleucid empire), but draws too far-reaching conclusions. For Dura, cf. Welles, *Studies pres. to Johnson*, 251, and *Aegyptus* 1959, 23. – In general, see F. Heichelheim, *Die auswärtige Bevölkerung des Ptolemäerreichs* (1925). F. Oertel, *Katoikoi*, *RE.* XI. – On the question of population in Egypt: above all, C. Préaux in many penetrating articles, also on Ptolemaic home policy: e.g. *Chr. d'Ég.* 1936, 111; *Les Grecs en Égypte d'après les archives de Zénon* (1947). Cf. also Kornemann, *Aegyptus* 1933, 644. Reekmans, *Chr. d'Ég.* 1949, 324. v. Schwind, *Studi in onore di Arangio-Ruiz* II 435. Bengtson, *Welt als Geschichte* 1951, 135 [also deals with the Seleucid empire; in my view he exaggerates the share taken by Orientals in actual government and administration]. van Groningen, *Mus. Helv.* 1953, 178. – A specially eloquent example of the complaint of a non-Greek (οὐκ ἐπίσταμαι ἑλληνίζειν): *P. Col. Zenon*, 66. – Gymnasium and Council: Kortenbeutel, *AfP.* 1937, 44. – On welfare policy: Westermann, *Am. Hist. Rev.* 1937–8. Lenger, *Studi … Arangio-Ruiz* I 483. – σῶμα λαϊκὸν ἐλεύθερον: Liebesny, *Aegyptus* 1936, 257. On wandering inside Egypt and flight cf. Braunert, *Journ. Jur. Papyr.* 1955–6, 211 [especially on the important and much disputed question of the meanings of ἰδία and ἀγαχώρησις]. – On the πίστεις, cf. e.g. Préaux, *Chr. d'Ég.* 1935, 109. – Differences of pay between Egypt and Delos: F. Heichelheim, *Wirt-schaftl. Schwankungen d. Zeit v. Alexander bis Aug.* (1930), esp. 103. – πολιτεύ-ματα: Ruppel, *Philol.* 1927, 268. Roux, *REG.* 1949, 281. – ἐπιγονή: v. Woess, *Sav.-Ztschr.* 1922. Pringsheim, ibid. 1924. Zucker, *RE.* XIX 915, also in: *Das neue Bild der Antike* I (1942), 377. A new, not unreasonable explanation of the men τῆς ἐπιγονῆς as private civilians *vs.* officials, is tried by J. F. Oates, *Yale Class. Stud.* 18 (1963); but the problem seems not yet finally solved. – Domestic policy of the first Ptolemy: Kornemann, *Raccolta Lumbroso* (1925), 235. Jouguet, *Bull. Inst. franç. d'archéol. orientale* 1930, 513. Heichelheim, *Chr. d'Ég.* 1932, 144. – State interest and racial policy: Préaux, *Chr. d'Ég.* 1935, 109; 1936, 111. – Potter's oracle, *P. Oxyr.* XXII 2332. Cf. Wilcken, *Herm.* 1905, 548. E. Visser, *Götter und Kulte im ptol. Ägypten* (1938). L. Koenen, *Ztschr. f. Papyrol. u. Epi-graphik* 2 (1968), 178. – Gymnasium as centre of Greek life even in the κῶμαι: Zucker, *Aegyptus* 1931, 485. H.-I. Marrou, *Hist. de l'éducation dans l'antiquité* (1960[5]). M. P. Nilsson, *Die hellenistische Schule* (1955), 83. – Slavery: its importance is asserted especially by Rostovtzeff; a somewhat different view: W. L. Westermann, *Upon Slavery in Ptol. Egypt* (1929); *RE.* Suppl. VI, under *Slavery; The Slave Systems of Greeks and Romans* (1955). Sacred slaves: W. Otto, *Abh. Bayr. Ak.* 1950. – Subjects: οἱ ὑφ' ἡμᾶς τασσόμενοι, or similar phrases, e.g. *OGI.* 56, 13; 90, 10. Welles, 27, 9; cf. also 34, 19. *SEG.* XII 368.

Chapter Three

SECTION I (p. 159). τὰ πράγματα: e.g. *P. Grenf.* II 27, 4; cf. *UPZ.* I 106; 144. Heuss (see III 3), 176 translates (hardly correctly, in spite of *OGI.* 332, 25): *Gebietsmacht.* The expression was also known to the Greeks of the Polis; the difference lies in the fact that in Hellenistic times no other word for the state existed. – Royal title and royal protocol: Aymard, *REA.* 1946, 107 = *Études* etc., 136. for Macedon: *RIDA.* 1950, 61 = *Études,* 100. – Constitutional law of the monarchy: M. L. Strack, *Die Dynastie der Prolemäer* (1897). E. Breccia, *Il diritto dinastico nelle monarchie dei successori d'Aless. Magno* (1903). E. Bikerman, *Institutions des Séleucides,* ch. 1. The importance of co-rule and joint rule as institutions has often been exaggerated, following Mommsen's *Staatsrecht* of the Principate (to say nothing of Kornemann's *Doppelprinzipat u. Reichsteilung*); on co-rule in Macedon cf. Robert, *REG.* 1951, 172 f., no. 136. For the role of women, cf. apart from Breccia: Kahrstedt, *Klio* 1910, 261, esp. 274. Koch, *ZfN.* 1924; for the parts played by Cleopatra II and III: W. Otto and H. Bengtson, *Abh. Bayr. Ak.* 1938. – Royal testaments: especially important is the last will of Euergetes II (*SEG.* IX 7); the connection that I have stressed in the text still holds, even though (with Schubart, *PhW.* 1932, 1077) we may conclude from the use of παρακατατίθεσθαι that the king speaks of his land as a property entrusted to him. – πρόγονοι: Tarn, *JHS.* 1933, 57. Edson, *Harv. St.* 1934, 213. Rostovtzeff, *JHS.* 1935, 56 [official Persian use?]. Welles (p. 81) shows that πρόγονοι, in diplomatic language, can sometimes mean the father only; but that use seems to be restricted to the founders of the dynasties. – ἀνακλητήρια: Otto, *Abh. Bayr. Ak.* 1934, 15. Cf. Bell and Skeat, *JEA.* 1935, 262. – Philip V: F. W. Walbank, *Philip V of Macedon* (1940). – F. Granier, *Die maked. Heeresversammlung* (1931), exaggerates the importance of the Hellenistic army assembly, especially as he continues to recognize it in much altered forms [cf., e.g., Ferguson, *Gnomon* 1935, 516; above all: Aymard, *REA.* 1950, 115 = *Études,* 143. *RIDA.* 1950, 61 = *Études,* 100. – βασιλεὺς βασιλέων: Griffith, *CP.* 1953, 145. – Diadem: H.-W. Ritter, *Diadem u. Königsherrschaft* (1965). – About the part played by the kings in inter-state relations, see Gschnitzer, *SB. Österr. Akad.* 1960, 15.

Grades of rank at court: Kortenbeutel, *RE.* XX 95 (*philoi*). M. Trindl, *Ehrentitel im Ptolemäerreich* (Diss. München 1942, only in typescript). K. M. T. Atkinson, *Aegyptus* 1952, 204. – Hetaeri: see Franke, *Gnomon* 1958, 206. – Guardianship: Pouilloux and Verdélis, *BCH.* 1950, 32. Aymard, *Aegyptus*

1952, 85 = *Études*, 230. *Historia* 1953, 49 = *Études*, 240; he assumes that there was no immediate right of succession for minors, but that seems to be contradicted by some of the events. – 'Family of the kings'; cf. Dölger, *Hist. Jahrb.* 1941, 397. – Royal edicts: F. Schroeter, *De regum hellenist. epistulis in lapidibus servatis quaestiones stilisticae* (1932), in the main outdated by Welles's book (see p. 275). On διάγραμμα and similar expressions, cf. Ehrenberg, *Herm.* 1930, 337 = *P. u. I.* 524, partly corrected and enlarged by Welles, *AJA.* 1938, 245. Bickerman, *RPh.* 1938, 295; cf. also Heuss (see III 3), 78. 98. Egypt: Lenger, *Chr. d'Ég.* 1944, 108; *RIDA.* 1948, 119. On *SEG.* IX 5, cf. Préaux, *Chr. d'Ég.* 1942, 133. Bickerman, *AHDO.* + *RIDA.* 1953, 251, who, however, takes the various concepts too precisely. Interesting is the inscription in Oliverio, *Doc. ant. dell'Africa ital.* II 2 (1936), no. 538, and *P. Hibeh* II, no. 198. – The 'Hellenistic monarchy' of Hiero is described in detail by Berve, *Abh. Bayr. Akad.* 1959 (cf. *Tyrannis bei d. Gr.*, 462). – Areus as a Hellenistic king: Ehrenberg, *RE.* III A, 1423. Eunus: Vogt, *Abh. Ak. Mainz* 1957, 18. – On the Pharaohs as precursors of the Ptolemies: F. K. Kienitz, *Die polit. Geschichte Ägyptens vom 7. bis zum 4. Jhdt.* (1953); on the epoch of the Persian satrapy: Bresciani, *Studi Classici ed Orientali* VII (1958), 132.

Ruler-cult: Out of a great mass of literature I mention: Kornemann, *Klio* 1901. L. Ross Taylor, *The Divinity of the Roman Emperor* (1931), ch. 1; above all: Wilcken, *SB. Berl. Ak.* 1938, 298. M. P. Nilsson, *Gesch. d. griech. Religion* II (1960²), ch. 3. F. Taeger, *Charisma* I (1958). *Numen*, Suppl. IV, 1959, 394. Large collection of material: L. Cerfaux et J. Tondriau, *Le culte des souverains dans la civilization gréco-romaine* (1957). Miss Taylor's attempt to prove a real ruler-cult for the Achaemenids is not convincing. On the old Babylonian divine monarchy, see C. J. Gadd, *Ideas of Divine Rule in the Anc. East* (1948). – Alexander as a god: doubts by Balsdon, *Historia* I (1950–2), 363; different view: Taeger, *HZ.* 172 (1951), 225; *Charisma* I 209. It need no longer be proved that the προσκύνησις had nothing to do with Alexander's deification; as to its significance with the Persians, see Méautis, *REA.* 1942, 305. – On ruler-cult in the cities: C. Habicht, *Gottmenschentum und griech. Städte* (1956) (but cf. Fraser, *CR.* 1958, 153). – 'Political religion': P. Wendland, *Hellenist.-röm. Kultur* (1912³), 126. – Secular and religious honours: Nock, *Harv.St.* 1930, 50. Habicht, op. cit. 211. – *OGI.* 212: L. Robert, *Études anatoliennes* (1937), 172. F. Sartori, *ΚΩΚΑΛΟΣ* 1957, 46. – Deification of Ptolemy Soter: Fraser, *Harv. Theol. Rev.* 1961, 141. – Identification with gods: the material in Tondriau, *Rev. of Rel.* 1948, 24. – Secondary names: E. Skard, *Euergetes – Concordia* (1931). Tryphon: the nickname of Euergetes I was taken over by Euergetes II. Otto and Bengtson, *Abh. Bayr. Ak.* 1938, 48, believe that the word at that time had acquired an 'honourable' meaning, something like 'the Magnificent'. This is quite possible, but the popularity of the third Ptolemy might be sufficient reason for using his nickname again. – ὁ μέγας: Spranger, *Saeculum* 1958, esp. 26 ff. – Demetrius Poliorcetes: Scott, *AJP.* 1928. Ehrenberg, *Die Antike* 1931

(= *Aspects of the Anc. World*, ch. 12). – Arsinoe Philadelphus: Pfeiffer, *Die Antike* 1926. G. Longega, *Arsinoe II* (1968). – Worship of the θεοὶ ᾽Αδελφοί during Arsinoe's lifetime: *P.Hib.* II 199; cf. Turner, *CR.* 1959, 165. *Greek Papyri*, 150. – Cult of the Ptolemies in Rhodes: Segre, *Bull. soc. d'arch. d'Alexandrie* 34 (1941), 29; cf. also 30 (1937), 286. – On the cult of Alexander in Alexandria: Plaumann, *AfP.* 1920, 77. – Antiochus III and Laodice: Welles, 36–7. Aymard, *REA.* 1949, 327. Roos, *Mnemos.* 1950, 54; 1951, 70. L. Robert, *Hellenica* VII 5; VIII 73; *REG.* 1951, 200; cf. also Welles, 44. – Cleopatra III: Otto and Bengtson, *Abh. Bayr. Ak.* 1938. Otto, *SB. Bayr. Ak.* 1939. – Commagene: *OGI.* 383 ff. Further literature in Nilsson, II 161. – On the monarchy in Sicily: W. Hüttl, *Verfassungsgeschichte von Syrakus* (1929), 128. Oath by the δαίμων of the king: e.g. *PSI.* IV 361. Cf. E. Seidl, *Der Eid im ptolem. Recht* (1929), esp. 18; 50. Kunkel, *Sav. Ztschr.* 1931, 240. Wilamowitz, *Glaube der Hellenen* II 307. Schubart, *AfP.* 1937, 15. These may have been ancient Egyptian ideas; but even then the oath by the δαίμων referred to the human nature of the king; a god had no δαίμων. It is often difficult to distinguish within the king's person between god and man. – φιλάνθρωπα (in sing. or plur.): Lenger, *Studi . . . Arangio-Ruiz* I 483. L. Koenen, *Eine ptolemäische Königsurkunde* (1957).

On the philosophy of the Hellenistic monarchy and the ideal king: J. Kaerst, *Studien zur Entwicklung und theoret. Begründung d. Monarchie im Altertum* (1898). W. Weber, *Zur Geschichte der Monarchie* (1919). E. R. Goodenough, *The Political Philosophy of the Hellenistic Kingship. Yale Class. Studies I* (1928). L. Delatte, *Les traités de la royauté d'Ecphante*, etc. (1942). Steinwenter, *Anz. Wiener Ak.* 1946, 250. M. Hammond, *City-State and World State* (1951), chs 3 and 4. Cf. also J. Keil, *Herm.* 1934, 452. Heuss, *X Congr. intern. di scienze stor.* II 208. On the forerunners of such theories, cf. Stroheker, *Historia* II (1953–4), 381. I have tried to show in *Alexander and the Greeks*, 73, that Aristotle's words ὥσπερ θεὸς ἐν ἀνθρώποις (*Pol.* III 1284a, 10) have nothing at all to do with Alexander, still less with the ruler-cult. My view has been largely adopted, but Welles in a recent paper holds firmly to the old view and even amplifies it (see below, III 3). – The question how far Alexander anticipated the political ideology of the Hellenistic age and, especially, the idea of the unity of mankind (cf. W. W. Tarn, *Alex. the Gr.* II, App. 24; against him: Badian, *Historia* 1958, 425) need not concern us here. His figure, anyway, exercised very little influence on the theory of monarchy [see Heuss, *Antike u. Abendland* IV 1954, 65, but cf. also Andreotti, *Historia* V (1956), 257]. – A different explanation of ἔνδοξος δουλεία (an honourable slavery before the law) is given by Volkmann, *Philol.* 1956, 52. *Historia* 1967, 155. – The appearance (as far as I know, the only one) of the expression ὁ βασιλικὸς νόμος in the inscription of the *astynomoi* at Pergamum (*SEG.* XIII 521, cf. XVI 735) (see Klaffenbach, *Abh. Deutsche Akad.* 1953) hardly proves that the theory of the king as the representative of the Nomos led to practical results. – Νόμος ἔμψυχος in Philo, *vita Mos.* I 162. II 4 f. (cf. *Abrah.* 5); critical text of late evidence: Delatte, *l.c.*

SECTION 2 (p. 179). In agreement with the general view, I have spoken in the text of 'professional bureaucracy', but I should like to point out that this description, justifiable as it may be, does not do justice either to the independent enterprise of Apollonius or to the activities of Zeno or to the position of the great strategi in the Seleucid empire or, on the other side, that of the Egyptian minor officials, forced into service. While the contrast to the Polis office is obvious, the difference from modern bureaucracy is equally unmistakable. – On detailed questions of administration, especially in Egypt, there exist a vast number of books and articles, only a few of which can be mentioned here. In general, cf. the works cited above (p. 276 f.). – ὁ ἐπὶ τῶν πραγμάτων: OGI. 247; 291 (cf. Welles, 61). Polyb. 5, 41, 1 f. Jos. Ant. Jud. XII 295. 2 Macc. 3, 7. The actual words of our sources often seem to point to a special appointment. Against the idea of a vizier we may also note that in OGI. 231, 26, the expression is used in the plural. General arguments – not entirely convincing – against their being a 'second after the king' in Hellenistic times (strictly he ought to be called 'the first after the king'): Volkmann, Philol. 1937, 285. – Apollonius and Zeno: M. Rostovtzeff, A Large Estate in Egypt (1922). C. C. Edgar, Zenon Papyri in the Univ. of Michigan Collection (1931), Introduction. R. Seider, Beiträge z. ptol. Verwaltungsgeschichte (1938), 43. C. Préaux, Les Grecs en Égypte (1947). – ὑπομνηματισμός: Bickerman, Aegyptus 1933, 349. – UPZ. I 106, 4: . . . καὶ] τοῖς ἄλλοις τοῖς τὰ βασιλικὰ πραγματευομένοις χαίρειν.

On provincial administration: Liebesny (see II 2). – Strategi: fundamental H. Bengtson, Die Strategie in der hellenist. Zeit. I–III (1937–52), also Aegyptus 1952, 378 (Carthage); cf. Aymard, REA. 1953, 132 = Études, 461. The criticism by Heuss, Gnomon 1949, 304, goes much too far. Otherwise, see, for example, Bilabel, RE. IV A, 184. Schwahn, RE. Suppl. VI, 1081. – Nomarch: R. Seider (see above), 15. Jurisdiction in every nomos by strategi and nomarchs: P.Hib. 198, 242 (later years of Philadelphus or early of Euergetes). – For the Seleucid division of satrapies, cf. Tarn, The Greeks in Bactria and India (1951²), 521, to pp. 1–4. – Epistrategos: V. Martin, Les epistratèges (1911). Skeat, AfP. 1937, 40. H. Bengtson, op. cit. III 121; another view in van't Dack, Aegyptus 1952, 437. – ἐπὶ τῆς Ἐρυθρᾶς καὶ τῆς Ἰνδικῆς θαλάσσης: Otto and Bengtson, Abh. Bayr. Ak. 1938, 22, 215. – Strategi of the Ionian League: Bengtson, Philol. 1937, 139. Strategi in Cyprus: Volkmann, Historia 1956, 452. Strategi in the Parthian empire: Rostovtzeff and Welles, Yale Class. Stud. 1931, 36. Bengtson questions any connection between the Hellenistic 'strategia' and that of the Polis, but in doing so, he at least overlooks the position of the strategi in the Hellenistic Leagues, and does not sufficiently stress that the Polis strategia could become a permanent office and, as such, could be the prelude to monarchy (Agathocles, Hiero). We must, of course, admit that the overwhelmingly regional character of the Hellenistic office of strategos meant something new. On the question of compulsory office: F. Oertel, Die Liturgie (1917). On the βασιλικὸς γραμματεύς: Kunkel, AfP. 1927, 179. – πρεσβύτεροι: Tomsin, Bull. Ac. Roy. de Belge

1952, 95. The quotation about the duties of an official is in *P. Teb.* III 703, 272 (3rd cent.): εὐτακτεῖν καὶ ἀκαμπεῖν ἐν τοῖς τόποις, μὴ συμπλέκεσθαι φαύλοις ὁμιλίαις, φεύγειν ἅπαντα συνδασμὸν τὸν ἐπὶ κακίαι γενόμενον. Cf. also *UPZ.* 144: τὰ παντ' οἰκονομεῖσθαι καθαρῶς καὶ δικαίως. In the letter of a strategos to the dioecetes we read (*BGU.* VIII 1764): πρότερον μὲν διὰ τὴν τύχην τοῦ θεοῦ καὶ κυρίου βασιλέως [καὶ τὴν παρὰ σοῦ] πρόνοιαν, εἶτα καὶ τὴν ἡμετέραν διὰ φόβου καὶ ἀγρυπνίας ἐξυπηρέτησιν. – Character of the administrative system: W. Schubart, *Verfassung u. Verwaltung d. Ptolemäerreichs* (1937). Welles, *Journ. Jur. Pap.* 1949, 21. Bengtson, *Mus. Helv.* 1953, 161. – Idealization of the Ptolemaic administration and jurisdiction: Hecataeus of Abdera in Diod. I, esp. 73–80. H. Braunert, *Saeculum* 1968, 47, tries to show that the philosophical concept of the mixed constitution is adapted to the reality of the social structure of Ptolemaic Egypt, and in the shape of Euhemerus' Utopian island had a direct influence on constitutional facts.

SECTION 3 (p. 190). The Hellenistic Polis: wide in scope and fundamental: A. H. M. Jones, *The Cities of the Eastern Roman Provinces* (1937). *The Greek City from Alexander to Justinian* (1940). Research on details, especially by L. Robert, has led to a good deal of addition and correction. Cf. also the discussion on Miletus in: *Atti X Congr. intern. di science stor.* (1957), 241. Welles, *l.c.* (ch. I) describes the Hellenistic and Roman periods of the Polis as the time not only of its widest extent, but also of its greatest importance in politics and culture. Of what Polis, which was not an imperial capital, except perhaps Rhodes, can that be maintained? Welles bridges the gulf between the old Polis and the Hellenistic Polis by finding a connecting link in the ideal state of the philosophers, in which the relations to a 'higher political authority' and the ruler-cult are already anticipated (see above, p. 282 f.). – Alexander and the Poleis: Bickerman, *REG.* 1934, 346. Ehrenberg, *Alexander and the Greeks* (1938), ch. 1. W. W. Tarn, *Alex. the Great* (1948), II, Appendix 7. D. Magie, *Roman Rule in Asia Minor* (1950), ch. 3 [chapters 4 and 5 should be consulted for the rest of this chapter, as far as Asia Minor is concerned]. E. Badian, *ASAI.* 37. My view agrees in a large measure with that of Mlle Préaux's (see below). In particular, she is right in rejecting the sharp distinction made by W. W. Tarn between δίδωμι and ἀποδίδωμι, the words with which the royal act of granting freedom is described in our sources. – Antigonus I: Heuss, *Herm.* 1938, 133; in some degree against him: Cloché, *L'antiquité class.* 1948, 101, also R. H. Simpson, *Historia* 1959, 385. – Kings and Poleis: P. Zancan, *Il monarcato ellenistico nei suoi elementi federativi* (1934). A. Heuss, *Stadt u. Herrscher d. Hellenismus* (1937) [cf. Bengtson, *DLZ.* 1939, 561. Bickerman, *RPh.* 1939, 335. Wüst, *Gnomon* 1939, 140]. Préaux, *Recueil de la soc. J. Bodin* VI (1954); VII (1956). – Cities of Macedon: Kahrstedt, *Herm.* 1953, 85. Bengtson, *Historia* III (1955), 462. A. Kanatsoulis, in several books on Macedon. – On the change of rule and, with it, of loyalties, cf. e.g. J. and L. Robert, *Mél. I. Lévy* (1953), 554. – Philip V and Lysimachia: text: *RPh.* 1939, 349. – Sacrifices ὑπὲρ τοῦ βασιλέως καὶ τοῦ δήμου (in Athens, the reverse order): Otto, GGA. 1914, 652. – New foundations: V. Tscherikower, *Die hellenist. Städtegründungen von Alex. d. Gr. bis auf die Römerzeit (Philol.* Suppl. XIX, 1927). – Partners in treaties: Polyb. 25, 2, 12; cf. Bickerman, *Philol.* 1932, 277. – ἐπιστάτου καὶ ἀρχόντων γνώμη: *SEG.* VII 62. Klaffenbach, *Philol.* 1948, 376. – Royal court of law in Dura: Welles, *Sav.-Ztschr.* 1936, 99. – Right of asylum: Seyrig, *Syria* 1939, 35. – The adoption of new citizens in the Hellenistic Polis, often following a suggestion by the rulers, were by decree of the Polis and (sometimes only) by inscription on the roll of citizens (πολιτογραφεῖν); cf. B. Keil, *Staatsaltert.*[2] (1914), 325. – Antiochus IV and Babylon: Rostovtzeff, *Yale Class. Stud.* 1932, 6. – On the disputed interpretation of Welles, 11–12, cf. Ehrenberg, *Alex. and the Greeks* (1938), 49. Kahrstedt, *OLZ.* 1939, 418. Rostovtzeff, *SEHHW.* 524. – On Hellenistic Jews in general: V. Tcherikover, *Hellenistic Civilization and the Jews* (1959). ἔθνος of the Jews: Bickerman, *REJ.* 1935, 4. – On the Council of Alexandria, *PSI.* 1160 is particularly important. Cf. Wilcken, *AfP.* 1930, 235; 1931, 255. Bell, *Aegyptus* 1932, 173. *Journ. Jur. Pap.* 1950, 25. Jouguet, *Bull. soc. arch. d'Alex.* 1948, 71. H. A. Musurillo, *Acts of the Pagan Martyrs* (1954), 83; also p. 108 on the Gerusia (see above, p. 266). – πολιτικοὶ νόμοι: Klaffenbach, *SB. Berl. Ak.* 1936. Bolla, *ÖJh.* 1939, Beiblatt, 169. – Cyprus: Mitford, *Aegyptus* 1953, 80. Volkmann, *Historia* 1956, 448. – Constitution of Cyrene: Taeger, *Herm.* 1929, 432. Ehrenberg, *Herm.* 1930, 332 = *P. u. I.* 538. Machu, *Rhist* 1951, 41. S. I. Oost, *CP.* 1963, 11. J. Siebert, *Metropolis und Apoikie* (1963), 68. Later protectorate: Arangio-Ruiz, *Rfil.* 1937, 266. Sometimes, I am speaking of a 'protectorate', while H. Braunert, *Historia* 1964, 80 (cf. II 2) replaces that word by the concept of 'hegemony'. It may sometimes be appropriate to use that expression, but it has far too vague a meaning, and Braunert's distinction between imperialism and hegemony is blurred. – Aspendus: Segre, *Aegyptus* 1934, 253. – Trierarchy in the Ptolemaic empire: Wilcken, *Raccolta Lumbroso* (1925), 93. – As to the nature of the Pergamene communities, cf. the inscription of Philadelphia (time of Attalus II); there we read of a κοινὸν τῶν πολιτῶν and of ephebes (F. Gschnitzer and J. Keil, *Anzeiger österr. Akad.* 1956, 223). – Alexandria as a world city: *Berl. Klassikertexte* VII 17 (first century B.C.).

Chapter Four

SECTION I (p. 205). The material and literature on Hellenistic religion are carefully discussed by M. P. Nilsson, *Gesch. d. griech. Religion* II (1950). Apart from him, cf. especially R. Reitzenstein, *Die hellenist. Mysterienreligionen* (1927[3]). F. Cumont, *Les religions orientales dans le paganisme romain* (1929[4]). U. v. Wilamowitz-Moellendorff, *Der Glaube der Hellenen* II (1932). – 'Religion de la culture': H.-I. Marrou, *Hist. de l'éducation,* 139, who, however, stresses 'la nuance personaliste' of the French word, as distinct from that of the German

Kultur, with its collective meaning. – For the combination of the abstract idea of divinity and personal deity, cf. e.g. the letter of Attalus II (Welles, 62) with his self-praise περὶ τῆς πρὸς τὸ θεῖον εὐσεβείας καὶ μάλιστα πρὸς τὴν Ἀθηνᾶν. – Sarapis: Roeder, *RE.* I A, 2394. Wilcken, *UPZ.* I. The date of his introduction, which is important for his original meaning, is disputed, but a safe *terminus ante quem* is the year of the death of Menander, that is to say, 291 at the latest; cf. Greipl, *Philol.* 1930, 159. Wilcken, *AfP.* 1930, 223. For the propaganda for Sarapis is especially interesting *P. Cairo Zenon* I 59034. Egyptians and Greeks as priests: cf. *I. v. Priene*, 195 = F. Sokolowski, *Lois sacrés de l'Asie Min.* (1955), no. 36, 20. S. wrongly assumes that all the priests in the Sarapeion in Alexandria were Egyptians; cf. on this point, P. M. Fraser, *Opuscula Atheniensia* III (1960), 1. Frazer was the first to question the view that Sarapis was a god of Ptolemaic imperialism, a *Reichsgott*. His own definition of Sarapis as a 'patron deity' of the Greeks in Egypt and especially at Alexandria seems rather too vague. C. B. Welles, *Historia* 1962, 271, tries to show that Alexander found the Sarapis cult at Rhacotis and took it over; that seems most unlikely, but his second point – that Alexandria was founded after, and not before, the march to the Ammoneion – seems sound. – 'Other religion': Wilamowitz, op. cit. 343. – Egypto-Hellenistic gods: W. Otto, *Priester und Tempel im hellenistischen Ägypten* (1905–8). W. Weber, *Ägypt.-griech. Götter im Hellenismus* (1912). *Die ägypt.-griech. Terrakotten* (1914). E. Visser, above II 2. – ἱερὸς πῶλος: Otto and Bengtson, *Abh. Bayr. Ak.* 1938, 71. In the syncretistic Isis, the two names of the Phrygian Mother goddess are combined, μεγάλη μήτηρ and μήτηρ θεῶν. – Asiatic gods in Egypt: Wilcken, *Festgabe f. A. Deissmann* (1927). – Tyche: Wilamowitz, *Glaube d. Hellenen* II 298. On the (Egyptian?) prehistory of Agathodaemon see Tarn, *JHS.* 1928, 213. Taeger, *Charisma* I 228. – Connection of Isis and Sarapis with Tyche and Agathodaemon: Tarn, ibid. 218. – Tyche and other city-goddesses: Schweitzer, *AJhb.* 1931, 203 and elsewhere. – Guardian deities of cities: Wilamowitz, op. cit. 357. – Dionysus in Egypt: Tondriau, *Chr. d'Ég.* 1946, 149. σπονδὴ Διονύσου and edict of Ptolemy IV (*BGU.* 1211): Eitrem, *Symb. Osloenses* 1937, 27. Dionysus in Pergamum: v. Prott, *Ath. Mitt.* 1902, 161. E. V. Hansen, *The Attalids of Pergamon* 401, 409; but cf. Taeger, *Charisma* I 346. In general cf. M. P. Nilsson, *The Dionysiac Mysteries of the Hellenistic and Roman Age* (1957). – σύνναοι θεοί: Nock, *HarvSt.* 1930, 1. – Temple states: see II 1. – ἀπόμοιρα: Longega (see III 1, p. 282), 111. – Judaea: E. Täubler, *Tyche* (1926), 116. Decree of Antiochus III: Bickerman, *Syria* 35 (1946–8), 67. Josephus actually says that the edict was valid κατὰ πᾶσαν τὴν βασιλείαν; naturally, that is nonsense, and a certain scepticism towards the whole story seems indicated.

SECTION 2 (p. 214). The recognition of the special character of Hellenistic law began with the book of L. Mitteis, *Reichsrecht und Volksrecht* (1891). Since then, the documentary sources (apart from the papyri, the cuneiform texts, and isolated Greek documents like the parchments of Avroman and Dura) and the

modern literature have grown enormously, and research is still in full flow. Cf.
the reports on literature, not confined to the papyri, in *AfP.*, by E. Seidl in: *Studia
et Documenta Historiae et Iuris* 1935 ff., also Wenger, *Studi in onore di P. Bonfante*
II (1929). – Greek documents from Mesopotamia and Iran: M. San Nicolò,
Beiträge zur Rechtsgeschichte im Bereiche der keilschriftlichen Quellen (1931).
Koschaker, *Sav.-Ztschr.* 1931, 427; *Abh. Sächs. Ak.* 1931, esp. 62. Rostovtzeff
(and others), *Excavations at Dura-Europos* (1929–52). Rostovtzeff and Welles,
Yale Class. Stud. II (1931). Welles in: *Papyri u. Altertumswissensch* (1934).
382. – Egypt: as an introduction for non-specialists in law, after Mitteis,
Grundzüge (see above, p. 277), we mention: E. Seidl, *Ptolemäische Rechtsgeschichte*
(1948), also Taubenschlag, *The Law of Greco-Roman Egypt* (1955²). *ADHO.* +
RIDA. 1952, 279. Préaux, *RIDA.* 1950, 349. H. J. Wolff, *Das Justizwesen der
Ptolemäer* (1962); cf. Modrejewski, *Sav. Ztschr.* 1963, 42. – Special courts:
E. Berneker, *Sondergerichtsbarkeit im griech. Recht Ägyptens* (1935). See there on
p. 47 on the οἱ ἄλλοι τῶν ἐπιπεπλεγμένων ταῖς προσόδοις. – Jurisdiction
for the βασιλικοὶ γεωργοί: Rostovtzeff, *Kolonat* 67. Schubart, *Einführung*
288; a different view in Mitteis, *Grundzüge* II. – On proceedings in court
before the cantonal strategi, cf. especially O. Guéraud, Ἐντεύξεις (1931). –
Athenaeus XV 697d: Bickerman, *Inst. des Sél.* 207, 3. Rostovtzeff, *SEHHW.* I
508. Meineke's correction (βασιλικόν for βασιλικῶν) will probably find no
longer any defender.

SECTION 3 (p. 218). In general: W. W. Tarn, *Hellenistic Military and Naval
Developments* (1931). M. Launey, *Recherches sur les armées hellénistiques* I. II
(1949–50). – Mercenaries: G. T. Griffith, *The Mercenaries of the Hellenistic World*
(1935). – Military settlers: F. Oertel, *Katoikoi. RE.* XI. The doubts (expressed,
for example, by Bouché-Leclerq, *Histoire des Séleucides* I 476) as to whether the
catoeci of the Seleucids like the Egyptian cleruchs formed a reserve army are
probably generally given up today. – Care for old age: Rehm, *Philol.* 1948,
267. – Citizen rights conferred on mercenaries: e.g. *Syll.* 529. *OGI.* 238.
Aspendus: see III 3. – Treaties with Cretan cities: e.g. *Syll.* 627; cf. Dunst,
Philol. 1956, 305. – Philip V's army prescriptions: Roussel, *RA.* 1934, 39; cf.
De Sanctis, *Rfil.* 1934, 515. Feyel, *RA.* 1935, 29. Welles, *AJA.* 1938, 245. F. W.
Walbank, *Philip V* (1940), 288, 291. – Egypt: J. Lesquier, *Les institutions
militaires de l'Égypte sous les Lagides* (1911); cf. Schubart, *GGA.* 1913, 610. –
Politeumata: see II 2 (p. 279). – Seleucid empire: Bickerman, *Inst.* 51. –
Pergamum: Rostovtzeff, *Cambr. Anc. Hist.* VIII 594. The Lilaia inscriptions
with their information about the Attalid army are published in the *Fouilles de
Delphes* III 4 (1954), nos. 132–5; cf. also R. Flacelière, *Les Aetoliens à Delphes*
(1937), 301.

SECTION 4 (p. 225). Modern research on the economy and finance of the
Hellenistic age began with U. Wilcken, *Griechische Ostraka* (1899). For the
massive literature that has appeared since then, see the general bibliographies.
More recent summaries: M. Weber, *Agrarverhältnisse im Altertum*, section 5,

printed in: *Gesammelte Aufsätze zur Sozial- und Wirtschaftsgeschichte* (1924), 154.
Wilcken, *Alexander und die hellenist. Wirtschaft* (*Schmollers Jahrbuch*, 1921).
Fundamental is the great work of Rostovtzeff, *SEHHW.* (above, p. 276); so
are some of his preparatory studies, e.g. *JEA.* 1920; *Anatolian Studies presented
to W. M. Ramsay* (1923). – Basic for Egypt: C. Préaux, *L'économie royale des
Lagides* (1939). Cf. also Heichelheim, *RE.* XVI 147 (*Monopole*). Suppl. VI 844
(*Sitos*). – 'New economic atmosphere': F. Oertel, *Anhang zu R. v. Poehlmann,
Gesch. d. sozialen Frage*, etc. II (1925³), 537. – Agriculture: M. Schnebel, *Die
Landwirtschaft im hellenist. Ägypten* I (1925). – The ground rent of the king's
peasants and the tax from land not immediately royal must not be treated as
identical, as H. Berve, *Alexanderreich* I 307, does. – *Lex Hieronica*: J. Carcopino,
La Loi de Hiéron et les Romains (1919). – On the Seleucid taxes, see Rostovtzeff,
Yale Class. Stud. 1932, 74. φόρος and δεκάτη: Welles, 41. Mittwoch, *Biblica*
1955, 352. – System of registration in Asia Minor: Westermann, *CP.* 1921. –
Grain in Egyptian economy: *P. Teb.* 703. Wilcken, *Chrestom.* 331. *PSI.* 400.
Private trade in grain: Kunkel, *AfP.* 1927, 212. – Ptolemaic imperial coinage:
Schubart, *ZfN.* 1921. – Movements of capital: F. Heichelheim, *Wirtschaftl.
Schwankungen der Zeit v. Alexander zu Augustus* (1930), 110. – My closing
remarks are linked to thoughts, expressed by M. Weber and Rostovtzeff. The
Hellenistic age as παίδευσις 'Ρώμης: cf. A. Aymard, *L'Orient et la Grèce*
(1953), 532. In a different sense, see p. 251.

Conclusion

Apart from the general literature mentioned above, p. 258 f., including
my *S. to S.* (1968), see for the Polis period my Oberlin (Charles B.
Martin) Lectures *Society and Civilization in Greece and Rome* (1964), for
the Hellenistic part my article on 'The Hellenistic Age' in the *Encyclopaedia Britannica* (1965). Both works contain much detail which would
be out of place in this chapter, and further bibliographical notes. – To
the question of the 'History of Mankind', cf. J. Vogt, *Wege zum
historischen Universum. Von Ranke bis Toynbee* (1961). *Saeculum* 1963, 41,
A. Heuss, *Zur Theorie der Weltgeschichte* (1968), and the discussion by
several authors *Saeculum* 1968, 1. – Some remarks on the innate
obstacles to Greek freedom: Larsen, *CP.* 1962, 230. – This concluding
chapter was the basis of a lecture which I delivered at Princeton
University and at Swarthmore College in autumn 1962.

Index

Index

I

II